AKBAR AND HIS INDIA

AKBAR AND HIS INDIA

Edited by

IRFAN HABIB

OXFORD
UNIVERSITY PRESS

OXFORD
UNIVERSITY PRESS

YMCA Library Building, Jai Singh Road, New Delhi 110001

Oxford University Press is a department of the University of Oxford. It furthers the University's objective of excellence in research, scholarship, and education by publishing worldwide in

Oxford New York
Auckland Cape Town Dar es Salaam Hong Kong Karachi
Kuala Lumpur Madrid Melbourne Mexico City Nairobi
New Delhi Shanghai Taipei Toronto

With offices in
gentina Austria Brazil Chile Czech Republic France Greece
Guatemala Hungary Italy Japan Poland Portugal Singapore
South Korea Switzerland Thailand Turkey Ukraine Vietnam

Oxford is a registered trade mark of Oxford University Press in the UK and in certain other countries

Published in India
by Oxford University Press, New Delhi

First published 1997
Oxford India Paperbacks 2000
Eighth impression 2008

ISBN-13: 978-0-19-564632-0
ISBN-10: 0-19-564632-0

Camera-ready-copy prepared by Shoaib Ahmad
Printed in India at Pauls Press, New Delhi 110 020
Published by Oxford University Press
YMCA Library Building, Jai Singh Road, New Delhi 110 001

Contents

Editorial Note

The 1992 national celebrations of the 450th birth anniversary of Akbar provided a much-needed impetus to research on Akbar and his times; and some of the results of such research are brought together in this volume. The original versions of many papers here published were presented at a seminar at the Centre of Advanced Study in History at Aligarh in October 1992, with the present editor as its Coordinator. Other material, comprising some papers, and most of the Documents and Reviews, has been especially contributed to this volume.

The volume was to appear as a publication of the Centre of Advanced Study in History. My work on it as Editor was nearly complete, when I was abruptly removed from my honorary position at the Centre in May 1996, as a minor by-product of the turn of the political winds, thankfully fleeting, of that fateful month. My removal from the Centre necessitated a change in the publication status of the volume and a redoing of much of the technical work, including the fresh preparation of the 'camera copy'. The volume now appears independently, but hopefully as the first in a series of collective studies, each devoted to a medieval theme, and with a structure similar to this volume's.

It may be helpful to mention that the transliteration system preferred here is that used by the *Epigraphia Indica* for the Indian languages and by Steingass's *Persian-English Dictionary* for Persian. But where some contributors have preferred other well-known systems, their transliteration has not normally been changed. Place-names usually carry modern spellings and do not bear diacritical marks.

Messrs Shoaib Ahmad and Munir Khan are responsible for the processing of the text and the preparation of the camera copy.

In bringing out *Akbar and His India*, especially at the last, difficult stage, I have been much helped by the advice and support of Professors M. Athar Ali, Iqtidar Alam Khan and Shireen Moosvi. I am greatly indebted to members of staff of the Centre's splendid library, who have continued to treat me as one of themselves. To all the contributors and to the Oxford University Press go my special thanks for their understanding and co-operation.

IRFAN HABIB

Aligarh
February 1997

Note to the Paperback Edition

Certain slips that were noticed in the original library edition (1997) were corrected in the reprint of 1998. This involved the repositioning of plates on pages 162 and 163 and on pages 285 and 286, and introducing important corrections in the text on pages 176,290, 291 and 293.

Opportunity has now been taken of this paperback edition to incorporate substantive alterations in the tables on pages 62 and 63 and in the text on pages 118-19, 137, 174 and 181.

Irfan Habib

1

Akbar's Initial Encounters with the Chiefs: Accident *vs*. Design in the Process of Subjugation

AHSAN RAZA KHAN

Territorial expansion on the part of powerful potentates, resulting in the overthrow or subjugation of lesser political entities , has been an integral part of the process of empire-building in Indian history. In medieval India, too, modern historians tend to look for explanations of the expansionist campaigns of empire-builders in the latter's urge to control strategic forts, routes and tracts, and the necessity to find openings to the sea for purposes of controlling or taxing trade and commerce.

Surveying the Mughal empire after it had been constituted, one comes across a large number of principalities under the control of autonomous and semi-autonomous chieftains who ruled hereditarily. Styled *rājas*, *rānas*, *rāwats*, *rāos* and by other similar designations, but appearing in the Persian chronicles generally as *zamīndārs*, these chiefs formed a formidable class. Their position and role under Akbar has been examined elsewhere.[1] Some of the chieftaincies stretched over distances of hundreds of kilometres, if Abū'l Fazl's geography can be trusted. The strength of the cavalry commanded by many chiefs exceeded the cavalry required to be maintained by the highest grandees of Akbar. In the course of his reign, Akbar evolved a policy towards this class which continued without any basic changes till the decline of the Mughal empire.[2] But what was the process of subjugation of chiefs under Akbar? Was it the

I have greatly benefited from discussions with my colleague Dr Chetan Singh in the course of preparing this paper.

[1] A.R. Khan, *Chieftains in the Mughal Empire during the Reign of Akbar*, Simla, 1977.

[2] S. Nurul Hasan, 'The Position of the *Zamīndārs* in the Mughal Empire', *Indian Economic and Social History Review*, I, No.4 (April-June, 1964), Delhi.

result of stray encounters or a set design? It is reported that leaving Persia for the reconquest of Hindustān, Humāyūn was advised by the Shāh of Iran to forge relations with the Rajputs rather than with the Afghans for the reason that the Rajputs were *zamīndārs*, and without the subjugation of the *zamīndārs* it was difficult to survive in India. Accordingly, on recovering the throne, Humāyūn not only followed this advice but allegedly passed it on as a *waṣīyat* or will to Akbar before his death.[3]

What one may well question is not that Akbar realized the importance of this class and forged powerful links with it but the assumption that the circumstances which brought him in contact with the chiefs were dictated not mainly by the exigencies of different situations but by a plan to carry out the so-called *waṣīyat* of Humāyūn. The scope of this paper is, therefore, limited to an inquiry into the circumstances leading to Akbar's initial encounters with the chiefs, though also drawing upon his subsequent relations with them. The study is confined to the region covered under the *ṣūbas* of Lahore, Delhi, Agra, Awadh, Allahabad, Bihar and Ajmer, as constituted in 1580.

I

To begin with the Punjab (the *ṣūba* of Lahore), where the chiefs of the *kohistān-i shimālī* (Northern Mountains) alone could muster a military strength of ten thousand *sawār* (cavalry) and one lakh *piyāda* (infantry),[4] Akbar's encounters with them started from the very beginning of his reign. It was owing to the activities of Sikandar Khān Sūr, who, having mobilized the support of the *zamīndārs* of the Punjab hills, had seized the revenues from the Punjab during Akbar's preoccupation with Hemū, that Akbar was forced to take notice of the hill chiefs of the Punjab.[5] The first to pay homage to Akbar was Dharam Chand, the Rāja of Nagarkot. Giving details of the circumstances of his submission, Abū'l Faẓl writes that, after Pīr Muḥammad Khān's campaign in pursuit of Sikandar Khān Sūr,

[3] Shaykh Farīd Bhakkarī, *Dhakhīratal-Khawānīn*, I (Karachi, 1961), pp.103-4.

[4] See Abū'l Faẓl, *Akbarnāma* (including its *takmila* by 'Ināyat-ullāh), Persian text, Bibliotheca Indica Series (Calcutta, 1877-78), III, p.683.

[5] Ibid., II, p.47.

when the emperor was encamped at Dhameri, a number of *zamīndārs*, including Dharam Chand, 'who was outstanding among his contemporaries on account of strength of retainers,' came and waited upon the emperor.[6]

However, the submission of the Rāja of Nagarkot and some other *zamīndārs*, not individually named, was only the beginning of the process, as a number of *zamīndārs* still supported Sikandar Khān Sūr. Hence, with a view to drawing away the *zamīndārs* from Sikandar Khān Sūr, the emperor sent Nāṣiru'l Mulk into the defiles with instructions to attack and plunder the *zamīndārs*. The Mughal commander succeeded in chastising many *rājas* of the mountains and capturing their baggage, as a result of which many were forced to abandon Sikandar's side.[7] A prominent chief of the Punjab hills who deserted Sikandar Khān Sūr and submitted to Akbar during the 2nd regnal year was Rāja Bakhtmal of Mau. He defected to the Mughals when Sikandar was besieged in the fort of Mankot.[8]

The submission of the powerful Gakkhar chief, Ādam Khān, in the same year was also a sequel to the campaign against Sikandar Khān Sūr. With the submission of Sikandar Khān and the capitulation of the fort of Mankot, Ādam Khān Gakkhar also saw the way the wind was blowing and offered submission to the emperor at Lahore.[9]

The last of the chiefs of the Punjab hills to attract Akbar's attention during his operations against Sikandar Khān Sūr was Rāja Kapūr Chand of Jammu. Before returning to Agra, the emperor appointed an army under the command of Khwāja 'Abdullāh and other *jāgīrdārs* of Talwandi against Kapūr Chand who had strengthened himself in the fort of Jammu. They are reported to have obtained a great victory and much plunder.[10]

Thus we notice that most of the prominent chiefs of the Punjab, namely Rāja Dharam Chand of Nagarkot, Bakhtmal of Mau, Ādam Khān Gakkhar, and Rāja Kapūr Chand of Jammu, apart from a number of other *rājas* whose territories are not mentioned by name, attracted the attention of the emperor principally in the course of his operations against Sikandar Khān

[6] Ibid., p.20.
[7] Ibid., p.50.
[8] Ibid., p.63.
[9] Ibid.
[10] Ibid., p.75.

Sūr. While some of them were subjugated, others were merely 'punished or forced to flee'.

The next encounter of Akbar with the chiefs of the Punjab hills was in the context of Bairam Khān's rebellion in the 5th year of his reign. When it was reported that Bairam Khān had sought shelter under Rāja Ganesh of Talwarah, the emperor moved in that direction and a part of the army advancing from the emperor's camp in the Sivaliks came to grips with what Abū'l Fazl calls the 'Hindu forces' and their hill chiefs (*rāyān* and *rājahā-i kohī*). The *rājas* were defeated, and many of them were put to the sword, while others fled.[11]

Some of the *rānas* and *zamīndārs* submitted to Akbar when the latter visited the Punjab to meet the threat posed by Mirzā Ḥakīm's intrusion in the Punjab in the 11th regnal year (1566). After Mirzā Ḥakīm's expulsion from the Punjab, the emperor celebrated his weighing ceremony at Lahore; some of the chiefs of the north came, paid homage and made offerings, while some others sent their sons and envoys and affirmed their allegiance.[12]

It was not until the appointment of Rāja Todar Mal to *ṣūba* Lahore in the 23rd year (1578) that we find the Mughals taking direct notice of the chiefs once again. Since the chiefs (*marzbāns*) of 'the Northern Mountains' were not yet obedient, he was ordered to subdue them. Consequently, many *būmīs* or chiefs of the hills submitted, while others were 'punished' or 'banished' from their territories.[13] The subsequent account of the chiefs of this *ṣūba* in our sources is in fact a story of the struggle of Akbar's officers against the chiefs, till almost the end of his reign. The rebellions and acts of defiance of the Mughal authority were fairly frequent, the major uprisings taking place in the 35th, 37th, 41st and 47th regnal years.[14]

In short, we see that Mughal encounters with the chiefs in this *ṣūba* during the first five years were the by-product of the military operations against Sikandar Khān Sūr and the rebellion of Bairam Khān, while in the 11th year they were the result of the expedition against Mirzā Ḥakīm. It was after these threats were over that the Mughals began to concentrate directly on the chiefs.

[11] Ibid., p.116.
[12] Ibid., p.278.
[13] Ibid., III, p.248.
[14] A.R. Khan, *op. cit.*, pp.52-3.

II

We now pass on to the *ṣūbas* of Delhi, Agra, Awadh and Allahabad. In these *ṣūbas*, too, the Mughals first encountered the chiefs in the course of the uprisings of the Afghans and the rebellions of the Mughal nobles. In the *ṣūba* of Delhi the two most powerful chiefs were Rāja Mittar Sen Katheriya of Lakhnor and the Rāja of Kumaun. While Mittar Sen is mentioned as one of the substantial *zamīndārs* of the territory of Sambhal, who ruled in his principality from the times of Humāyūn[15] and had earlier even come to possess Sambhal,[16] the *marzbān* or chief of Kumaun is mentioned as one of the great *būmīas* of Hindustān.[17] According to Firishta, he commanded an army of eighty thousand, inclusive of cavalry and infantry, and was one of the five great *rājas* of North India ruling over a number of other *rājas*.[18]

Mittar Sen attracted the attention of Akbar in the 5th year (1560) when he supported the uprising of the son of Sikandar K͟hān Sūr and G͟hāzī K͟hān Tanwar in the territory of Sambhal. Muḥammad Ṣādiq K͟hān was sent against them, and, as Abū'l Faẓl tells us, Ṣādiq K͟hān became the 'instrument of punishment of this crew'.[19]

The Rāja of Kumaun, too, despite the resources at his command, did not receive Akbar's attention until the 26th year (1581). It was only in the context of 'Arab Bahādur's rebellion and the extension of his activities to the territory of Sambhal that the Mughals took cognizance of the Rāja, for the latter, along with Rām Sāh, Makat Sen, *Rāja* Karan and many other *zamīndārs*, had joined hands with 'Arab Bahādur. Ḥakīm 'Ainu'l-Mulk, the *faujdār* of Sambhal, succeeded in creating dissension in the camp of the rebels and won over the above-named four chiefs, who were 'brought into the way of good service'.[20]

[15] *Akbarnāma*, I, p.185.

[16] 'Abdu'l Qādir Badāūnī, *Muntak͟hab al-Tawārīk͟h*, Persian text, Bibliotheca Indica Series (Calcutta, 1864-9), I, p.425.

[17] *Akbarnāma*, III, p.533.

[18] Muḥammad Qāsim Hindū Shāh 'Firishta', *Gulshan-i Ibrāhīmī*, popularly known as *Tārīk͟h-i Firishta* (Kanpur, 1884), II, p.420.

[19] *Akbarnāma*, II, p.104.

[20] Ibid., III, p.349.

In *ṣūba* Agra, the submission of the powerful Bhadauriya *zamīndārs* of Hatkant, described by Abū'l Faẓl as the strongest place in the vicinity of the capital,[21] where even Sher Shāh had to station 12,000 cavalry, was the result of court politics.[22] As Bairam Khān was always suspicious of Adham Khān, and, hence, wanted to keep him away from the court, he assigned that *pargana* to him in the 3rd regnal year with the purpose of keeping him occupied with the Bhadauriyas. Consequently, writes Abū'l Faẓl, 'that country came under *'amal* (tax-administration) and the recalcitrant elements received punishment'.[23] Later on, Rāja Bikramājīt Bhadauriya and his uncle, Rai Mukand, entered Mughal service and were granted *manṣabs*.[24]

The most powerful chief of *ṣūba* Agra was Rāja Madhukar Bundela of Orchha. He was the only chief in the region who invited Akbar's attention because of his own activities. Abū'l Faẓl says that as the Rāja was bent upon recalcitrance, an expedition was sent to Orchha in the 18th year (1573), which 'brought that country under *'amal*' and 'the power of the turbulent elements was reduced'.[25]

In Awadh, the most prominent chief was Ḥasan Khān Bachghoti. Abū'l Faẓl writes that he was 'one of the prominent *zamīndārs* of Hindustān and was distinguished on account of (the number of) his kinsmen, brethren and retainers' and lived in places of strength.[26] Ḥasan Khān emerged on the scene when he stirred trouble for the Mughals, first in alliance with Jalāl Khān Sūr, a prominent Afghan leader, in the 2nd regnal year,[27] and afterwards in alliance with Mabāriz Khān's son, Sher Khān, in the 6th year.[28] In the former year he was instrumental in mobilizing the support of the Afghans and creating trouble in the *sarkār* of Sambhal; in the latter year he fought the Mughals under the banner of Mubāriz Khān's son, and commanded a wing of the Afghan army. On both the occasions the rebels were defeated and forced to flee.

[21] Ibid., II, p.78.
[22] 'Abbās Khān Sarwānī, *Tārīkh-i Sher Shāhī*, MS Elliot No.371, Bodleian Library, ff.89a-b.
[23] *Akbarnāma*, III, p.77.   [24] See A.R. Khan, *op.cit.*, p.149.
[25] *Akbarnāma*, III, p.77.   [26] Ibid., II, p.56.
[27] Ibid.   [28] Ibid.

Of other chiefs of Awadh, Rāja Mān of Gonda and the *zamīndār* of Guwarikh also figure in the Mughal chronicles on account of the support they extended to Ma'ṣūm Khān Farkhūndī during his rebellion in the 25th year (1580). The former soon deserted Ma'ṣūm Khān Farkhūndī, while the latter, under the threat of Shahbāz Khān, sent Ma'ṣum Farkhūndī away from his territory.[29]

Another chief the Mughals encountered in Awadh was Rāja Sansār Chand of the forest country of Gorakhpur. From the only contemporary reference to him we notice him extending shelter to Yūsuf Muḥammad, the son of Sulaimān Uzbek, when the latter came to the Rāja after escaping from prison at Agra. The Rāja then helped Yūsuf Muḥammad capture the fort of Gorakhpur from the brother of Pāinda Muḥammad Khān Sag Kāsh. Subsequently, after the defeat of the allied rebel forces by the Mughals, the Rāja fled to his territory.[30]

The *zamīndārs* of Bahraich and of the hills north of Bahraich also submitted to the Mughals in the course of their operations against Ma'ṣūm Khān Farkhūndī and 'Arab Bahādur. It was after Ma'ṣūm Khān Farkhūndī's defeat by Waz Khān and Mehtar Khān near the city of Bahraich, which had been captured by Ma'ṣūm Khān along with its neighbouring territory, that the chiefs (*būmīs*) of that territory submitted to the Mughals during the 26th year (1581).[31] The *zamīndārs* of the hills north of Bahraich also appear in the context of the rebellion of 'Arab Bahādur in the 31st year (1586). They had extended support to 'Arab Bahādur and with their help he had constructed a fort in those hills.[32] But later on, it was on account of one of the *zamīndārs* of that region, Kharak Rāi, and his son Dūlā Rāi, who had turned hostile to 'Arab Bahādur and joined hands with the Mughals, that the rebellion of 'Arab Bahādur was suppressed, and he met his death at Dūlā's hands.[33]

Another chief the Mughals encountered in the hills bordering *ṣūba* Awadh was Rāja Ranka of Ajmer. His territory lay in the

[29] Ibid., III, p.340; see also A.R. Khan, *op.cit.*, pp.151-2.

[30] Bāyazīd Biyāt, *Tadhkira-i Humāyūn wa Akbar*, ed. M. Hidayat Husain (Calcutta, 1941), pp.316-7.

[31] *Akbarnāma*, III, p.370.

[32] Ibid., p.492.

[33] Ibid., p.493.

Sivalik hills when approached from the side of Awadh. According to Badāūnī, he was a *zamīndār* of some grandeur, and *qaṣba* Wajrāil which was at a distance of two days journey from Ajmer, the capital of the Rāja, was a part of his territory. The Mughal expedition to Rāja Ranka's territory was the by-product of the transfer of *pargana* Lucknow from Ḥusain Khān to Mahdī Qāsim Khān causing annoyance to the former who in protest abandoned Lucknow and marched towards the territory of Rāja Ranka. But Ḥusain Khān had to affect a retreat because of the inclement weather, shortage of provisions and resistance offered by the people of the hills.[34]

In *ṣūba* Allahabad the most powerful chief was Rāja Rām Chand of Bhatta who ruled over a large territory to the south of Allahabad from his capital at Bandugarh, one of the most redoubtable forts.[35] In the beginning Akbar took no notice of him. But when Ghāzī Khān Tanwar and other Afghans in the course of their struggles against the Mughals went to Bhatta, the emperor sent Āṣaf Khān, the *jāgīrdār* of Karra, along with a number of other commanders, to Bhatta, to induce Rāja Rām Chand to hand over the Afghan rebels. Due to the approach of the rainy season, the Mughal forces were unable to pressurize the Rāja and had to beat a retreat.[36] It was in the 8th year (1563) that Āṣaf Khān once again led an expedition to Bhatta. A well-contested battle was fought in which Ghāzī Khān Tanwar and some other Afghans were killed and the Rāja was forced to retreat to Bandugarh.[37]

To sum up, we notice that in the *ṣūbas* of Delhi, Agra, Awadh and Allahabad, the Mughals came in contact with the chiefs mostly in the context of the uprisings of the Afghans, namely Sikandar Khān Sūr's son, Ghāzi Khān Tanwar, and Mubāriz Khān's son, Sher Khān, or in the context of the rebellions of the Mughal nobles, namely Ma'ṣūm Khān Farkhūndī, 'Arab Bahādur and Yūsuf Muḥammad Uzbek, or as a result of feuds between Mughal nobles.

[34] Badāūnī, II, pp.125-6.
[35] Ibid., III, p.728.
[36] Ibid., II, p.148.
[37] Ibid., pp.182-3.

III

The pattern of Akbar's initial encounters with the chiefs in *ṣūba* Bihar was not very different from the preceding *ṣūbas*. In this *ṣūba*, the powerful Ujjainiya chief, Rāja Gajapatī, was the first to come in contact with the Mughals. When we first notice him in the 17th year of Akbar's reign (1574), we find him serving under Khān-i Khānān Mun'im Khān in his expedition against Zamaniya held by Dāūd Khān, the son of Sulaimān Khān Karrānī, ruler of Bengal.[38] But the sojourn of the Ujjainiya chief with the Mughals did not last long, for in the 21st year (1576) we find him attacking Mughal possessions in the east in alliance with Dāūd Khān Karrānī; and subsequently his son, Dalpat Ujjainiya, lent support to the rebels, 'Arab Bahādur and Ma'ṣūm Khān Kābulī, provoking Mughal military action against the Ujjainiyas.[39]

The submission of Rāja Sangrām, the *zamīndār* of Kharagpur, and Pūranmal, the Rāja of Gidhaur, in the 19th year was clearly the by-product of the military operations against the Afghans of the east. On his way to Bengal when Mun'im Khān seized the *qaṣbas* of Surajgarh and Munger from the Afghans, the above-mentioned chiefs, along with a number of other *zamīndārs* of the vicinity, 'bound themselves to the saddle-straps of eternal dominion'.[40] However, both the chiefs later defied the Mughals, the chief of Gidhaur openly sheltering the rebel Ma'ṣūm Khān Kābulī.[41]

Udai Karan, the *zamīndār* of Champaran, also figures for the first time in the course of the Mughal–Afghan struggle. When Muẓaffar Khān led an expedition to recover Hajipur from the Afghans in the 20th year (1575), Abū'l Fazl tells us that Udai Karan, the *zamīndār* of Champaran, 'joined the ranks of the sincere ones' or, in Beveridge's translation, Udai Karan 'became one of the single-minded', and rendered useful service in recovering the fort of Hajipur from the Afghans.[42]

Many other chiefs came in contact with the Mughals as a result of Muẓaffar Khān's expedition against the Afghans in south Bihar. After the capture of the fort of Rohtas, when the

[38] Ibid., vol.III, p.22.
[39] Ibid., pp.168-87, 186-9, 323-4, 331.
[40] Ibid., pp.107-8.
[41] Ibid., pp.321.
[42] Ibid., pp.136-7.

Khan was hunting in the jungles and hills, he obtained 160 elephants as booty from the rājās of the hills. And, while on his way back to Hajipur, when he encamped at Seor (985/1577-78), the Rāja of Seor sent him 30,000 rupees and 20 elephants by way of *peshkash*.[43]

The submission of Mādho Singh, the *būmī* of Kokra, to Shahbāz Khān in the 30th year was also a corollary to his successful campaign against the Afghans. Since Mādho Singh, relying on the inaccessible mountains held his head in pride, the imperial forces proceeded to plunder him and obtained much booty. Consequently, Mādho Singh undertook to pay the revenue.[44]

The *zamīndār* of Kalyanpur, the precursor of modern Hatwa Raj, also figures in the accounts of the military operations against the rebels Nūr Muḥammad and 'Abdu'l Ghafūr in the 27th year. When pursued by Khān-i A'ẓam Mirzā Koka the rebels fled to Kalyanpur for shelter.[45] Although they did not actually receive shelter at Kalyanpur, there is no evidence of the submission of the chief of Kalyanpur to the Mughals on this occasion.

Anant Chero, the powerful Chero chief, was probably the only chief of Bihar who attracted the attention of the Mughals independent of their concern for the Afghans or the rebels. It was in the 35th year (1590) when the trouble from the side of the Afghans and the Mughal rebels was over that Rāja Mān Singh, having subdued the chiefs of Kharagpur and Gidhaur, led an expedition against Anant Chero and obtained a large booty.[46]

Thus, we see that with the exception of Mān Singh's expedition against the Cheros, the initial encounters of the Mughals with the chiefs in this *ṣūba* were essentially a fall-out of the Mughal expeditions against the Afghans and the Mughal rebels.

VI

We now turn westward to *ṣūba* Ajmer, where Rāja Bhārmal, the Kachhāwa chief of Amber, was the first to come in contact with

[43] 'Ārif Qadahārī, *Tārīkh-i Akbarī* (Rampur, 1962), pp.225-6.
[44] *Akbarnāma*, III, p.479. [45] Ibid., pp.396-7.
[46] Ibid., p.576.

Akbar. He came into prominence because of his alliance with Ḥājī Khān Afghan in the very first year of Akbar's reign. The Rāja was with Ḥāji Khān when the latter besieged Majnūn Khān Qāqshāl, the Mughal *jāgīrdār*, in the fort of Narnaul. As the Mughals were pressed hard, the Rāja intervened and arranged the peaceful capitulation of the fort. The Rāja then sent Majnūn Khān to the court. Pleased with this, the emperor invited him to the court. The Rāja responded to the invitation and waited upon Akbar later in the same year.[47] However, it was the internal tussle between Bhārmal and his nephew, Sūja, for the chiefship of Amber and the hostility of Sharfuddīn Ḥusain Mirzā, the Mughal *jāgīrdār* of Mewat, who was siding with Sūja, which drove the Rāja to seek shelter with Akbar and join his service in the 6th year.[48]

The initial submission of the Hādā chief, Rāi Surjan, was the by-product of Akbar's action against Ādham Khān, the governor of Malwa. As Ādham Khān, after his conquest of Malwa from Bāz Bahādur, had begun to assume airs of independence, the emperor marched in person against him. When he reached near Ranthambor, Rāi Surjan on hearing of the presence of the emperor near his territory, sent *peshkash* to him and offered his submission.[49]

The conquest of Jodhpur from Chandra Sen in the 8th year (1563) was the outcome of Ḥusain Qulī Khān's expedition against the rebel Sharfuddīn Ḥusain Mirzā. Having taken Ajmer and Merta from the Mirzā's men, the imperial commander availed of the opportunity to attack and seize Jodhpur from Chandra Sen before terminating his expedition.[50]

Rāi Kalyānmal of Bikaner first figures vis-à-vis Akbar in the context of his extending shelter to Bairam Khān.[51] But it was in the 15th year (1570) when the emperor, after strengthening the fort of Ajmer, moved to Nagaur and prolonged his stay there 'for subduing oppressors', and 'for political reasons', that Kalyānmal came to him and entered imperial service.[52] It was

47 Ibid., pp.22 & 45.

48 Ibid., pp.155-8.

49 Ibid., p.140.

50 Ibid., p.197.

51 Ibid., p.105; see also Niẓāmuddīn Aḥmad, *Ṭabaqāt-i Akbarī*, II, (Calcutta, 1931), p.147.

52 *Akbarnāma*, II, pp.357-9; *Ṭabaqāt*, II, pp.229-30.

on this occasion that Rāwal Har Rāj, the chief of Jaisalmer, also offered submission to him.[53]

Akbar's initial encounter with the Deora chief of Sirohi and Abugarh was an offshoot of his Gujarat campaign in the 17th year. After the failure of a stratagem on the part of the Deora chief's men to kill Khān-i Kalān Mīr Muḥammad Khān Atka, heading the vanguard of the Gujarat expedition, the emperor retaliated by personally leading an abortive expedition to Sirohi. On account of the urgency of resuming the march to Gujarat the task of subjugating the chief of Sirohi was, however, postponed.[54]

The chief of Dungarpur, too, attracted the attention of Akbar in the course of his Gujarat campaign. After the successful conclusion of his Gujarat expedition, when the emperor on his return journey was encamped with his army near Dungarpur in the 18th year (1573), he availed of the opportunity to send an expedition to subdue the chief of Dungarpur. A battle was fought, but it was not until the 21st year (1576), that he was subdued.[55] Likewise, the ruler of Banswara was not taken notice of till after the conquest of Gujarat. He paid homage to the emperor only when the latter encamped in his territory on his way to Malwa in the 21st year.[56]

The Afghan chieftaincy of Jalor first figures in relation to the Mughals in the context of Sharfuddīn Ḥusain Mirzā's rebellion. When the rebel Mirzā was driven out from Nagaur and Ajmer in the 8th year, he retired toward Jalor.[57] However, it was in the 21st year (1576), that the chief of Jalor was forced to pay homage to Akbar.[58]

Lastly, the powerful Sisodia Rānā of Mewar also attracted Akbar's attention in the course of his operations against the Afghans and the sons of Muḥammad Sulṭān Mirzā. The Rānā came into conflict with Ḥājī Khān Afghān in the course of his fight from Alwar in the first year of Akbar's reign.[59] As Ḥājī Khān was the major concern of the Mughals, the Rānā was not taken notice of. But in the 7th year, the Rānā acted in a hostile manner by giving shelter to Bāz Bahādur.[60] No action still was

[53] *Akbarnāma*, II, p.359.

[54] Ibid., pp.4-5, 189-90; *Ṭabaqāt*, II, pp.236-7; see also Badāūnī, II, p.140.

[55] *Akbarnāma*, III, pp.40 and 196.

[56] Ibid., p.194-5.

[57] Ibid., II, p.196.

[58] Ibid., III, pp.189-90.

[59] Ibid., II, p.146.

[60] Ibid., p.169; *Ṭabaqāt*, II, p.157.

taken against him until an opportunity came Akbar's way during the rebellion of Muḥammad Sulṭān Mirzā's sons in Malwa in the 12th year (1567), which forced Akbar to march in person to Malwa. Abū'l Faẓl writes, 'at the time of sublime camp was pitched in the environs of Gagraun *on account of making arrangements for the Malwa campaign* [emphasis mine], Āṣaf Khān and Wazīr Khān, who had fiefs in his neighbourhood, went off in accordance with orders to attack the fortress of Mandalgarh', which was held by Rawat Ballo Solanki for the Rānā.[61] Consequently, the capture of Mandalgarh which was an offshoot of the Malwa campaign, paved the way for the conquest of Chittor in the 12th year and the subsequent long struggle with the Rānā.

Thus, we notice a close association between the Mughal military operations against the rebel nobles, Ādham Khān, Sharfuddīn Ḥussain Mirzā and Muḥammad Sulṭān Mirzā's sons, and the initial encounters of the Mughals with the Hāḍā chief of Ranthambor, the Rāṭhor chief of Jodhpur and the Sisodia chief of Mewar, respectively. In the case of Mewar, the refuge given by the Rānā to Bāz Bahādur, the fugitive Afghan ruler of Malwa, is also noteworthy, while the Kachhāwa chief of Amber first figures in the context of Ḥājī Khān Afghān's siege of Narnaul. As for the Kachhāwas, an additional reason for Bhārmal's coming closer to Akbar was the internal struggle for the chiefship of Amber. The chieftaincies bordering upon Gujarat, namely Sirohi, Dungarpur and Banswara, only came into contact with Akbar in the course of his Gujarat campaigns.

To sum up, we see that Akbar's initial encounters with the chiefs, leading in many cases to their partial or total subjugation, and in some other cases unfolding the process of subjugation, were largely the by-products of the Mughal military operations against the Afghans or rebel Mughal nobles, or by-products of court politics. However, regarding the chieftaincies in the south-western part of *ṣūba* Ajmer, the encounters were a corollary to his Gujarat campaigns. The chiefs, howsoever powerful, were too localized to pose any major threat to the Mughals. Their territorial ambitions were limited to their surrounding areas. Hence Akbar did not have any need to put his military resources

[61] *Akbarnāma*, II, pp.301-3 and 313ff.

heavily against them so long as the threat from the Afghans and the Mughal rebels existed. On the contrary, the Afghans and the Mughal rebels operated in wide areas, and it was they who kept the Mughal forces occupied. Defeated and driven by the Mughals from their territories it was they who yet principally occupied Akbar's attention during these early years. The chiefs became a primary concern of the Mughal court only when the threat from the Afghans and the rebels was over.

2

Akbar and the Rajput Principalities: Integration into Empire

S. INAYAT A. ZAIDI

Official sources for Akbar and his empire, the *Akbarnāma* and the *Ā'īn-i-Akbarī*, tend to divide the people of his empire, excluding the nobility and its dependants, into two classes, namely, the sub-ruling groups and the 'subjects': the former are styled *zāmīndārs*, *būmīān*, *marzbānān* and *aqwām*, and the latter *ra'iyat* and *mardum*.[1] The terms did not have any religious connotation, and Akbar, being the emperor (supreme to all), considered it his task to look after the interests of both categories. His concern for the first led him to integrate the ruling groups within the Mughal imperial system. On the one hand, by defeating independent rulers, Akbar curtailed the power of local ruling groups; on the other, he increased their power and prestige by turning them into a part of an imperial ruling class.

This was a departure from the policy of his predecessors and gave a radical turn to the Indian polity. The conventional policy hitherto was of subjugating a local chief, exacting a heavy sum of *peshkash* ('offering' or tribute),[2] and then leaving him free in his dominion. But Akbar brought the chiefs to the centrestage by giving them the opportunity to serve the empire as military commanders and so treating them at par with the Turani and Irani nobles.

The earlier policy of extracting *peshkash* and demanding military service whenever needed not only adversely affected the interests of the local rulers but also their *ra'iyat* (subjects)

[1] Cf. Irfan Habib, *The Agrarian System of Mughal India*, Bombay, 1963, pp. 136-41. The word *zamīndār* was used for Hindu chiefs outside the areas of direct control of the Sultanate in the 14th century (*The Cambridge Economic History of India*, Vol.I, ed. T. Raychaudhuri and Irfan Habib, Cambridge, 1982, p.58).

[2] Iqtidar Alam Khan, 'The Nobility Under Akbar and the Development of his Religious Policy, 1560-80', *JRAS*, 1968, pp.29-36.

who eventually bore the brunt of the burden. Thus the interests of the chief and his subjects became identical and they were equally keen to throw off the yoke of the centre. But Akbar, by a policy of 'give-and-take', linked the interests of the chiefs with the central power and created a strong bond at a higher level;[3] both worked hand in hand to exploit the *ra'iyat*, through imperial assignment of *jāgīrs* to the chiefs and the latter's assistance, in return, in the expansion of imperial territories.

By the sixteenth century, the Rajput chiefs had obtained a formidable position among the indigenous powers. Recognizing their military potentialities in terms of men and war animals,[4] Akbar recruited them into the Mughal ruling hierarchy. He did not restrict the entry in the Mughal service only to the chiefs but kept the doors open also for leaders *(sardārs)* of lower-level clans as well. They too were assigned *manṣabs* and were treated on an equal footing with their chiefs in Mughal service, subject only to the *manṣab* hierarchy.

These recruited chiefs (nobles) required soldiers to maintain their military contingents according to the assigned *manṣabs*. Consequently a larger number of persons, initially, were peasants-soldiers.[5] In addition to their income from land, these troopers began to earn extra amounts by rendering military service to the Mughal *manṣabdārs*. Thus the Rajput chiefs as well as their soldiers brought a certain amount of wealth to their regions, out of the income earned by serving the empire: there was little drain in the opposite direction by way of tribute, which was not expected once a *manṣab* had been awarded.

[3] Akbar established matrimonial alliances with major *zamīndār* famlies. 'Ārif Qandhārī and Abū'l Faẓl both link these marriages with Akbar's policy of winning over the chiefs by peaceful means. (*Tārīkh-i-Akbarī*, ed. Muizuddin Nadvi, *et al.*, Rampur, 1962, pp.47-8; *Akbarnāma*, ed. Agha Ahmad Ali, Calcutta 1873-87). See also Afzal Husain, 'Marriages among Muslim Nobles as an Index of Status and Aristocratic Integration', *Proceedings of the Indian History Congress*, Muzaffarpur, 1972; S. Inayat A. Zaidi, 'Matrimonial Ties between the Mughal Ruling Family and the Kachawāha Clan', *Proceedings of the Indian History Congress*, Jadavpur, 1974.

[4] The *Ā'īn-i-Akbarī* testifies to both. Abū'l Faẓl records in detail the number of horsemen and infantry maintained by the different Rajput clans. *Ā'īn-i-Akbarī*, ed. Blochmann, I, pp.508-13 (*ṣūba* Ajmer).

[5] S. Inayat A. Zaidi, 'Organization and Composition of the Contingents the Kachawāha Nobles', *Studies in History*, II, No.1,1980.

Akbar also let the Rajput chiefs into the highest ranks of the nobility by assigning them high administrative offices such as those of *ṣubadārs* (governors), *faujdārs* (commandants), *dīwāns* (revenue officers) and *qil'adārs* (castellans), in different parts of the empire.[6]

Akbar thus gave a radical turn to the relationship between the centre and the landed magnates. At the earlier stage of recruitment of the Rajput chieftains in imperial service, Akbar seems to have followed the traditional policy in which, after the subjugation of a chief, his territory was left with him with an obligation to render military service whenever required. Such an arrangement could not obviously be made, however, with the relations of the ruling Rajput chiefs, who had joined Akbar's service after their friction with their own chiefs. An alternative course was to seize some territory from the principal chief and assign it in *jāgīrs* to other Rajput nobles. The assignment of *jāgīrs* to both chiefs and their relations assumed significance after specific numeral ranks for nobles were fixed in 1573-4.[7] Now the Rajput chiefs, whose salary bills exceeded the *jama'* of their principalities, had to be assigned *jāgīrs* in other parts of the empire. We come across evidence that, in 1573, Mān Singh held Khichiwāra in Malwa in *jāgīr*.[8] Sometime before 1578, Kachawāha nobles were given *jāgīrs* in the Punjab, when they were posted there.[9]

Akbar also seems to have made attempts to establish complete control over some Rajput principalities. Thus, taking advantage of succession disputes among the descendants of Rao Maldeo, Akbar kept Jodhpur under direct imperial control for nearly

[6] Ahsan Raza Khan, *Chieftains in the Mughal Empire during the Reign of Akbar*, Simla, 1977, pp.115, 209; S. Inayat A. Zaidi, 'Political Role of the Kachawāha Nobles During Jahangir's Reign', *Proceedings of the Indian History Congress*, Hyderabad, 1978.

[7] A.J. Qaisar, 'Note on the Date of Institution of *Manṣab* under Akbar', *Proceedings of the Indian Hisotry Congress*, 1961, pp. 156-7; Shireen Moosvi, *The Economy of the Mughal Empire, c.1595*, Delhi,1987, p.202, fn 2.

[8] *Akbarnāma*, III, p.43; Muhta Nainsi, *Muhta Nainsi rī Khyāt*, ed. Badri Prasad Sakaria, Rajasthan Oriental Research Institute, Jodhpur, 1960, I, p.342.

[9] *Akbarnāma*, III, p.248; also see S. Inayat A. Zaidi, 'The Origin of the Institution of Watan Jagir', *The Quarterly Review of Historical Studies*, No. 4,Calcutta, 1980-1.

twenty years (1563-83).[10] But after witnessing persistent resistance, Akbar decided to grant Jodhpur to his favourite officer, Udai Singh, popularly known as Moṭa Rāja.[11]

In 1572-3, when Nagarkot, which was part of the territory of the rebel ruler Rāja Jai Chand, was assigned in *jāgīr* to Rāja Bīrbar by Akbar, it aroused vehement opposition.[12] Akbar then handed over Nagarkot back to the chief and a treaty was entered into between the imperial court and the Rāja.[13]

In 1573-4, Akbar decided to fix the *manṣabs* of his nobles and introduced *dāgh* (brand) regulations.[14] He decided to fix afresh the *jama*' (assessed income) of the empire to meet the salaries of the *manṣabdārs* and soldiers. To assess the *jama*', Akbar deputed *karorīs* to different parts of his empire.[15] They were also sent to the Rajput principalities. Yet, when in 1575 the *karorīs* arrived at Bikaner and Sambhar to assess the *jama*' of these regions, the chiefs did not allow them to do so.[16]

In 1592-3 Akbar, taking advantage of the succession issue, made an attempt to keep Bhatta under direct imperial control.[17] Subsequently, in 1598-9, it was assigned to prince Dāniyāl.[18] But the strong resistance of the chiefs (*sardārs*) of Bhatta forced Akbar to reassign it to its ruler Bikramājīt in 1602-3.[19]

These cases were, however, largely exceptions. Akbar left the *waṭans* (or 'home' principalities) in the possession of the chiefs. Initially, he assigned only the fort (which was also the seat of residence or palace of the chief) coupled with the hereditary title of Rāo or Rāja to every succeeding chief. This was recognized as his hereditary right; but this too needed the

[10] *Akbarnāma*, II, p.197; *Banke Das ri Khyāt*, R.O.R.I., Jaipur, 1956, p. 21. In 1572, Jodhpur was entrusted to Rāi Singh of Bikaner (*Akbarnāma*, III, P.5; Badāūnī, *Muntakhab u't Tawārīkh*, ed. by Aḥmad Alī *et al.*, Bib. Ind. Series, II, p.140).

[11] Muhta Nainsī, *Mārwār rā parganā rī Vigat*, ed. Fateh Singh, R.O.R.I., Johdpur, 1968, Vol. I, p.76.

[12] *Akbarnāma*, II, p.270.

[13] Ibid., III, p.36. Cf. A.R. Khan, *Chieftains in the Mughal Empire*, p.57 f.n. 114.

[14] *Akbarnāma*, III, p. 69.

[15] *Muntakhab u't Tawārīkh*,, II, p.189.

[16] *Dalpat Vilās*, ed. Rawat Saraswat, Sadul Research Institute, Bikaner, 1960, p.33; *Muhta Nainsī rī Khyāt*, I, p.306. See S. Inayat A. Zaidi, 'The Origin of the Institution of *Waṭan Jāgīr*', 641, 648.

[17] *Akbarnāma*, III, pp.648.

[18] Ibid., pp.717, 728, 740.

[19] Ibid., p. 788.

emperor's confirmation, as we shall see. At the time of the accession of Udai Singh in 1583, Akbar gave him only the fort of Jodhpur.[20] Similarly, in 1602-3, Duryodhan was entrusted with the fort of Bandugarh,[21] and the chief was accorded the status of the commandant of the fort.[22]

We also find that parts of the erstwhile principalities of the chiefs were assigned to other nobles and sometimes annexed to the Khālisa (imperial territory). In 1572, Sanganir, a *maḥal* of *pargana* Amber, was given in *jāgīr* to Rām Dās Udāwat by the emperor.[23] In 1597, village Punvaliya of *pargana* Amber was granted in *udak* (revenue-free grant) to Dharm Rām Joshi, a Brahman.[24] In the 1570s some part of Nagarkot was seized and included in the *Khāliṣa*.[25] In 1596, Paithan, a *maḥal* of the principality of hill Rāja Bāsū, was assigned in *jāgīr* to Mirzā Rustam.[26] The case of the Sirohi principality deserves special attention. In 1576-7, after Rāo Surtān's submission, the whole principality of Sirohi and Abugarh was placed under the administrative charge of Sayyid Hāshim Bukhārī.[27] The territory was assessed, and the *jama 'dāmī* fixed.[28] The principality used to be assigned in *jāgīr* to the *ṣūbadārs* of Gujarat for maintaining 2000 *sawars* (horsemen) for imperial service.[29] What is

[20] *Marwar rā parganā rī vigat*, I, p.76; Shyamal Das, *Vīr Vinod*, reprint, Delhi, 1986, III, pt.III, p.815.

[21] Thus the understanding that there was an assignment of whole of his dominion as his *waṭan jāgīr* after the chief joined Mughal service needs reconsideration. (M. Athar Alī, *The Mughal Nobility Under Aurangzeb*, Reprint edition, Bombay, 1970, p.70; S. Nurul Hasan, '*Zamīndārs* under the Mughals', *Land Control and Social Structure in Indian History*, ed. Robert Eric Frykenberg, Wisconsin, 1969/Delhi edition, 1979, p.21.)

[22] *Akbarnāma*, III, p. 788.

[23] Niẓāmu'ddīn Aḥmad, *Ṭabaqāt-i-Akbarī*, 1594 ed. B.De, Bib. Ind., Calcutta, II, p.442; 'Abdu'l Bāqī Nahāwandī, *Ma'āṣir-i-Raḥīmī*, 1616, ed. Hidayat Husain, Bib. Ind., I, p.804; *Muhta Nainsī rī Khyāt*, I, p.331.

[24] The document is preserved in the old record files of the Rajasthan State Archives, Bikaner.

[25] J. Hutchinson, *History of the Punjab Hill States*, Lahore, 1933, pp.73-4, 146; *Gazetteer of Kangra District*, cited in A.R. Khan, *Chieftains in the Mughal Empire*, p.42.

[26] *Akbarnāma*, III, p.712.

[27] Ibid., p.197.

[28] *Ā'īn-i-Akbarī*, II, p.251.

[29] 'Alī Muḥammad Khān, *Mirāt-i-Aḥmadī*, Suppl., ed. Saiyid Nawab Alī, Baroda, 1927-8, p.226. The chiefs of Sirohi were accorded the status of *zamīndārs*, but their tracts were assigned to other *jagīrdārs* (I. Habib, *Agrarian System of Mughal India*, pp.184-5).

even more important, Akbar, visualizing the strategic significance of the region and the previous subordination of the Sirohi chiefs to the Sisodia Rānās of Mewar, attenuated the Rāo's power by alienating half of his principality from him and assigned it in *jāgīr* to Jagmal Sisodia, the brother of Rānā Pratāp, who was in Akbar's service.[30]

Many chiefs of the status of *ṭhikānadārs* and *paṭṭadārs* from the territories of the chiefs were also taken directly into imperial service and their seats (*ṭhikānas*, *paṭṭas*) were considered assignments separate from those of the previous chiefs. Obviously this move had a dual effect in that it (i) curtailed the territorial possessions of the higher chiefs; and (ii) broke or weakened clan solidarity. Now the sub-chiefs were directly accountable to the emperor, instead of their erstwhile chiefs.

In the Kachawāha territory of Amber, the possessions of Deosa, Naraina, Lawan, Sambhar and Amarsar were accorded the status of permanent *jāgīrs* of different *sardārs*.[31] Similarly, the large territory controlled by Rāo Māldeo and his successor Chandar Sen was assigned in *jāgīrs* to their *sardārs*. The cases of Merta, Jaitaran, Sojat, Siwana and Jalor are worth citing.[32] The *ṭhikānadārs* of Sisodia Rānās of Mewar who had accepted Akbar's hegemony were assigned their *ṭhikānas* as *jāgīrs*. Rāo Surjan Hāḍā and Rāo Durga Chandrawat after their acceptance of Akbar's suzerainty were given back their *ṭhikānas*, Bundi and Rampura, in *jāgīr*.[33]

That the assignments made to the chiefs and their erstwhile vassals in their *waṭans* were different from the ordinary *jāgīr* was because of their non-transferable nature. A terminological distinction between the two appears to have taken place towards the end of Akbar's reign. In the wake of the continuous systematization of the administrative institutions, Akbar, while

[30] *Akbarnāma*, III, p. 413; *Muhta Nainsī rī Khyāt*, I, pp. 131-2. Jagmal entered into matrimonial relations with the Deora chiefs of Sirohi. He married the daughter of Mān Singh Deora, the immediate predecessor of Rāo Surtān. Mān Singh did not have any male issue. Therefore, Surtān, being a close relative, became his successor.

[31] *Akbarnāma*, III, pp.156-7; *Muhta Nainsī rī Khyāt*, I, pp.304, 308.

[32] *Mārwār rā parganā rī Vigat*, II, p.495; *Akbarnāma*, II, pp.34, 80-2.

[33] *Vīr Vinod*, pp.983-4. Rāo Surjan and Rāo Durga were *manṣabdārs* of 2000 and 1500 respectively. (*Ā'īn-i-Akbarī*, I, p.161; *Ṭabaqāt-i-Akbarī*, II, p.446.)

making a distinction between *z̲āt* and *sawār* ranks around 1596-7,[34] seems to have also conceived of the distinction between the ordinary *jāgīr* and the *waṭan jāgīr*.

An apparent distinction between ordinary *jāgīr* and *waṭan jāgīr* is specifically noticed for the first time around 1604 in Akbar's *farmān* to Rāja Rāi Singh of Bikaner. It is stated in the document that 'whereas the said *maḥal* (Shamsabad) has been attached to the *jāgīrs* of the Rāṭhors since long, we have as a token of great favour bestowed both the *parganas* (Shamsabad and Nurpur) upon him (Rāo Rāi Singh) as a *waṭan jāgīr*'.[35]

From this reference to the assignment of *waṭan jāgīr* it emerges that:

(i) the *waṭan jāgīr* was given on a permanent basis;

(ii) the emperor could create *waṭan jāgīr* at his will for a noble in any part of the empire; and

(iii) the noble, for whom the *waṭan jāgīr* was created, was expected to have had a long association with the place.[36]

Akbar possibly realized also that confining the attachment of the Rajput chiefs to their patrimonies would fortify local loyalties, but the creation of a *waṭan jāgīr* far away from their patrimonies would compel a merger of the chiefs' own interests with those of the empire.

Since the chiefs joined Mughal service and were assigned the *manṣabs*, they were paid through the assignment of revenues in the form of a *jāgīr* equivalent to their salary claim. Out of this, a portion of the revenues was always assigned to the chiefs in their *waṭans*. Thus the revenues assigned to the chiefs in their *waṭans* were a part of their salaries and not an extra privilege.[37] In other words, it was held by Akbar that the revenues assigned to chiefs in their *waṭans* were in lieu of their military service and not simply by virtue of their hereditary right. The nature of this assignment continued to be like that of an ordinary

[34] S. Moosvi, *The Economy of the Mughal Empire*, p.206.

[35] The *farmān* is preserved in the State Archives of Rajasthan, Bikaner.

[36] Ibid. From the *Ā'īn-i Akbarī* we learn that *pargana* Shamsabad was in the *zamīndārī* of the Rāṭhors and the predecessors of Rāi Singh belonged to Shamsabad. (*Ā'īn-i-Akbarī*, ed. Blochmann, II, p.507.)

[37] The revenues of *waṭans* were always adjusted in the salary bills of the Rajput *manṣabdārs*. For Jodhpur see *Mārwār-rā paraganā rī Vigat*, I, pp.76-7, 83, 93; II, pp.488-9.

(*tankhwāh*) *jāgīr* in all other respects, barring one only, that it would remain immune from transfer. It seems that the amount of revenues supposedly yielded by the chiefs' *waṭans* was not treated as fixed, as has been postulated by some scholars.[38] It seems to have varied from time to time.[39] But it had become a convention that a portion of revenues would always be assigned in *waṭan* to every succeeding chief, as token of his hereditary chiefdom.

In addition to their *waṭan* assignments, a substantial amount of revenues was also assigned in ordinary *jāgīrs* in tracts contiguous to the *waṭan*. Since this assignment also might remain with the chiefs, for more than one generation or for long periods, they often misconstrued it as their *waṭan*, while the Mughal chancery continued to consider the assignment to be of ordinary nature and, therefore, subject to resumption and transfer whenever occasion demanded. This conflict of understanding came to the surface in 1693 when *jāgīrs* in the *parganas* adjacent to Amber were not assigned to Rāja Bishan Singh. The Rāja immediately submitted a petition to the Mughal court. He claimed *waṭandārī* rights on the unassigned *jāgīrs* on the ground that since the time of Rāja Mān Singh (1589–1614), the *parganas* of Deoli, Baswa, Newai and Phagi had always been assigned to the Amber rulers. The emperor thereupon instituted an enquiry as to the real nature of the *jāgīr*.[40]

The concept of permanent interest in the form of *waṭan jāgīr* was strengthened by Akbar by not dispossessing the chiefs in ordinary circumstances. But he made it clear, through his intervention in determining succession, that the final authority rested with him. Indeed, his regent Bairam Khān asserted this right early enough when, in 1557, he deposed Bakht Mal of Mau on account of his reluctance in accepting Akbar's suzerainty, and put his brother Takht Mal in his place.[41] In 1576, Akbar deposed Duda, the eldest son of Rāo Surjan Hāḍā

[38] S.P. Gupta, *The Agrarian System of Eastern Rajasthan*, Delhi,1986, p.2.

[39] Satish Chandra, Presidential Address to the Eighth Session of the Rajasthan History Congress, Ajmer, 1975; G.D. Sharma, *Rajput Polity*, Delhi, 1977, pp. 26-7.

[40] *Vakīl's* Report (Persian), preserved in Rajasthan State Archives, Bikaner.

[41] *Akbarnāma*, II, p.63.

of Bundi, on the charge of collaborating with Rānā Pratap a[illegible] transferred the chiefship to his younger brother Bhoj Hāḍā. Similarly, when there was a dispute over the succession of Jodhpur between Rāo Māldeo's sons, Rām Rāi and Chandar Sen, Akbar set aside the claims of both and declared their brother, Udai Singh, popularly known as Mota Rāja, to be the chief of Jodhpur.[43] Again, in 1592, when Balbhadr Baghela, the chief of Bhatta, died, his *sardārs* raised his son Bikramājīt as his successor. When Akbar came to know of this, he rejected the succession on the ground that his approval had not been sought.[44] The *sardārs* resisted for a long time, but Akbar installed Duryodhan, a younger son of Balbhadr on the gaddi.[45]

Thus while Akbar recognized the sentimental attachments of the Rajput chiefs with their patrimonies and so refrained from unnecessarily uprooting the old chiefs from their *waṭans*, he yet systematically integrated their principalities into the empire. The chiefs were reconciled to this by the offers of *jāgīrs* and administrative offices in other parts of the empire.

This move produced far-reaching effects on the Rajput chiefs themselves. Their vision shifted from local interests to larger bureaucratic ambitions. An interesting aspect of this was that the Rajput chiefs' *jāgīrs* in the far-flung regions of the empire brought them closer to other Rajput clans and families with whom previously they had no relations or intercourse. The Rajput chiefs of Rajasthan and of Eastern and Central India began to establish matrimonial relations with each other.[46] The Rajput *jāgīrdārs* also employed many local persons in their *jāgīrs* who later accompanied the chiefs to their patrimonies

[42] *Muhta Nainsī rī Khyāt*, I, p.112; Sūrya Mal Misr, *Vamsh Bhaskar*, ed. R. Asopa, Jaipur, V, pp.2324-48.

[43] *Mārwār rā pargana rī vigat*, I, p.76; *Vīr Vinod*, III, p.815.

[44] *Akbarnāma*, III, pp. 641, 648.

[45] Ibid, pp.641, 648; *Muhta Nainsī rī Khyāt*, I, p.313: Shāh Nawāz Khān, *Ma'āṣir u'l Umarā'*, 1742-7, ed. Maulvi Ashraf Alī, Calcutta, 1890, II, pp. 137-8.

[46] In 1590-1, Pūran Mal of Gidhaur gave his sister in marriage to Rāja Mān Singh's brother Chandra Bhan. Balbhadr Baghela, the chief of Bhatta married the daughter of Rāja of Bikaner (*Akbarnama*, III, pp.576, 630). For similar marriages contracted in Bengal, Bihar, Orissa and Central India, see ibid., pp.716-7; *Bānke Dās rī Khyāt*, pp.124, 141-2; *Muhta Nainsī rī Khyāt*, I, p.132.

and settled there. On the other hand, many Rajputs of Rajasthan settled in other parts of the empire. There they founded new settlements and towns, and built temples and mosques with their own resources (e.g. Mān Singh's mosque at Raj Mahal). Thus an integration of class interests underlay the growth of a composite polity under Akbar. Though no concept of 'nation' could exist at that time, in the modern sense of the word, the integration of the Rajput principalities within the Mughal empire was certainly a step forward in the process of imparting a political entity to the geographical concept of India.

3

Akbar's Annexation of Sind — An Interpretation

SUNITA ZAIDI

The Arghūns and the Tarkhāns, who formed sister lineages of the Mughals, successively held sway over Sind for the most part of the sixteenth century. Both Bābur and Humāyūn generally maintained friendly relations with them.[1] Humāyūn, after his defeat by Sher Shāh, approached Mīr Shāh Husain, the Arghūn ruler, for help, but the latter could hardly oblige him in the circumstances. During the period he was a fugitive in Sind, Humāyūn's wife Ḥamīda Bāno gave birth to Akbar at Umarkot, the seat of a chiefdom of the Sodha Rajputs in the Thar desert, in 1542.[2] Thus Akbar can be said to have had certain special links with the region which should have made him interested in the territory. But the sources, particularly the official historian Abū'l Fazl, stress other important reasons behind Akbar's desire to conquer the territory. The route through Sind to Qandhār,[3] passing through Siwi and the Bolan Pass, made Sind a strategic prize. Its possession too meant an outlet to the sea for the Mughal possessions in the Punjab. Furthermore, to control Sind meant denying the Portuguese an alternative port and hinterland, should there be a confrontation with the Mughal authorities in Gujarat or the Arabian Sea.[4]

[1] Mīr Muḥammad Ma'ṣūm, *Tārīkh-i Ma'ṣūmī*, ed. U.M. Daudpota, Poona, 1938, pp.147, 162-5, 196; Mīr 'Alī Shīr Qāni', *Tuḥfat-al Kirām*, Hyderabad (Pakistan), 1971, III, pp.56-7, 121-2.

[2] Gulbadan Begam, *Humāyūn-nāma*, edited and translated A. Beveridge, Lahore, 1974, p.157; Hājī Muḥammad 'Ārif Qandhārī, *Tārīkh-i Akbarī*, Rampur, 1962, p.15; Niẓāmu'ddīn Aḥmad, *Ṭabaqāt-i Akbarī*, tr. B. De, Calcutta, 1939, II, p.90.

[3] *Akbarnāma*, III, pp.917-21.

[4] When 'Īsā Tarkhān (1554-66) was on an expedition against Sulṭān Maḥmūd of Bhakkar, Pedro Barreto raided Thatta and plundered the city, many persons being killed. (*Tārīkh-i Ma'ṣūmī*, p.206; Saiyid Ṭāhir Muḥammad Tattawī Nasyānī, *Tārīkh-i Ṭāhirī*, ed. Nabi Bakhsh Baloch, Hyderabad (Pakistan), 1964, pp.111-4; Frederick Charles Danvers, *The Portuguese in India*, I, p.508.)

Akbar must have wanted also to control the resources of the region. A variety of cotton and silk cloths were produced and exported from Sind.[5] It was famous for its crafts of ivory and ebony inlay on wooden furniture,[6] leather, palanquins and chariots.[7] There were salt-pits, and antimony and iron mines.[8] Indigo was also a product of much commercial significance.[9] These items were largely exported. This was one reason why Portuguese merchants maintained a constant presence at Thatta.[10]

Once he had established his authority firmly by the 1560s Akbar might therefore have been expected to attempt the subjugation of the Tarkhān chiefdoms. The Tarkhān rulers were also aware of this and, therefore, were not averse to tendering nominal allegiance to Akbar. But Sind had strong defensive barriers in having the sea and the Rann in the south and south-east, and hills and deserts in the west and north-west. Because of its natural geography the region had many pastoral, nomadic and semi-sedentary tribes from whose support the Tarkhāns draw strength. The only important path of entry from the north could be barred at two strategic points: (1) Bhakkar at the Rohri-Sukkur gorge, and (2) Sehwan, covering the narrow Lakhi pass above the head of the delta. With these two forts held firmly, the tribes could be used to harass the supplies of the invader.

The chronicles differentiate between two kinds of tribes. The tribes with hereditary chiefs are described as being led by *marzbāns* or *zamīndārs*, and tribes without political organization are simply styled *ulūs* or *mardum*.[11] The primitive character of

[5] There were 1000 families of weavers in Sehwan, 3000 families in Nasarpur and 3000 families in Thatta. *The English Factories in India*, ed. W. Foster, Oxford, 1906-27: 1634-36 vol., pp.128-9; Francisco Pelsaert, *Jahāngīr's India*, tr. W.H. Moreland, Cambridge, 1925, p.32; Fray Sebastian Manrique, *Travels of Father Sebastin Manrique, 1629-43*, tr. C.E. Luard, Hakluyt Society, London, 1927, pp.238-9; Niccolao Manucci, *Storia-do-Mogor*, tr. W. Irvine, London, 1907-8, II, p.427. See also Irfan Habib, *An Atlas of the Mughal Empire*, Delhi, 1982, pp.15-16.

[6] *Jahangir's India*, p.32.

[7] *Travels of Father Sebastian Manrique*, II, p.239.

[8] Abū'l Fazl, *Ā'īn-i Akbarī*, ed. Blochmann, Calcutta, 1866-67, I, p.556; *Mazhar-i Shāhjahānī*, pp.49, 60, 232.

[9] *Ā'īn-i Akbarī*, I, p.556.

[10] In order to inculcate a feeling of security among the merchants, the Portuguese governor of Ormuz used to have one agent at Thatta *(Akbarnāma*, III, pp.920-1).

[11] Ahsan Raza Khan, *The Chieftains in the Mughal Empire during the Reign of Akbar*, Shimla, 1977, p.61.

some of these tribes is evident from their superstitious practices. The depiction as 'liver-eaters' (*jigar khwār*) by Abū'l Faẓl disapprovingly,[12] shows the primitive traits of some tribesmen. Their pastoral character is shown by their paying the revenue in the form of livestock,[13] and also from the items offered at religious shrines.[14] Abū'l Faẓl has furnished the names of the main tribes, estimated their armed strength in numbers, and indicated the regions where they were concentrated.[15]

Name of tribe	Military strength	Region
1. Baloch Kalmātī	20,000 cavalry	Siwistan (Sehwan) to Lakhi
2. Nahmardī	3,000 cavalry 7,000 infantry	Sehwan to Kirthar Range
3. Baloch Nazharī	1,000 cavalry	Ditto
4. Baloch Kalmātī	4,000 cavalry	'Karah' hills near Kachh Gandawa
5. Bhaṭṭī	-	Uch to Gujarat
6. Sodha, Jareja and other tribes (Samejas)	-	From Bhakkar to Nasarpur and Umarkot.

It thus required considerable preparation to subjugate and establish a firm administration in Sind. The Tarkhān rulers made endeavours to keep up good relations with Akbar as kinsmen by claiming a common descent from Timur. Mirzā Bāqī Tarkhān sent his daughter Sindhī Begam to marry Akbar, but the latter did not accept this proposal.[16] By rejecting the proposed marital alliance,

[12] *Ā'īn-i Akbarī*, tr., II, p.340.
[13] *Maẓhar-i Shāhjahānī*, pp.94-5, 183-4.
[14] Ibid.
[15] *Ā'īn-i Akbarī*, tr., II, pp.338-9.
[16] *Tārīkh-i Ma'ṣūmī*, p.143; Mirza Kalich Beg, *History of Sind*, Karachi, 1902, II, pp.108-11.

Akbar made it clear that he wanted total submission. He sent an expedition in 1571 under the command of Muḥibb 'Alī Khān, but it failed to achieve success.[17] In 1586, Akbar himself went to Lahore with the intention of supervising the expedition to Thatta. He also deputed Ṣādiq Khān to lead an expedition into Sind, but, though he got some initial success, he failed to defeat Jānī Beg, the ruler of Central and Lower Sind. Ṣādiq Khān could not get beyond the *sarkār* of Nasarpur. To ward off further military pressure, Mirzā Jānī Beg agreed to pay homage personally and to issue coins in Akbar's name with the inclusion of the name of Akbar in the Friday sermon (*khuṭba*).[18] He, however, later offered excuses for not coming to the court personally.[19]

In 1589-90, when 'Abdu'r Raḥīm Khān-i Khānān was deputed to conquer Qandhar, he thought of conquering Thatta first. When Mirzā Jānī Beg came to know about the Khān-i Khānān's planned expedition to Qandhar, he offered a military contingent to accompany him. The latter imprisoned the emissary and continued with his march into Sind. The Khān-i Khānān also sought reinforcements. Rāi Singh of Bikaner and Rāwal Bhīm of Jaisalmer, who had experience in desert fighting, were asked to join him by the Thar route. Rāwal Bhīm and Mirzā Farīdūn were sent to the Rānā of Umarkot to win over his support.[20]

After fairly energetic resistance, Mirzā Jānī Beg was forced to accept the Mughal terms. He had to accept the position of *banda-i dargāh* ('servant of the court') by coming to the court personally. Akbar made him realize that, from now on, he was no more a ruler of Sind in his own right, but simply a noble of Akbar's court. He was granted the *manṣab* of 3000 and assigned Multan in *jāgīr*. It is significant that even Thatta was given over in *jāgīr* to Mirzā Shāhrukh.[21] But after this assertion of his sovereign power and depreciation of the status of Mirzā Jānī Beg, within two months Akbar again assigned Thatta in *jāgīr* to the latter. Still, the status accorded to Jānī Beg was not very high in the Mughal hierarchy. Only after the political integration of Sind into

[17] *Akbarnāma*, II, pp.526-7.

[18] *Tārīkh-i Ṭāhirī*, pp.170-1; 'Alī Shīr Thattavī, *Tuḥfat-ul Kirām*, ed. Husamuddīn Rashidi, Hyderabad, 1971, III, pp.153-4.

[19] *Akbarnāma*, II, pp.526-7.

[20] *Akbarnāma*, III, pp.917-21, 925, 929, 930, 971.

[21] Ibid., pp.979, 985-6.

the empire had been completed did Akbar permit the marriage of the daughter of Jānī Beg with Mirzā Īrij, the son of Khān-i Khānān.[22] The Khān-i Khānān himself married a niece of Rānā Megh Rāj of Umarkot, presumably to emphasize direct links with an important local ruler, till now mainly within the Sind orbit.[23]

Akbar's decision to restore Thatta within a short period to Mirzā Jānī Beg might have been due to political considerations. He had realized that it would be difficult for the newly appointed Mughal officials to govern the region because of its geographical and social complexities. The Tarkhāns, having established a rapport and understanding with the local people, might act as useful intermediaries in bringing the people of the region closer to the Mughal state. Therefore, after Akbar's temporary annoyance with Mirzā Jānī Beg at Asirgarh,[24] the latter still obtained an increase in his *manṣab*.[25] Jānī Beg, to be close to Akbar, had become a member of the select set of Akbar's spiritual disciples (*irādat gazīnān*),[26] thus professing his fidelity to an ideology which was fairly directly linked to the needs and aspirations of a centralized state.[27]

In 1601, after Mirzā Jānī Beg's death, his son Mirzā Ghāzī Beg, who had had a short tussle with Akbar,[28] was assigned Thatta in *jāgīr* with a *manṣab* of 5000.[29]

After annexation Sind was given the status of a *ṣūba* with five *sarkārs*, namely Thatta, Chachgan, Nasarpur, Chakarhala and

[22] Ibid., pp.940, 979.

[23] Shaikh Farīd Bhakkarī, *Zakhīrat-u'l Khawānīn*, ed. Moin-ul Haq, Karachi, 1961, II, p.317; Shāh Nawāz Khān, *Ma'āṣir-u'l Umarā*, ed. Maulvi Ashraf Alī, Calcutta, 1890, I, p.63.

[24] Mirzā Jānī Beg offended Akbar by his remark during the campaign against Khandesh that he would have defended his territory for a hundred years if he had a fort like Asir ('Abdu'l Bāqī Nihāwandī, *Ma'āṣir-i Raḥīmī*, Calcutta, 1931, III, p.302).

[25] In 1598, his *manṣab* was increased to 3500 (*Akbarnāma* III, p.1071). At the time of his death, he held the *manṣab* of 5000 (*Tuzuk-i Jahāngīrī*, ed. Saiyid Aḥmad, Aligarh, 1863-4, p.64; Saiyid Mīr Muḥammad, *Tarkhān-nāma*, ed. Husamuddīn Rashidi, Hyderabad (Pakistan), 1965, p.83).

[26] 'Abdu'l Qādir Badāūnī, *Muntakhab-u't Tawārīkh*, ed. Ahmad Ali, Kabir al-din Ahmad and W.N. Lees, Bib. Ind., Calcutta, 1864-69, II, p.304.

[27] M. Athar Ali, 'Akbar and Islam', presented to the Indian History Congress, Calicut, 1976.

[28] *Ma'āṣīr-ul Umarā*, III, pp.866-7; Ansar Zahid Khan, *History and Culture of Sind*, Karachi, 1980, p.61.

[29] Idrākī Beglārī, *Beglārnāma*, Ms. Br. M., 1814; *Ma'āṣīr-i Raḥīmī*, II, p.350; *Akbarnāma*, III, p.839.

Siwistan.[30] It is significant that Akbar did not assign *sarkār* Siwistan and the port of Lahari Bandar to Mirzā Jānī Beg, but included these in the *khāliṣa* (imperial territory).[31]

Sarkār Siwistan (Sehwan) had many pastoral tribes and keeping them under control proved a tedious task. Therefore, it began to be assigned directly in *jāgīr* to some powerful nobles.[32] The *jāgīrdārs* of Siwistan, perhaps to keep the local populace in control, used to sub-assign portions to their officials and grant *jāgīrs* to their troopers.[33]

There was constant conflict between the Mughal officials and the tribes on account of the collection of land revenue. Even Mirzā Jānī Beg seems to have faced the problem in *sarkār* Thatta where the Kehar and Nakmara tribes used to plunder settled peasants. Jānī Beg suppressed them by force.[34] Bakhtyār Beg, the *jāgīrdār* of Sehwan, had to expel the recalcitrant Machi tribe from *Pargana* Nirun Qila and he encouraged the *ra'iyatī* (revenue-paying) tribe of Pahwars to settle there. The name of the *pargana* was changed to Akbarabad.[35]

It is not correct to suppose that the annexation did not affect the system of administration.

The magnitude of the land revenue and the method of assessment changed with the annexation. Akbar seems to have raised the land revenue demand from a third to one half of the produce.[36] Yūsuf Mīrak, writing in the early years of Shāhjahān's reign, sympathizes with the peasants and praises the Tarkhāns for realizing the revenue at moderate rates, whereby the region and the people had become prosperous.[37] In Sind, *ghalla-bakhshī* (crop-sharing) had been the main form of collection of land revenue, and even now it formally continued.[38] But Akbar's officials preferred to realize the revenue in cash. Bakhtyār Beg, the *jāgīrdār* of Sehwan during Akbar's reign, refusing to accept the revenue

[30] In the *Ā'īn-i Akbarī*, Thatta is not formally treated as a separate *ṣūba*; it was deemed a *sarkār* of the *ṣūba* of Multan, but it was itself divided into five *sarkārs*, like other *ṣūbas* (*Ā'īn-i Akbarī*, I, p.557). See Sunita Zaidi, 'Problems of the Mughal Administration in Sind, during the First Half of the Seventeenth Century', *Islamic Culture*, LVII, no.2, April 1983, p.153.

[31] *Akbarnāma*, III, pp.985-6.

[32] Ibid.; *Maẓhar-i Shāhjahānī*, p.189.

[33] *Maẓhar-i Shāhjahānī*, pp.144, 164-5.

[34] Ibid., pp.34-5.

[35] Ibid., pp.65-6, 67.

[36] Ibid., pp.51, 204, 207, 209-10, 220.

[37] Ibid.

[38] *Ā'īn-i Akbarī*, I, p.556; *Maẓhar-i Shāhjahānī*, p.51.

in kind, demanded it in cash.[39] Since the peasants would now become dependent on the vagaries of the market, the demand for money payment must have fallen heavily on them.

Though before Akbar the Sind rulers seem to have made large revenue grants even to the local headmen, namely, the *arbābs* and *muqaddams* (*zamīndārs*), Akbar was not in favour of granting away revenues in such a manner to this class.[40] Overall Akbar's measures proved successful in enhancing the total *jama 'dāmī* of the *ṣūba*. Between 1595 and 1633, the total *jama*' increased from 6,61,152,893 *dāms* to 9,30,28,000 *dāms*.[41]

The continuance of Mirzā Jānī Beg and later his son G͟hāzī Beg as *jāgīrdārs* and governors of the *ṣūba* should not be seen as an argument against the centralizing tendencies of the Mughal state.[42] In 1611, after G͟hāzī Beg's removal from the governorship of the *ṣūba*, none of his family members were assigned charge of the *ṣūba*, quite contrary to the pronouncements of Sanjay Subrahmanyam.[43] This removal of the Tark͟hān family from Sind is all the more remarkable in that the family remained important, with Mirzā 'Īsa Tark͟hān holding the governorship of Gujarat for more than four years under Shāhjahān.[44] Their position was thus almost effortlessly reduced from independent rulers to high-level bureaucrats, and the assignment of *manṣabs* to them meant that

[39] *Maẓhar-i Shāhjahānī*, pp.94-5.

[40] Ibid, pp.185, 190-1. In fact Akbar took various measures to reduce the *madad-i ma 'āsh* grants systematically (*Ā'īn-i Akbarī*, I, p.197).

[41] *Ā'īn-i Akbarī*, I, p.557; Sunita Zaidi, 'Problems of the Mughal Administration in Sind', op.cit., p.153.

[42] Chetan Singh, 'Centre and Periphery in the Mughal State: The Case of Seventeenth Century Panjab', *Modern Asian Studies*, XXII (2), 1988, pp.299-318. See also his book *Region and Empire: Punjab in the Seventeenth Century*, Delhi, 1991, pp.34-5. Those who hold such views appear to ignore the working of the *manṣab* system, particularly of the *sawār* ranks, under which a stipulated ratio of troopers of different ethnic groups, was to be maintained.

[43] For governors during Jahāngīr's reign, see Irfan Habib, 'The Family of Nūr Jahān during Jahāngīr's Reign — A Political Study', *Medieval India - A Miscellany*, I, Aligarh, 1969, pp.79-94; and for Shāh Jahān's reign, M. Athar Alī, 'Provincial Governors under Shāh Jahān', *Medieval India — A Miscellany*, III, Aligarh, 1975; *Tārīk͟h-i Sind*, pp.228-35. Sanjay Subrahmanyam's claim that the family members of Mirzā Jānī Beg held the *ṣūba* till the middle of the seventeenth century occurs in his paper, 'The Mughal State — Structure or Process? Reflections on Recent Western Historiography', *IESHR*, XXIX, no.3, 1992, p.310, f.n.42.

[44] 'Alī Muḥammad K͟hān, *Mir'āt-i Aḥmadī*, ed. Syed Nawab Alī, Baroda, 1928, I, pp.216-19.

they had become employees of the state, detached from their regional moorings.

Sind, upon its annexation, was territorially broken up into the set imperial divisions of *sarkārs* and *parganas* on the same pattern as established for the rest of the empire after 1580. This was more than an act of map-making. Akbar and his successors were determined to force all local authorities to adjust themselves to a standard imperial system. What happened to Sind after Mughal annexation shows how implausible are some of the recent questionings of the centralizing processes of the Mughal empire and the application to it of the concept of the 'Segmentary State'.[45]

[45] Cf. Burton Stein, *Peasant State and Society in Medieval South India*, Delhi, 1980, p.23.

4

The Mughal Annexation of Sind — A Diplomatic and Military History

FATIMA ZEHRA BILGRAMI

The annexation of Sind to Akbar's empire was an event of considerable strategic significance as it secured access to the Arabian Sea for the Panjab, an important province in Akbar's dominions. For long, Akbar had had to tolerate independent rulers in Sind. At the beginning of his reign Upper Sind (from Bhakkar to Sehwan) was ruled by Sulṭān Mahmūd Khān,[1] and Lower Sind by the Tarkhāns who captured power in 1555 by overthrowing their kinsmen, the Arghūns. In the same year the Portuguese ransacked Thatta;[2] but this, fortunately for Sind, proved to be no more than a passing incident.

Mughal interference in Sind commenced from 1567-8, with the arrival of imperial troops at Bhakkar under the command of Mujāhid Khān and Muḥibbullāh Khān.[3] Sulṭān Maḥmūd was busy at that time in his struggle with Mirzā Muḥammad Bāqī Tarkhān.[4] He was now forced to confront the imperial forces, and various skirmishes took place.[5] Ultimately, he pacified Akbar by offering him his daughter (Bhakkarī Begum) in marriage (1572); and he was then recognized as the permanent

[1] For Sulṭān Maḥmūd Bhakkarī, see Mīr Ma'ṣūm, *Tārīkh-i Ma'ṣūmī*, ed. Daud Pota, Bombay, 1938, pp.218, 222-8, 232-8; and 'Alī Sher Thattavī, *Tuḥfat al-Kirām*, ed. Hussamuddin Rashidi, Hyderabad 1971, Vol.III, Supp. pp.120-2; 192,194-200.

[2] *Tārīkh-i Ma'ṣūmī*, p.207; Mīr Muḥammad Thattavī, *Tarkhān-nāma*, ed. Hussamuddin Rashidi, Hyderabad, 1965, p.46; Muḥammad Ṭāhir Nisyānī, *Tārīkh-i Ṭāhirī*, ed. Nabi Bakhsh Khan Biloch, Hyderabad, 1964, pp.111-2.

[3] Abdū'l Bāqī Nahāvandī, *Ma'āṣir-i Raḥīmī*, ed. by M. Hidayat Husain, Calcutta, 1925, Vol.II, pp.338-9; *Tārīkh-i Ma'ṣūmī*, pp.228-35; *Tuḥfat al-Kiram*, III, pp.143-4.

[4] *Tārīkh-i Ṭāhirī*, pp.147, 151; *Tuḥfat al-Kiram*, III, p.143; *Tārīkh-i Ma'ṣūmī*, pp.211-4; *Tarkhān-nāma*, p.56.

[5] *Tārīkh-i Ma'ṣūmī*, pp.233-4; *Tuḥfat al-Kirām*, III, pp.14-44. See also *Ma'āṣir-i Raḥīmī*, II, pp.336-9.

ruler of Bhakkar. Sulṭān Maḥmūd had no son, and so during his last illness in order to avoid the transfer of Bhakkar over to the Tarkẖāns he requested Akbar to appoint imperial officials to take charge of the principality.[6] After his death (1574), Upper Sind was thus incorporated in the Mughal empire, and from 1574 imperial governors were successively appointed to administer it.[7] When Akbar divided his empire into *ṣūbas* in 1580, the area was consolidated as a *sarkār* (the *sarkār* of Bhakkar), and assigned to *ṣūba* Multan, as may be seen from the particulars of the latter *ṣūba* given in the *Ā'īn-i Akbarī*.[8]

The next round of Mughal operations in Sind started in 1586, with Muḥammad Ṣādiq H̱ān's arrival as Governor at Multan.[9] He was assigned the *jāgīr* of Bhakkar and entrusted with the task of reducing the Tarkẖān principality of Thatta.[10] Before starting for Sīwistān (Sehwan) in the Tarkẖān dominions, Ṣādiq H̱ān sent a portion of his army to Pātar (Pat) to fight with the troops of Mirzā Jānī Beg, the Tarkẖān ruler. In the first two encounters, the imperialists succeeded and many soldiers of Jānī Beg's army were slain or captured.[11] Subḥān Qulī Arghūn, the commander of the Tarkẖān forces, was made prisoner and twelve *ghurābs* (galleys) were seized.[12] Inspired by these victories, Ṣādiq H̱ān marched towards

---

[6] *Tārīkẖ-i Ma'ṣūmī*, p.235.

[7] *Ma'āṣir-i Raḥīmī*, II, pp.340-2; *Tārīkẖ-i Ṭāhirī*, p.147; *Tuḥfat al-Kirām*, III, p.313. The details of their appointments, transfers and dismissals are given in *Tārīkẖ-i Ma'ṣūmī*, pp.235-6.

[8] *Ā'īn-i Akbarī*, ed. H. Blochmann, Bib. Ind., Calcutta, 1866-7, Vol.I, p.554. Cf. Irfan Habib, *Atlas of the Mughal Empire*, Delhi, 1982, Map 5A, & Notes, pp.13-4.

[9] Abū'l Faẓl, *Akbarnāma*, III, pt.II, Calcutta, 1887, p.495.

[10] *Tārīkẖ-i Ma'ṣūmī*, p.248; *Tarkẖān-nāma*, p.66, *Tārīkẖ-i Ṭāhirī*, p.169.

[11] *Tārīkẖ-i Ma'ṣūmī*, p.248. *Tarkẖān-nāma*, p.67. *Akbarnāma*, III, p.492, contains references to only one battle and its participants, while the *Ma'āṣir-i Raḥīmī*, II, p.343, mentions two encounters. A passage from the *Beglārnāma*, pp.224-5, 228, shows that Mirzā Bāqī had died sometime after the first battle of Patar and his successor, Mirzā Jānī, the governor of Siwistan, was now away from the place, being engaged in a civil war with his uncle Muẓaffar Mirzā over the succession. For details, see *Tuḥfat-u'l Kirām*, III, pp.150-1.

[12] So *Tārīkẖ-i Ma'ṣūmī*, 249. 'Only two *ghurābs* (galleys) were captured and a large number of the soldiers of both sides were killed' (*Tarkẖān-nāma*, p.67).

Sehwan and besieged the fort.[13] Mirzā Jānī Beg was now keen to establish cordial relations with Akbar, and he wrote submissive letters after receiving an imperial *farmān*.[14] He also promised in one letter to send his cousin, Shāh Ru<u>kh</u>, to the Court with proper presents.[15]

A reference in the *Tārī<u>kh</u>-i Ṭāhirī*[16] shows that this letter was sought to be dispatched through Ṣādiq <u>Kh</u>ān, who did not forward it to the emperor and continued the siege. A graphic description of the siege is given by contemporary historians.[17] Ṣādiq <u>Kh</u>ān's army could not succeed in storming the fort and was pushed back to a distance of one *kuroh* from Sehwan by fire from guns within the fort.[18]

Meanwhile, hearing of the news of the siege, Mirzā Jānī Beg arrived in the vicinity of the Indus.[19] His boats were commanded by <u>Kh</u>usrau <u>Kh</u>ān and land forces by Abū'l Qāsim Sulṭān.[20] We have conflicting statements from the historians regarding this battle. According to Abū'l Faẓl, 'having failed to take Sehwan, Ṣādiq <u>Kh</u>ān came to Nasrpur, collected spoils and retired before Jānī Beg's arrival'.[21] Mīr Ma'ṣūm's description is slightly different: Muḥammad Ṣādiq raised his siege and arrived opposite the Lakhi Hill; Mirzā Janī Beg's war

[13] *Tārī<u>kh</u>-i Ma'ṣūmī*, p.249; *Tar<u>kh</u>ān-nāma*, pp.67-8, *Beglārnāma*, p.229; *Ma'āṣir-i Raḥīmī*, II, p.343; *Akbarnāma*, III, p.495.

[14] *Tārī<u>kh</u>-i Ṭāhirī*, pp.170-1, and *Tuḥfat al-Kirām*, III, pp.153-4. After Mirzā Bāqī's death, a *farmān* was issued to Jānī Beg, asking him to pay homage and to use Akbar's name in his coins and the *<u>kh</u>uṭba*. Mirzā Jānī, admitting the emperor as his superior, accepted this demand.

[15] *Tārī<u>kh</u>-i Ṭāhirī*, pp.170-1; *Tuḥfat al-Kirām*, III, pp.153-4.

[16] After a prolonged siege, writes Ma'ṣūm Bhakkarī, 'they laid a large mine which blew up the gate and walls in front of the fort; Muḥammad Ṣādiq (<u>Kh</u>ān) ordered that no one should enter the fort without his permission. When smoke and fumes cleared away, the garrison erected another wall and began to fire their cannon and muskets' (*Tārī<u>kh</u>-i Ma'ṣūmī*, pp.248-9).

[17] The *Akbarnāma* (III, p.751) tells us that some of the walls were demolished by mines, but the Mughals could not proceed further because the earthen parapet was very high. Meanwhile the garrison, because of the delay, was able to construct another wall. According to the *Ma'āṣir-i Raḥīmī*, II, p.343, 'mine and covered passage (*sābāṭ*) were laid and the walls of the fort were damaged'. This operation is referred to also in the *Tārī<u>kh</u>-i Ṭāhirī*, p.172; *Tar<u>kh</u>ān-nāma*, p.67; and *Tuḥfat-u'l Kirām*, III, p.154.

[18] *Tar<u>kh</u>ān-nāma*, p.67.

[19] *Tārī<u>kh</u>-i Ma'ṣūmī*, p.249; *Ma'āṣir-i Raḥīmī*, II, p.343.

[20] *Beglārnāma*, p.230.

[21] *Akbarnāma*, III, p.495.

boats came within a short distance of the troops, and fired from cannon and muskets.[22] From the *Tarkhān-nāma*[23] it appears that the battle which ensued was quite fierce, but the Tarkhāns got the upper hand, and Ṣādiq Khān could not penetrate to any point beyond the Lakhi Hill. Ṭāhir Nisyānī provides some further details: 'Jānī Beg's army', he writes, 'comprised the following racial groups of the local tribes of Sind: Mughals, Sindis, Sameja, Summahs, Somrahs, Ghor, Palija and Numkara. The Sindis used to make night attacks upon the imperial army, and steal their animals, camels and mules. Hearing the news of Jānī Beg's arrival, the whole Mughal army took to flight till they reached the borders of Bhakkar.'[24] We have two more versions. Idrākī Beglār says that as Muḥammad Ṣādiq Khān could not resist these two lions (Abū'l Qāsim Beglār and Khusrau Khān), he retreated to Bhakkar, and 'the fear of the enemy [Mughals] was completely erased from the hearts of the people'.[25] According to the *Ma'āṣir-i Raḥīmī*, the tables turned in favour of Mirzā Jānī Beg, who captured the muskets and artillery of the imperial forces. Indeed, Nahāvandī attributes to the prestige of Akbar the bare survival of the remaining soldiers; otherwise not a single person of Ṣādiq Khān's army could have returned safe.[26] At the same time, Mirzā Jānī Beg very diplomatically sent his envoy, Sayyid Jalāl, to the imperial court with a petition and presents.[27] Akbar summoned the envoy, and Sayyid Jalāl truthfully informed him of the large numbers of men who had perished in these battles. Afterwards Akbar granted him leave to depart, sending his own envoy Ḥakīm 'Ain-u'l Mulk, along with costly garments and an elephant for Mirzā Jānī Beg, who thereupon acknowledged nominal submission to the emperor. A *farmān* recalling Ṣādiq Khān to the imperial court was also

[22] *Tārīkh-i Ma'ṣūmī*, p.188.
[23] *Tarkhān-nāma*, p.67.
[24] *Tarikh-i Ṭāhirī*, pp.172-3.
[25] *Beglārnāma*, p.230.
[26] *Ma'āṣir-i Raḥīmī*, II, p.345.
[27] Abū'l Faẓl (*Akbarnāma*, III, p.509) also refers to a petition and mentions 1586 as the date of the arrival of Sayyid Jalāl, and 1587 as the date of Ṣādiq Khān's return to the court. In *Ṭabaqāt-i Akbarī*, II, Calcutta, 1931, pp.406-7, the date of Ṣādiq Khān's arrival is given as 1588. It is stated in *Tarkhān-nāma*, p.66, that Mirzā Jānī Beg sent gifts and *peshkash* (presents) through his confidential people, accompanied by Mīr Jalālu'ddīn bin Mīr Sayyid 'Alī Shīrāzī, the Shaikh-u'l Islām of Thatta.

dispatched.[28] This represented clearly a setback to Akbar's plans, though the incident was now treated for public consumption as merely the result of an unauthorized action on Ṣādiq Khān's part.

The annexation of Sind entered its last phase when in 1590 Akbar appointed 'Abdu'r Raḥīm Khān-i Khānān as commander-in-chief to lead an expedition against it. We have varying interpretations from contemporary historians regarding the reasons for this shift to an aggressive design once again.

According to Ma'ṣūm Bhakkarī, 'the emperor was determined to bring Mirzā Jānī Beg under subjection. He had then made Lahore his capital, but Mirzā Jānī Beg, imitating the example set by Mirzā Shāh Ḥasan, had not put the neck of obedience in the halter of submission and pretended himself to be independent. So the Khān-i Khānān was deputed to conquer the territory of Thatta and to chastise the Balochīs'.[29] From the *Akbarnāma*[30] too it appears that Jānī Beg caused Akbar much annoyance, because he failed to render personal homage. This statement is supported by Niẓāmu'ddīn[31] and Firishta,[32] and seems to have represented the official explanation of the campaign given out at the Mughal court.

Among the Sind histories, the *Tarkhān-nāma* tells us that the enemies of Mirzā Jānī Beg, motivated by self-interest, poisoned Akbar's mind against him, stressing the Mirzā's vanity and arrogance, and arguing that since he had driven back the imperial forces, he intended to assume the insignia of royalty.[33]

[28] *Tārīkh-i Ma'ṣūmī*, p.249; *Tarkhān-nāma*, p.69; *Tārīkh-i Ṭāhirī*, p.173; 'Abdu'l Qādir Bādāūni, *Muntakhab al-Tawārīkh*, II, p.359; *Ṭabaqāt-i Akbarī*, II, pp.406-7. *Maktūbāt-i 'Allāmī*, p.105, also refers to Ḥakīm 'Ain-u'l Mulk's journey to Thatta.

[29] *Tārīkh-i Ma'ṣūmī*, p.249. *Ma'āṣīr-i Raḥīmī*, II, p.345, attributes Mirzā Jānī's haughtiness and misbehaviour towards Ṣādiq Khān which infuriated Akbar, so that state necessity demanded the punishment of 'Mirzā Jānī, Afghāns and Baluchis'. So the Khān-i Khānān, who had recently arrived from Gujarat, received the governorship of Bhakkar and Multan, and was sent to punish Mirzā Jānī and conquer Sind.

[30] It was decided to send an army against him and he was asked to come personally or send his troops; otherwise he would be punished after the return of the royal forces (from Qandhar) (*Akbarnāma*, III, p.585). *Akbarnāma*, B.M. Add.27, 247, f.390a, provides more details.

[31] *Ṭabaqāt-i Akbarī*, II, p.411-12.

[32] *Tārīkh-i Firishta*, II, p.623.

[33] *Tarkhān-nāma*, p.70.

The *Beglārnāma* sees the decision as a belated response to the discomfiture suffered by Ṣādiq Khān: when the defeated forces returned to the capital, Akbar became furious and decided to send 'Abdu'r Raḥīm Khān-i Khānān to capture Thatta.[34] Ṭāhir Nisyānī holds Mirzā Jānī responsible for this calamity: 'After sending the letter of submission through Mirzā Shāh Rukh, Jānī Beg became satisfied; setting aside his good virtues, he indulged in pleasures and became a debauch. The wise men of the country interpreted it as a sign of his decay as well as of his country; this state of affairs lasted... till the imperial forces entered Sind to remove the heat of his mind.'[35]

Abū'l Fazl, however, introduces a variant version, which is *prima facie* hard to reconcile with these statements. The Khān-i Khānān's appointment as Governor of Multan, he says, was made for the Qandhar expedition, and he was ordered to march via Baluchistan (i.e. through the Derajat and the Southern Sulaiman Range).[36] But he, preferring the larger gains of Thatta than the smaller ones of Qandhar, did not follow the prescribed route, and preferred to march via Bhakkar (and the Bolan Pass).[37] Abū'l Fazl in his letters to the Khān-i Khānān expresses his resentment at the change of the planned route, urging him not to postpone his Qandhar campaign in favour of that against Siwistan (Sehwan).[38] In a letter (Sept.-Oct.1591) written from Lahore, he says, 'the fourth [source of] unhappiness is that the Khān-i Khānān diverted his attention from Qandhar, and has wrongfully proceeded towards Thatta'.[39]

[34] *Beglārnāma*, p.231.

[35] *Tārīkh-i Ṭāhirī*, pp.174-5.

[36] *Akbarnāma*, III, p.585; also Abū'l Fazl's letter in *Maktūbāt-i 'Allāmī*, Lucknow 1270/1853, p.88.

[37] B.M. MS Add. 27, 247, which contains an earlier version of the *Akbarnāma*, supplies more details on 'Abdu'r Raḥīm Khān-i Khānān's invason of Sind, and some of its passages (ff.390, 391-394) slightly differ in wording from the printed text. It appears from this manuscript (f.392) that the Khān-i Khānān adopted the route via Bhakkar (as Multan and Bhakkar were assigned to him in *jāgīr*) avoiding the shorter Ghaznin-Bangash route from where he could have easily reached Qandhar. Some of his companions urged him to follow this route, but in vain.

[38] *Maktūbāt-i 'Allāmī*, pp.78-9. According to Riazul Islam, the letter is dated, 15 December 1589 and written from Jalalabad (*A Calender of Persian Documents,* Vol.I, Karachi, 1979, p.105).

[39] *Maktūbāt-i 'Allāmī*, p.84. See *Akbarnāma*, B.M. MS, Add. 27,247, f.393a.

Almost the same thing is repeated in another letter, wherein he considers the conquest of Qandhar 'a prelude to the conquest of Persia' and blames those ill-wishers of the K͟hān-i K͟hānān for alienating his mind from that project.[40]

In the next letter, however, Abū'l Fazl changes his position and only expects from the K͟hān-i K͟hānān that, after settling the affairs of Thatta, he would march to Qandhar to subdue Khurasan and Iran.[41] This change of view must have come about because the K͟hān-i K͟hānān had secured royal assent to his change of plans, and, in a letter written from Lahore (1591), Abū'l Fazl, indeed, goes so far as to congratulate him for the campaign he had undertaken for Qandhar, Thatta and other places (in that order), adding instructions about his personal conduct during these expeditions.[42]

Whatever may have been the precise circumstances which led to the invasion of Sind, it is apparent that Akbar permitted a diversion from Qandhar only because he too was anxious to bring Sind under his control, and subdue or expel Mirzā Jānī Beg.

The *Ma'āṣir-i Raḥīmī*[43] vividly describes the large-scale military preparations of the K͟hān-i K͟hānān's march from Lahore to Sind along with war elephants, musketeers and artillery. Officers who accompanied the expedition included Shāh Beg Kābulī, Sayyid Bahāu'ddīn Buk͟hārī, Farīdūn Barlās, Sher K͟hān, Janish Bahādur, Bak͟htyār Beg, Kara Beg Turkmān, Muḥammad K͟hān Niāzī and the historian Mīr Ma'ṣūm.[44] The last named had just arrived at Lahore from Gujarat and the *parganas* of Darbela, Kakri and Chanduka (in *Sarkār* Bhakkar) were assigned to him in *jāgīr*;[45] he arrived at Bhakkar (12 December 1590), a few days ahead of the K͟hān-i K͟hānān. K͟hwāja Muqīm *Bak͟hshī* was sent to perform the duties of *Bak͟hshī* of the army.

[40] *Maktūbāt-i 'Allāmī*, p.88. [41] Ibid., p.99.

[42] Ibid., p.91.

[43] *Ma'āṣir-i Raḥīmī*, II, p.358. Faizi composed a chronogram, '*Qaṣd-i Tatta*' (999/1590-91).

[44] *Tārīk͟h-i Ma'ṣūmī*, p.252. For the long list of officials, *Akbarnāma*, III, p.585. B.M. MS, Add. 27,247, ff. 392a-393a, contains still more details.

[45] *Ma'āṣir-i Raḥīmī*, II, p.359. It seems that Jānī Beg was unaware of the entire design. Abū'l Fazl says that when K͟hān-i K͟hānān stationed his troops at Bhakkar, an envoy from Jānī Beg came to him and represented that his

The Khān-i Khānān arrived at Bhakkar (1590) and, after a few days' stay, marched towards Sehwan.[46] He found the gates of that fort closed upon him. On the advice of his commanders, he decided to reduce Sehwan, before proceeding towards Thatta. Batteries were accordingly set around the fort and a *sābāṭ* (covered passage) was constructed.[47] At this time, writes Abū'l Faẓl, fire broke out in the fort and consumed its stores. On hearing of this, the imperial troops moved rapidly by land and water. Those who went by water rowed past the fort and took Lakhi Hill.[48] In the beginning, writes Ṭāhir Nisyānī,[49] the Khān-i Khānān tried to invest and capture the fort, but afterwards he thought it a waste of resources for the possession merely of a few mud walls, especially when he could push on and seize the capital Thatta as well as the person of the ruler of the country. Contrary to this, the *Akbarnāma*[50] says that Sehwan was the gateway of the country and its siege could not be abandoned; no injury had been caused to the royalists from the cannon and musket shots of the garrison in any case.

Leaving a group of soldiers to continue the siege, the Khān-i Khānān marched southwards. Jānī Beg ordered the construction of a ditch and a fortress at Bohiri (near Nasrpur) after demolishing houses.[51] A body of troops was sent towards

---

master, being unable to come personally (because of the pressure of 'strife-mongers'), was prepared to send his forces to assist the imperial army in the Qandhar campaign. But the envoys were imprisoned and the imperial troops marched ahead (*Akbarnāma*, III, p.602; B.M. MS, Add. 27, 247, f.392b).

[46] Abū'l Faẓl's description of the fortress of Siwistan or Sehwan is as follows: 'This fort of the ruler is situated on the bank of the Indus on the top of a ridge. The glacis (*khākrez*) is 40 yards and the wall seven yards high. Near it there is a lake, 8 *kurohs* in length and six in breadth. Three branches of the river join it' (*Akbarnāma*, III, p.602).

[47] *Tārīkh-i Ma'ṣūmī*, p.252; *Tarkhān-nāma*, p.70.

[48] *Akbarnāma*, III, p.602: 'It is like Garhi in Bengal and Barahmula in Kashmir'. The *Tārīkh-i Ṭāhirī*, p.181, narrates the hardships suffered by the Khān-i Khānān in the course of his journey through Lakhi Hills, 'the key of the country, stretching away from river Indus towards Sun, [with] its narrow passages and rebellious inhabitants who never acknowledged a master'.

[49] *Tārīkh-i Ṭāhirī*, p.181.

[50] *Akbarnāma*, III, p.602. For further details, B.M. MS, Add.27, 247, f.393.

[51] Bohiri or Bhiri Juheja, a small town, 10 miles from Nasrpur. Abū'l Faẓl does not mention Bohiri; he only says, 'at the pass of Nasirpur, a place which lies on the side of the river, and the other streams, he constructed a fort and

SIND

MUGHAL ANNEXATION, 1591

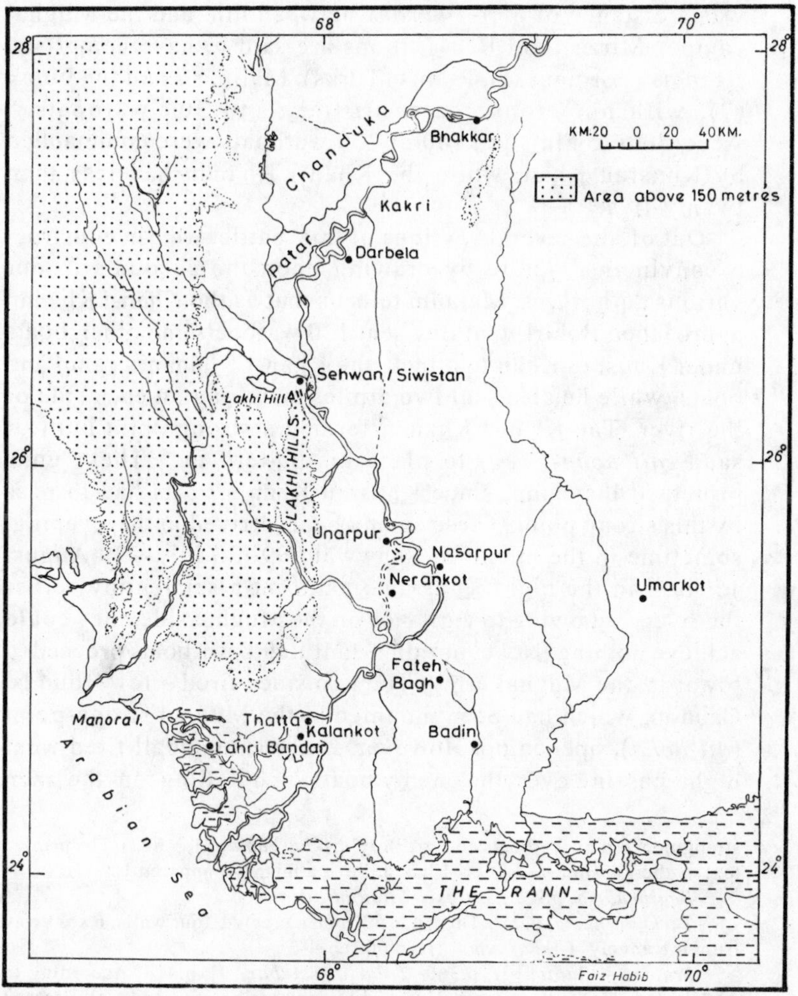

Sehwan under Dastām Beg; and Jānī Beg entrenched himself at Bohiri along with his soldiers, numbering 60,000.[52] There was a distance of 6 or 7 *kurohs* between him and the Mughal camp.[53] Mirzā Jānī Beg's troops are said to have comprised *firangīs* (Portuguese), Rūmīs (Turks), Mālibārīs and the Lūtak (?), with numerous boats, artillery and 300 warboats.[54] According to Ma'ṣūm, 100 or 200 warboats were commanded by Khusrau Khān, while the Khān-i Khānān had less than twenty-five.[55]

Out of the several versions of this battle, we can construct a convincing picture by drawing upon the accounts in our various authorities. Ma'ṣūm tells us that as the Khān-i Khānān approached Bohiri, Jānī Beg sent 120 warboats and other boats under Khusrau Khān to attack the Khān-i Khānān's camp and boats, while he also sent two armies marching on each side of the river. The Khān-i Khānān formed a strong point built of sand (*qil'acha-i reg*) to place his battery in.[56] These guns protected his camp, since Khusrau Khān's boats had to pass by this strong point. These enemy boats arrived in the evening, sometime in the month of Shawwāl 999 (23 July – 20 August 1591).[57] In the night Khusrau Khān sent a small army across the river; but owing to vigilance on the Mughal side, they could achieve nothing. Next morning, Jānī Beg's warboats proceeded towards the Mughal army. The two sides fired a few rounds. Cannon, which had been mounted at the Mughal strong-point (*qil'acha*), opened up. However, every cannonball fired went high, passing over the enemy boats, and falling on the men

strengthened it by warboats and artillery' (*Akbarnāma*, III, p.602). The printed text of the *Tarkhān-nāma*, p.71 has Lohiri, a misprint apparently.

52 *Beglārnāma*, p.232; *Ma'āṣir-i Raḥīmī*, II, p.360.

53 *Tarkhān-nāma*, p.71. 'The Khān-i Khānān erected four walls, 6 *kos* away from the enemy' (*Akbarnāma*, III, p.602).

54 *Ma'āṣir-i Raḥīmī*, II, p.360; *Ṭabaqāt-i Akbarī*, II, p.414. According to Abū'l Faẓl, Jānī Beg was accompanied by many tribesmen and well-dressed servants (*Akbarnāma*, III, p.602).

55 Khusrau Khān, belonging to a family claiming descent from Changez Khān, had served in various capacities under the Tarkhāns. He was reputed to be a great builder and constructed many bridges, mosques, and wells around Thatta and Makli (*Tuḥfat-u'l Kirām*, III, pp.214-6).

56 *Tārīkh-i Ma'ṣūmī*, pp.251-2.

57 Ibid, 252. 'The enemy could not come to close quarters owing to the shallowness of water' (*Akbarnāma*, III, p.602).

whom K̲h̲ān-i K̲h̲ānān himself had sent across the river.[58] The
guns were then lowered and they succeeded in hitting some 8
or 9 enemy warboats. The Sind warboats carried carpenters
to repair the damage, and so the engagement was prolonged.
At last, the Sind warboats began to withdraw. The K̲h̲ān-i
K̲h̲ānān's warboats, setting forth in pursuit, overtook them,
whilst the army stationed on the other side of the river also
attacked them.[59] K̲h̲usrau K̲h̲ān commanded his boats well,
keeping himself in the rear while sending some other warboats
to join the fight.[60] The battle continued till the evening, and
fire was continuously exchanged. The Sind warboats had to
struggle against the current of the river.[61] By the end of two
hours after mid-day a large number of their men had been
killed by cannonballs.[62] The Mughals not only used cannon
but also engaged in close fighting with spear and dagger.[63]
Some boats containing Portuguese soldiers now fell into their
hands.[64] An imperial warboat attacked K̲h̲usrau K̲h̲ān's *g̲h̲urābs*

---

[58] 'Hearing the news of Jānī Beg's arrival by land, Farīdūn Barlās and others
on a dark night left the river' (*Akbarnāma*, III, p.602).

[59] *Tārīk̲h̲-i Ma'ṣūmī*, p.252. For details, B.M. MS Add. 27, 247, f 393b.

[60] According to *Tārīk̲h̲-i Ṭāhirī*, pp.184-5, and *Tarkhān-nāma*, pp.72-3, Mirzā
Jānī in consultation with his soldiers decided to send a flotilla under the command
of K̲h̲usrau K̲h̲ān while the land force was under his own command. K̲h̲usrau K̲h̲ān
attacked the imperialists according to a plan under which a body of soldiers was
to remain on the boats whilst another would advance by land. But K̲h̲usrau K̲h̲ān
was deceived by his own people who were jealous of him and anxious for his
defeat. They did not turn up with reinforcements. K̲h̲usrau K̲h̲ān waited in vain
and protected his boats during the night by raising a wall of sand-bags. In the
morning he retreated.

[61] Abū'l Faẓl says that they (Sindis) were moving upstream, but were forced
down by the strength of the current (*Akbarnāma*, III, p.602).

[62] *Tārīk̲h̲-i Ma'ṣūmī*, p.252, *Akbarnāma*: B.M. MS, Add 27,247, f.393b.

[63] *Akbarnāma*, III, p.602. 'Fighting was horrible and many people were killed
or captured or drowned amidst the uproar of the river. Those who were seized, got
safety of life. A huge amount of booty came into the possession of the imperialists.
Ten or twelve galleys filled with Turkish, Malabar and Frankish soldiers sank into
the river. The K̲h̲ān-i K̲h̲ānān was so impressed with the bravery of rival forces
that he thought of composing a *Fathnāma* or of erecting a minaret of their heads'
(*Ma'āṣir-i Rahīmī*, II, p.362). According to *Akbarnāma* (III, p.603), 1000 of Jānī
Beg's men were wounded and 200 killed, while the Mughals suffered fewer
casualties.

[64] Four *g̲h̲urābs* (galleys) full of men were captured and in one of them
was the ambassador of the Portuguese settlement of Hurmuz (*Akbarnāma*, III,
p.603). Ṭāhir Nisyānī gives his name as Charkas Daftir and counts him as the

(galleys), but suddenly its powder magazine caught fire, burning many soldiers to death, and Khusrau Khān was thereby enabled to escape.[65] A significant victory was thus achieved by the Khān-i Khānān.

Afterwards, the imperial forces marched towards the fortress built by Mirzā Jānī Beg ('New Nasrpur'), but after a prolonged siege they found its reduction difficult.[66] One night they assaulted the fortress but gained no success. Moreover the Mughals faced a shortage of provisions.[67] As Jānī Beg had stopped all movement of supplies, and most of the territories and *parganas* of Sind were in his hands, the Khān-i Khānān decided to move towards Jun in southern Sind; and the siege was lifted.[68] Provisions were meanwhile sent by boat to the Mughal troops facing Sehwan.[69]

The Mughal officers decided to disperse among various parts of Sind:[70] One party was to move towards Sehwan, another

---

chief of the merchants of *Firang*, who came yearly from Hurmuz (*Tārīkh-i Ṭāhirī*, p.185).

[65] According to Nahāvandī (II, p.361) fire broke out in one of Jānī Beg's *ghurābs*. It appears from *Akbarnāma*, III, p.603, that 'royal *ghurābs* pursued Khusrau Khān, and injured him. They wanted to seize him; suddenly a gun burst and the boat was torn into pieces'. See *Tārīkh-i Ma'ṣūmī*, p.253; *Tarkhān-nāma*, p.73.

[66] *Tārīkh-i Ma'ṣūmī*, p.253, *Ma'āṣir-i Raḥīmī*, II, p.353; *Akbarnāma*, III, p.603. The *Beglārnāma*, pp.233-4, provides more details and says that 'frustrated in their designs, the imperialists decided to vacate the place and proceeded towards Shahgarh where Abū'l Qāsim was posted. Afterwards they moved towards Lar; finally they reached Sehwan and besieged the fortress'. It is stated in *Ma'āṣir-i Raḥīmī*, II p.263, that Khān-i Khānān, being unable to conquer the fortress, diverted his attention away from Nasrpur. Mirzā Jānī and his supporters planned to make night attacks upon the Mughal camp, but some of them hesitatingly remarked that they were facing Khān-i Khānān, not Ṣādiq Khān. See also B.M. MS, Add 27,247, f.393 a-b.

[67] Abū'l Fazl also speaks of the abundance of food in the enemy fort and shortage of provisions in the Mughal camp (*Akbarnāma*, III, pp.606, 608). *Ma'āṣir-i Raḥīmī*, III, p.263, says that the Khān-i Khānān informed the emperor [of these difficulties] and asked for help and received money and provisions along with Rs 1,50,000. Again, Rs 1 lakh and one lakh maunds of grain, a hundred big guns and numerous gunners and reinforcements were sent under Rāi Singh by way of Jaisalmer. See also *Ṭabaqāt-i Akbarī*, II, p.414.

[68] *Ma'āṣir-i Raḥīmī*, II, p.363. 'The enemy had the strength of men and the help of the peasantry and were waiting for rains' (*Akbarnāma*, III, p.608).

[69] Ibid., p.608.

[70] The *Tarkhān-nāma*, p.74, suggests that this plan was proposed to the

towards Thatta,[71] a third to Badin and Fateh Bagh.[72] Abū'l Faẓl, whose version is slightly different from that of Ma'ṣūm, also mentions Agham[73] and Umarkot among places which the Mughal troops now occupied.[74] Shāh Beg was sent to storm the fortress of Shahgarh, built by Shāh Qāsim Arghūn.[75] The force led by Bahādur Khān, Bakhtyār Beg, Ḥasan 'Alī 'Arab, Jān Beg and Maqṣūd Beg marched against Sehwan and besieged it.[76] When the siege was tightened, the garrison asked Jānī Beg for assistance, failing which they threatened to surrender the fortress.[77] Following the advice of Girya Mehta,[78] and paying heed to the requests of Abū'l Qāsim and Khusrau Khān, Mirzā Jānī Beg, along with 10,000 soldiers,[79] moved towards Sehwan.[80] Hearing the news of his arrival (at a place 6 *kurohs* distant), the Mughal forces arrayed themselves near Lakhi Hill. Here they were joined by fresh

---

Khān-i Khānān by Girya (Ghoria) Mehta, a traitor in Jānī Beg's forces, to compel Jānī Beg to come out from his fortress and join battle.

71 Most of the soldiers moved to Thatta 'to plunder the town to get supplies and harass the enemy' (*Akbarnāma*, III, p.608).

72 Dharū Bahādur, Khān Qūrdār and others were sent towards Badin (ibid., p.608).

73 Shāh Beg Khān, Muḥammad Khān Niāzī, Qāsim Koka, Murtaẓā Qulī, Dād Mal, Dūda Beg and others were sent to capture Agham, and to watch the activities of Mirzā Jānī Beg (*Akbarnāma*, III, p.608; B.M. MS, Add. 27, 247, f.395b).

74 Mirzā Farīdūn and Rāwal Bhīm were sent towards Umarkot, because the imperial control had slackened there (ibid., pp.606; 608; B.M. MS, f.395b).

75 *Tārīkh-i Ma'ṣūmī*, p.254.

76 *Tārīkh-i Ma'ṣūmī*, p.254; *Ma'āṣir-i Raḥīmī*, II, p.364. Abū'l Faẓl says that Sayyid Bahāu'ddīn, Qara Beg and Bakhtyār Beg were sent towards Sehwan along with stores (*Akbarnāma*, III, p.608; B.M. MS, Add. 27, 247, f.393b).

77 *Tārīkh-i Ma'ṣūmī*, p.254; *Ma'āṣir-i Raḥīmī*, II, p.363. The enemy was disturbed on account of their families (*Akbarnāma*, III, p.608).

78 Girya allegedly induced his master to leave the fortress of Nasrpur and to shift to Sehwan, stating that if the latter fell into Mughal hands, the gates of the country would be opened. Girya's plan was successful, for when Jānī Beg marched to Sehwan, the Mughals occupied Bohiri (*Tarkhān-nāma*, pp.74-75). Abū'l Faẓl says that the fort of Sehwan was invested by the imperialists under difficult circumstances (*Akbarnāma*, III, p.608).

79 *Tārīkh-i Ma'ṣūmī*, p.255; *Ma'āṣir-i Raḥīmī*, p.365. *Akbarnāma*, III, p.609, gives the number of his soldiers as 5000. See also *Ṭabaqāt-i Akbarī*, II, p.417. *Tarkhān-nāma*, p.77, puts the figure at 6000.

80 Abū'l Faẓl states that Jānī Beg proceeded to Sehwan to seize the boats already there; the *Ṭabaqāt-i Akbarī* (II, p.416) says that the performance of

reinforcements under Muḥammad Khān Niāzī, Bahādur Khān and Daulat Khān, along with artillery and boats; and now they numbered 12,000.[81] A description of the preparations, the stationing of troops, different wings of the army, their commanders and the ensuing conflict is given by Abū'l Fazl[82] and Ma'ṣūm Bhakkarī.[83] Ṭāhir Nisyānī, whose father Ḥasan was a participant in this battle, provides further details.[84] All the authorities say that in the beginning Jānī Beg put the Mughals under much pressure.[85] Bitter encounters took place, and the dense smoke and fire made distinction between foe and friend very difficult.[86] Though Jānī Beg fought bravely, a large number of his soldiers were killed or captured.[87] He remained in the battlefield along with 400 soldiers, but seeing no hope of success took to flight.[88] His soldiers in the fort[89] tried to stop the fleeing troops as they were pursued by the Khān-i Khānān's men. Jānī Beg's elephant rushed upon

---

the Sehwan troops was not satisfactory, so he went there to punish them. See also *Ma'āṣir-i Raḥīmī*, III, p.366; *Tarkhān-nāma*, p.77; *Beglārnāma*, p.234.

[81] *Tārīkh-i Ma'ṣūmī*, p.255; *Mā'aṣir-i Raḥīmī*, p.365; *Akbarnāma*, III, p.609; *Ṭabaqāt-i Akbarī*, II, pp.416-7.

[82] *Akbarnāma*, III, p.609.

[83] *Tārīkh-i Ma'ṣūmī*, p.255.

[84] The Khān-i Khānān's soldiers, in order to distinguish themselves, fixed arrows in their turbans, while the soldiers of Mirzā Jānī Beg tied green branches to their turbans. Mirzā Jānī Beg promised his soldiers that whosoever would bring an enemy head would receive 500 *kabars*. But Girya, who better understood the financial conditions of the state, reduced the reward to 50 *kabars*. In spite of this small amount of money, the starving people plunged themselves into the fight (*Tarikh-i Ṭāhirī*, p.183). The *Tārīkh-i Ṭāhirī* tells us (p.183) in a gloss that 1 *kabar* = *12 mīrīs*, and 72 *mīrīs* = 1 *ṭanka*. In other words, 1 *ṭanka* = 6 *kabars*. Since in Akbar's time 20 *ṭankas* were worth a rupee, 500 *kabars* would have been the equivalent a little above 4 rupees.

[85] *Akbarnāma*, III, p.609; *Ma'āṣir-i Raḥīmī*, p.367; *Tārīkh-i Ma'ṣūmī*, p.255.

[86] *Akbarnāma*, III, p.609; *Ma'āṣir-i Raḥīmī*, p.367; *Tārīkh-i Ma'ṣūmī*, p.255; *Beglārnāma*, p.236.

[87] *Tārīkh-i Ma'ṣūmī*, p.255. According to Abū'l Fazl, 300 men of Jānī Beg's side were killed and 100 of the imperial troops (*Akbarnāma*, III, p.609). The *Tarkhān-nāma*, p.79, gives the number of the slain (on both sides) as 8000, an incredible figure. For the details of the contest between Rāja Dharul Mal (son of Todar Mal) and Jānī Beg, see *Ma'āṣir-i Raḥīmī*, II, p.367; *Akbarnāma*, III, p.609; and *Tarkhān-nāma*, p.79.

[88] *Tārīkh-i Ma'ṣūmī*, p.255; *Akbarnāma*, III, p.609; B.M. MS, f.396a.

[89] Namely, Shāh Qāsim Arghūn, Khusrau Khān Charkas, Mullā Muḥammad Farahī, 'Alī Sulṭān Ghaznavī and Ḥasan. According to Abū'l Fazl, the fort was destroyed by the Khān-i Khānān (*Akbarnāma*, B.M. MS, f396a).

his own men, which created further havoc in his army.[90] Leaving the battlefield by a small vessel Jānī Beg reached Unarpur, 20 *kurohs* from the site of battle.[91] Here he built a fort surrounded by a deep and broad moat and entrenched himself there.[92] After a few days the Khān-i Khānān arrived and besieged the fortress. Afterwards all passages were stopped and supplies were cut off.[93] Meanwhile fresh reinforcements and provisions brought relief to the Mughal forces,[94] while the scarcity of food caused starvation in the enemy camp.[95]

In the meantime much had happened at Thatta:

After the Khān-i Khānān's arrival at Thatta, Mirzā Jānī Beg in a state of disappointment wrote to his father (Mirzā Pāyanda) to vacate the city (of Thatta) and move to the fort of Kalānkot (Tughralābād), that he had rebuilt for this day. Announcements were made for people to leave the city within three days. The flight started. The people in a hurry, being unable to carry their belongings, buried them beneath their houses. Even the porters demanded high rates and charged half or a third of the value of goods carried. After its desolation, the city, which was populous and flourishing, was consumed in flames; it burnt for about a month, because of its wooden houses. Whatever remained was plundered by groups of vagabonds who entered the city. As for those who were inside the fortress, their inconveniences were great. There was nothing to drink except the blood of their liver and nothing to eat except the flesh of their dead horses. No sign of smoke was to be seen from any chimney except that produced by cannon and musket. Bread was dearer than life, lips became saltless in the vain desire for salt. In the state of confinement, Mirzā Jānī Beg heard the news of the death of his father and his son, Abū'l Fatḥ, but his own

[90] *Akbarnāma* III, p.609; *Tārīkh-i Ṭāhirī*, p.191; *Tarkhān-nāma* p.79; *Ma'āṣir-i Raḥīmī*, II, p.367.

[91] Anarpur or Unarpur, 4 *kos* from Halakandi and 40 *kos* from Sehwan (*Akbarnāma*, III, p.614). According to *Tārīkh-i Ma'ṣūmī*, p.256, it was 20 *kurohs* from the battlefield.

[92] *Tārīkh-i Ṭāhirī*, pp.191-2, *Tārīkh-i Ma'ṣūmī*, p.256; *Beglārnāma*, p.239; *Tarkhān-nāma*, p.79.

[93] *Ma'āṣir-i Raḥīmī*, II, pp.368-9; *Ṭabaqāt-i Akbarī*, II, p.416.

[94] *Akbarnāma*, III, pp.608,615.

[95] 'On account of strangeness of the land and the refractoriness of the peasantry, provisions became scarce and food became dear. There was also much sickness. The extraordinary thing was that it (also) attacked the people of Sind'. (*Akbarnāma*, III, p.614). It seems that, in spite of imperial assistance, the Mughals too were not in an altogether happy position, when they accepted the peace proposals of Jānī Beg (*Akbarnāma*, III, p.615).

position was also helpless.[96]

The K͟hān-i K͟hānān, who was well informed of the situation, summoned all his troops from different areas.[97] Nerunkot,[98] Shahgarh and Badin came into the possession of the Mughals.

Contemporary sources provide much information about the siege of Jānī Beg's fort at Unarpur. A suitable site was chosen by the Mughals, its three sides surrounded by water. They dug trenches leading towards the fort, and at the same time carried sand forward to fill the ditch surrounding the fort.[99] Abū'l Faẓl offers clearer details. After the custom of the Ottomans, the Mughals raised mounds of sand and carried forward their batteries and set about filling up the moat. From within, the enemy made sorties to remove the sand.[100] The K͟hān-i K͟hānān made a pledge that nobody would take rest or wash himself till the ditch was filled. Ustād Yār Muḥammad K͟hān, the architect (*ma'mār*), who had recently arrived from Iran, was ordered to build a high tower to set the battery on, so as to command the citadel.[101] These measures greatly alarmed Mirzā Jānī Beg; but he did not show his fear and often came out of the fortress.[102] As the batteries advanced, active fighting commenced. The struggle was fierce and a large number of people were slain. Suddenly, however, both parties agreed to a truce.

Historians differ regarding the circumstances of the peace negotiations. According to Abū'l Faẓl, 'the garrison, troubled,

---

[96] *Tārīk͟h-i Ṭāhirī*, pp.194-5. Niẓāmu'ddīn also says that the people slaughtered their animals and ate them (*Ṭabaqāt-i Akbarī*, II, p.417). Abū'l Faẓl tells us that the air in the fort had become dangerous on account of the number of dead bodies, and the condition of the survivors had become critical (*Akbarnāma*, III, p.616).

[97] Abū'l Faẓl mentions it in connection with the siege of Sehwan stating that contingents which were sent to Thatta, did not perform well since wicked people were allowed to set fire to the city (*Akbarnāma*, III, p.608).

[98] Abū'l Faẓl refers to the capture of Nerunkot and praises its strength (*Akbarnāma*, III, p.614).

[99] *Tārīk͟h-i Ma'ṣūmī*, p.256.   [100] *Akbarnāma*, III, p.615.

[101] *Ma'āṣir-i Raḥīmī*, II, pp.368-9.

[102] It is said that Jānī Beg wanted to leave the fort or to move elsewhere, but Abū'l Qāsim advised him to stay as many Arg͟hūn and Tark͟hān families resided there (*Beglārnāma*, p.239). Abū'l Faẓl mentions a group of Arabs and Kurds among the residents of the fortress, who quarrelled with Qāsim 'Alī (*Akbarnāma*, III, p.614; B.M. MS, Add. 27,247, f.396a).

begged for peace and the Mughal army accepted it because of the shortage of food'.[103] Similar statements are made by Ma'ṣūm Bhakkarī[104] and 'Abdū'l Bāqī Nahāvandī.[105] Ma'ṣūm says the Mughal officers advised the Khān-i Khānān against accepting a truce since Mirzā Jānī Beg was now as good as in their hands. The Khān-i Khānān, however, overruled them, and took what ultimately appeared to the historian himself to be a wise decision. But the Sind historians, Idrākī Beglār[106] and the author of the *Tarkhān-nāma,*[107] say that the appeal for peace came from the Khān-i Khānān's side. Ṭāhir Nisyānī says that when the Khān-i Khānān's envoy reached the presence of Jānī Beg, the latter was sitting along with his few soldiers, 'pierced with wounds, wearing blue garments to mourn his dear ones — father, son and the soldiers, but the same grandeur, the same majesty as before, was manifest from his countenance so that it astonished the envoy'.[108] He departed along with Mirzā Jānī Beg's envoy, Rifāqat 'Alī Kābulī. It is alleged that some nobles of Mirzā Jānī Beg were already in secret correspondence with the Khān-i Khānān.[109] Mirzā Jānī Beg, acceeding to the Khān-i Khānān's proposal, at last accepted the following terms:

(1) Siwistan, with the fort of Sehwan, was to be surrendered to the Mughals.[110]

(2) The Khān-i Khānān was to acquire 20 *ghurābs*(galleys)[111] from Jānī Beg.

[103] *Akbarnāma*, III, p.614, B.M. MS, Add. 27,247, f.396a.

[104] *Tārīkh-i Ma'ṣūmī*, p.256, according to which the Khān-i Khānān in accepting proposals of the truce, thought of proposing a *manṣab* of 5000 for Jānī Beg.

[105] 'The imperial forces were proceeding towards victory; Jānī Beg sued for peace' (*Ma'āṣir-i Raḥīmī*, II, pp.370-1).

[106] *Beglārnāma*, p.239, says that the Khān-i Khānān sent Miānjī, a pious man, for the peace negotiations, and Jānī Beg accepted his offer.

[107] *Tarkhān-nāma*, p.79.

[108] *Tārīkh-i Ṭāhirī*, pp.197-9. According to Mīr 'Alī Sher Thattavī, 'on this occasion the Khān-i Khānān sent a message to Jānī Beg to this effect: What if by the revolution of time some fighting took place between us. The bravery you have shown will long be remembered. But you must remember that on one side you have the emperor of the world, before whom brave warriors rub their foreheads', etc. (*Tuḥfatu'l Kirām*, III, p.159).

[109] *Tārīkh-i Ṭāhirī*, p.199; *Tuḥfatu'l Kirām*, III, p.160.

[110] *Akbarnāma*, III, p.615; *Tārīkh-i Ma'ṣūmī*, p.256.

[111] Thirty *ghurābs* (galleys) according to *Tārīkh-i Ma'ṣūmī*, p.256, and

(3) The soldiers of both sides were to be allowed to sell and purchase freely in each other's markets.[112]

(4) Jānī Beg was given three months' time to make his preparations to meet the Khān-i Khānān personally.[113]

(5) Jānī Beg should accept Mirzā Iraj, the Khān-i Khānān's son as a son-in-law, and after the rains should go to the Court.[114]

It was decided that the siege should be abandoned first. Afterwards, 'on 16th Khūrdād (26 May 1592) batteries were dismantled and betrothal ceremonies were performed'.[115]

After this agreement, Mirzā Jānī Beg moved to Thatta, and Sehwan was surrendered to the Mughals.[116] The Khān-i Khānān preferred to stay at Sun (20 *kurohs* from Sehwan) to spend the rainy season there.[117]

From here the process of annexation of Sind took a new turn. First of all, there was much anxiety felt by Jānī Beg on the imperial demand that he should send his wives and sisters to the court in advance.[118] Abū'l Fazl also says that Jānī Beg did not go to the court in accordance with the agreement, but sent a message that he would undertake his journey after collecting the autumn revenue.[119] This unnecessary delay caused annoyance in the Mughal camp. Jānī Beg's envoy was kept in custody and all the three wings of the army hastened towards Nasrpur.[120] Jānī Beg came out from Thatta and

---

Tarkhān-nāma, p.80. *Akbarnāma* III, p.615, and *Ṭabaqāt-i Akbarī*, II, p.417, mention only twenty.

[112] *Tārīkh-i Ṭāhirī*, p.199.

[113] *Akbarnāma*, III, p.615; *Ṭabaqāt-i Akbarī*, II, p.418; *Ma'āṣir-i Raḥīmī*, II, p.371. Mirzā Jānī Beg, says Mīr Ma'ṣūm, expressed his wish to go to Thatta, with the promise of meeting the Khān-i Khānān. The Mughal commanders hesitated to accept the treaty; they feared that after reaching Thatta, Jānī Beg would change his mind.

[114] *Akbarnāma*, III, p.615. This provision is not mentioned in *Tārīkh-i Ma'ṣūmī*, p.256.

[115] *Akbarnāma*, III, p.615. Jānī Beg's other daughter was married to Jahāngīr's son, Prince Khusrau.

[116] 'On this day Rustam, the governor of Sehwan, made over the fort to Ḥasan 'Alī 'Arab, and Maqṣūd Āqā; and all of Siwistan was added to the Empire' (*Akbarnāma*, III, p.616).

[117] Ibid., p.616; *Beglārnāma*, p.240; *Tarkhan-nāma*, p.80; *Tuḥfatu'l Kirām*, III, p.161.

[118] *Tārīkh-i Ṭāhīrī*, ff.92b, 94a, 95b.

[119] *Akbarnāma*, III, p.634. [120] Ibid.

arrived at the distance of 3 *kurohs* from the Mughal camp. He kept his rear open to provide safe access to the river.[121] After a small skirmish the Mughals plundered the Mirzā's camp. He enquired the reason of the violation of the treaty, but was told that the Mughals were compelled to take this action owing to the reported arrival of the Portuguese.[122] The spoils were restored to him with apologies, and the relations of friendship were renewed.

In the beginning of winter, the Khān-i Khānān arrived at the river of Fath Bagh, some 20 *kurohs* from Thatta. Here, in a pleasant atmosphere, he met Mirzā Jānī Beg, and both professed delight in greeting each other.[123] Both of them arranged feasts at their residences and invited all the grandees present. The Khān-i Khānān now went to Thatta,[124] and here both of them met several times.[125] They went together for sight-seeing and hunting, and also visited Tughralābād, Lahri Bandar and the Manora Island (near Karachi).[126] The Khān-i Khānān gave Jānī Beg the assurance that he would recommend his case to the emperor and his territory would be restored to him. Afterwards, Mirzā Jānī Beg moved to Tughralābād and

[121] Ibid.

[122] The Khān-i Khānān asked him to surrender his fleet so that in future pirates may be dealt with by its assistance (*Akbarnāma*, III, p.634).

[123] *Tarkhān-nāma*, p.80.

[124] Commenting on the Khān-i Khānān's visit, Abū'l Fazl says that 'his ostensible move was to see the place but his real intention was to secure the lower part of the river' (*Akbarnāma*, III, p.634).

[125] *Tarkhān-nāma*, p.80. Here Abū'l Fazl's version is a little different: 'After visiting Thatta, the Khān-i Khānān went to Lahri Bandar. He despatched Shāh Beg Khān, Bakhtyār Beg, Farīdūn Barlās and others to go forward with the Mirzā. He left someone in Thatta and returned by land. Near Fath Bagh he arrived in person on 29 Bahman (20 February)' (*Akbarnāma*, III, p.634).

[126] Several anecdotes of their friendly relations are recorded in contemporary works (*Maqālāt-u'sh Shu'rā*, pp.526-7; *Tuhfatu'l Kirām*, III, p.161). The following is related from *Tarkhān-nāma*, pp.80-1: The Khān-i Khānān and Mirzā Jānī Beg went together on boats in the 'billowing open sea'. The Khān-i Khānān and his nobles, since they had never been out on the sea, were greatly disturbed and became suspicious of Jānī Beg's intentions. Meanwhile the Mirzā's followers advised him to get rid of his guests (by drowning them), but he strongly objected. He brought his own vessel near the Khān-i Khānān's boat and entertained him. Mirzā Jānī was not merely a man of letters and poet but also possessed a sense of humour. Abū'l Fazl also praises his scholarly attainments (*Akbarnāma*, III, p.783).

the Khān-i Khānān went to Thatta to take charge of the affairs of the province which now became a part of the Mughal empire (1000/1592).

The *Ma'āṣir-i Raḥīmī* tells us that the success was celebrated with great rejoicings. Ustād Yār Muḥammad Khān was ordered to construct a pandal for the occasion. Offerings were made and rewards were conferred on the soldiers. Panegyric poems (*qaṣīdas*) were composed by the poets in the train of the Khān-i Khānān, such as Mullā Shakebī Isfahānī, Naẓīrī Nīshāpūrī, 'Urfī Shīrāzī, Būiqulī Beg Baqāī, Ghayūrī Shustarī, Muḥammad Sharīf Qawī, Mīr Mughīṣ Mahwī, Ḥayātī Gīlānī and Kāmī Khurāsānī.[127]

It is said that Mullā Shakebī wrote a *maṣnawī* '*Sāqīnāma*' for this occasion and recited the following verses:

> A Humā (mythical bird), which was moving over the Heavens,
> You seized and freed from delusion.

The Khān-i Khānān gave him 12,000 *ashrafīs* in reward; and Jānī Beg himself gave the poet a handsome reward as he felt delighted and said, 'It is by God's mercy that you called me the noblest of the birds. Had you called me an ugly crow, who would have checked your tongue?'[128]

Meanwhile an imperial *farmān* was received ordering that Khān-i Khānān should come to the court along with Jānī Beg. Leaving Bahā'u'ddīn to guard the country,[129] the Khān-i Khānān arrived at the court (1593) accompanied by Jānī Beg and other nobles.[130] Jānī Beg was kindly treated by Akbar and was honoured with the rank of 3000.[131] Soon he gained the emperor's favour and confidence. Two of his daughters were already married in the royal family. On the Khān-i Khānān's

[127] *Ma'āṣir-i Raḥīmī*, II, pp.374-5. For these *qaṣīdas*, see *Tuḥfatu'l Kirām*, III, pp.259-75.

[128] *Maqālāt-u'sh Shu'rā*, pp.526-7; *Tārikh-i Ṭahirī*, p.207; *Tuḥfatu'l Kirām*, III, p.161; Farīd Bhakkari, *Zakhīrat al-Khawānīn*, Karachi, 1961, I, p.39.

[129] *Akbarnāma*, III, p.634. According to *Tārīkh-i Ma'ṣūmī*, p.257, Daulat Khān Lodī and Khwāja Muqīm were left to administer the country on the Khān-i Khānān's behalf.

[130] For the list of nobles, see *Akbarnāma*, III, p.634; *Muntakhab-al-Tāwārīkh* II, p.386.

[131] It was then increased to 3500. *Akbarnāma*, III, p.721. Mirzā Jānī's rank is variously given. The *Tārīkh-i Ma'ṣūmī* p.376, mentions his rank as 4000 or 5000. In *Ma'āṣir-i Raḥīmī*, II, p.376, it is put at 3000 at one place

recommendation all the territories of Jānī Beg, including Thatta,[132] were restored to him except Siwistan[133] and Lahri Bandar.[134] The nobles who served in Sind as well as the notables of Thatta who visited the Court, were rewarded handsomely.[135] Abū'l Faẓl quotes Akbar's letter, written to Shāh 'Abbās Ṣafavī, soon after the conquest of Sind and despatched through Ẓiā-u'l Mulk, which refers to Jānī Beg's visit and the restoration of Thatta to him.[136] In his absence Thatta was governed by his son Ghāzī Beg.[137] The last statement of Abū'l Faẓl, which relates to Jānī Beg, but which is not corroborated by any other historian, is that 'though some courtiers represented that he should be restrained from returning, their suggestions were not proper'.[138] Mirzā Jānī Beg stayed in the imperial court and remained on good terms with the emperor.[139] He even counted himself as a member of the emperor's spiritual disciples.[140] He accompanied Akbar when the latter besieged the fortress of Asirgarh.[141] Jānī Beg died at Burhanpur in 1599 or 1600 from an attack of apoplexy

---

and 4000 at another (II, p.349). It appears from the *Tuzuk-i Jahāngīrī* (tr., I, p.131) that he had held the rank of 5000 *zāt* and 5000 *sawār*. See, however, M. Athar Ali, *Apparatus of Empire*, Delhi, 1985, Entries A 196, 332, 427, 497, 758, showing that when he died he had not risen above 3500; his *sawār* rank remains unknown. All higher ranks assigned to him appear to be fictitious.

132 Thatta was previously given to Shāh Rukh (*Akbarnāma*, III, p.638, B.M. MS, Add. 27, 247, f.406a).

133 Siwistan, which had been annexed as a *peshkash* (offering to the emperor) in the first instance was given in *jāgīr* to Bakhtyār Beg (ibid., p.642).

134 Bandar Lahri in the Indus delta was included in the *Khāliṣa* (ibid., p.642).

135 The nobles from Thatta were: Shāh Qāsim Arghūn, Khusrau Bahāīkhān, Dastān, Saifullāh 'Arab, and Nadīm Koka. Every one received princely favours. Among the court nobles, Shāh Beg Khān was made an officer of 2500, and Sayyid Bahāu'ddīn of 1000 (*Akbarnāma*, III, pp.634, 638; B.M. MS, Add. 27,247, f.466b).

136 *Maktūbāt-i 'Allāmī*, p.23.

137 *Tārīkh-i Ma'sūmī*, p.257; *Tārīkh-i Ṭāhirī*, p.205.

138 *Akbarnāma*, III, p.643, tr. p.986.

139 Several stories relating to their cordial relations are alluded to by the *Beglārnāma*, pp.241-2; *Tārīkh-i Ṭāhirī*, pp.204-5; and *Tuḥfatu'l Kirām*, III, pp.164-5.

140 *Muntakhab al-Tawārīkh*, II, p.305.

141 A reference in *Zakhīrat al-Khawānīn*, II, p.21, shows that on this occasion Mirzā Jānī Beg lost Akbar's favour because of his comments relating to the surrender of the fortress by the ruler of Khandesh.

or brain fever.[142] His body in accordance with an imperial *farmān* was taken to Thatta by Khwāja Muḥammad Qūr Begī. Makli near Thatta is his final resting place.[143]

[142] *Tārīkh-i Ma'ṣūmī*, p.257; *Tuḥfat u'l Kirām*, III, p.165. According to *Tārīkh-i Ṭāhirī*, p.208 and *Akbarnāma*, III, p.783, he died because of excessive drink. Abū'l Faẓl mentions 1601 as the year of his death. See also *Ma'āṣir al-Umarā*, I, p.527.

[143] *Tuḥfatu'l Kirām*, III, p.165.

5

Disappearance of Coin Minting in the 1580s? — A Note on the *Alf* Coins

NAJAF HAIDER

For quite some time numismatists and historians have expressed their sense of mystification at the virtual absence of coins of almost all denominations from the major mints of the Mughal empire during the period A.H. 989–99 (1581-2 to 1590-1).[1] The coins seem to reappear in A.H. 1000 (1591-2) in large numbers with the mint-name Urdū Ẓafar Qarīn and with the date *alf* or 1000 inscribed on them.

Among scholars who have reflected on this phenomenon, John S. Deyell appears to have been the most imaginative. According to him it was the result of the 'simultaneous closing of the mints' during the entire decade of the 1580s. He suggested that the primary function of the Mughal mints was to remint the previously accumulated coins or the obsolete coins of the current regime, and once this process was complete the mint operations became uneconomical. This, in his view, happened in A.H. 988-9. Deyell thus discounts the share of the freshly supplied bullion in the total output of the inland mints. But he himself concedes that the absence of gold coinage is difficult to explain since very little of it was available for reminting either from the previous regime or from out of current circulation.[2] He still concludes by saying:

[1] P.L. Gupta, 'The Gold Mohars of Akbar', *Indian Numismatic Chronicle*, Vol.IV, part II, 1965-6, pp.157-8; Irfan Habib, 'The Economic and Social Setting', in Michael Brand and Glenn D. Lowry (ed.), *Fathpur Sikri*, Marg Publication, Bombay, 1987, p.79; John S. Deyell, 'The Development of Akbar's Currency System and Monetary Integration of the Conquered Kingdoms', in J.F. Richards (ed.), *The Imperial Monetary System of Mughal India*, Delhi, 1987, pp.33-5.

[2] John S. Deyell, *op.cit.*, pp.33-4.

If several major mints faced this cost squeeze for a few years, becoming only marginally profitable, the government may have decided to suspend all recoinage throughout the empire pending further reorganization of the mints.[3]

P.L. Gupta, no less exercised over this vacuum, has been more cautious. In his opinion, the mints simply stopped giving their names to the coins they uttered, which uniformly took the name Urdū for reasons presumably linked to a reorganization of the mints.[4] This, however, does not explain why the years from A.H. 989 to 999 should be missing.

Before offering an explanation for the decade-long 'disappearance' of coins it is desirable to survey the relevant nuimismatic evidence. Table I is based on the specimens collected from several museum catalogues,[5] and counted chronologically. Table II is derived from treasure trove reports of the Lucknow Museum, similarly arranged.[6] Our count begins from A.H. 980 and ends at A.H.1007 or 44 Ilāhī year, and covers the output of eleven mints. Table I clearly bears out the numismatists' concern: with the notable exception of the Ahmadabad mint, which shows continuous minting of silver coins well into the Ilāhī years, representation of silver coins from every other mint stops at A.H. 989 (A.D.1581-2) and begins only in A.H.

[3] Ibid., p.34. Deyell (p.35) also offered alternative explanations such as falling demand for money after the Karori experiment had been abandoned, or failure of the mint reorganization of 1577-8, and scandalous mismanagement.

[4] P.L. Gupta, *op.cit.*; also see Deyell, *op.cit.*, Appendix 5.6, for criticism of Gupta's arguments: 'The Question of the Mint name "Urdu" and the closing of the Mints', pp.61-2.

[5] S. Lane-Poole, *The Coins of the Moghul Emperors of Hindustan in the British Museum*, London, 1892; H. Nelson Wright, *Catalogue of the Coins in the Indian Museum, Calcutta*,Vol.II, pt.III: *Mughal Emperors of India*, Oxford, 1908; C.J. Brown, *Catalogue of Coins in the Provincial Museum, Lucknow: Coins of the Mughal Empeors*, 2 Vols., Oxford, 1920; C.R. Singhal, *Supplementary Catalogue of Mughal Coins in the State Museum, Lucknow*, Lucknow, 1965; R.B. Whitehead, *Catalogue of Coins in the Punjab Museum, Lahore*, Vol.II, *Coins of the Mughal Emperors*, Oxford, 1934; M.K. Hussain, *Catalogue of Coins of the Mughal Emperors (Treasure Trove Collections,Bombay)*, Bombay,1968; V.P. Rode, *Catalogue of Coins in the Central Museum, Nagpur*, part I, Bombay,1969; and R.B. Whitehead, *Catalogue of Coins, Illustrative of the History of the Rulers of Delhi up to 1858 A.D. (Delhi Museum)*, New Delhi,1990.

[6] I am grateful to Professor Shireen Moosvi for allowing me access to the information she has collected on U.P. treasure troves.

1000 or Ilahi year 37(A.D.1591-2).[7] The gold coins too stop around A.H. 989. Even in the Ahmadabad mint they do not re-appear. With regard to the copper coins, the story is the same in the tri-metallic mints, though it is a little different in the mints of Ajmer, Dogaon and Narnol which worked solely in copper.[8] Coins from these mints continue appearing with Hijri dates up to the year 1000.

Apart from the coins struck from various mints in A.H.1000 and onwards, a large number of coins appear in all the three metals from the mint Urdū Ẓafar Qarīn (lit. Camp associated with Victory) bearing the date *alf* or 1000.

Table II largely strengthens the impression obtained from Table I, though some variation is noticeable in case of Delhi and Lahore. As in Table I, silver coins are almost non-existent in the decade A.H.990-9. (Gold coins hardly occur in the treasure troves during the entire period covered, there being only two from Agra, of A.H. 985 and 987, while copper coins seem less affected.) The number of coins belonging to the mint Urdū Ẓafar Qarīn in A.H. 1000 is very high, and is only next to Ahmadabad, which in any case offers an exception to the entire trend. The occurrence of large quantities of mintless coins in Table II may be due to an important difference between the two sets of numismatic evidence we have consulted. While the treasure trove reports do not examine the coins as severely as the museum catalogues, the latter represent holdings which have a tendency to exclude or reject duplicates, particularly when they appear in large numbers.[9]

The question, therefore, is whether the gap shown in Tables I and II is real, and the Mughal mints did actually close down, or there is some other explanation. The matter assumes comp-lexity because if no mint was working in this period, one has

[7] The Lahore mint, however, resumes representation in 36 Ilāhī year (A.H. 999/A.D. 1590-1). See Table I.

[8] Ajmer started minting silver coins after Akbar, but at least five silver coins of A.H. 970 from the Narnol mint have been published.

[9] See for this point John S. Deyell, 'Numismatic Methodology in the Estimation of Mughal Currency Output', *IESHR*, XIII, No.3, 1976, pp.375-92, esp. p.395 (Table I). The published treasure trove reports from the Lucknow Museum suffer from the same problem. See for instance A.K. Srivastava, *Coin Hoards of Uttar Pradesh*, Vol.1, Lucknow, 1981, which shows a similar tendency to ignore counts of duplicates.

to explain why Bāyazīd Bayāt was appointed suprintendent (*dārogha*) of the Fatehpur Sikri mint in A.H. 993 (A.D.1585), a fact we know of as a certainty.[10]

It would seem that there is an explanation, and a very simple one at that. The critical information is given in a passage in the *Muntakhab u't Tawārīkh* of 'Abdul Qādir Badāūnī under A.H. 990 (1582-3):

And having thus convinced himself that the thousand years from the prophethood of the apostle, the duration for which Islam (lit. religion) would last, was now over, and nothing prevented him from articulating the desires he so secretly held in his heart; and the space (*basāṭ*) became empty of the theologians (*'ulamā*) and mystics (*mashā'ikh*) who had carried awe and dignity and no need was felt for them; he [Akbar] felt himself at liberty to refute the principles of Islam, and to institute new regulations — obsolete and corrupt but considered precious by his pernicious beliefs. The first order which was given was that on all coins be written *alf* (1000) and the *Tārīkh-i Alfī* be written from the demise (*riḥlat*) of the Prophet.[11]

Badāūnī thus makes it quite clear that all coins of the empire were made to bear the date *alf* or 1000 at least ten years before the year was actually due. The order was thus implemented and all the coins struck from A.H. 990 from the mints listed in Tables I and II bore a single date. Though Badāūnī does not expressly say so, a new mint-name too replaced the actual mint-names, this name being 'Urdū Ẓafar Qarīn'. When the *alf* year (1000) came round, the decision to revert to the previous system was apparently taken, but with the use of the Ilāhī instead of the Hijri year.[12] Therefore, all the mints in question must have continuously worked during the 1580s, but without putting their specific names on the coins. Since the measure seems to have

[10] Bāyazīd Bayat, *Tazkira-i Humāyūn wa Akbar*, ed. Hidayat Hussain, Bib. Indica, 1941, p.373.

[11] 'Abdu'l Qādir Badāūnī, *Muntakhab u't-Tawārīkh*, ed. William Lees and Ahmad Ali, Bib. Ind., Calcutta, 3 Vols., 1864-9; Vol.II, p.301. The information has not been hidden from the eyes of the numismatists and has been used to prove a rather different point. See U.S. Rāo, 'On Alf Coins of Akbar', *Journal of Numismatic Society of India*, Vol.XXV, 1963, p.249 and n.

[12] The Ilāhī era was introduced in A.H. 992 (1584-5) (H.S. Hodivala, *Historical Studies in Mughal Numismatics*, Bombay, 1976, p.14). But the Ilāhī coins do not appear before A.H. 1000 (except for the Lahore mint, where they appear a little before this year).

affected only the gold and silver mints, the copper mints remained exempt.

As we would expect from our solution, the coins from Urdū Ẓafar Qarīn in our Tables would be placed under A.H.1000, and their number is the largest in all the metals in relation to the respective output of the other mints in the preceding and following decades. Similarly, there is a dramatic spurt in the production of the mintless coins from 19 in A.H. 999 to 65 in A.H.1000 and then a sudden decline to 8 in A.H.1001(Table II.) This might mean that in certain mints even the name Urdū Ẓafar Qarīn was not given to the coins struck through the decade A.H. 990–9.

Why was this measure undertaken at all? To put *alf* on the coins might have had some ideological significance; but why remove the mint-name? A solution to this might possibly be located in what Monserrate says on the basis of his observations in 1580-2. He speaks of a system of imperial control which Akbar had imposed on the business of the money-changers (*ṣarrāfs*), forcing them to conduct their business according to his regulations.[13] One way of regulating the exchange business seems to have been to deny the money-changers any opportunity to levy discount and premium on the coins belonging to particular mints and years.[14] Akbar might have thought that this could best be done by a system of minting which precluded any mint identification along with removing differences of years (all coins being *alf* coins).[15]

It may also be noted that the original memorandum of Todar Mal, which belongs to the 27th Ilāhī year (1582), instructs the

[13] *The Commentary of Father Monserrate, S.J., on his journey to the Court of Akbar (1590-91)*, tr. J.S. Hoyland and S.N. Banerjee, London, 1922, p.207.

[14] See Irfan Habib, 'The Currency System of the Mughal Empire (1556-1707)', *Medieval India Quarterly*, IV, 1971, pp. 4-6, on the system of discount and premium (the sources are cited entensively in the footnotes). I am currently engaged in a detailed study of the monetary practices of Mughal *ṣarrāfs*.

[15] John S. Deyell alludes to the theoretical possibility of such a motive in his arguments (*op.cit* p.33).

[16] Abū'l Faẓl, *Akbarnāma*, British Museum, Add. 27247, f.330b; tr. Shireen Moosvi, 'Todar Mal's Original Memorandum on Revenue Administration, March 1582', *Proceedings of the Indian History Congress*, 49 Session, Dharwad, 1988 (1989), pp.245ff.

mint officials to remit newly struck coins to the treasuries to be exchanged for coins of previous years (*sikka sanwāt-i guẕashta*), paid apparently into the treasury as state dues through the agency of the local revenue and treasury officials (*karori* and *foṭadār*) and the money-changers (*ṣarrāf*) in accordance with elaborate state regulations on weight, value and fineness.[16] The injunctions are subsequently reiterated specifically for the money-changers (*ṣarrāf*) and conclude with a warning against any deviation.[17]

It seems however that the efforts towards monetary management of this kind failed to produce the desired effect, and in the 39th regnal year of Akbar it was revealed that the revenue officials (*'amalguzār*) of the *k͟hāliṣa*, assignment holders (*tuyūldār*) and money-changers (*ṣairafī*) were demanding pure coins (*sikka-i k͟hāliṣ*), while levying discount (*ṣarf*) even on coins of full weight and fineness (*naqd-i durust 'aiyār tamām wazn*). It was only when an official, K͟hwāja Shamsuddīn, appointed solely on this mission, laboured for about two months that things were apparently set right and the defaulters (*k͟hiyānat peshagān*) were cornered.[18]

The occurrence of silver coins with the correct years and mint names from Delhi and Lahore in certain years as shown in Table II could perhaps be explained in terms of concessions granted to these mints to strike normal coins either partially or fully for reasons that were presumably financial. The two cities participated considerably in importing horses from Central Asia and Persia and a substantial amount of silver coins flowed out of the importing regions (Rs 28.4 lakhs a year by one estimate).[19] It is likely that the merchants involved in the transactions preferred the more familiar and identifiable set of coins over the *alf* or mintless coins. Similarly, the explanation for the Ahmadabad mint being exempted from this measure may lie in its coveted position as a major recipient of bullion from the

[17] Ibid. In the revised and final version of *Akbarnāma* (Vol.III, ed. Aḥmad Alī, Calcutta 1887, p.383) the proposed regulations are summarized, but the emphasis on imperial control is retained.

[18] Abū'l Faẓl, *Akbarnāma*, Vol.III, p.651. Also see Irfan Habib, 'Currency System of the Mughal Empire', *op.cit.*, p. 5n.

[19] Shireen Moosvi, *The Economy of the Mughal Empire c.1595: A Statistical Study*, Delhi, 1987, p.379.

west with a more organized and assertive money-changing busi-ness, and the circulation of *maḥmūdīs* and rupees exchanging at market rates at Surat. These explanations, however, are pre-liminary. A more detailed study of the currency systems of these regions is required to resolve these subordinate questions.

TABLE I

A. SILVER COINS IN MUSEUM CATALOGUES: A.H. 980-100

Years (Hijri/ Ilāhī)	Agra	Delhi	Fateh-pur	Lahore	Patna	Jaunpur	Narnol	Urdū Ẓafar Qarīn	Mintless	Ahmadabad
980	4	1		4	1	1			5	
981	4			2					4	2
982	1								1	7
983	3	1		2	1	5			4	7
984	2	1		5		2			7	3
985	3	5	3	3		2			7	3
986	1	1	7	5	1				6	4
987			10	9	6	5			5	7
988			8	4	1	2			1	5
989			6	4		1			2	2
990									4	5
991									3	5
992/29									3	4
993/30									1* + 11	5* + 4
994/31									2	5
995/32									7* + 3	7
996/33									12* + 1	5
997/34									13* + 4	4
998/35									24* + 5	2
999/36				11*					7* + 8	4
1000/37		4*		18*				28	9* + 4	4* + 5
1001/38		1*		25*				1	8*	1
1002/39		4*		18*					8*	23*
1003/40		1*		11*					9*	7*
1004/41		1*		4*						1*
1005/42		1*		2*						2*
1006/43		3*								2*
1007/44	1	1*		2*					2*	

B. COPPER COINS IN MUSEUM CATALOGUES A.H. 980 — 1007

Years (Hijri/ Ilāhī)	Agra	Delhi	Fatehpur	Lahore	Patna	Jaunpur	Ajmer	Dagaon	Narnol	Urdū Zafar Qarīn	Mintless	Ahma-dabad
980	1			3			4	2	7		1	2
981		4		1			4	1	2		1	3
982	3	2	1	2			4	2	2		1	5
983	2	1		2			1	5	3		1	2
984	1			1			1	4	3		1	3
985	2	1	4					3	3		2	3
986	2	1	10	2			1	4	3		1	3
987		2	9	10		1	1	3	3		4	2
988	3	3	5	4			1	5	3		1	
989	1		1	2			2	2	1		1	
990							1	2	.			
991							3	2	1			
992/29							3	2	2			
993/30							2	5	1			
994/31							3	4	1		1*	
995/32							1	2				
996/33							1	1			6*	
997/34							2					
998/35										2*		
999/36					6*		2	2 + 1*		3*		
1000/37				5*	12*			1		4* + 19		
1001/38				15*	11*		1	1		4*		
1002/39				8*	20*					1*		
1003/40	1*			4*	3*		2	1		1*		
1004/41							2	3		2*		
1005/42										3*		
1006/43												
1007/44							2*			37		

* Ilāhī year coin(s)

C. GOLD COINS IN MUSEUM CATALOGUES A.H. 980– 1007

Years (Hijri/ Ilāhī)	Agra	Delhi	Fatehpur	Lahore	Patna	Jaunpur	Ajmer	Dagaon	Narnol	Urdū Ẓafar Qarīn	Mintless	Ahma-dabad
980	1					1					1	5
981	4										2	4
982	12											8
983	1			4		1					1	2
984	2				3	1					2	2
985				3	2						1	
986			5	1							1	3
987			2	2	3							1
988			2	4						1	2	4
989										1	1	
990												
991												
992/29												
993/30											1*	
994/31												
995/32											1*	
996/33											3*	
997/34												
998/35												
999/36												
1000/37										16	1*	
1001/38												
1002/39												
1003/40												
1004/41												
1005/42												
1006/43												
1007/44												

* Ilāhī year coin(s)

SILVER COINS IN U.P. TREASURE TROVES, A.H. 980–1007

Years (Hijri/ Ilāhī)	Agra	Delhi	Fatehpur	Lahore	Patna	Jaunpur	Ajmer	Dagaon	Narnol	Urdū Ẓafar Qarīn	Mintless	Ahma-dabad
980	7			2		4			1		12	3
981	3					3					9	4
982	5										4	23
983	4			1		2					11	20
984	9			1		5			1		21	6
985	10	40	4			7					24	8
986		1	6	3							27	6
987			5	6						1	6	
988			2	1	1					1	3	12
989			3			2				1	2	2
990	1										8	18
991										1	2	12
992/29		2									6	12
993/30											14	16
994/31		1										13
995/32											17	16
996/33				2							17	22
997/34		1		6							22	14
998/35		2	2	1							24	20
999/36		2		4							19	11
1000/37		2		9		1				24	65	28
1001/38		2		6							8	40
1002/39		3		7							1	36
1003/40				5					1		1	28
1004/41		10		8					1	1	6	24
1005/42	1	6.5		15						2	7	22
1006/43		3		5		2					4	15
1007/44	1	1		10								19

6

Akbar's Farmāns — A Study in Diplomatic

IQBAL HUSAIN

In the construction of his imperial administration, Akbar paid personal attention to the *daftar-i sanad,* as the *Ā'īn* describes it. In this paper an attempt is made to discuss the procedure followed in the preparation and issue of Akbar's *farmāns* concerning land grants, which constitute the bulk of his surviving *farmāns*. Hopefully, this will serve as a tentative effort towards constructing the foundations of the science of Mughal imperial diplomatic, about which so little exists in modern writing.

It may be assumed that Akbar's chancery built on the traditions left by Bābur and Humāyūn; so we may begin with a study of Bābur's *farmāns*.

Bābur's *farmān* of 13 Ziqa'd 933/11 August 1527 refers to the assignment of 2,000 *tanka-i siyāh*[1] in *suyūrg̲h̲āl*[2] to Qāẓī Jalāl of *pargana* Batala.[3] In another *farmān*[4] issued on 24 Ẕīqa'd 933/22 August 1527 Bābur restored an old *suyūrg̲h̲āl* grant. Interestingly, Bābur's *farmān* of 8 Rabī' I, 934/2 December 1527, addressed to the *Dīwāns* of Muḥammad Sulṭān Bahādur[5] confirms village Auhadpur,[6] *ṭappa ḥavelī qaṣba* Fathpur Sandi[7]

[1] Not 5000 as read by M. Momin, *Chancellery and Persian Epistolography Under the Mughals*, Calcutta, 1971, p.76 (hereafter *Chancellery*). The original of the *farmān* is in India Office: I.O.4438:(1),

The *tanka-i siyāh* was a copper coin also called *tanka-i Dehlī* or *tanka-i Murādī*. Cf. Irfan Habib, *The Agrarian System of Mughal India*, Bombay, 1963, p.381.

[2] The *Ā'īn* designates a charity grant as *suyūrg̲h̲āl*: when paid in cas̲h̲, it was *waẓīfa*, and when in the form of land, *milk* or *madad-i ma'āsh*. (*Ā'īn*, Vol.I, p.278).

[3] I.O. 4438:(1).

[4] *Mughal Documents*, 1526-1627, p.44.

[5] Probably Muḥammad Sulṭān Mirzā, the grandson of Sulṭān Ḥusain Mirzā K̲h̲urāsānī, a favourite of Bābur.

[6] A village in tahsil Hardoi, District Hardoi (District Census, Hardoi, 1971, p.118).

[7] A village in tahsil Bilgram, District Hardoi (District Census, Hardoi, 1971, p.118).

with a *jama*' of 800 *tanka-i siyāh* and 250 *bighas* of land, in favour of Qāẓī Dā'im,[8] son of Ilāhdād, in *madad-i ma'ash*. Here the term *suyūrghāl* is not used.[9]

Some of the notable characteristics of Bābur's *farmāns* seem to have been retained in the *farmāns* of Akbar, issued in the early years of his reign. For example, Bābur's *farmāns*, on their top, carry an invocation: '*Huw al-Ghanī*' (He is rich). Below the invocation are inscribed in *tughrā* the words, '*Farmān-i Ẓahīru'ddīn Muḥammad Bābur Pādshāh Ghāzī*'. Just below the *tughrā* appears a round seal with two circles. The inner circle reads 'Ẓahīru'ddīn Muḥammad Bābur' prominently.[10] The outer circle carries the names of Bābur's ancestors back from 'Umar Shaikh to Amīr Timūr. It, however, seems that Humāyūn did not stick to the invocation *Huw al-Ghanī*. His *farmān* of 27 Zīqa'd 960/4 November 1553 carries the invocation *Allāh-u Akbar*,[11] an invocation that Akbar was to use in his later years.

II

Momin notes with some surprise that the *Ā'īn-i Akbarī*, our chief source of knowledge of Mughal institutions, does not make any reference to the working of the chancery as a distinct department under the Mīr Munshī or State Secretary.[12] The *Ā'īn*, however, provides ample evidence that there existed two well organized departments which together fulfilled the functions of *dāru'l inshā'*. The *Ā'īn*, says, 'His Majesty has appointed fourteen zealous, experienced, and impartial clerks, two of whom do daily

[8] He was the son of Qāẓī Ilāhdād, who is said to have acquired the post (*manṣab*) of *qaẓā* in Bilgram. Ghulām Ḥusain Farshūrī, *Sharā'if-i 'Uṣmānī*, MS, Research Library, CAS in History, A.M.U., Aligarh, pp.115, 119. Āzād Bilgrāmī, who gives a biography of Qāẓī Ilāhdād, is silent about Qāẓī Dā'im. See *Ma'āṣir-al Kirām*, I, Agra 1910, pp.227-8.

[9] Incidentally Bābur's *farmān* of July-August 1530 addressed to the *'āmils*, *wazīrs*, *mutaṣaddīs* and others refers to the confirmation of an earlier grant of 'villages and *waẓīfa*' to Qāẓī 'Abdu'l Ḥalīm and brothers in *Sarkār* Tātār Khān. In this *farmān* neither the term *sayūrghāl* nor *madad-i ma'āsh* appear. See *Oriental College Magazine*, May 1933, p.119.

[10] I.O. 4438: (1); also Bābur's *farmān*, Maulana Azad Library, Aligarh.

[11] *Oriental College Magazine*, May 1933, pp.119-20.

[12] *Chancellery*, p.30.

duty in rotation.' The *Ā'īn* further provides details of duty performed by these men. This included 'the writing down of the orders and actions of His Majesty and whatever the Heads of the Department report... such as appointments to *manṣabs*; contingents of troops; *jāgīrs*; *irmās* money; *suyūrghāl* (grant-land).' Further, 'after the diary has been corrected by one of His Majesty's servants, it is laid before the emperor, and approved by him. The clerk then makes a copy of each report, signs it, and hands it over to those who require it as a voucher, when it is signed by the *Parwānchī*, by the *Mīr 'Arẓ*, and by that person who laid it before His Majesty. The report in this state is called *yād-dāsht*, or memorandum.' There were 'several copyists who write a good hand.' For the issuance of *sanads* (documents), the *Ā'īn*, in its next chapter, refers to a set procedure and the existence of a *daftar* or office. It says that His Majesty had made himself acquainted with this department and brought it into proper working order. He appointed honest and experienced writers, and entrusted the *daftar* to impartial officers under his immediate control.[13] These quotations from the *Ā'īn* have been given to establish that the functions of the chancery or the traditional *dāru'l inshā'* were shared by two departments, and one of them was supervised by the emperor himself.

III

The *Ā'īn* refers to two categories of *farmāns*, namely, *farmān-i ṣabtī* and *farmān-i bayāẓī*.[14] The *farmān-i ṣabtī* was issued mainly for appointments to *manṣabs*, to the office of *Wakīl*; to the post of *sipahsālār* (governor), etc. The *farmān-i bayāẓī* was issued for assignments of *jāgīrs* without prior branding and descriptive roll (*be-dāgh o maḥallī*)[15] for taking charge of a newly conquered territory; and assignment of *milk* and *suyūrghāl*.[16] A large number of documents of the category here called *farmān-i bayāẓī* have survived, and many have been published.[17] Many

[13] Abū'l Faẓl, *Ā'īn-i Akbarī*, I, tr. Blochmann, Calcutta, 1977, pp.268-70.

[14] *Ā'īn*, tr. Blochmann, I, pp.270-4. Cf. Momin, *Chancellery*, Chapter II.

[15] Cf. S. Moosvi, *JRAS*, 1981, pp.180-3.

[16] *Ā'īn*, tr. Blochmann, I, pp.270-1.

[17] To cite a few, Goswamy and Grewal, *The Mughals and the Jogis of Jakhbar*;

are still lying unpublished, being in the possession of individuals or in libraries.[18]

These *farmāns* in their standard form came to be written in fine *nasta 'līq* on the front, with the reverse (*ẓimn*), containing a detailed record of the processing of the proposal for its issue, with dates of imperial approval and confirmation, names of recording officers, other details not given in the front, and seals and endorsements of officers, the entire text being in the cursive or *shikasta* script. This form came to be firmly established under Akbar. But all his earlier *farmāns* are in a highly stylized pre-*nasta 'liq* semi-cursive *riqā*' hand, which has a large number of *shikasta* forms. In fact, the *riqā'* script continued to be used for the main text of Akbar's *farmāns* until the later years of his reign.[19] The *nasta 'līq* was introduced as an alternative mode of writing under Akbar himself;[20] and under Jahāngīr the *riqā*' for the front of the *farmān* was totally abandoned.

Every *farmān* of Akbar's reign begins with an invocation. Documents issued by the Ottomans also invariably had an invocation such as *lā* (None but He), *Huwa* (He is), *Huw-al Mu'īn*, and so on.[21] The early Safavid *farmāns* granting *suyūrghāl* also have similar invocations, *Huw Allāh Subḥāna-hu* followed by *Yā 'Alī*.[22] We note that in the early *farmāns* of Akbar's reign *Huw al-Ghanī* generally appears as the invocation, just as in Bābur's *farmāns*.[23]

J.J. Modi, *The Parsees at the Court of Akbar*, Bombay, 1903; K.M. Jhaveri, *Imperial Farmans*, 1577-1805, Bombay, 1928; A. Ansari, *Administrative Documents of Mughal India*, Delhi, 1984; and 'Abdu'l Bāri Ma'nī, *Asānīd-uṣ Ṣanādīd*, Ajmer, 1952.

[18] See for example the Farangi Mahal and Khairabad Documents, CAS in History, Aligarh; J.S. Mathur Collection, Bikaner Archives.

[19] *Farmān* of 40 Ilāhī/1596 in Modi, *Parsees at the Court of Akbar*. Bombay, 1903, p.93.

[20] Eg. *Farmān* of 41 *Ilāhī*/1595-6 in *Mughals and Jogis of Jakhbar*, Plate of Doc., 11, on p.57.

[21] S.M. Stern, *Documents from the Islamic Chanceries*, Oxford, 1965, pp.83, 87, 88, 89, 90. (hereafter *Islamic Chanceries*). Fīroz Shāh Bahmanī's *farmān* (1397-1422) also carries an invocation: 'God is Great, worthy of praise'. (*Allāh al Ḥamdah-i aulā*). Yusuf Husain Khan, *Farāmīn wa asnād-i Salāṭīn-i Dakkan*, Hyderabad, 1963, pp.1-2.

[22] *Islamic Chanceries*, pp.174, 180.

[23] Batala Document, I.O. 4438:(1); and Aligarh *farmān*, Maulana Azad Library.

Ultimately, the invocation *Huw al-Ghanī* was substituted by *Allāh-u Akbar*. Badāūnī says that in 983/1575-6 Akbar enquired about people's reaction if he ordered the words *Allāh-u Akbar* ('God is Great') to be cut on the imperial seal, and the dies of his coins. The majority of those present supported the proposal but Ḥājī Ibrāhīm argued that it might cause confusion, suggesting instead: '*La Zikr Allāh-u Akbar*' ('Speaking of God Almighty'). This latter proposal was strongly resented by the emperor.[24] Badāūnī says explicitly that the use of the invocation *Allāh-u Akbar* at the head ('*unwān*) of imperial rescripts and official documents began only in 1584;[25] and it is indeed only from this year that the invocation appears at the head of Akbar's surviving *farmāns*.[26] Abū'l Qāsim Namakīn says that the invocation '*Allāh-u Akbar*' was adopted for the sake of brevity.[27] The suspicion about the change of invocation from '*Huw-al Ghanī*' to '*Allāh-u Akbar*', voiced by Momin,[28] becomes hard to understand when one finds that a *farmān* of Humāyūn also carries the same invocation.[29]

IV

Just below the invocation was set the words '*Farmān-i Jalālu'd-dīn Muḥammad Akbar Pādshāh Ghāzī*'[30] in *ṭughrā* characters, which is in conformity with the style of Bābur's *farmāns*.[31] In Akbar's *farmāns* the *ṭughrā* is far less stylized than on the *farmāns* of his successors. In some later *farmāns* of Akbar, the

[24] 'Abdu'l Qadir Badāūnī, *Muntakhab-u't Tawārīkh*, ed. Lees and Aḥmad 'Alī, Calcutta, Vol.II, p.210.

[25] Badāūnī, *Muntakhab-u't Tawārīkh*, II, p.338.

[26] See *Mughal Documents*, pp.63-64 (Nos.70, 71).

[27] *Munsha'āt-i Namakīn*, f.3b, cited in *Chancellery*, p.63n.

[28] *Chancellery*, p.63.

[29] *Oriental College Magazine*, May 1933, pp.119-20. The appearance of *Huw a'l Ghanī* on Jhaveri, *Imperial farmāns*. Docs., IV & V, along with *Allāh-u Akbar* is not relevant, since both these documents, lacking the initial two half-lines and written in uncharacteristic *nasta'līq*, are forgeries. On some of Akbar's *farmāns* the invocation '*Huwa'l Akbar*' ('He is Great') also appears. See *Mughal Documents*, pp.56,58,59.

[30] *The Parsees at the Court of Akbar*, pp.93-4, 119-20; Jhaveri, Documents Nos.II, IV and IVA; Akbar's *farmān* 5 Jamāda I 983/12 August 1575, CAS in History, Aligarh; *Mughals and Jogis of Jakhbar*, p.56.

[31] Batala Documents, I.O. 4438 (1); and Aligarh *farmān*.

name 'Muḥammad' was omitted, e.g. in that of Ilāhī 41/1595-6, issued to a Brahman grantee in *pargana* Pathankot;[32] but it occurs in the seal and *ṭughrā* of the *farmān* issued in Ilahi 43/1598 to the temples of Vrindavan.[33]

In the early *farmāns* of Akbar we do not find the *shanjarfī* square seal which is a distinct feature of the *farmāns* of his successors.[34] It is well known that the use of seals or signet rings has been an ancient practice.[35] Bābur's *farmāns* assigning *suyūrghāl* carry a large round seal. The inner circle carries the name of the emperor with titles while the outer circle gives the names of his ancestors up to Amīr Timūr. This seal is also used in Akbar's *farmāns* where in the inner circle the name of Akbar is given with titles, and in the outer the names of his ancestors, beginning from Timūr down to Humāyūn. The seal was reduced in size and improved in appearance. The style of writing was also changed from *riqā'* character to *nasta'līq*.[36] We are not in a position to determine the exact date of the introduction of this seal in Akbar's *farmāns*. Abū'l Fazl, however, suggests that in the beginning of Akbar's reign Maulānā Maqṣūd made these seals. After some time Tamkīn made another small round seal which was improved by 'Alī Aḥmad.[37] This seal was known as *uzuk* and used on *farmān-i ṣabtī*, and the larger one, with names of Akbar's ancestors, was in the beginning used only for diplomatic correspondence, but later on used for all documents.[38] That is why both the seals, *uzuk* and the larger one, are generally found on Akbar's *farmāns* conferring *suyūrghāl* grants.[39] However, it does not seem to have become a general practice to use the larger one. There are many *farmāns* of Akbar which carry

[32] *Mughals and Jogis of Jakhbar*, pp.57-9.

[33] Original in National Archives of India.

[34] *The Mughals and the Jogis of Jakhbar*, pp.76-7; Farangi Mahal Document No.2, CAS in History, Aligarh.

[35] For a detailed discussion see, *Chancellery*, pp.64-5.

[36] *Ā'īn*, vol.I, p.54 says that Maulānā Maqṣūd, the seal engraver, cut in a circular form upon a surface of steel, in *riqā'* characters; and afterwards he cut another seal in the *nasta'līq* characters. For the seals, see *The Mughals and the Jogis of Jakhbar*, p.57; Jhaveri, Documents Nos.II, IV and IVA; *Asnād-uṣ Ṣanādīd*, pp.3,5.

[37] *Ā'īn*, I, p.54.

[38] Ibid.

[39] *Farmān*, Maulānā Azad Library, Aligarh, No.28: *The Mughals and the Jogis of Jakhbar*, p.57: *The Parsees at the Court of Akbar*, Doc. No.1 and 2.

only one small round seal. Its position also varies.[40] This departs from the norms of affixing seals as prescribed by Abū'l Faẓl. According to the *Ā'īn* the imperial seal was to be put above the *ṭughrā* lines on the top of the *farmāns*;[41] but this in practice is seldom the case.

Abū'l Faẓl also describes how seals of various officials were affixed.[42] It transpires that the seals were to be affixed in an hierarchical order on the *farmāns*, i.e. the first that of the *Wakīl*, below it that of the *Mushrif Dīwān*, and a little below that of the *Ṣadr*. Abū'l Faẓl further says that when Shaikh 'Abdu'n Nabī and Sulṭān Khwāja held the office of *Ṣadr*, they used to put their seals opposite to that of the *Wakīl*.[43] In none of the *farmāns* under study, do the ministers' seals appear on the front side (except that of the emperor). The *ẓimn* or reverse, however, bears all the seals of officials, and the order of the seals thereon seems to have been as described by Abū'l Faẓl. For example, the *ẓimn* of Akbar's *farmān* of 983/1575-6, after an endorsement on the left corner, carries the round seal of *'Abdu'n Nabī ibn-i Aḥmad al-Hanafī Khādim-i 'ilm-i ḥadīṣ'*. On the right-hand corner appears the round seal '*Ghayāṣu'ddīn 'Alī gasht Āṣaf Khān az 'ināyat-i Shahinshāh-i Walī*'.[44] Just below the seal of 'Abdu'n Nabī is a round seal reading '*Todar Mal, banda-i dargāh, Rām kī panāh*',[45] followed by two other round seals of '*Shāh Manṣūr Ghulām-i Shāh Akbar*' and '*banda-i kamtarīn Parkhotam bin Chālnīdās*'.[46] Similarly, on the right hand corner and below the seal of Āṣaf Khān is a small seal reading '*Lashkar Khān banda-i Shāhī Mīr Bakhshī 'ala mutawakkilullāh il Malik musta'ān*'. All the seals appearing on the left or right corner of the *farmān* are followed by endorsements of the respective departments with dates.[47]

[40] See: Jhaveri, Docs. No.II, IV A: *Asnād-uṣ Ṣanādīd*, pp.3,5; Khairabad Documents, CAS in History, Aligarh, No. 100.

[41] *Ā'īn*, I, p.274.

[42] *Ā'īn*, I, pp. 273-4.

[43] Ibid., p.273.

[44] Akbar's *farmān*, CAS in History, Aligarh, Old MS No.29. For the life and career of Āṣaf Khān, see Ṣamṣām-u'd Daulah, *Ma'āṣir-ul Umarā*, I, pp.280-1; also see M. Athar Alī, *The Apparatus of Empire*, Delhi, 1985, pp.6,9.

[45] Akbar's *farmān*, CAS in History, Aligarh, MS No.29. Also see 'Akbar and the Temples of Mathura', by Tarapada Mukherjee and Irfan Habib, *Proceedings of the Indian History Congress, 48th (1987) Session*, pp.246-8.

[46] Akbar's *farmān*, CAS in History, Aligarh, MS 29.

[47] Ibid.

V

It is noteworthy that the first two lines of Akbar's *farmāns* are always half lines. The text of each line tends to be crowded upwards on the left side. This feature is also found in Bābur's *farmāns*.[48] It appears that this style already existed in Iran.[49] The use of two half-lines at the head of the text seems to have been treated as an imperial prerogative in Akbar's later years; but these occur in Bairam Khān's *ḥukm* of 966/1558, as also Mun'im Khān's *ḥukm* of Ṣafar 974/August-September 1566. But both these *ḥukms* carry the formula '*Ba-farmān-i Jalālu'ddīn Muḥammad Akbar Pādshāh Ghāzī*' at the top, and both the officers not only held the title of Khān-i Khānān but also the office of the '*Wakīl-us Salṭanat*' or King's Representative or Regent at the respective times.[50] The two initial half- lines in Ḥamīda Bānū Begam's *ḥukm* of Ramaẓān 989/Sept-Oct 1581, are similarly explained by her very high status as the Queen Mother.[51]

The initial sentence of the *farmāns* assigning *madad-i ma'āsh* grants or confirming such earlier grants carry different initial phrases (*khiṭābs*), such as:

(i) *dar īn waqt farmān-i 'ālīshān wājib al-iṭā'at wal izān sharaf-i ṣudūr yāft*.[52]

(ii) *dar īn waqt farmān-i 'alīshān 'inayat nishān*.[53]

(iii) *chūn mawāzī....*

(iv) *dar īn waqt ḥukm farmudem....*[54]

(v) *chūn ba mūjib-i farmān-i 'ālīshān*[55]

(vi) *ḥukkām-i kirām wa dīwāniyān wa 'ummāl wa mutaṣaddiyān....*[56]

[48] Batala Doc. I.O. 4438: (1); Bābur's *farmān*, Maulānā Azad Library, Aligarh.

[49] Shāh Ismā'īl's *farmān* dated 25 June 1508, reproduced by Martin in *Islamic Chanceries*, ed. S.M. Stern, Oxford, 1965, p. 246.

[50] Information on Bairam Khān's *ḥukm* is derived from Professor Irfan Habib who has a xeroxed copy of the document; Mun'im Khān's *ḥukm* is reproduced with translation by Iqtidar Alam Khan, *The Political Biography of a Mughal Noble, Mun'im Khān Khān-i Khānān, 1497-1575*, New Delhi, 1973, pp.96-7.

[51] Jhaveri, Doc.II.

[52] Akbar's *farmān*, Khairabad Documents, CAS in History, Aligarh.

[53] *The Parsees at the Court of Akbar*, p.119.

[54] Jhaveri, Doc. No.II, *Asnād-uṣ ṣanādīd*, p.5.

[55] *The Mughals and the Jogis of Jakhbar*, p.59.

[56] Akbar's *farmān*, Maulana Azad Library, No.28.

The above mentioned are a few examples gleaned from Akbar's *farmāns* by way of illustration. Interestingly, the beginning of Bābur's Batala and Aligarh *farmāns* is similarly: '*dar īn waqt farmān-i jahān muṭā' wājibu'l-ittibā*', etc. Bābur's *farmān* reproduced in the *Oriental College Magazine* has altogether a different beginning: *'Umrā'-i nāmdār wa wuzrā-i kifāyat shi'ār wa mutaṣaddiyān*, etc. The difference in the beginning may be ascribed to the nature of the *farmāns*. Bābur's Batala and Aligarh *farmāns* refer to fresh assignments of *madad-i ma'āsh* grants, whereas the *farmāns* published in the *Oriental College Magazine* refer to an earlier grant of *mawāzi'*, *arāẓī* and *waẓīfa* (villages, lands and cash allowance).[57] It seems that the pattern set by Bābur's *farmāns* was followed by Akbar's chancery: Modi's Doc. Nos.1and 2 which refer to fresh land grants, begin with the phrase: *dar īn waqt farmān-i 'ālīshān sharaf-i ṣudūr yāft*'.[58]

VI

The last portion of Akbar's *farmāns* contains the exhortation to officials as to what they should do. This portion invariably begins with the words *Mī bāyad*, 'it is necessary'. Some times these letters are written just like other letters; some times the word *Mī* is made much larger and thicker to indicate that the operative or hortatory portion began from there.

The text of this portion tended to be increasingly standardized in the *farmāns* for *madad-i ma'āsh* grants, which now invariably contained a list of taxes from which the grantees were to be deemed exempt. It may be marked that some of these cesses bore designations which were not in actual use in India, and seem to have been borrowed from Safavid usage.

Practically all of Akbar's *madad-i ma'āsh farmāns* refer to the exemption from cesses such as (a) *māl o jihāt* and (b) *ikhrājāt-i 'awāriẓāt* which in turn included (i) *qunalgha*, (ii) *dāroghgāna*, (iii) *maḥtarifa*, (iv) *muhrāna*, (v) *ẓābiṭāna*, (vi)

[57] *Oriental College Magazine*, May 1933, p. 119.

[58] *The Parsees at the Court of Akbar*, pp.93-4, 118-9. In the Khairabad *farmān* the phrase '*farmān-i, 'ālīshān wājib-u'l iṭā'at wa'l iẕ'ān*' is used. Khairabad Documents, CAS in History, Aligarh.

jarībāna, (vii) *ṣad doi qānūngoī*,(viii) *takrār-i zirā'at*, (ix) *peshkash*, (x) *sāvrī*, (xi) *jalkar*, (xii) *bankar*, (xiii) *Kharj-i naishkar*, (xiv) *bāghāt*, (xv) *salāmī*, (xvi) *faujdārī*, (xvii) *dah nīm*, (xviii) *shikār*, and (xix) *begār*.[59] The precise itemization of these cesses, however, varied from *farmān* to *farmān*. The list of these exemptions was considerably more extensive as compared with that in Bābur's *farmāns*, two of which confine exemptions to *māl o jihat* only.[60] In the third *farmān* of Bābur the list comprises, *sā'ir mutwajjihāt, taufīr, 'ushr, dāroghgāna* and *shiqdārāna wa kul ikhrājat-wa kul takālif-i dīwānī wa lawāzim-i sulṭānī*.[61]

VII

A few words may be said about Badāūnī's much quoted statements in regard to *a'imma* or land grantees. According to Badāūnī in A.H. 983/1575-6 Akbar gave orders that the *a'imma* of the whole empire should not be let off by the *karorīs* (imperial revenue-collectors) unless they brought their *farmāns* for verification by the *ṣadr*.[62] Akbar personally enquired into the grants of the leading shaikhs and 'ulamā (religious divines and scholars) by granting them private interviews and assigned them some lands, if he was satisfied with their deserts and merits. But those who had disciples, or held spiritual soirées or held forth pretensions to miracles, were punished (by withdrawal of their grants). The *a'imma* generally suffered greatly, on account of the emperor's general order of verification.[63]

We have a large number of Akbar's *farmāns* which refer to the personal appearance of the *madad-i ma'āsh* holders before the court. The land grants were often renewed with reductions in the total grant either due to the deaths of the original grantees or of co-sharers or, later, on account of a change in the measuring instrument from *ṭanāb-i san* (measuring rope) to *ṭanāb-i bāns* (bamboo-rod), or a change in the unit of measure-

[59] *Oriental College Magazine*, May 1933, pp.119-20. It may be noted that the cesses mentioned at (b), (i), (x), (xviii) and (xix) were levied by the Safavids in Iran also: see *Islamic Chanceries*, pp.189-90, 201-2.

[60] Batala Docs. I.O. 4438:(1); and *Oriental College Magazine*, May 1933, p.119.

[61] Bābur's *farmān*, Maulana Azad Library, Aligarh (display-case).

[62] *Muntakhab-u't Tawārīkh*, II, pp.204-5, 278-9.

[63] Ibid.

ment from *gaz-i Sikandarī* to *gaz-i Ilāhī*.[64] Here it may be pointed out that even before Akbar's order of A.H. 983, the *madad-i ma'āsh* holders were appearing before the court and presenting *farmāns* by way of offering proof of their genuine claims as grantees.[65]

It seems that, with a view to stricter verification, Akbar's *farmāns* concerning the *madad-i ma'āsh* grants had assumed by 1567 a set pattern or style. The *ẓimn* (reverse) by and large provided the summary of the *farmān* which was recorded in the office of the *wakīl*, *mīr bakhshī*, *ṣadr* and other officials, and the seal of each officer was affixed to confirm the respective endorsement. The copy of each *farmān* was preserved in the *daftar-i khāṣa* (imperial chancery). In case of loss of the original *farmān*, the grantee could obtain a copy, as is evident from the Kota *farmān* of November 1567.

VIII

The text in the front of the *farmān* ended with the date, the scribe so writing and spacing the text that no blank space might be left in the last line. Until the institution of the Ilāhī era, promulgated in 1584, all *farmāns* of Akbar were dated in Hijri years and months.

One notices that during the period of the use of the Hijri calendar, while most *farmāns* bear the full date, i.e. date of the month along with the year, some only give the month. This can be easily seen in the calendar compiled by S.A.I. Tirmizi where documents nos. 35 and 38, which are *farmāns* of Akbar, give only the month and the year.[66] A more noteworthy question is whether Akbar ever used a regnal era with Hijri months as was to be done later by Shāhjahān and succeeding Mughal emperors. The evidence of two Vrindavan '*farmāns*' dated1 Sha'bān 3rd regnal year (*'ahd-i ānḥaẓarat*) and 1 Sha'bān 16th regnal year (*julūs-i muqaddas-i hijrī*) is of no importance, because both

[64] For a detailed discussion, see *Agrarian System of Mughal India*, pp.353-66.

[65] To quote a few by way of illustration, see Akbar's *farmān*, MS, No.29 and Khairabad Doc.No.100, CAS in History library, Aligarh; Kota Doc. in possession of Dr Abdul Matin, Tibbiya College, Aligarh; *Asnād-uṣ Ṣanādīd*, p.3; *Mughals and the Jogis of Jakhbar*, Docs. I & II.

[66] *Mughal Documents*, pp.54, 55.

of them are obvious forgeries.[67] Of all other known *farmāns* there are only two (Tirmizi Docs.12 and 14) which give regnal years. The first of them, a *farmān* to Shaikh Ḥasan as *mutawallī* merely gives the year 5. It also gives (apparently on the *ẓimn*) the name and titles of Shaikh 'Abdu'n Nabī. Now Shaikh 'Abdu'n Nabī became *ṣadr* only in 971/1563-4, whereas Akbar's fifth regnal year could not have possibly gone beyond 1560-1. Thus either the document is not genuine or the date has been misread through an erasure of two figures: the year might originally have been 975.[68] One must then doubt if the other *farmān*, Tirmizi Doc.14, has a correctly deciphered date at all and really contains the term *julūs*, for the phrase *julūs-i muqaddas-i hijrī*, 'regnal year of *hijrī*', is a contradiction in terms.

In 992/1584, Akbar promulgated the Ilāhī Era, whose epoch was put at 10 March 1556 (vernal equinox). This was a strictly solar era.[69] But it could actually be used only after its promulgation at the beginning of the 29th Ilāhī year, or 21 March 1584 (Gregorian).[70] But, possibly, it took some further time before the chancery shifted to the new era. A *farmān* of Akbar, dated 7 Jumādā II 992/6 June 1584, in favour of the Jains, a land-grant *farmān* of 2 Sha'bān 992/30 July 1584 and a *jāgīr*-assignment *farmān* of 15 Rajab 993/3 July 1585, are all dated in the Hijri calendar.[71] The use of the Ilāhī calendar appears first, among surviving documents, in a *parwāna* of Ṣādiq Khān, dated 20 Ābān 33 Ilāhī and 5 Ẕī'l Ḥij 996, the Ilāhī date corresponding to 11 November 1588 and the Hijri to 27 October 1588 (a misreading of the Hijri date is possible).[72] The next Ilāhī date occurs in a *ḥukm* of 'Abdu'r Raḥīm Kḥān-i Khānān, dated 9 Āẕar 33 Ilāhī and 11 Muḥarram 997, both corresponding to 30 November 1588.[73] The earliest *farmān* of Akbar after 1585 in

[67] Vrindavan Research Institute, Nos.2 and 36. Cf. T. Mukherjee and I. Habib, *PIHC,* 48th (Goa) session, p.235.

[68] For the *farmān* (Tirmizi, Doc.12), see *Farāmīn-i Salāṭīn*, pp.2-3, and *Mu'īnu'l Auliyā*, pp.66-7. There is no justification for Tirmizi inserting *Julūs* in the date, since the word is not present in the document.

[69] *Akbarnāma*, Bib. Ind., II, pp.9-14.

[70] Ibid., III, p.431.

[71] *Mughal Documents*, pp.62-4 (Docs. Nos. 68, 70, 71).

[72] Blochet, Suppl. Pers 482, f.113b.

[73] Jhaveri, Doc., III A.

Tirmizi's calendar was issued in1592 and apparently bears an *Ilāhī* date alone. But there is a slightly later *farmān* in a copy contained in an eighteenth-century collection of documents relating to Bilgram: this gives 21 Tīr 37 *Ilāhī* and 2 Shawwāl 1000, both corresponding to 12 July 1595 as the date of issue.[74] This suggests that till this time it was customary to use both dates, *Ilāhī* as well as hijri, in some imperial *farmāns*.

Subsequently, Akbar's *farmāns* tended to omit the hijri dates altogether. Of some sixteen *farmāns* after 1592 calendared by Timrizi, only three bear hijrī dates in addition to *ilāhī*; only one has a hijrī date alone.[75] The last would have to be checked for the decipherment of its date. It would, indeed, seem from the *farmān* conferring land-grants on the temples of Vrindavan and Mathura issued on 19 Shahréwar 43 Ilāhī/11 September 1598, with its detailed *ẓimn* and dates of various stages of processing, that the Mughal chancery had by now shifted completely to *ilāhī* dates, with no mention of hijri dates even as a convenient mode of cross-checking.[76]

[74] *Sharā'if-i 'Uṣmānī*, CAS in History, Aligarh, MS, ff.57b. 589. In its text the *farmān* also gives a double date for the presentation of Qāẓī Kamāl before Akbar, 19 Āẕar 36 Ilāhī/24 Ṣafar 1000, both corresponding to 11 December 1591. Tirmizi, calendaring this *farmān* as his Doc. No.86 (pp.67-8), omits the *Ilāhī* date altogether.

[75] *Mughal Documents*, Docs. Nos. 107, 108, 110 and 117, pp.74-5, 77.

[76] See T. Mukherjee and I. Habib, *PIHC*, 48th (Goa) session, pp.238-40. (The Christian dates given as equivalents to the *Ilāhī* in this paper need correction.) Akbar's *farmāns* issued to Kaikubad Parsi of Nausari also carry only *Ilāhī* dates. See Documents Nos.1 and 2 in *The Parsees at the Court of Akbar*, pp.93 and 119.

7

Akbar's Personality Traits and World Outlook — A Critical Reappraisal

IQTIDAR ALAM KHAN

Akbar's contribution to the establishment of Mughal authority in Hindustān on a firm basis has engaged the attention of modern historians for a long time. Some of the recent researches on Akbar, however, have tended to focus on the factors contributing to the rise of his policy of religious tolerance based on the principle of *ṣulḥ-i kul*, or 'Absolute Peace'. Akbar's 'religious policy' is often viewed in these studies as being linked to his transformation of the nobility into a composite ruling group including within its ranks a fairly large number of Shī'as and Rajputs. There has been far less concentration on the nature of Akbar's personal world outlook and of the ideological influences that went to shape it and his religious policy in the last twenty-five years of his reign. Athar Ali has recently re-examined this aspect in his article 'Akbar and Islam',[1] which in turn has given rise to several significant questions bearing on the basic character and motivations of Akbar's 'religious policy'. Perhaps the two most relevant questions are: (a) To what extent did Akbar's personal world outlook influence his religious policy? and (b) What was the response of the different sections of his subjects to his religious views and, more importantly, to the measures adopted by him. These questions assume special significance in view of the contemporary testimony of Badāūnī and the Jesuits suggesting that, from 1581 onwards, Akbar had ceased to be a Muslim. Shaikh Aḥmad Sirhindī's insistance that Akbar's tolerant attitude towards the non-Muslims stemmed

[1] Athar Alī, 'Akbar and Islam' in *Islamic Society and Culture: Essays in Honour of Professor Aziz Ahmad*, ed. Milton Israel and N.K. Wagle (New Delhi, 1983).

basically from his hostility to Islam further underlines the significance of his personal beliefs for a proper assessment of Akbar's policy of religious tolerance.[2]

In this paper an attempt is made to trace the development of Akbar's world view from his accession in 1556 to his death in 1605. While doing so, I shall also be focusing on the two questions identified above. To the extent permitted by the new evidence that I plan to present in this paper, I shall also be suggesting a reconsideration of some of the positions taken by Athar Ali.

II

The textbook explanations for Akbar's natural inclination towards religious tolerance, in terms of his being influenced by the broad-mindedness of his parents and teachers of Sunnī and Shī'a persuasions who had no use for sectarian bigotry, undoubtedly appeal to common sense. But it may be pointed out that the supposition of some of the textbook writers that Akbar's mother, Ḥamīda Bāno Begam, was a Shī'a[3] has no basis. On the contrary her brother, Mu'aẕẕam Beg, became involved, in 1546, in the Sunnī bigots' assassination of Humāyūn's *wazīr*, Khwāja Sulṭān Rushdī, an Iranian and Shī'a. This strongly suggests that he and possibly the other members of the family, including Ḥamīda Bāno, were Sunnīs.[4] It cannot, however, be denied that Akbar's tutors including the two Irani Shī'a's, Bairam Khān and Mīr 'Abdu'l Laṭīf Qazvīnī, and the Sunnī Tūrānī, Mun'im

[2] For a thorough examination of Badāūnī's and Shaikh Aḥmad Sirhindī's assessment of Akbar, in addition to Irfan Habib's memorable piece, 'The Political Role of Shaikh Aḥmad Sirhindī and Shāh Walīullāh' (*Proceedings of Indian History Congress*, Aligarh, 1960 23rd Session), reference may also be made to Athar Abbas Rizvī's pioneering work, *Muslim Revivalist Movements in Northern India in the Sixteenth and Seventeenth Centuries* (Agra, 1964) and his more recent study, *Religious and Intellectual History of Muslims in Akbar's Reign* (New Delhi, 1975).

[3] Cf. Ishwari Prasad, *The Mughal Empire*, Allahabad, 1976, p.346.

[4] Abū'l Faẓl, *Akbarnāma*, ed. by Agha Aḥmad Alī, Calcutta, 1877, p.254, and Bāyazīd Bayāt, *Tārīkh-i Humāyūn-wa-Akbar*, ed. Hidayat Husain, Calcutta, 1941, p.74. For an interpretation of this evidence, see my article, 'Wizarat Under Humāyūn (1545-1555)', *Medieval India Quarterly*, V, No.1, 1963, Aligarh, p.76.

Khān, were largely above sectarian prejudices. About Mīr 'Abdu'l Laṭīf Qazvīnī, it is asserted by Abū'l Faẓl that for his rejection of sectarian prejudices he was condemned by bigots of both the sects.[5] So far as Bairam Khān is concerned, notwithstanding what some of the eighteenth-century Persian chroniclers, like Khāfī Khān and Shāh Nawāz Khān, write of his sectarian partiality (*ta'aṣṣub*), contemporary evidence presents him as a person who, seemingly, did not attach much significance to the Shī'a–Sunnī divide.[6] On the other hand, Mun'im Khān counted among his closest friends 'Alī Qulī Khān, who was well known for his Shī'a beliefs.[7] It is, therefore, reasonable to imagine that the contribution of these early teachers and counsellors of Akbar to his natural inclination towards religious tolerance was not inconsiderable.

In a discussion of the influences that made Akbar's mind receptive to ideas promoting religious tolerance, one must also take into consideration the cultural ethos of the Timurids down to Humāyūn's time. Tīmūr is reported to have respected all religions alike. This climate of religious tolerance appears to have by and large persisted in the Timurid polity down to the time Akbar came to the throne.[8] The Timurid cultural ethos perhaps had something to do with the considerable influence that the *Yāsā-i Chingezī* continued to exercise on the minds of the successive Timurid rulers (with the doubtful exception of Abū Sa'īd Mirzā) down to Akbar's time. According to 'Alāu'ddīn 'Aṭā Juwainī, the *Yāsā-i Chingezī* required the ruler 'to consider all sects as one and not to distinguish them from one another'. It was in pursuance of this principle that Chingīz Khān, in Juwainī's words, 'eschewed bigotry and preference of one faith to another, placing some above others'.[9] The climate of

[5] *Akbarnāma*, II, p.20.

[6] For a discussion of this evidence see my article, 'The Mughal Court Politics During Bairam Khān's Regency', *Medieval India-A Miscellany*, I, Aligarh/Bombay, 1969. Attention is invited to f.ns.20,36,56,59.

[7] Mun'im Khān's close relations with 'Alī Qulī Khān Uzbek and Bairam Khān are discussed in my *The Political Biography of a Mughal Noble: Mun'im Khān Khān-i Khānān 1497-1575*, New Delhi, 1973, pp.59, 85, n.3.

[8] For the continuing influence of *Yāsā-i Chingezī* in the Timurid polity down to Humāyūn's reign, see *The Political Biography of a Mughal Noble*, Introduction, pp.IX-XIV.

[9] *T'ārīkh-i Jahān-gushā*, ed. Mirza Muhammad, I, London, 1912, pp.18-19 (tr. J.A. Boyle, I, Manchester, 1958, p.26).

religious tolerance promoted within the Timurid polity by the influence of *Yāsā-i Chingezī* is also highlighted by the absence of persecution of Shī'as in the Timurid principalities.

The increasing presence of Shī'a Iranīs in the nobility after Humāyūn's return from Iran (1545),[10] without giving rise to Shī'a–Sunnī tensions in any appreciable measure is eloquent testimony to the Mughal empire in India, being, from the beginning, a very different type of state from the Sultanates it replaced in different parts of the Indian subcontinent. It is worth noting that, before the induction of a large number of Iranī Shī'as in Humāyūn's service, in no other state ruled by a Muslim dynasty did the Shī'as and Sunnīs coexist in the nobility in such remarkable amity. The Safavid empire, where the rulers, claiming to be the *imāms* of the Islamic community the world over, severely repressed elements suspected of Sunnī leanings, was no exception to this rule. Thus it might be safely suggested that the influence of the *Yāsā-i Chingezī,* to the extent it survived in the Timurid polity till the middle of the sixteenth century, was an important element in Akbar's cultural heritage, inducing him to be broadminded towards other religious beliefs. Akbar's intolerant attitude towards the Shī'as and Mahdavīs during the sixties may conversely be explained as a partial consequence of the erosion of the influence of the original Mongol tradition with the passage of time.

For a proper appreciation of the way Akbar's world outlook gradually evolved and of his becoming, from around 1581, strongly committed to the principles of *ṣulḥ-i kul*, it is also important to keep in view some of the traits of his personality recorded by contemporary observers.

According to Monserrate, Akbar had 'a somewhat morose disposition' to which he attributes the latter's excessive interest in 'various games'.[11] That Akbar's extraordinary interest, during his early years, in hunting and elephant fights verged upon obsession is borne out even by Abū'l Faẓl. Abū'l Faẓl obviously finds it embarrassing to report Akbar's senselessly endangering his life repeatedly in hunts or while witnessing

[10] Afzal Husain, 'Growth of Irani Elements in Akbar's Nobility', *Proceedings of Indian History Congress*, 1975, 36th Session, pp.166-79.

[11] Antonio Monserrate, *Commentary on his Journey to the Court of Akbar*, tr. by J.S. Hoyland and annotated by S.N. Banerjee, Calcutta, 1922, p.197.

elephant fights or tackling *mast* elephants. He has devoted a whole chapter in the *Akbarnāma* to Akbar's 'inclination for elephants'. At another place, noticing Akbar recklessly endangering his life by mounting a *mast* elephant in 1561, Abū'l Faẓl has quoted a not very bright saying of Akbar from this period, suggesting that he thus endangered his life deliberately: if he had displeased God in any manner, 'may that elephant finish us, for we cannot support the burden of life under God's displeasure.'[12] This, incidentally, also points to Akbar's being vaguely dissatisfied and apologetic about his own conduct in society as well as in religious matters at this time.

This psychological factor in Akbar's personality also appears to have manifested itself in the occasional fits of depression and melancholy that he is reported to have suffered down to 1578. The last fit of this nature is reported from 1578; it came in the midst of a hunting expedition. On this occasion Akbar fell unconscious for some time. It appeared, according to Abū'l Faẓl, as if he was dying.[13] That these fits, which were characterized by Abū'l Faẓl and by Akbar himself as spiritual experiences, recurred down to 1578 and are not reported from the subsequent period when Akbar had developed a new world view identified with *ṣulḥ-i kul*, goes to suggest that these had something to do with the mental tensions of the earlier phase of his life.

The dichotomies of Akbar's religious beliefs and intellectual commitments during the seventies are illustrated by the perplexing questions that he is reported to have posed to the Muslim religious divines during the first phase of discussions in the '*Ibādat Khāna* (1575-8). These uncertainties and dichotomies were partly also fed by Akbar's general inquisitiveness and questioning temperament as well as by his eagerness to conform to an accepted code of ethical and legal behaviour, a trait of personality that he seems to have inherited from his father. Two scientific experiments made by Akbar in the seventies illustrate his questioning temperament in general. 'Ārif Qandahārī mentions his not very successful attempt at cross-breeding a male deer with a *barbarī* goat. This experiment produced a non-productive hybrid deer.[14] The other experiment,

[12] *Akbarnāma*, II, p.152. [13] *Akbarnāma*, III, pp.241-2.

[14] 'Ārif Qandahārī, *Tārīkh-i Akbarī*, ed. Muīnuddīn Ghauri, Azhar Ali and Imtiaz Ali Arshi, Rampur, 1962, pp.42-3.

involving six new-born infants, was aimed at testing the theory of *zubān-i qudrat*, or natural language, a notion having its origin, possibly, in the speculative philosophy of classical Greece. The notion of *zubān-i qudrat* certainly had no validity in the Islamic theological tradition.[15]

During the same period Akbar seems to have been exposed for the first time to philosophical discourses (*sukhnān-i ḥikmat*), so strongly disapproved by post-Ghazālī Islamic theology. Among the persons who introduced him to an Islamized version of Greek philosophy in the early seventies, Shaikh Mubārak and his sons, Faiẓī and Abū'l Faẓl, were the most prominent. Akbar in one of his sayings admits to finding these discourses so enchanting (*dil-āwez, dilrubā*) that it was difficult for him to keep away from them.[16] It was in consequence of Akbar's growing interest in philosophy and his raising questions about religion in general that the process of re-examining the important aspects of Islamic theology and jurisprudence (*fiqh*) began in the *'Ibādat Khāna* around 1578. The ball was set rolling, according to Badāūnī, by Shaikh Mubārak when he raised a question regarding the position of *Imām-i 'Ādil vis-à-vis* the *Mujtahid*. It was this discussion which led to the signing of a *Maḥẓar* (1579) by the leading theologians that recognized Akbar as the *Bādshāh-i Islām*.

One knows from unimpeachable evidence, including some of Akbar's own sayings recorded after 1581, that in his early years he was not only a practising Muslim but also had a very intolerant attitude towards Hindus. He regretfully admits of having forced many Hindus, during those early years, to be converted to Islām.[17] Akbar was then looked upon by orthodox

[15] *Akbarnāma*, III, p.393. According to Abū'l Faẓl the experiment was started in the 24th R.Y./11 March 1579 – 10 March 1580, by confining a few new-born children in a house specially built for the purpose in total seclusion; nurses appointed to look after them had orders not to speak in their hearing. It was concluded with Akbar's visit to that house on 9 August 1582. All the children used in this experiment failed to pick up any language proving Akbar's contention that 'speech came to every tribe from hearing'.

[16] *A'īn-i Akbarī*, III, Nawal Kishore, 1893, pp.182-3.

[17] See Akbar's sayings, *A'īn-i Akbarī*, III, p.181; also *Zubdatūt Tawārīkh*, tr. Elliot and Dowson, *History of India as told by its own historians*, London, 1964, VI, p.189, where Shaikh Nūru'l Ḥaq says that until A.H. 986/1578 A.D., Akbar used strictly to observe the daily five prayers.

Muslim elements as a pious Muslim committed to defending Islām against infidelity. Rizqullāh Mushtāqī, a well known Shaikhzāda of Delhi, writing around 1580, says that Akbar was sent by God to protect Islām from being suppressed by Hemū.[18] In one of his passing remarks, Badāūnī suggests that during the early years of his reign Akbar was under the influence of the *Naqshbandiya* order.[19]

However, it seems that his attitude towards Hindu religious rites and forms of worship was no longer contemptuous and hostile after 1562, when he married the daughteers and nieces of a number of Rajput chieftains. Badāūnī says that during Akbar's early youth (*'unfuwān-i shabāb*), he used to perform *hom*, a form of fire worship in the company of his Hindu wives.[20] Akbar was perceived by many of his contemporaries in these years as being not averse to performing Hindu rites, his Islamic orientation notwithstanding. This impression is reinforced by measures like the announcement of the abolition of Pilgrimage Tax (1563) and *Jizya* (1564) or the establishment of an *in'ām* grant for the support of a temple at Vindravan (1565).[21]

However, during the same period, he had a manifestly suppressive attitude towards the Muslim sects condemned by the orthodox as heretical. The Iranian nobles, mostly Shī'as, were encouraged and used against the discontended Tūrānīs throughout the sixties.[22] But at the same time their freedom to profess and practise their faith was sought to be restricted. A

[18] *Wāqi'āt-i Mushtāqī* MS, Br. Library, Or. 1929, f.94a.

[19] 'Abdu'l Qādir Badāūnī, *Muntakhab u't-Tawārīkh*, III, ed. Aḥmad 'Alī and Lees, Calcutta, 1864-9, p.74.

[20] *Muntakhab u't-Tawārīkh*, II, p.261. Lowe's comment that *hom* was a substitute for *soma* juice offered by Parsees (*Muntakhab u't-Tawārīkh*, tr., Calcutta, 1924, p.269, f.n.1) is obviously a slip. Badāūnī's reference here is to a Hindu ritual. For a more viable explanation see John T. Platts, *A Dictionary of Urdu, Classical Hiṇdi and English*, reprint, New Delhi, 1977, p.1242. This term is explained as denoting 'an oblation with clarified butter, a burnt offering, a sacrifice', etc.

[21] See *Akbarnāma*, Vol.II, pp.190,203-4; Tarapada Mukherjee and Irfan Habib, 'Akbar and the Temples of Mathura and its Environs', 48th session, *PIHC*, Goa 1987, pp.235, 237.

[22] For the improvement in the position of Irani nobles during the sixties, see my article, 'The Nobility under Akbar and the Development of His Religious Policy', *Journal of the Royal Asiatic Society*, 1968, p.31, & f.n.7; and *The Political Biography of A Mughal Noble*, pp.xvi-xvii.

glaring example of this was the exhumation, in 1567, of Mīr Murtaẓā Sharīfī Shīrāzī's remains from the vicinity (*jawār*) of Amīr Khusrau's tomb in Delhi at the suggestion of Shaikh 'Abdu'n Nabī. The argument was that a 'heretic' could not be allowed to remain buried so close to the grave of a renowned Sunnī saint. It was no doubt an extreme action: even Badāūnī has criticized it as a very unjust act.[23] Akbar's *farmān* to 'Abdu's Ṣamad, the *muḥtasib* of *pargana* Bilgram, around 1572, directing him to 'help in eradicating heresy and deviationism from the *pargana*' is an indication that the restrictive attitude towards Shī'ism continued to persist till the early seventies.[24]

Akbar's hostility towards the Mahadavīs was still more pronounced. This was maintained down to 1573 when he is reported to have suppressed them harshly in Gujarat. It was in the course of this suppression that the leading Mahadavī divine, Miyān Muṣṭafā Bandagī was arrested and brought to the court in chains.[25]

Akbar came increasingly under the influence of pantheistic *ṣūfī* doctrines, roughly from 1571, and this caused a momentous turn in the development of his world view. It paved the way for his eventual rejection of what he regarded as Islām professed by the traditional divines (*faqīhān-i taqlīdī*) in favour of a new and entirely different concept of Islam which transcended the limits demarcating the different religions (*kesh'hā*) and the essence of which, according to Akbar, was not in reciting the article of faith or getting circumcised, but in one's readiness and capacity to fight against overpowering worldly desires or urges (*nafs-i ammāra*). Akbar was exposed to these ideas way back in the sixties when he first came into contact with the Chishti *khānqāhs* at Ajmer and Sikri. Still earlier his contacts with Shaikh Ghauṣ Gawālyarī could also have provided him with an opportunity to become familiar with pantheistic doctrines

[23] *Muntakhab u't-Tawārīkh*, III, p.321.

[24] *Sharā'if-i 'Uṣmānī*, MS, Department of History, Aligarh, ff.26a-32a. Also see 'The Nobility Under Akbar and the Development of His Religious Policy', f.n.17.

[25] 'Alā'uddaulāh Qizvīnī, *Nafā'is u'l-Ma'āṣir*, MS., Br. Library, ff.62 a&b; Ghauṣī Shattārī, *Gulzār-i Abrār*, MS., John Rylands Library, f.207b. Also see a detailed examination of the evidence in Athar Abbas Rizvi, *Muslim Revivalist Movements in Northern India in the Sixteenth and Seventeenth Centuries*, (Agra, 1965), pp.116-8.

of *fanā* and *waḥdat u'l-wujūd*. Already by 1573, Akbar had come to regard Shaikh Mu'īnuddīn Chishtī as his spiritual preceptor. In one of his conversations with Miyān Muṣṭafā Bandagī, Akbar is reported to have declared: 'Haẓarat Khwāja Mu'īn-u'ddīn Chishtī is my preceptor... Any one who says that he was misguided (*gumrāh*) is an infidel. I shall kill the person saying this with my own hands.'[26] This is confirmed by Badāūnī's testimony to the effect that by 1577 Akbar was regularly practising the spiritual exercises prescribed in the Chishtī *silsilah*. Some time after 1575, he even tried to learn the art of performing *chilla-i ma'kūs* [concentrating on God while suspended head down in a well for forty days and nights], from Shaikh Chāya Laddha.[27]

The influence of pantheistic sufic doctrine of *fanā* seems to have provided an impetus to Akbar's interest in philosophy. In the company of Shaikh Mubārak, Abū'l Faẓl, Ghāzī Khān Badakhshī, Ḥakīm Abū'l Fath and other rationalist thinkers, during 1578-82, he eventually became familiar with the systematic exposition of the doctrine of *waḥdat ul-wujūd* by Ibn al-'Arabī in a larger philosophical perspective. As Irfan Habib points out, the pantheism of Ibn al-'Arabī, despite lacking a rational basis, was capable of becoming a strong ideological challenge to the post-Ghazālī conventionalism in Islam. It was this quality of the impact of Ibn al-'Arabī's ideas on Akbar and, more importantly, on his socio-political perceptions during 1578-82, that is characterized by Abū'l Faẓl as the elevation of 'intellect (*khirad*)' to a 'high pedestal (*buland pāigī*)'. The idea suggested by Ibn al-'Arabī that all that is not a part of divine reality is an illusion, in turn, led Akbar to the notion that all religions are either equally true or equally illusory,[28] a suggestion that was bound to be sharply denounced by all the shades of orthodox opinion as a deviation from the true path. It was equally unacceptable to the Jesuit fathers then present at the court. Commenting on Akbar's assurance in 1581 to Jalāla Roshanī of the freedom to practice his cult, Monserrate observed:

[26] *Majālis*, Maktaba Ibrahimia (Haidarabad), A.H. 1367, p.58.

[27] *Muntakhab u't-Tawārīkh*, II, p.201 and III, p.110.

[28] Irfan Habib, 'Reason and Science in Medieval India', (cyclostyled), paper presented at South Asian Studies Conference, Australia, 1981 (unpublished).

'the King cared little that in allowing everyone to follow his religion he was in reality violating all'.[29] The emergence of this new ideological trend at the court seems to have confused many of the quite learned people regarding Akbar's world view. 'Abdu'l Qādir Badāūnī for instance viewed the intellectual climate at the court around 1581 as the truimph of Shi'ism over orthodoxy.[30] This was, in any case, another decisive point of departure in Akbar's world view, taking him much farther away from the accepted Islamic beliefs and practices than was ever possible within the parameters of the pantheistic notions of Islamic mysticism.

III

The development of Akbar's world view subsequent to his being deeply influenced by the pantheistic philosophy of Ibn al-'Arabī is identified with the concept of *ṣulḥ-i kul* (absolute peace). This concept was formulated by him, or for him by Abū'l Fazl, in such a manner that it was elevated from the status of a mystic notion alluding to the state of *fanā* to that of a concept denoting a principle capable of promoting amity among divergent groups in a culturally pluralistic situation. In a revealing restatement of Alberuni's famous passage criticizing Brahmans for their intellectual insularity, Abū'l Fazl has tried to project the idea that social strife was caused in India primarily by the absence of the spirit of *ṣulḥ-i kul*. He goes on to suggest in the same passage that the absence of the spirit of *ṣulḥ-i kul* in India was caused mainly by the preponderance of an attitude of imitation (*taqlīd*) and by the suppression of intellect and reason.[31]

After 1581 Akbar's identification with *ṣulḥ-i kul* tended to make him part company with the mainstream tendency of orthodox Islam in so far as there was no place in his vision for

[29] *Commentary on his Journey to the Court of Akbar*, pp.132-3.

[30] *Muntakhab u't-Tawārīkh*, II, p.211, where Badāūnī accuses Mullā Muḥammad Yazdī, who had arrived from *Wilāyat* (Iran) only recently, for trying to attract Akbar towards Shī'a beliefs. In III, p.74, while commenting on Shaikh Mubārak's career, he suggests that it was the 'Iraqis' or Iranis (*Shī'as*?) who came to dominate Akbar's court-circle about this time.

[31] *Ā'īn-i Akbarī*, III, pp.3-4.

the prescribed prayers and the unquestioned acceptance of prophethood. It was much closer to the teachings of the contemporary Nirguna Bhakti sects which criticized both Hinduism and Islam for being formalistic and divisive. The conceptualization of man's relations with God articulated by Akbar in one of his less well-known statements reveals its proximity in certain important respects to the one found in the teachings of Nirguna Bhakti. Replying to a query from Murād in 1591, Akbar tells him:

Devotion to the Matchless One (*Bechūn*) is beyond the limits of the spoken word whether in respect of form (*jism*), material attributes (*jismānīat*), letter (*ḥarf*) or sound (*ṣaut*). Devotion to the Matchless One is (also) matchless. If God so wishes, (you) shall enter into the private chamber of this wonderful divine mystery. At present, the auspicious preamble (to the discourse on the subject) is this that he (Murād) may decorate with agreeable sincerity and praiseworthy actions the page of his disposition (*safha-i khāṭir*) and endeavour for gaining our pleasure so that with this blessing this other fortunate house of devotion (to God) may be opened (to him).[32]

Emphasis on the absoluteness of Divine Reality and a subtle suggestion, in this passage, that one could reach it not through formal prayers, but only by cultivating the self and with the help of a preceptor, recall to mind the teachings of Kabīr and Nānak.

It is again very much like the contemporary Bhakti cults that in Akbar's system there was strong emphasis on the role of a preceptor. As he tells Murād in the above passage, the latter could hope to have access to Divine Mystery only with the help and guidance of Akbar, who was in the position of his preceptor. The status of perceptor in Akbar's system, in turn, began to be perceived as that of the *insān-i kāmil* (Perfect Man) of Islamic mysticism.

This new world-view reflected itself with its distinct tilt towards rationality as well as (with all its inconsistencies) towards the norms of moral behaviour that Akbar prescribed, not only

[32] *Akbarnāma*, MS. (possibly Abū'l Faẓl's first draft), Br. Library, Add. 27, 247, ff.401b-404b, carries the text of a memorandum containing Akbar's orders on queries and requests sent to him by Murād upon appointment to Malwa in 1591. This memorandum is not included in the final draft. The statement of Akbar cited above can be read on f.402a of the same MS.

for his personal devotees (*arbāb-i irādat*), but also for ordinary
members of the court elite. It is also revealed majestically in
Abū'l Faẓl's theoretical expositions on the concept of kingship. He defines kingship dually, as *farr-i īzadī* or Divine Light,
and as originating in a social contract between society and the
ruler.[33] In addition to these are Akbar's sayings[34] and other documents reproduced by Abū'l Faẓl, projecting a new set of cultural values rooted in rational experience but not violating the
spirit of *ṣulḥ-i kul*. Some of these values appear astonishingly
'modern', and are imbued with compassion.

This is for example suggested by Akbar's numerous observations recorded by Abū'l Faẓl reflecting on the duty of the
ruler to work for the welfare of the common people or highlighted by statements revealing Akbar's deep respect and concern for women. I should like to reproduce his reply to Murād
(1591) for the transfer of a *dāk-chaukī* man, Bahādur, to his
camp. Akbar recorded the following order: 'Bahadur's wife is
not agreeable to his going (there). If presently we (are able to)
persuade her, we shall send Bahādur as well. Otherwise after a
few days we shall depute him to carry a *farmān* by *dāk-chaukī*.
Then you may detain him (there).'[35] The regard here for
Bahādur's wife's opinion and to his vague hope that he might
eventually succeed in persuading her to change her mind are
quite revealing, especially since the person concerned was a
mere *dāk-chaukī* messenger. Similarly, one of his sayings where
he ridicules Hindu men for seeking salvation in the other world
by inducing their wives to perish in fire and the one in which he
criticizes Muslim personal law for the daughters' receiving 'a
smaller share in the inheritance, although it is better that the
weaker should receive a large share',[36] are refreshingly original
and compassionate.

Akbar's strong disapproval of meat-eating is also rooted not
in his religious beliefs but basically reflects his natural com-

[33] For Abū'l Faẓl's expositions of these theories see the relevant sections
of *Ā'īn-i Akbarī*, particularly the section entitled, *Riwāī-i Rozī*.
[34] *Ā'īn-i Akbarī*, III, pp.177-91. Some of these sayings are recorded in
Akbarnāma as well, with reference to the actual occasions where Akbar is
supposed to have uttered them.
[35] *Akbarnāma*, MS., Br. Library, Add. 27, 247, f.403b.
[36] *Ā'in-i Akbarī*, III, pp.184, 190.

passion for living beings (*jāndārān*). He shames the meat-eaters for having converted 'their inner sides, where reside the mysteries of Divinity, into a burial ground of animals'. And, again: 'I wish my body, made of elements (*jism-i 'unṣarī*), was big like that of an elephant so that these flesh-eating ignorant ones would have satisfied their hunger with my flesh, and so spared other living beings'.[37] What is important about this sentiment is that it is not sought to be supported by any religious sanction or appeal. This is one of those cultural norms recommended by Akbar that seem to carry the imprint of his very private reflections not fully assimilated in the structure of beliefs and ideas that he was trying to evolve. These were his reflections not as the *Insān-i Kāmil* or *Pīr-o-Murshid* of the official discourse, but as a very sensitive and intelligent private man who had missed the opportunity of receiving formal education.

Akbar's socio-religious outlook, based on *ṣulḥ-i kul,* developed, and created ideological space for itself, largely through a polemical dialogue with mainstream Islamic orthodoxy within the framework of comparative religion. At an ideological plane the tendency identified with *ṣulḥ-i kul* was critical of Hindu beliefs and practices as well, but this aspect remained all the time in the background, possibly because none of the Hindu sects thus criticized responded to the challenge.[38] The reaction of orthodox Muslim theologians was generally sharp. It was this continuing polemic between a large section of the orthodox theologians and the protagonists of *ṣulḥ-i kul* which continued for about twenty-five years (roughly the second half of Akbar's reign), that appears to have given rise to a widely held belief towards the end of Akbar's reign that he was very hostile

[37] *Har Sih Daftar*, Nawal Kishore, 1862, p.123.

[38] Akbar's rejection of 'divine incarnation' (*ḥulūl*) theory is reflected, as suggested by Athar Alī ('The Religious World of Jahāngīr', *Proceedings of Indian History Congress*, Calcutta, 51st Session 1990, p.298, f.n.57), in the saying that in India no one sets a claim to prophethood because of the theory of divine incarnation. Abū'l Fazl's calling Todar Mal a simpleton (*sāda lauḥ*) for his attachment to his private idols and his disapproving references to Todar Mal's bigotry (*kīna tozī*) are pointers to the ideological reservations that existed between him and Todar Mal. The *Dabistān-i Mazāhib* quotes a well argued statement of Akbar criticizing Brahmans for believing in the doctrine of incarnation.

to Islam and was trying to undermine its position within the Mughal empire. Badāūnī and Shaikh Aḥmad Sirhindī seem to represent the more extreme or outspoken reaction of this genre. It should, however, be kept in mind that the exaggerated reaction of Badāūnī and Shaikh Aḥmad Sirhindī was not fully shared by many, even perhaps a majority, of the contemporary orthodox *'ulamā*. A large number of such persons noticed by Badāūnī himself in the third volume of *Muntakhab u't-Tawārīkh* as men of great piety and learning are also mentioned as maintaining close contacts with Akbar's court during the time when the polemics of the supporters of *ṣulḥ-i kul* against orthodox Islam were at its height. This is also suggested by some of the occasional statements of the most eminent theologians of the time, Shaikh 'Abdu'l Ḥaq Muḥaddis̤, and his son, Shaikh Nūru'l Ḥaq. Although both of them were critical of some of the new ideas promoted by Akbar, yet seemingly they did not share the alarmist view of Akbar's policies taken by Badāūnī. As late as 1605, Shaikh 'Abdu'l Ḥaq could find it possible to conclude his book, *Tārīkh-i Ḥaqqī*, with a prayer where Akbar is referred to as the reigning *Pādshāh*, who was expected to act as the defender of Islam. In the same year, Shaikh Nūru'l Ḥaq went out of his way in remarking that Akbar's motives in encouraging religious discussions were misunderstood by the common people.[39] These passages obviously imply an assessment of Akbar's role as king and of his motives in starting religious discussions, qualitatively different from those of Badāūnī and Sirhindī.

IV

I should like to conclude this paper with a few comments on the doubt raised by Athar Ali regarding Ni'matullāh[40] and Muhammad Sadiq's[41] testimony corroborating Badāūnī's and Sirhindī's allegations that Akbar had adopted a repressive attitude towards the practitioners of orthodox Islam.

[39] See translations of the relevant passages of *Tārīkh-i Ḥaqqī* (p.181) and *Zubd u't-Tawārīkh* (p.191) in Elliot and Dowson, VI.

[40] *Tārīkh-i Khān Jahānī* ed. Saiyed Muhammad Imamuddin, Asiatic Society of Pakistan, Dacca, 1962, pp.670-1.

[41] *Ṭabaqāt-i Shāh Jahānī*, MS., Aligarh Muslim University Collection No.226, f.451, cited in Athar Alī, 'Akbar and Islam', pp.170-1.

Athar Ali doubts the veracity of these statements by pointing out that an exceptionally large mosque was built by Mān Singh at Raj Mahal in 1592. Regarding this mosque he also quotes the popular tradition recorded in the Archaeological Survey's report that the structure 'was originally intended for a temple, but was afterwards turned into the Jama Masjid for fear of the Emperor'. He seems to argue that the reports pertaining to the closing down of mosques could have been an exaggeration of the difficulties caused by the reduction in 'the flow of financial patronage' to Islamic institutions. He thinks that 'given Akbar's own religious views', 'a persecution' of the practitioners of orthodox Islam does not appear plausible.

There is now available some more rather firm evidence supporting Badāūnī's and Sirhindī's version in its essentials. This evidence needs to be taken into account before one makes up one's mind on the position taken by Athar Ali.

Before I come to an examination of this additional evidence, it may be considered whether the building of a mosque by Mān Singh at Raj Mahal in 1592 is much relevant to the present discussion. One might suggest that the restrictive attitude with regard to Islamic practices and institutions mentioned by Badāūnī and Sirhindī might have appeared at a time later than 1592, perhaps around 1600.

There is an explicit reference to the attempt at closing down the mosques and prohibiting *namāz* in congregation in a '*farmān*' issued by Prince Salīm, during his rebellion of 1601, to local *ḥākims* (governors, etc.). Its text is reproduced by Rafī'u'ddīn Ibrāhīm Shīrāzī in his *Taẕkiratu'l Mulūk*. As I have argued elsewhere, although Rafī'u'ddīn Ibrāhīm Shīrāzī (d.1626) wrote his book at Bijapur early in the seventeenth century, he sometimes reproduces new information and documents on the history of Akbar's reign, the veracity of which cannot be reasonably doubted.[42] Salīm's '*farmān*' of 1601 reproduced by him seems to be one such piece. It reads: 'At the instigation of some mischeivous persons, my father has abolished the arrangements for the maintenance of *k͟haṭīb*, *mu'aẕẕīn* and *imām*

[42] See my article, 'The Taẕkiratu'l Mulūk by Rafī'uddīn Ibrāhīm Shīrāzī as a source on the History of Akbar's Reign', *Studies in History*, II, No.1, New Delhi, 1981, pp.41-4.

in the mosques and has prohibited the performance of *namāz* in congregation. He has converted many of the mosques into store-houses and stables. It was improper on his part to have acted in this manner. They [recipients of the '*farmān*'] should resume the paying of stipends for the maintenance of the mosques, the *khaṭīb*, the *mu'azzin* and *imām* and should induce people to offer prayers. Anyone showing slackness in this respect would be duly punished.'[43]

This '*farmān*' leaves little doubt that towards the turn of the century there was a general impression that in some of the mosques *namāz* in congregation was prohibited by Akbar's orders. That Salīm should try to win the sympathy of the Muslims by playing upon this issue during his rebellion is quite understandable. It also suggests that, in Salīm's perception at the time (1601), the feeling of hurt among Muslims over Akbar's attitude towards Islam was so deep and widespread that many of them could be roused to support him against his father over this issue.

A story narrated by 'Abdu'l Bāqī Nahāvandī in *Ma'āṣir-i Raḥīmī* (compiled, 1614) offers corroborative evidence. He reports that after Dānyāl's appointment to the newly conquered '*ṣūba* of Deccan and Khandesh' (1601), Akbar had written to him ordering him to destroy the *jāma' masjid* at Asirgarh 'and raise [in its place] a temple on the pattern of Hindus and [other] infidels of Hindustān'. According to this story, however, Dānyāl was wise enough 'not to enforce that order by ignoring it and whiling away the time' so that 'the demolition of a mosque and building of a temple in its place during the time of the kings of Islam was avoided'.[44]

Regarding this story one may note that it was recorded by 'Abdu'l Bāqī Nahāvandī in the context of his employer 'Abdu'r Rahīm Khān-i Khānān's role in the Deccan as the *atālīq* of Dānyāl. There is thus an implicit suggestion in the manner this story is recorded that the credit for ignoring Akbar's extraordinary order should partly go to the Khān-i Khānān who was then next in command to Dānyāl. This story is not recorded by any other known authority. Possibly 'Abdu'l Bāqī Nahāvandī's source

[43] *Tazkiratu'l Mulūk*, MS. Br. Library, Add. 23,883, f.224b.
[44] *Ma'āṣir-i Raḥīmī*, II, ed. Hidayat Husain, Calcutta, 1925, p.474.

of information for the story was 'Abdu'r Raḥīm Khān-i Khānān himself. Moreover, such a story being recorded in a text identified with 'Abdu'r Raḥīm Khān-i Khānān tends to suggest that at the time of its writing (i.e. 1614), Akbar's restrictive measures against orthodox Islam around 1601 were such common knowledge that an allusion to it in a historical text's passing observation was not expected to be considered offensive by Jahāngīr as well as his courtiers.

In the memorandum already cited, containing orders recorded by Akbar on requests and queries sent by Murād from Malwa some time in 1591, we find a query by Murād to the effect that if some one in his camp was found performing prayers 'in the manner of imitating theologians (*fuqhā-i taqlīd shi'ār*)', whether he was to be 'forbidden' or was to be 'left in his ways'. Akbar's response suggests that a person performing *namāz* was considered deserving 'admonition' (*nasīḥat*) by his superior so as to 'help' him to come to 'the path of reason' (*rāh-i 'aql*)'. But Murād is also warned that such a person is not to be forced to abandon his rites of worship, as this would amount to violation of *ṣulḥ-i kul*.[45] This document clearly points to two aspects of the situation: firstly that some of the princes/nobles commanding armies or administering different regions were not clear in their minds, around 1591, if they should prohibit the performance of *namāz* offered by individuals serving with them, and, secondly, that official policy at this time (1591) was for the Mughal administrators to 'admonish' but not pressurize such persons to bring them 'to the path of reason'. One might suggest that this was perhaps the beginning of the drift towards a situation that, some time prior to Salīm's revolt in 1601, led to a general impression that Akbar had withdrawn all support to maintenance of mosques, and even ordered the destruction of some.

This seems, however, to have been a brief phase. The attempt to discourage *namāz* in congregation and compliance with other decrees of Islam was apparently given up by Akbar before *Ā'īn-i Akbarī* was completed by 1601. This is attested to by a casual statement of Abū'l Faẓl in the *Ā'īn-i Akbarī* where he talks of Akbar practising 'external as well as spiritual

[45] *Akbarnāma*, MS. Br. Library, Add. 27,247, f.404a.

austerities in the worship [of God] which render silent the slanders [spread] by the ritualists of this age [*rasmiyān-i rozgār*]'. Blochmann reads this passage as suggesting that Akbar occasionally joined 'public worship in order to hush the slandering tongues of the bigots of the present age'.[46] This rather loose rendering of the relevant line is not implausible. In the above passage, the expression, *riyāẓat-i ṣūrī* (external austerities) is perhaps an allusion to the observance of *namāz* by Akbar which, according to Abū'l Faẓl, silenced the 'slanderous' criticism of Akbar by *rasmiyān*, or those who considered the form or ritual of worship as of primary importance. It is a candid admission of the fact that, towards 1601, Akbar's beliefs and his attitude towards *namāz* were being widely criticized. This, perhaps, made him concerned about the reaction of common Muslims, forcing him to soften his attitude on the performance of *namāz*. One could explain the appreciative references to Akbar's role as King by Shaikh 'Abdu'l Ḥaq Muḥaddiṣ and Shaikh Nūru'l Ḥaq in 1605 also in the light of this possible softening in Akbar's attitude towards Islam during the last four years of his reign.

The hurt that was seemingly caused to Muslims by Akbar's hostile attitude to Islam during 1591-1601 was, apparently, healed considerably in the last four years of his reign. At the time of his death, in any case, there were no signs of widespread discontent against his policies among Muslims as well as among a majority of orthodox theologians. On the other hand, at the time of Akbar's death in 1605, the impression of even a theologian like 'Abdu'l Ḥaq was that, despite all his 'innovations', he remained a Muslim king.

[46] *Ā'īn-i Akbarī*, Nawal Kishore, 1882, I, p.105. Compare H. Blochmann, *Ā'īn-i Akbarī*, English translation, Calcutta, 1873, p.163.

8

Akbar and the Jains

PUSHPA PRASAD

Akbar's religious thought was woven from different threads which are not always easy to identify. Different influences worked on his mind in varying degrees at different times. The historical material and contemporary records of Akbar's reign make it clear that Akbar was keen to know the principles and doctrines of all contemporary religions. Many scholars have already discussed the various aspects of Akbar's relations with the Jains, notable among them being Chimanlal Dahyabhai Dalal, V.A. Smith and Kalipad Mitra.[1] In this paper an attempt is made to examine afresh Akbar's attitude towards the Jains from the evidence of contemporary Jain sources. Most significant within these are the *Hīrasaubhāgyama-hākāvya* (Samvat 1646/1589 of Devo Vimal Gani, the *Karmachandravaṁśaprabhandha* (S. 1650/1593) of Jayasoma, the *Bhānucandracarita* of Siddhi Chandra and *Akbar Pratibodha Rāsa* (S.1658/1601) of Jinchandra Sūri.[2] Later Jain literary accounts of the seventeenth century too have been utilized. Sixteenth-century inscriptions found in Jain temples in Gujarat and at Agra also furnish information about the activities of the Jains during the reign of Akbar.[3]

Abū'l Fazl writes that representatives of many creeds gathered at the '*Ibādat Khāna* (House of Worship) to join the

[1] Chimanlal Dahyabhai Dalāl, 'Hīravijaya Sūri or the Jains at the Court of Akbar'. *Jaina Sāsana*, Benaras S.Y. 1910, pp.113-28; V.A. Smith, 'The Jain teachers of Akbar', *Bhandarkar's Commemoration Volume*, Poona 1917, pp.265-76; Kalipada Mitra, 'Jain Influence at the Mughal Court', *Proceedings of Indian History Congress*, 1939, pp.1059-71.

[2] Devovimal Gani, *Hīrasaubhāgyamāhākāvya*, ed. K.P. Parab, *Kāvyamālā*, No.67, (Bombay 1900); Jayasoma, *Karamchanda vaṁsaprabandhkāvyaṁ*, ed. G.S. Ojha, *New Review*, No.58, (Baroda, 1939); Siddhi Chandra, *Bhānu Chandra Charitra*, ed. Sri Mohan Lal Dali Chanda Desai, *Singhi Jain Series*, No.15 (Calcutta, 1941); Jinachandra Sūri, *Akbar Pratibodha Rāsa*, ed. Aghar Chand Nahata, *Atihāsika Jain Kāvya Saṁghra*, pp.58-78, (Calcutta, S.Y. 1944).

[3] G. Buhler, 'The Jain inscriptions from Satrunjaya'. *Epigraphia Indica*, II, pp.34-86; Puran Chand Nahar, *Jain Inscriptions*, II, p.142, No.1628.

discussions:'*Sufi* philosopher, orator, jurist, Sunnī, Shī'a, Brahman, *Jatī*, *Siūra*, Charbaka, Nazarene, Jew, Sabi, Zoroastrian and others enjoyed exquisite pleasure'.[4] The term *Jatī* (Sanskrit, '*Yati*') in the above passage refers to Jains, not Buddhist monks; and '*Siūra*' (Sanskrit *Śvetāmbara*, Prakrit *Seyambara*) to the Śvetāmbara Jains.[5] It is relevant to quote Badāūnī, who writes, 'Moreover *samanīs* and Brahmans managed to get frequent private audiences with His Majesty'.[6] Here the term *samanī* (Sanskrit *Śramaṇa*; Prakrit *Samana*) means a devotee or a monk. Lowe has taken *samanīs* to be Buddhist monks, though it refers to Jain ascetics, now commonly called *yati*.[7]

It is clear that the three terms *Yati*, *Siūra* or *Sevarā*, and *Samanīs* referred to the monks of the Śvetāmbara sect. Pinherio, a Portuguese priest, states in a letter from Lahore in 1595 that 'he (Akbar) follows the sect of Jains (Vertoi)'.[8] Smith rightly states that Akbar never came under Buddhist influence in any degree whatsoever. No Buddhist monk took part in the religious discussions held at Fatehpur Sikri.[9] Consequently, his knowledge of Buddhism was extremely limited. On the other hand, many Jains visited the imperial court or resided there at various times during the period 1578-1605.

'The list of the learned men of the Age' given by Abū'l Faẓl in his concluding section of the *Ā'īn-i Akbarī* includes Jain saints. Harījī Sūr is in the first category (at no.16) among those who 'understand the mysteries of both the worlds'. Bijaya Sen Sūr (no.139) and Bhānu Chand (no.140) are mentioned in the fifth category of those who 'understand sciences, resting on testimony'.[10] These refer to Hīravijaya Sūrī, Vijaya Sen Sūri and Bhānu Chandra

[4] Abū'l Faẓl, *Akbarnāma*, tr. H. Beveridge, III, 1921, p.365.

[5] Monier Williams, *Sanskrit English Dictionary*, s.v. Abū'l Faẓl refers to the Śvetāmbaras as *Sewra* while taking brief notices of nine schools: Nyāya, Vaiśeṣika Mīmāṁsa, Vedānta, Sāṁkhya, Pātanjal, Jaina, Buddha and Nāstika (*Ā'īn-i Akbarī*, tr. Jarrett, III, Calcutta, 1918, p.143). He also says, 'the writer had personal knowledge of both the orders and his account of Digambars has been written, as it were, in the dark; but having some acquaintance with the learned of the Śvetāmbara order, who are also known as *Sewra*, he has been able to supply a tolerably full notice' (p.222).

[6] Badāūnī, *Muntakhab al-Tawārīkh*, tr. W.H. Lowe, Delhi, 1973, p.265.

[7] Ibid., fn.l.

[8] V.A. Smith, *Akbar the Great Mogul*, Delhi, 1962, p.189.

[9] Ibid., p.116.

[10] *Ā'īn-i Akbarī*, tr. H. Blochmann, I, pp.606, 617.

Upādhyāya. All these Jain priests belonged to the *Tapā gaccha* of the Śvetāmbara sect. Hīravijaya Sūri was the supreme pontiff of the *Tapā gaccha*, and a disciple of Vijayadan Sūri; he attained the status of *Guru* in 1566.[11] He was invited by Akbar in 1582 while he was returning from Kabul. At Agra the whole Jain community headed by Thānsingh[12] and others celebrated the occasion of Sūrī's arrival with great eclat and paid homage to the monk.[13]

Sanskrit works and inscriptions provide many details about Hīrāvijaya Sūri. The impression made on the emperor during the course of his meetings with Sūri is said to have been profound, when the Jain divine held forth on matters such as 'resurrection' and 'redemption', the misery of life, and 'the idea of personal God'.[14] As a token of his admiration Akbar offered Sūri a large number of religious books. The monk declined at first to accept them but consented when pressed by Abū'l Faẓl and Thānsingh. All these books were placed in a library at Agra, under the charge of Thānsingh.[15]

From the inscription of the Palitana temple of V.S.1639/ 1582-3, it appears that Sūri persuaded the emperor to issue an edict 'forbidding the slaughter of animals for six months to abolish the confiscation of the property of deceased persons, the *sujijia* tax and *śulk*, to set free many captives, snared birds and animals, to present the sacred place Śatrunjaya to the Jains, to establish a Jain library, and to become a saint like King Śrenik, who converted the head of the Lumpakas Meghaji, made many people adherents of *Tapā gaccha*, caused many temples to be built in Gujarat and other countries, and made many natives of that country of Malwa, etc., undertake pilgrimages to Śatrunjaya'.[16]

Akbar also issued a *farmān,* dated 6 June1584, ordering his officials not to allow slaughter of animals during the twelve days of the Jain *Paryuṣaṇa* festival, in places where the Jains were settled.[17]

[11] Muniraj Vidyavijaya, *Sūrishwar ane Samrāt* (Bhavanagara S.Y.1976), v. 22-83, 78-83, 84-92, 94-8, 101-6.

[12] He was converted to Jainism by Siṁhavimālā, a Jain Tapāgacchiya Sadhu. *Bhānuchandra Carita*, *op.cit.*, p.26.

[13] Ibid. [14] Ibid., pp.26-7.

[15] Ibid.

[16] Legard Jacob, 'Inscriptions from Palitana,' *Journal of the Bombay Branch of the Royal Asiatic Society*, No.II, pp.56-63.

[17] For the Persian transcript of this *farmān*, see *Sūrishwar ane Samrāt*,

Other Jain sources inform us that Akbar conferred upon the *āchārya* the title of '*Jagad Gurū*' or 'world preceptor'.[18] In its celebration birds in cages were set free on the banks of Damara. However, in Nahata's *Yugapradhān Śrī Jinachandra Sūri*, there is a quotation from the *Praśnottara Granth* of Jayasom Upādhyaya of *Kharatara Gaccha*, where the latter has deduced that Akbar never conferred the title *Jagad Gurū* upon Hīravijaya Sūri.[19] According to him it was conferred on him by his devoted followers. But Desai, on the basis of epigraphic and literary evidence, argues that Akbar actually did bestow on him the title of *Jagad Gurū*.[20]

Hīravijaya Sūri left Agra for Gujarat in 1585 and left behind his disciple Shānti Chandra at the Mughal court. At the time of his departure Hīravijaya Sūri conferred the title of Upādhyaya upon Shānti Chandra.[21] Shānti Chandra is the author of a panegyric on the emperor. The work is composed in Sanskrit and is entitled *Kṛpa-rāsa-kośa* (Treasury of the merciful deeds of the emperor).[22] He used to recite these verses in the presence of the emperor who held him in high esteem. When Shānti Chandra started for Gujarat in 1587, Akbar is said to have issued a *farmān* prohibiting the slaughter of animals and proclaiming the abolition of the *jizya* tax. Animal slaughter was prohibited for six months in the year. These six months consisted 'of the previously ordained 12 days which included 8 days of *Paryuṣaṇa*, the *Nauroz* day, all Sundays, days of Sophian, *Id*, equinoxes,the month of his birth-days, [the Ilāhī month of] of *Mihir*, the month of Rajab and the birth days of his sons'.[23]

On 6 Azur 35 Ilāhī (6 November 1590), Akbar did in fact issue a long *farmān*, which bears all the marks of Abū'l Fazl's penmanship. It states the requirements of the doctrine of *Ṣulḥ-i Kul*

Appendix, pp.375-8. For its English translation, see *Bhānuchandra Charita*, Appendix II, pp.77-8. The *farmān* has also been published in the *Journal of the University of Bombay*, IX, pp.9-10: cf. S.A.I. Termizi, *Mughal Documents*, New Delhi, 1982, p.62 (No.68). An English translation of the copy of the *farmān* sent to *suba* Malwa, was printed in John Malcolm, *Memoir of Central India*, 2nd ed., London, 1824, II, pp.163-5 *n*.

[18] Smith, op.cit., pp.267-8.

[19] *Yugapradhān Śri Jinachandra Sūri*, pp.103-4.

[20] Bhānu Chandra, *Vivek Vilas tika*, Verse 3, cf. *Bhānuchandra Charita*, Appendix I, p.37.

[21] Ibid., p.27.

[22] Ibid., p.8, Chapter I, V.127.

[23] *Hīra Saubhāgya Mahākāvya*, Chapter 14, Verses, 273-4.

(Absolute Peace), refers to Hīr Bijai Sūr Sewrā (Hīravijaya Sūri) as an eminent ascetic who had come to the court, and calls upon all officers, including Ḥājjī Ḥabībullāh, by name, to extend full tolerance to the Jains.[24]

After the departure of Shānti Chandra, Bhānu Chandra, a disciple of Sūrachandra, continued to stay at Mughal court till the end of Akbar's reign. He even continued to stay during the reign of Jahāngīr. Details of Bhānu Chandra's stay at Akbar's court are given in the Jain biographical work *Bhānu-Chandra charita* written by his disciple Siddhi Chandra. Bhānu Chandra had the title of '*Prājña*' [Pandita] conferred on him by Hīravijaya Sūri.[25] During his stay at the court Bhānu Chandra distinguished himself by his intellectual attainments. He composed a commentary in Sanskrit on one thousand names of the Sun, *Sūryasahastranāma*, and explained and taught their significance to Akbar.[26] The first thing that the emperor did after entering the court was to repeat one thousand names of the Sun as given to him by Bhānu Chandra with great devotion.

The extent of Bhānu Chandra's influence on Akbar in political and religious spheres is to be inferred from some of the incidents he describes. He writes that on hearing the news of the defeat of Jām Sattojji Satrasāl, a *zamīndār* of Gujarat, in 1591, Akbar offered Bhānu Chandra a *pūrṇapātra* — a box filled with valuable things.[27] But the *āchārya* requested him to release the rebel prisoners in lieu of this present. As a result of this, a *farmān* was issued and given to Bhānu Chandra who immediately got it despatched to Gujarat to secure the release of the prisoners.[28]

Siddihi Chandra tells us that Bhānu Chandra keenly desired to have a halting place for Jain monks in the city of Lahore. On one occasion when he was late in making his way to the royal court, the emperor asked him the cause of his being late. Bhānu Chandra replied that his residence was far away. Thereupon the emperor granted a piece of land to the Jain community (in the Lahore fort). A magnificent temple was erected there providing living room

[24] Mohan Lal Dalichand Desai, *Jain Sāhityano Saṁkshipta Itihās*, text facing p.545.

[25] *Bhānuchandra Charita*, p.27.

[26] Hīrananda Sastri, 'Akbar as Sun Worshipper', *The Indian Historical Quarterly*, IX, (1933), pp.137-8.

[27] *Bhānuchandra Charita*, pp.29-30.

[28] M.S. Commissariat, *A History of Gujarat*, II, (Delhi 1957), pp.233-4.

for the monks. An idol of Jain *tīrthānkara* Shāntināth was consecrated in this temple.[29]

In another instance, when a daughter was born to Prince Salīm, Akbar was told that the constellation under which she was born boded ill for her father. So Bhānu Chandra suggested the performance of *Aśṭottara-Śata-snātra* (108 baths to be given to the idol of Jina in its temple), which would effectively avert this evil.[30] This ceremony was accordingly arranged by Thānsingh and Mantri Karma Chand.[31] Both Akbar and Salīm stood in front of the Jina idol and listened to the recitation by Bhānu Chandra of the *Bhaktāmara-stotra*, a sacred hymn in Sanskrit composed by Mantung Sūri in honour of Ādināth Jaina. (It begins with the word *Bhaktāmara*.) The emperor took some *snātra* water from the gold pot and applied it to his eyes and passed it on into the *harem*. He then made gifts of gold *muhrs* to all those present and, after being excused by the *āchārya*, returned to his palace.[32]

Akbar wished to bestow the title of *Upādhyāya* upon Bhānu Chandra. But he was told that the privilege of granting the title was confined only to the head of the Jain Sangh. Thereupon Abū'l Faẕl sent an imperial *farmān* to Hīravijaya Sūri, the head of the *Tapā gaccha* residing at Radhanpur. Hīravijaya Sūri confirmed the contents of the *farmān* and sent consecrated *vāsakṣepa* and a letter of appointment to Bhānu Chandra, thus making him competent to hold the title of *Upādhyāya*.[33]

Later in 1592 Bhānu Chandra accompanied Akbar during his second visit to Kashmir. There he requested the emperor to abolish the taxes on piligrims visiting the Śatrunjaya hill, and a *farmān* to this effect was issued.[34]

[29] Rishabha Dās, *Hīravijaya Sūri Rāsa*, text published in *Ānanda Kāvya Mahodhadi*, V, Verses 36-7, p.182. Here the construction cost is said to have been Rs 20,000.

[30] *Hīravijaya Sūri Rāsa*, Verses 38-44; *Suriswara ane Samrāt*, p.154.

[31] Karm Chand was an Oswal Bania of Bacchavat family. He was a minister of Ṛāo Kalyān Singh and then of Rāi Singh of Bikaner. After the annexation of Gujarat, Tarsūn Khān plundered Sirohi (1577) and took away about a thousand Jain metal idols to Agra. The Mantri is said to have received them back in 1583: they were taken to Bikaner where they were placed in the temple of Chintāmani. He later left the service of Bikaner and was given an appointment at Akbar's Court. See *Yugapradhān Śrī Jina Chandrā Sūri*, pp.213-39.

[32] Ibid., pp.85-7; *Hīravijaya Sūri Rāsa*, p.183.

[33] *Bhānuchandra Charita*, p.33; *Hīra Saubhāgya kāvya*, p.741, verses, 285-6.

[34] *Bhānuchandra Charita*, p.34.

It seems that Akbar's desire for meeting Jain leaders never weakened. On one occasion, he wished to know from a leading Jain Durjanasalya as to whom Hīravijaya Sūri had appointed as his successor. He replied that a great and austere ascetic named Vijayasen Sūri had been selected.[35] On hearing of this the emperor issued a *farmān* inviting Vijayasen Sūri to present himself at the court. The Jain *āchārya* reached the court on 31 May 1593 along with a hundred disciples. He was recieved by Abū'l Faẓl and Bhānu Chandra. One of his pupils, Nandivijaya, performed 8 *avadhānas* (attending eight things at a time). The emperor was highly impressed and conferred the title *Khwushfahm* (a man of sharp intellect) upon this pupil.[36] Vijayasen Sūri, accompanied by *Vācaka* Bhanu Chandra, paid several visits to the emperor.[37]

According to the *Vijayapraśasti Kāvya* the Brahmans felt jealous of the exālted position enjoyed by the Jain āchārya at the Mughal court. Therefore they sent Rājā Rāmdās (Kachhwaha) to tell Akbar that the Jains were atheists. The Emperor asked that a debate be arranged on the subject of the existence of God in the assembly hall and invited the learned, including Brahmans. Vijayasen Sūri proved from the Jain scriptures the falseness of the accusation and convinced the Brahmans, 'Shaikhs' (Muslim scholars), the emperor and others, that the Jain conception was similar to that expounded in the Saṁkhya philosophy of the Brahmans. It earned him the tittle *Savāi Hīravijaya Sūri*,[38] i.e. a quarter greater than his master Hīravijaya Sūri!

On another occasion Vijayasen Sūri convinced the emperor of the necessity of prohibition of cowslaughter, and of repealing the law which empowered the state to confiscate the property of those persons who died heirless and sanctioned the taking of captives in war. This information is corrobrated by a Palitana inscription dated S.Y.1650/1593 or 1594.[39]

[35] Durjanaśalya was an Oswal Bania of the Jadia *gotra* of Lahore. He led a Jain congregation on a pilgrimage to Sauripura *tīrth*, where he repaired the temple and the Jain idol consecrated there. He was a staunch adherent of Hīra Sūri. *Bhānuchandra Charita*, p.38.

[36] This is confirmed by Jahāngīr's *farmān* of 1610, issued in favour of the Jains, which refers to 'Nand Bijai, given the title of *Khwush fahm*' (Desai, *Jain-Sahityano Sam Kshipta*, p.553).

[37] *Bhānuchandra Charita*, p.38; *Hīra Saubhāgya Kāvya*, Chapter XIV, pp.742-3, verses 287-90.

[38] *Bhānuchandra Charita*, p.10.

[39] G. Buhler, 'Jain Inscriptions from Gujarat', *Epigraphia Indica*, II, pp.53-4.

Akbar desired Vijayasen Sūri to perform the ceremony at Lahore, to solemnize the grant of the title of *Upādhyāya*, to Bhānu Chandra. On this occassion Abū'l Faẓl gave away 600 Rupees and 108 horses in charity.[40] A Jain inscription from Gujarat offers the additional information that Vijayasen Sūri now recieved the title of *Kālī Saraswati* from Akbar. Vijayasen Sūri left the court in 1595-6.[41]

In the meantime Hīravijaya Sūri sent two of his best pupils, Bhava Chandra and Siddhi Chandra, to the court. Siddhi Chandra was a scholar of Sanskrit and Persian and made a profound impression on Akbar. He performed the 108 *avadhānas* (attending to 108 things at a time) — a marvellous feat of memory. The emperor being much pleased, conferred upon him as well the title of *Khwush-fahm*. Thereafter he stayed permanently at the court till late in Jahāngīr's reign.[42]

Siddhi Chandra in his biography of his master Bhānu Chandra Upādhyāya also gives an account of the merits and virtues of Akbar and Abū'l Faẓl. Of the emperor he writes: 'There is not a single art, not a single branch of knowledge, not a single act of boldness and strength which was not attempted by young Akbar'. He compares him to the son of Kauśaliya [i.e. Rāma], and further claims: 'Thieves and robbers were conspicuous by their absence in his empire. His glory was as white as the moon because he had defeated all his enemies. His religious fervour never made him intolerant as is shown by his degree of regard for all the six systems of philosophy. He took interest in all the arts and all branches of learning. He had three valiant sons viz Śekhujī, or Salīm; Pahādī, or Murād; and Dānaśāh, or Dānyāl'.[43]

About Abū'l Faẓl, Siddhi Chandra writes that 'he was endowed with eight qualities of intellect:desiring to hear, inquiring again, listening, understanding, reflecting, removing doubts by the excercise of reasoning, fixing a thing in mind, and putting it into practice'. He had gone through 'the ocean of literature', and he was the best amongst all learned men. He had mastery over various schools of philosophy, Jainism, Mimāṁsā, Buddhism, Śānkhya

[40] Jina Vijaya, *Prāchīn Jain Lekha Saṁghra*, II, No.454.

[41] Johannes Klatt, 'Extracts from the Historical Records of Jains', *Indian Antiquary*, XI, (1882), p.256.

[42] *Bhānuchandra Charita*, p.41.

[43] Ibid., pp.23-4.

Vaiśeṣika, Cārvaka, Jaiminīya, Pātanjali, Yoga, Vedānta, vocabulary and lexicography, music, dramaturgy, rhetoric, prosody, astrology, politics, mathematics, palmistry, veterinary science, etc. And 'in appreciation of his service, when Murād was in trouble, the Emperor [Akbar] conferred on him the title of '*Dalathambhan*' (Pillar of the army)'.[44]

At the time of Akbar's third visit to Kashmir in 1597 Siddhi Chandra and Bhānu Chandra accompanied him. The emperor was severely wounded while witnessing an antelope-fight. The animal's horn penetrated his thigh. During these days nobody except Bhānu Chandra and Abū'l Faẓl, who enjoyed Akbar's full confidence, were allowed to be near him. After his recovery Akbar sent five hundred cows to the halting places of the Jain monks for the purpose of distribution among them.[45]

The emperor at one point for some reason issued an order to stop the erection of a new Jain temple dedicated to Chintāmaṇi Pārāśavanāth at Agra. Siddhi Chandra by his personal influence got the order cancelled and obtained the emperor's sanction for temple construction to be carried on.[46]

At the same time Jains of the *Kharatara gaccha* began to erect a temple in the interior part of Mount Vimalacala in Saurashtra. Due to their rivalry with the members of the *Tapā gaccha*, the latter raised objections to this and approached the emperor. Akbar, under the influence of Bhānu Chandra Upādhyāya of the *Tapā gaccha*, issued a *farmān* forbidding the construction of the temple.[47]

There was a threat of demolition of the temple at Satrunjaya from Mirzā Khurram (son of Mirzā 'Azīz Koka, posted as *faujdār* of Sorath in AH 1009/ 1600-01).[48] Siddhi Chandra, through his influence on Akbar, succeeded in getting an imperial order issued for its protection.[49] Vijayasen Sūri, *pattadhara* (head of the *Tapā gaccha*) had occasion to exercise his influence on Akbar when Prince Salīm held sway over Gujarat and appointed different *sāmantas* (magnates) over it.[50] Apparently, this referred to the period, around

[44] *Bhānuchandra Charita*, Chapter I, Verses 39-65, 66-7.

[45] Ibid., p.42.

[46] Ibid., p.43; *Hīra Saubhāgya Kāvya*, Chapter XIV, Verse 152.

[47] *Bhānuchandra Charita*, p.43.

[48] *Mir'āt-i Aḥmadī*, ed. S. Nawab Alī, Baroda, 1928, I, p.183.

[49] *Bhānuchandra Charita*, p.46.

[50] Ibid.

1601, when Salīm revolted; and he might possibly have appointed officers over Gujarat. We are told that difficulties arose in connection with the orders (issued formerly by Akbar) prohibiting animal slaughter and abolishing piligrim taxes, etc. Now these taxes and the practice of animal slaughter were again revived. Under these circumstances Vijayasen Sūri approached the Emperor. As a result, a comprehensive *farmān* dated 1601 was issued confirming the earlier orders in favour of the Jains. From a *nishān* of Prince [Dānyāl], issued to 'the officers of *ṣūba* Gujarat and *sarkār* Surat' on 25 August 1601, in pursuance of the imperial *farmān* aforementioned, it would seem that Dānyāl was given some authority over the *ṣūba,* though Mirzā 'Azīz Koka was the *de facto* governor. In the prince's *nishān,* the *farmān* is cited for a reference to 'Bijaiser Sūr Seora (Vijayasen Sūri), the successor (*khalīfa*) of Hīr Bijay Sūr (Hiravijaya Sūri)' and calls upon all officials to protect Jain temples. It also asks them to protect Jain ascetics from popular anger raised by the unreasonable allegation that the current failure of rains was due to their magical devices.[51]

Several Jain priests of the rival *Kharatara gaccha* of Śvetāmbara sect also attained some influence with Akbar during the same period.

The earliest reference to their influence occurs in the writings of Hanskīrtti. In Samvat year 1625/1568, when Akbar was at Agra, a religious discussion was held at his court between Buddhisāgara of *Tapā gaccha* and Sādhu Kirtti of *Kharatara gaccha* at the time of the celebration of *Poṣadha* in the presence of learned scholars such as Aniruddha, Mahadeva Miśra and others. Sadhukirtti was deemed victorious, and Akbar conferred upon him the title of '*Vadīndra*'.[52]

In the *Akbar Pratibodha Rāsa* it is stated that in 1591, at Lahore, Akbar heard through Karm Chand of the Jain teacher Jinachandra Sūri, who was a great teacher of the *Kharatara gaccha*. Akbar invited him to the court. Sūri reached Lahore on 14 February 1592 accompanied by thirty-one Jain monks. Karm Chand escorted him to the court and the Emperor requested him to be present at all religious debates and discussions. Seeing the respect accorded to him by the emperor the people called him '*Bade Gurū*' (Great teacher).[53]

[51] Desai, *Jain Sahityano Saṁkshipta Itihās*, text facing p.552.

[52] *Atihāsika Jain Kāvya Saṁghra*, pp.135-8.

[53] *Yugapradhāna Śri Jina Chandra Sūri*, pp.73-84; *Atihāsika Jain Kāvya Saṁghra*, pp.58-78.

One day Sūri heard of the demolition of temples near Dvārkā by Navarang Khān. There upon he requested the emperor to protect all Jain temples. Akbar is alleged to have issued a *farmān* in 1592, proclaiming the grant of Śatrunjaya and other Jaina holy places to the Jains.[54]

Before starting on his second visit to Kashmir, Akbar called Jinachandra Sūri for his '*dharma lābha*' (religious blessings). At that time the court was held in the garden of Rājā Rāmdās, and was attended by Prince Salīm, several vassal rulers, learned Brahmans and pandits. Jinachandra Sūri along with his pupils also attended. One of his pupils, Samayasundra, read out a work known as *Aṣṭalakshi*, composed by him. He explained to the Emperor that there was a short sentence consisting of three simple Sanskrit words *Rājño dadate soukhyam* (the king alone can bestow pleasure) which could be interpreted in eight hundred thousand ways and grammatically this sentence had 10,22,407 meanings. Akbar praised him for his vast erudition.[55] Mansingh, Harshvilās and his other disciples accompanied Akbar to Kashmir. When he reached Srinagar, he gave protection to all living beings, like fish, for eight days. Samayasundra and Guṇavinaya were invested with the title of *Upādhyāya*. At the same time Akbar conferred the title '*Yugā Pradhān*' on Jinachandra Sūri and the title *āchārya* on Mānsingh who became famous as Jinasimha Sūri. Fishing and animal slaughter were prohibited on that day.[56]

The *farmān* dated 1592 given to Jinachandra Sūri was lost. Upon this his pupil, Jinasimha Sūri (Mānsingh) applied to the emperor for another *farmān*. Akbar readily granted a *farmān* in 1603-4, prohibiting the slaughter of animals and meat-eating during the twelve days of the *Paryuṣaṇa*.[57]

On the basis of the above evidence, which undoubtedly contains much exaggeration in some parts, one can say that Jain teachers belonging to both the groups, the *Tapā* and *Kharatara gaccha* of the Śvetāmbara sect, were received and patronized at Akbar's court, where they explained the tenets and doctrines of Jainism.

[54] *Epigraphia Indica*, II, p.37.

[55] *Yugapradhāna Śrī Jinachandra Sūri*, pp.91, 95. *Karmachandra Mantri Vaṁsa Prabandha*, Verses, 400-3.

[56] *Yugapradhāna Śrī Jina Chandra Sūri*, pp.99-101.

[57] *Bhānuchandra Charita*, pp.81-82; *Yugapradhān Śrī Jinachandra Sūri*, p.278.

It is probable that Akbar was attracted to Jainism, especially on account of its belief in non-killing, and compassion towards all living beings, and in the doctrine of the transmigration of souls. We also see how firmly Akbar acted to protect the sect, small as it was, against any act of intolerance, and went out of his way to assuage the feelings and senisitivities of the Jains during the last twenty-five years of his reign. He thereby won for himself a lasting good name in Jain tradition.

9

Science and Superstition under Akbar and Jahāngīr: The Observation of Astronomical Phenomena

SHIREEN MOOSVI

The occurrence of singular astronomical phenomena, such as comets, meteors and eclipses, has fascinated all civilizations. These have seemed to introduce into the fixed dispersal of the stars and the regular movements of the moon and planets an unforeseen, rare disturbance that aroused curiosity as well as fear. The rational spirit directed that the reason for the uncommon be looked for; and solar and lunar eclipses, indeed, stood explained in ancient times. The positions of heavenly bodies, marked in specific moments of time, had simultaneously come to signify the fortunes of individuals; and thus astronomy and astrology had long been unified into a single 'discipline'. It was natural for priests and astrologers to attach meanings to rare events (even when foreseen, like eclipses) and irregular occurrences (unforeseen, like comets) for the fate of peoples, sovereigns and ordinary beings. On eclipses, the brilliant Brahmagupta had taken issue with Varāhamihira, in order to support the priest against the scientist — a controversy made immortal by Alberūnī's wise comments.[1]

It should thus be of no little interest to see how the Mughal emperors reacted to curious and unpredicted astronomical phenomena. One must remember that their basic assumptions about astronomy derived from Aristotle and Ptolemy, though over the centuries much had been added to the Hellenistic heritage by observation. Their ancestor Ulugh Beg (fifteenth century) had built a celebrated astronomical observatory and left a book of tables (*zīj*) which remained authoritative in all its essentials for *zīj* compilations in India down to Sawā'ī Jaisingh (d.1745). The Mughal astronomers used astrolabes, sun-dials, sand-glasses and

[1] *Alberūnī's India*, tr. E.C. Sachau, London, 1910, II, pp.107-14.

water-clocks of considerable accuracy. (Some of these instruments may be seen in the accompanying black-and-white enlargement of details of an astronomer and his tools from an album of paintings in Jahāngīr's library.[2])

Side by side with the Hellenistic and Arab heritage, the Mughals were also becoming familiar with Indian astronomical and mathematical tradition. The famous Indian text-book on mathematics, Bhaskara's *Līlāvatī,* was translated into Persian at Akbar's court in 1587 by the famous poet Faiẓi, the elder brother of the official historian Abū'l Faẓl.[3] Neither the Hellenistic-Arab nor the Indian tradition was immune from superstition, which could often be clothed in apparently logical hypotheses. Their influence was obvious in the attitudes displayed by the Mughal emperors and their court when comets appeared or eclipses of a singular nature occurred.

In what follows, the descriptions of these phenomena in the Mughal accounts of the reigns of Akbar and Jahāngīr are explored. Whether the observations recorded have any scientific value

[2] Reproduced from the margin of a folio in Jahāngīr's album, Naprstek Museum, Prague, in Lubor Hajek, *Indian Miniatures of the Mughal School*, Prague, 1960, plate 18.value is for professional astronomers to judge.

[3] Cf. Storey, *Persian Literature*, II, part 1, London, 1972, pp.4-5.

is for professional astronomers to judge. But they certainly shed light on the Mughal attitude to the wonders of the universe that surrounded them.

Comets and Meteors

During the one and a half centuries that cover the period of the Great Mughals (1556-1707), seven appearances of comets are recorded, being 'remarkable' in the sense of being distinctly visible to the naked-eye.[4] Of these the comets of 1577 and 1618 are reported to have been bright enough to be seen even in day-time.[5] The comet of 1577 was of singular significance and Kepler made observations of it, noting that it seemed to occupy the same position among the stars whether viewed from Uraniburg or from Prague, 400 miles apart. He therefore concluded that comets were much farther from the earth than the moon. However, he wrongly assumed that comets moved in straight lines.[6] Both these comets are described in Mughal accounts. Other comets (including Halley's comet in its two appearances, 1607 and 1680) were either not noticed or were not held to be of significance enough to find mention in major Indian historical works.

The appearance of the comet of 1577 is recorded by 'Ārif Qandahārī, writing mainly in 1579,[7] and by Abū'l Faẓl, from whom we have two accounts, a short and direct description contained in an earlier draft of his *Akbarnāma*,[8] and an edited, polished one in the final text of the same work.[9] His contemporary Badāūnī also reports the sighting of this comet.[10]

'Ārif records that on the night of Thursday, 25 Sha'bān 985 (7 November 1577) a bright star appeared in the west inclining towards the south with numerous tiny stars flowing from its top, making it look like a cypress tree: it remained visible for four

[4] George F. Chambers, *The Story of the Comets*, Oxford, 1910, p.137. The years of their appearances were 1556, 1577, 1607, 1618, 1661, 1680 and 1689.

[5] Ibid., p.8.

[6] Ibid., p.48. It is evident that the comet remained visible in Europe for quite some time, allowing Kepler to carry out observations from different places.

[7] 'Ārif Qandahārī, *Tārīkh-i Akbarī*, ed. Muinud-Din Nadvi, Azhar Ali Dehlevi, and Imtiyaz Alī Arshi, Rampur, 1962, pp.231-2.

[8] British Library MS. Add.27,247, f.291a & b.

[9] Abū'l Faẓl, *Akbarnāma*, III, ed. Aḥmad Alī, Calcutta, 1987, pp. 222-4.

[10] 'Abdu'l Qādir Badāūnī, *Muntakhab-ut Tawārīkh*, II, ed. Aḥmad Alī and W.N. Lees, Calcutta, 1864, pp. 240-1. It is mentioned under A.H. 984 (1576-7).

gharīs (1 hour, 36 minutes) in the cities of Agra, Delhi and Lahore. It disappeared in the month of Shawwāl of the same year (12 December 1577 – 9 January 1578) and became known as the long tailed-star (*sitāra-i dum-i darāz*).[11]

'Ārif Qandahārī's description does not particularly give the impression of any apprehensions or nervousness shown by the court on the appearance of this comet. He reproduces some verses from an ode composed on the occasion by one of Akbar's court poets, Sherī,[12] where the comet is treated as a brilliant sight, comparable with similar things of value and splendour in the world.

'Ārif Qandahārī prefaces the ode, which seemingly assigns no bad or evil aspects to the comet, with the rather bland statement that it was under the influence of this comet that Shāh Ismā'īl of Persia, son of Shāh Ṭahmāsp, was assassinated on 14 Ramaẓān of the same year (26 November 1577).

Abū'l Faẓl does not seem to have known of or used 'Ārif's work. According to his earlier draft, it was in November 1577, when Akbar was just laying down the foundation of a new fort, Mol Manoharnagar, not far from Fatehpur Sikri, that a spectacular comet made its appearance after sunset in the west (but inclining to the north) and visible till two hours before dawn. This strange spectacle shook the hearts of the people, for the appearance of this unfamiliar comet was regarded as an extremely bad omen. The historian Badāūnī, in his usual sarcastic vein, writes that since Shāh Manṣūr, Akbar's harsh minister of finance, wore a turban with a long tail he was suitably dubbed a comet (lit. 'tailed star', *sitāra-i dumbāla*). He goes on to add that Shāh Ismā'īl of Iran was assassinated and the evil influence of this comet became evident in that country.

The emperor Akbar, at this time barely thirty-five years of age, took the matter more seriously. According to the first version of the *Akbarnāma*, he directed his famous minister Rāja Todar Mal to collect astronomers to carry out research on the matter and to predict the consequences. After careful consideration, the astronomers, led by Jotik Rāi,[13] an accomplished astrologer, concluded reasonably that the comet held no danger for India. In

[11] 'Ārif Qandahārī, pp.231-2.

[12] He is mentioned by Abu'l Faẓl in the list of Akbar's court poets (*A'in-i Akbarī*, I, p.262).

[13] Jotik Rāi is a title given to an astrologer; the holder of this title is mentioned

his final text[14] Abū'l Faẓl perhaps thought that his sovereign's anxiety might seem a weakness, and so glosses over these details and instead appears more concerned with purely scientific matters. He gives the exact date of the comet's appearance as 25 Ābān, 22 Ilāhī (7 November 1577) and says that when the sun was auspiciously placed in Scorpio, this heavenly star-like sign appeared in Sagittarius in the west, but inclined to the north. It had a bright head and a long tail. He further reports that in some countries it remained visible for five months. The astrologers predicted that in some parts of Hindustān grain would be dear, and also identified the places where this would occur. He then comes forward with an explanation more suitable to the good repute of his sovereign, namely that it was because of His Majesty's own pure being that the comet caused no damage to India, the generous gifts by the emperor to 'Muslims and Brahmans' playing their due part!

Both the first and final versions of the *Akbarnāma* agree in this, however, that the comet had dire effects in Iran, causing the deaths of two sovereigns, Ṭahmāsp and Ismā'īl, just before and after the appearance of the comet, and much bloodshed in the interval.

In the final version Abū'l Faẓl uses the opportunity of the appearance of this comet to sum up the knowledge of comets and meteors that had been assembled by his time. Here he considers these phenomena as belonging to the realm of physical sciences (*ḥikmat-i ṭaba'ī*) and testifies to the existence of monographs on them, including Greek treatises and an alleged work of Ptolemy that sets the distance between the sun and a comet as eleven signs apart.[15] Abū'l Faẓl seems to consider meteors and comets as of terrestrial origin, and says that they are created by the action of solar light on the elements of the earth. The particles burnt by the

at two other places in the *Akbarnāma*, once when he was sent for an errand to the chief of Baglana (*Akbarnāma*, III, p.30) and the next when he was consulted for finding the auspicious moment for the emperor's entry into the capital (ibid., p.38). Blochmann's suggestion that Jotik Rāi means a Hindu 'Court-Astrologer' is not warranted. (*Ā'īn-i Akbarī*, I, tr. Blochmann, Calcutta, 1927, p.442 *n*).

[14] *Akbarnāma*, III, pp.222-4.

[15] Ptolemy did not mention comets at all (C.L. Poor, *The Solar System*, London, 1908, p.273). The Arabic book on comets *Ẕawāt al-Awāib*, attributed to him and translated into Latin as well, is not authentic, being held by Carmody to be an amplification of the non-authentic *Centilquium*. See *Encyclopaedia of Islam*, 2nd ed., 1, p.1101.

solar rays become extremely light and get mixed in the atmosphere and ascend. These dispersed particles are called 'vapour' or 'smoke' (*dukhān*). This 'vapour' is the cause of clouds, rain, storms, thunder, lightning and the like. This viscous smoke on reaching the higher layers of the atmosphere, which is mixed with fire, is set alight and is called a meteor (*shahāb*). When it descends to the earth 'the vulgar' see it as 'a falling star'. If the smoke is not very fine, owing to its density, it does not get dispersed but starts burning and, appearing to us as a comet, assumes various forms, similar to a tailed body, spread-out hair, a spear, a many-horned head, etc. The comets' periods of visibility are both long and short. Abū'l Faẓl then makes a distinction in the terms used for comets according to their shape. The *ẕuẕuāba* (lit. possessed of forelocks) is the one like hair spread-out (*gesūdār*); the *ẕuẕanab* (lit. possessed of tail) is the tailed one (*dumdār*). He carefully uses the terms *ẕuẕanab* for the comet of 1577, although he himself in the earlier version of his work and his contemporary Badāūnī, had used the term *ẕuẕuāba* for it, so that the distinction was, perhaps, not generally a recognized one. The Indian astronomers, adds Abū'l Faẓl, had identified more than a hundred comets,[16] while the Greeks had determined seven categories, but held the *ẕuẕanab* and *ẕuẕuāba* to constitute the major (and most ominous) kinds of comets. He attributes to the Greeks the statement that the *ẕuẕuāba* appears in the east at dawn, the *ẕuẕanab* in the west at sunset.

Abū'l Faẓl goes on to give short notices of three previous comets, that of A.H. 662 (A.D.1264) that was visible in CentralAsia, and China, and of A.H. 803 (1400-1) visible in Asia Minor. Both these comets were observed in Europe and fall among the category of comets that were visible at daytime. Abū'l Faẓl, however, mentions another comet of A.H.837/1433-4, that he describes as having had the most disastrous effects. It appeared as a tailed one but later changed its form and became spear-like. This comet is not apparently considered a significant one in European works.

Jahāngīr provides an interesting description of the comet of 1618 which seems to be based on careful observation. He records

[16] Alberūnī says that the Indian scholars differ on the number of comets: some think there are 101 and others that there are 1000 (Edward C. Sachau, *Alberūnī's India*, II, London, 1910, p. 236).

in his diary that a few days before 18 Ābān 13 R.Y. (= 3 November 1618, Greg.), a luminous vapour appeared at night 3 *gharīs* (1 hour 12 minutes) before dawn; every night it rose one *gharī* (24 minutes) earlier. First its shape was like that of a staff, but later it looked like a javelin, with both ends very narrow, the middle thick, curving like a sickle. Its rear was towards the south, the front towards the north. At the time of writing (presumably 3 November 1618), it rose full one *pahr* (one fourth of the night, equalling three hours at the equinox) before dawn. The astronomers determined, by use of their astrolabes, that it extended across 24 degrees of the sky at different times.[17] While it moved with the heavens (in the Aristotelian-Ptolemaic conception of the universe), it had a movement of its own: initially in Scorpio, it moved into Libra. As the comet faded sixteen days after the above date (3 November), a star appeared in its position with a tail two or three yards long, but with no luminosity in the tail. As Jahāngīr wrote on, eight nights passed with this appearance being maintained. He promised to record its disappearance and its effects, if any, but fails to do so.

The way Jahāngīr describes this comet shows little trepidation on his part at the appearance of this ominous sign. He almost cheerfully informs us that the astrologers in their books called this type of comet 'spear-like' (*ḥarba*) and had recorded that its appearance means weakness of the rulers of Arabia and the victory of their enemies against them.[18] Nevertheless, Mu'tamad Khān, while he gives essentially the same details about the comet, goes on to describe its evil effects: it caused an unprecedented plague epidemic which had anticipated its appearance by a year and lingered on for twenty years. He even considers the rebellion of Khurram (Shāhjahān) (1622) a consequence of this comet's appearance, and so concludes that there was much bloodshed and no household remained unaffected by its appearance.[19]

There is only one detailed description of the fall of a meteorite. The reporter is Jahāngīr himself. He records that on 30 Farwardīn, of the 16th regnal year (Rabī' II, A.H.1030 = 19 April 1621) in

[17] The comet of 1618 is reported to have had a vibrating tail (*Story of Comets*, p.25).

[18] *Tuzuk-i Jahāngīrī*, ed. Syud Ahmud, Ghazipur and Aligarh, 1863-64, p. 250.

[19] Mu'tamad Khān, *Iqbālnāma-i Jahāngīrī*, Vol. 3, Nawal Kishore, Lucknow, 1870, p. 552.

one of the villages of the *pargana* of Jalandhar, a frightful commotion occurred and such a terrible noise came from the east that the residents of the village were deadly shaken with fear. A light appeared falling from the heavens as if there was a rain-shower of fire from the sky.[20] When people regained their senses, a rapid messenger was sent to the '*āmil* (revenue collector) of the *pargana*, Muḥammad Sa'īd, who at once rode to the village. He found that ten by twelve yards of ground had burnt so intensely that no sign of vegetation remained, and the earth was still hot. He had the ground dug out; the deeper they dug the greater was the heat, till they found a piece of burning red-hot iron so hot that it seemed to have come from some 'sphere of fire'. After some time it cooled down and was sent to the emperor in a sealed packet. Jahāngīr found that its weight was 160 *tolas* (4.24 lb. avdp.). He handed it over to his master smith, Dāūd, for making a sword, a dagger and a knife. He was informed that it was too brittle for hammering and would go to pieces. The emperor ordered it to be mixed with ordinary iron. By mixing three parts of the meteor, or 'lightning iron' (*āhan-i barq*), with one part of other iron, two swords, one dagger and a knife were made. Jahāngīr says that the swords were as good as those of Yemen and of 'the South' (Deccan), and were sufficiently flexible to bend and regain form. He got them tested in his own presence and found them to match well with the best swords. He named one of them *Shamshīr-i Qaṭa'ī* (cutting-sword) and the other *Barq Sarisht* (lightning-like) and a poet composed a quatrain about them emphasizing their celestial origin: 'Out of lightning fell raw iron in his reign.' The date was worked out in the chronogram, *Shu'la-i Barq-i Bādshāhī* ('The flash of the Royal Lightning').[21]

It is evident that the fall of the meteorite was treated by Jahāngīr quite rationally. His description suggests that this was a siderite (composed of metal, chiefly of iron and nickel) and not an aerolite (of stone). Since it was a small piece of hardly 3.3 lb. avdp. theforce with which it must have struck the earth could not have been very great.

[20] It seems that the narrators were so terrified that they inverted the sequence of events and reported that the sound came first and the light afterwards.

[21] *Tuzuk*, pp. 327-8. The weight of 160 *tolas* is converted into lb. avdp. on the basis of 1 *tola*=185.5 grains, which seems to have remained constant (Irfan Habib, *Agrarian System of Mughal India*, Bombay, 1963, pp.367 ff.).

Eclipses

It is rather surprising that out of the 56 eclipses of the sun (39 in the reign of Akbar, and 17 in that of Jahāngīr)[22] only one solar eclipse during Akbar's reign and two in the reign of Jahāngīr are recorded. If Abū'l Fazḷ chooses to provide information only about the eclipse of 1590, this may perhaps be because the astronomers had predicted that it would be a total or annular one.

There are two accounts of this eclipse given by Abū'l Fazḷ, in the first and in the final version of his *Akbarnāma*. The earlier version records the eclipse under 35th regnal year (1590). It does not mention any precise date, but puts it between two events dated Saturday, 7 July and Saturday, 15 September 1590.[23] The final version in the published text gives the precise date as 23 Amardād 35 Ilāhī;[24] but 23 must be an error for 8 Amardād, since *hasht* (8) written in Persian could easily be misread as *bist* (20). 8 Amardād corresponds to 31 July 1590 (Gregorian) which precisely is the date of an annular solar eclipse in India given according to Beveridge in *L'Arch's tables*, a French reference work.[25] R. Schram too gives the date of this eclipse as 21 July 1590 (Julian), i.e. 31 July (Gregorian).[26]

Unlike the appearance of comets and the fall of meteorites, eclipses could be predicted well in advance. As commented upon by Alberūnī the Indian astronomers, since ancient times, well understood the phenomenon notwithstanding the prevalent myths and superstitions.[27] But among Indians a solar eclipse was taken to be a bad omen and a total or annular one especially so. Akbar, notwithstanding his commitment to rationality, was not immune to these superstitions.

The earlier account contained in the first draft of the *Akbarnāma* reveals that he was quite concerned over the effects of the predicted eclipse of the sun. Since the belief was that if, at the time of the eclipse, clouds obscured the sun, the evil effect would be nullified,

[22] These have been counted from R. Schram's table of solar eclipses observable from India, given in R. Sewell, *The Indian Calendar*, London, 1896, pp.125-6.

[23] Add. 27,247, f.387b.

[24] *Akbarnāma*, III, p.579.

[25] *Akbarnāma*, III, tr. H. Beveridge, Indian Reprint, 1993, p.877 *n*.

[26] R. Sewell, *The Indian Calendar*, Table A, p.125.

[27] Alberūnī, *Alberuni's India*, II, pp. 107-14.

the emperor called upon the Brahmans to perform their rituals for gathering the clouds at the required moment. But the Brahmans failed and retired abashed. Barely half a *gharī* (12 minutes) had remained and the sky was still clear. The emperor himself now prayed to the Almighty, and lo! – the clouds duly came, bringing rain and obscured the sun at the moment of eclipse. Despite the eclipse, there remained ample brightness, a testimony to the fact that the eclipse was not complete. But, adds the historian, owing to the clouds obscuring the view, the embarrassment of the astronomers at their prediction (of a total eclipse) not having been fulfilled, was also mitigated.

Since it is difficult to imagine that Akbar's astronomers did not know that the moon, being near apogee, the eclipse predicted would not be total, but annular, leaving a ring of the sun all around the moon, the reason for there being more light than expected could possibly be that at Lahore the eclipse was only partial. The error in prediction for that place could lie in the inaccurate determination of the longitude of Lahore, which Abū'l Fazl himself gives (in relation to that of Delhi) with an error amounting to 6°40'.[28] In this period the longitudes were, in any case, extremely difficult to determine with much accuracy.

In his final version Abū'l Fazl appears to have suitably edited the account in keeping with his projection of Akbar's personality. The emperor's own alarm has again been edited out of his account; even the Brahmans are shown to have prayed on their own and not at the command of the emperor. It would have been dismaying to admit that the one who proclaimed that 'the acclaiming of Reason and rejection of Tradition is so brilliantly clear as to stand in no need of argument,'[29] remained himself vulnerable to the prevailing superstition about comets and eclipses.

As for eclipses, the superstition appears to be so strong that even Jahāngīr succumbed to it, as is brought out from the statements made in his memoirs. He mentions two solar eclipses and one lunar eclipse;[30] the first solar eclipse dated by him to 28 Ramazān A.H.1019 (14 December 1610, Greg.) and the other on Sunday 9

[28] Cf. Irfan Habib, 'Cartography in Mughal India', *Medieval India–A Miscellany*, IV, p. 132.

[29] *Ā'īn-i Akbarī*, II, ed. Blochmann, Calcutta, 1867, p.237.

[30] *Tuzuk*, pp.76-7, 88, 138.

Farwardimah [28 Ṣafar] 1024, corresponding to 29 March 1615. The first date broadly suits Schram's date of 5 December 1610 in the Julian calendar; but the second is an exact date, since according to Schram the solar eclipse took place on 19 March 1615 (Julian), which corresponds to 29 March (Gregorian), a Sunday. Jahāngīr makes the date firm by giving to the next day, a Monday, the Hijri date of 29 Ṣafar.

About the solar eclipse of December 1610, Jahāngīr gives no details, except to tell us that to ward off the evil influences he weighed himself against precious metals and gave away these and other articles and animals (horses, elephants and bullocks) in alms at Agra and at other places.[31] On the eclipse of March 1615 he is a little more forthcoming, perhaps since it was near total. He says that the eclipse began 12 *gharīs* (4 hours, 48 minutes) after dawn, beginning from the west. At the maximum extent of the eclipse, four-fifths of the sun was covered (as seen from Agra); and the eclipse lasted about 8 *gharīs* (3 hours, 12 minutes). Again, precious metals, animals and cereals were distributed among the needy and the deserving.[32]

The lunar eclipse that gets mention was a total one, and occurred on Saturday, 13 Shawwāl A.H.1018 (=20 January 1609). It began 4 *gharīs* (1 hour, 36 minutes) after dusk, and stage by stage the moon became covered, the eclipse lasting for 5 *gharīs* (2 hours) of the night. On this occasion as well, Jahāngīr weighed himself against gold, silver, cloth, and grain and gave these and other things and animals worth 15,000 Rupees to ward off the evil effect of the eclipse by his alms, as he says quite frankly.[33]

This preliminary study of statements in Mughal historical records about astronomical phenomena suggests that this information, even if it adds little to modern scientific knowledge, may yet have its own importance in the history of astronomical theory and tradition. For the historian of intellectual development,

[31] Ibid., p.88. [32] Ibid., p.138.

[33] *Tuzuk*, pp. 76-77. It is not clear whether Jahāngīr's 5 *gharīs* cover only the total eclipse, for, in that case, these would slightly exceed the maximum possible time (1 hour, 42 minutes) or are inclusive of the period of the partial eclipse, which could have lasted for a further two hours or more. Jahāngīr could, however, have been using the smaller night *gharīs* (each of 22 minutes, 24 seconds) (Cf. 'Abdu'l Ḥamīd Lāhorī, *Pādshāhnāma*, Bib. Ind., Calcutta, 1866-72, II, pp.337-9), in which case the duration of the eclipse as counted by him was 1 hour, 52 minutes.

the curious marriage between science and superstition that appears in the union of astronomy and astrology (comparable to that between chemistry and alchemy) should always remain of interest. It should remind us once again that the struggle between reason and superstition has not been a simple, straightforward process; one has been so intertwined with the other as to make the story a very complex one, full of curiosities and advances and retreats of the scientific spirit.

10

Scientific Concepts in Abū'l Fazḷ's *Ā'īn-i Akbarī*

IQBAL GHANI KHAN

It is quite obvious from some European and indigenous accounts of Akbar's character that he had more than a passing interest in science and technology. His minister and spokesman Abū'l Fazḷ devotes several sections to things scientific and technological in his *Ā'īn-i Akbarī*. The section entitled *Ā'īn-i Paidā'ish-i Filizzāt* ('Description of Genesis of Metals') contains the Aristotelian theory of four elements of all matter and natural phenomena. Aristotle said that all worldly phenomena are built up of the four elements, namely fire, water, earth and air. This is not the fire, water, earth and air as we know them, but different aspects of a primary matter which he called protyle. Each aspect displays different qualities and the potential forms contained in the protyle became manifest under the influence of the four fundamental qualities, namely hotness, wetness, coldness and dryness. These qualities were never met with by themselves, but in pairs, e.g. air is hot and wet; fire is hot and dry; earth is cold and dry; and, finally, water is cold and wet.[1]

In addition, Aristotle explained the cyclical rhythms in nature such as evaporation, rain, snow and floods by using the concept of 'dry' and 'wet exhalations'. For example, earthy parts get heated and mix with air and constitute what he called a 'dry exhalation' (*du<u>kh</u>ān* of Abū'l Fazḷ). These 'dry exhalations' would combine with the 'wet exhalations' within the earth's crust to give birth to

[1] Olaf Pedersen and M. Pihl, *Early Physics and Astronomy—A Historical Introduction*, London, 1974, p. 146. For details of the debate see Rene Taton, ed., *A General History of Science, Medieval and Ancient*, London, 1963; also some good surveys in classics like Benjamin Farrington, *Greek Science*; J.D. Bernal, *Science in History*, London, 1957, pp.140 ff; Julian Marias, *A History of Philosophy*, Dover, 1967; S. Sambursky, *The Physical World of the Greeks*, London, pp.14-15. For the Indian versions of this theory, see *Susrut Saṁhita*, vol. 2, quoted in B.V. Subbaroyappa, et al., *A Concise History of Science in India*, New Delhi, 1971, pp. 455-60.

minerals and metallic ores.[2]

The 'translation phase' of the reception of Greek scientific works in early Islam (c.A.D.800), when learning and criticism of authority were not considered to be signs of irreligion, Aristotle's ideas were questioned and then adopted after modification. The form in which they reached medieval India is reflected in the *Ā'īn-i Paidā'ish-i Filizzāt*.[3] Thus Abū'l Faẓl writes, 'God has manifested, in various forms, the four basic elements (namely, fire, water, earth and air). Fire is hot, dry and relatively light. Air is relatively warm and light. Water is cooler and heavier, while earth is cold, dry and absolutely heavy. Heat causes lightness; moisture imparts heaviness; wetness renders a body easily separable; while dryness prevents divisibility. In this wonderful way do the four elements become manifest as natural phenomena (*āṣ̤ār-i 'ulwīya*, e.g. rain, snow, lightning); secondly, as stones; thirdly, as plants; and, fourthly, as animals.'[4] Abū'l Faẓl then goes on to describe the wet and dry exhalations introduced by Aristotle and which he calls *dukhān* and *bukhār*. These two combine in the earth's atmosphere to give rain, snow, hail, etc. Below the earth's surface they combine to produce earthquakes, volcanoes and minerals.[5] It may be said that, compared to the Aristotelian theory, Abū'l Faẓl's elements and qualities as well as terminology are more specific and relative to each other. Furthermore he also incorporates Chinese Duality (in its Jabirian form) when he considers sulphur and mercury to be the building blocks of all minerals and metals in the earth's crust. Thus the Aristotelian wet and dry vapours combine in a variety of ways to produce an array of sulphurs and mercuries (symbiotic and hot chemicals). These sulphurs and mercuries then combine to give five classes of minerals and 'the Seven Metals'.

This leads to Abū'l Faẓl's acceptance of the theoretical basis of alchemical beliefs. Without any qualifying remarks, he writes, 'Although sulphur and mercury are the component parts of the Seven Metals there arise various forms from a difference in their

[2] Cf. Pedersen and Pihl, *Early Physics*, pp. 146, ff.

[3] For details on the translation phase, see O'Leary, *How Greek Sciences Passed to the Arabs*, London, 1957; also F.E. Peters, *Aristotle and the Arabs*, N.Y., 1968, and George Sarton, *Introduction to the History of Science*, Harvard, II.

[4] *Ā'īn-i Akbarī*, Nawal Kishore, Lucknow, I, pp. 37-8.

[5] Ibid., I, p.38.

purity, or from the peculiar circumstances of the mixture, or from a variety of the action of the component parts on one another. Thus silver will result when neither of the two components is mixed with earthly particles, when they are pure and perfectly united and when the sulphur is white and less in quantity than the mercury. When both are in equal proportions, and the sulphur is red as well as capable of imparting colour, gold will originate'.[6] And so he goes on until the formation of all the seven metals has been explained. However, while concluding he does seem to retreat a little when he comes to explain the possibility of transformation of metals from one to the other. Ascribing the idea to 'the practitioners of the art (of alchemy) (*ahl-i ṣan'at*)', he writes that tin is silver in a state of leprosy and bronze is crude gold, and that the alchemist like the physician can cure them back to their true state, using the methods of opposition and similarity.[7]

Abū'l Fazl's own practical mind was more concerned with how to classify metallic zinc which was being mined and extracted at Zawar (near Udaipur), but which was 'nowhere to be found mentioned in the books of knowledge (*nāmahā-i ḥikmat*)'.[8] So he introduces this metal by its local name (*jast*) and Persian term for zinc-oxide (*rūḥ-i tūtiya*), and then tries to explain its importance by enumerating and describing its uses in alloys such as brass, *kaulpatr* and *sīm-i sokhta*.

The Classification of Minerals

Having explained the origins of minerals, Abū'l Fazl takes pains to classify them too. While, on the one hand, he uses the Aristotelian criteria of wetness, dryness, hotness and coldness, on the other, he uses highly scientific criteria such as al-Bīrūnī's and al-Khāzinī's tables on specific gravity.[9]

The classification of minerals was a major matter of interest among Arab chemists such as Jābir ibn Ḥayyān, Zakarriya al-Rāzī and Abū Sīna, and their efforts helped greatly in the development of scientific method and of chemistry.

[6] Ibid., I, p.39. [7] Ibid.

[8] Ibid.

[9] The criteria such as hardness, solubility, colour, lustre, and fracture were developed by Theophrastos (c.372-288 B.C.), a pupil of Aristotle, in his *De Lapidus* (George Sarton, *A History of Science*, p.560).

The desire for finer categories finally led al-Bīrūnī to take up where Archimedes had left off, and he set about compiling a very long and accurate table of the specific gravities and relative densities of a large variety of minerals.

The exactitude and applicability of this concept to commercial use fired the imagination of Abū'l Faẓl and he inserted a whole chapter on this subject entitled 'On the Heaviness and Lightness of Every Substance'. The theoretical base of this chapter, which is largely full of tables, is rather simple. According to Abū'l Faẓl, 'some bodies are lighter (despite their larger size) than others, because due to the incomplete union of the dry and wet exhalations, air has entered the inter-particular spaces within the body. This makes them larger but lighter than those in which the mixing is more perfect.'

This reference to interparticular space and the resort to Atomism (when he talks of air entering the space between the particles (*ajzā'*) in the various bodies) is an example of Abū'l Faẓl's ability to accept a new theory if he found it to be in consonance with his own rationalism.[10]

Nonetheless, coming back to specific gravity (or relative density), Abū'l Faẓl reproduces a versified 'ready reckoner' which allows one to memorize the relative weights of mercury, bronze, tin, gold, lead, iron, brass, copper and silver, both in numbers and in *jummal* or *abjad* enumeration (in terms of given numerical weights of letters).

He also describes an instrument similar to the Ellenmeyer Flask of recent years (*āla al-makhrūṭiya*) which allowed one to measure the relative amounts of water displaced by equal weights of different substances. Various types of balances are also described in the *Ā'īn.*[11] Abū'l Faẓl ends this chapter with detailed tables on the relative weights as well as loss in weight of substances as wide ranging as gold, silver, pearls, crystal, precious stones and alloys.[12] The weightage given to this concept and to the devices used for detraining relative weights is reflective not just of intellectual exactitude, but also of the fact that many nobles were indulging in

[10] *Ā'īn.*, I, p. 40.

[11] Incidentally, atomism as a theory was highly disliked and refuted by Aristotle. Cf. *Ā'īn*, I, pp. 40-1. See J.D. Bernal, *Science in History*, London 1957, pp. 133-45.

[12] *Ā'īn*, I, pp. 40-1. Cf. al-Khāzinī's *Mīzān al-Ḥikmat*, Hyderabad, 1940, pp.79-82.

the sale and purchase of precious metals and stones and thus needed to know ways of detecting the genuine from the counterfeit.[13]

The appearance of such accurate and detailed tables shows that sixteenth-century Indian science was not lacking in methodological quantification and exactitude. In fact, on the question of quantification, it is interesting how Abū'l Faẓl relates the chapter on the origin of metals to a sub-section on alloying or the chemical combination of metals. For example, while describing the formation of *safīdrūī* (or white bronze), he writes: 'This alloy is known as *kānsī* in Hindi and is said to contain copper and tin in the ratio 4:1... Another bronze contains copper and lead in the ratio 8:3 and is known as *rūī* in Persian or *bhangār* in Hindi.'[14] For making brass, three different copper and zinc percentages are specified, namely with 72% copper, 67% copper and 58% copper.[15]

For fabricating more complex alloys such as having three to eight constituent metals, quantities were fixed by first putting together the simple, two-element alloys and, then, once their constituent ratios were fixed, combining these to form larger metal complexes such as *haft-josh* and *ashṭ-dhāt*. Incidentally, Akbar's own interest in technology enabled him to 'invent' an alloy made up of two parts white bronze and one part copper, which was 'beautiful and lustrous'.[16] Although it was a part of the usual sycophancy to credit new inventions to the emperor, in this case one could believe Abū'l Faẓl, for Akbar's work in the workshop has been remarked upon by contemporary Jesuit writers as well.[17]

On Sounds

Akbar enjoyed discussions on science, and interesting accounts of discussions on the movement of sound and on colours are available in the *Ā'īn*, though they are more in the form of digressions than direct or consistent description. Thus, sound is

[13] See Al-Bīrūnī's *Kitab al Jamāhir fī Ma'arifat ul Jawāhir,* Hyderabad, A.H. 1355.

[14] An entire treasury of precious stones is described in the *Ā'īn,* I, p.14.

[15] *Ā'īn.*, I, p.37.

[16] Ibid., p. 40.

[17] See Monserrate, *Commentary on his Journey to the Court of Akbar,* tr. J.S. Hoyland and S.N. Banerjee, Cuttack, 1922, p.201; and Du Jarric's account in *Akbar and the Jesuits,* tr. C.H. Payne, London, 1926.

dealt with in a chapter on calligraphy, the linkage being established when Abū'l Faẓl takes about the letters of the alphabet and then how they sound. It is here that he draws upon the theories propounded by the secret brotherhood of rationalists, the Ikhwān u'ṣ ṣafā and Ibn Sīnā, when he says, 'sound is produced by the striking together or the breaking of any hard substance. In both cases the air lying in between is set into wave-like motion and thus the state known as sound, is produced.'[18]

Thus we have atoms and we have wave-theory on the propagation of sound, both in very clear, unambiguous terms. More information on the modifying influences on sound follows, but space does not permit us to go into these details here.

On Colours

Just before the chapter on calligraphy and painting, Abū'l Faẓl gives a short note on the basic colours and how the various shades are produced. Echoing Aristotle's hypothesis on the rainbow, Abū'l Faẓl writes, 'White and black are believed to be the origin of all colours. They are looked upon as extremes and the component parts of all colours. White, when mixed in large proportions with a little black, will yield yellow, white and black in equal amounts will yield red; white and a lot of black will yield green. Other colours may be formed by compounding these basic colours in varying quantities. Besides it must be borne in mind that cold makes a wet body white and a dry body black; while heat renders that which is 'wet', black; and white, that which is 'dry'. These two factors (hotness and coldness) produce each in its place, a change in the colours of a body and are both capable of being acted upon (*qābil*), as well as receptive to (*muqtaẓā*) the influence of heavenly bodies (chiefly the sun).'[19] The theory of colours as stated in the *Ā'īn-i Akbarī* constitutes a typical example of the way in which Aristotelian concepts became embedded in the Indo-Islamic system of scientific beliefs. At such points one wonders why the well researched writings of Ibn al Haytham (*c*.A.D.965-

[18] *Ā'īn.*, I, p.127. Ibn Sīnā, *Risāla al Mausīqī,* Hyderabad, A.H.1353, p.10, and *Rasā'il Ikhwān u'ṣ Ṣafā,* Bombay, 1886, I, p.1188.

[19] *Ā'īn*, I, p.126.

1010) on light and colours which is presented in his *Kitāb al Manāẓir* (Book of Optics) were ignored by Abū'l Faẓl. As a matter of fact, what al Haytham was doing was revolutionary in that he was introducing experiments and apparatus to study the behaviour of light. Perhaps, his ideas were too dangerous for the Establishment and he had to leave Baghdad and seek refuge under the more tolerant Ayyubid rulers of Cairo. A greater tragedy for science in Islamic civilization was the failure of subsequent opticians and physicists to take up and turn into a tradition the methodology introduced by Haytham.[20] In fact a survey of scientific writing in medieval India has produced just one text on colours, and that is probably a copy of Quṭbuddīn Shīrāzī's *Sharḥ-i Manāẓir*.[21]

Though al-Bīrūnī too failed to absorb anything Haytham had said (perhaps because they were contemporaries and he was unaware of his writing) his advice to all the followers of Aristotle would have done Abū'l Faẓl a world of good. Al-Bīrūnī had said, 'The misfortune of these people is that (which arises) from their exaggeration in taking sides with the opinions of Aristotle entirely. It also lies in their belief which excludes the possibility of error in it, in spite of their knowledge that he was one of the deep thinkers, but not one of those who are infallible.'[22]

The *Ā'īn-i Akbarī* also contains chapters on assessing the purity of gold in all its various grades. While describing the imperial mint Abū'l Faẓl goes into the extraction of gold, silver and copper from the ore and their purification up to the exacting standards set by the mint-masters.[23] Apart from metallurgy Abū'l Faẓl also goes into other areas of chemical technology, such as when he explains the extraction of perfumes, the making of soap, the cooling of water by the use of saltpetre, the manufacture of paper and even ways of distilling alcohol.[24]

There are chapters on other areas of technology, such as the metallurgy of cannon and hand-gun fabrication; the geared devices for cleaning or smoothening the bores of 16 gun-barrels at a time;

[20] See details in Omar bin Saleh (tr.), Ibn al-Haytham's *Kitāb al Manāẓir* (Optics), Chicago, 1980.

[21] Ms. No.2335 Arabic, Raza Library, Rampur; Cf. A. Rahman, M.A. Alvi, et al., *Science and Technology in Medieval India — A Bibliography*, New Delhi, 1982.

[22] E.S. Kennedy (tr.), *Al Bīrūnī's Kitāb Ifrād al Maqāla fī Amr al Ẓalāl* (on Shadows, etc.), Aleppo, 1976, I, p.32.

[23] *Ā'īn*., I, pp.18-32.

[24] Ibid., I, passim.

and the geared mills that grind wheat in a moving carriage.[25]

Apart from the concepts just analysed, the *Ā'īn* also has sections on veterinary science and natural history, on medicine, on physical and mathematical geography which describe ways of determining the linear extent of a degree of longitude or latitude and hence the circumference of the earth. Calendering the solar year accurately was a major problem and a way out was sought by the introduction of the Ilāhī calendar. This in itself is a highly problematic area of science.

The Hindu sciences were not neglected either and much of the last portion of the *Ā'īn* is devoted to the Hindu sciences (and to Indian and Ptolemaic geography).

Finally, it was Akbar himself who must be credited with patronizing and promoting men like Abū'l Faẓl and Fat'ḥullāh Shīrāzī, men who could help him introduce more scientific syllabi in the schools and more effective techniques in technology, and to initiate discussions on scientific theories.[26] Nonetheless, the socio-economic and ideological stimulants that this was producing were not apparently provocative enough to bring about a paradigm change[27] in the structure of Indian science. Hence Abū'l Faẓl's lament in the *Ā'īn* that exchanges between scientists of various religious persuasions were not taking place because of 'the blowing of the chill blast of inflexible custom (*taqlīd*) and the low flicker of the lamp of wisdom.' That the old methodological-ideological framework of 'science' had not been breached is evident from the rest of his remarks: 'From time immemorial, the exercise of inquiry has been restricted, and questioning and investigation have been regarded as precursors of infidelity. Whatever has been received from father, kindred or teacher is considered as a deposit under Divine sanction and a malcontent is reproached with impiety or irreligion. Although a few among the intelligent of their generation admit the imbecility of this procedure in others, yet they will not stir one step in a practical direction themselves'.[28]

Fortunately, in the age of Akbar, there were exceptions.

[25] See Irfan Habib, 'Akbar and Technology' in this volume.

[26] See M.A. Alvi and A. Rahman, *Shāh Fat'hullāh Shīrāzī, a 16th Century Indian Scientist*, New Delhi, 1976.

[27] On the idea of 'paradigm change', see T.S. Kuhn, *The Structure of Scientific Revolutions*, Chicago, 1970.

[28] *Ā'īn-i Akbarī*, III, tr. Jarrett, rev. Sarkar, Oriental Reprint, 1978, pp.4-5.

11

Akbar and Technology

IRFAN HABIB

In April 1580 the Jesuit father Francis Henriques reported from Fatehpur Sikri that 'Akbar knows a little of all trades, and sometimes loves to practise them before his people, either as a carpenter, or as a blacksmith, or as an armourer, filing.'[1] Rudolf Acquaviva soon afterwards, in July, referred to Akbar's taking delight in 'mechanical arts',[2] and in September Monserrate claimed to 'have even seen him making ribbons like a lace-maker and filing, sawing, working very hard.'[3] In his *Commentary* written later, Monserrate recalled that

> Zelaldinus [Akbar] is so devoted to building that he sometimes quarries stone himself along with the other workmen. Nor does he shrink from watching and even himself practising for the sake of amusement the craft of an ordinary artisan. For this purpose he has built a workshop near the palace where also are studios and work-rooms for the finer and more reputable arts, such as painting, goldsmith work, tapestry-making, carpet and curtain-making, and the manufacture of arms. Hither he very frequently comes and relaxes his mind with watching those who practise their arts.[4]

These statements by Jesuit witnesses are important, since they suggest that Abū'l Faẓl's claims of Akbar's great interest in craft and technology are not mere products of courtly flattery. Akbar had a natural inclination towards industrial crafts; and this was undoubtedly a source of his concern with technological innovation.

[1] *Letters from the Mughal Court: The first Jesuit Mission to Akbar (1580-83)*, ed. [& tr.], with an Introduction by John Correia-Affonso, Bombay/Anand, 1980, p.22.

[2] Ibid., p.56.

[3] Ibid., p.81.

[4] Monserrate, *Commentary on his Journey to the Court of Akbar*, tr. J.S. Hoyland and S.N. Banerjee, Cuttack, 1922, p.201. See also Pierre du Jarric's account based (ultimately) on Jesuit letters in *Akbar and the Jesuits*, tr. C.H. Payne, London, 1926, p.206 ('the next moment he would be seen shearing camels, hewing stones, cutting wood, or hammering iron').

'Prefab' and Movable Structures

An early testimony to Akbar's interest in technology comes from 'Ārīf Qandahārī. Writing in 1579, he says:

His high and majestic nature is such that when he journeys, the tents of His Majesty's encampment are loaded on five hundred camels. There are eighteen houses, which have been made of boards of wood, each including an upper chamber and balcony, that are set up in a suitable and attractive place. At the time of departure, each board is dismantled, and, at the time of encamping, the boards are joined together by iron rings. The insides of these houses are clothed with covers of European brocade and European velvet, and the outside thereof are covered with broadcloth.[5]

The spplementing of tents by wooden boards to create prefabricated and movable structures was an interesting innovation, which, though described later in some detail by Abū'l Faẓl in the *Ā'īn-i Akbarī*, appears to have escaped general attention, especially since Blochmann's translation[6] does not bring out the fact that the structures were essentially of wood, not of cloth or canvas. I offer a fresh translation of the passage in the *Ā'īn-i Akbarī*:

The *Ā'īn* of Encampment and Campaign: It is difficult to describe all of it, but a little of what is arranged during hunting expeditions and journeys to nearby places is put into writing, and an illustrative account offered. First, the *Gulālbār* is a wonderful fortress which His Majesty has created. In it the enclosure is very solid, and passage is closed or opened with lock and key. It is not less than 100 *gaz* by 100 *gaz* in area. On its eastern side, is set up a large tent-hall (*bārgāh*), with two high masts (*sargha*), containing 54 chambers [i.e. with 54 smaller poles around them], 24 *gaz* in length, 14 *gaz* in width.[7] Inside [the *Gulālbār*], a large wooden *rāwaṭī* stands, and around it they have other curtained pavilions. Adjacent to it is put up a two-chambered (*do-āshyāna*) wooden building, and that is the place of worship for His Majesty. Outside of it, in select order, 24 wooden *rāwaṭīs*, each 10 *gaz* in length and 6 *gaz* in width, are raised, each set

[5] 'Ārif Qandahārī, *Tārīkh-i Akbarī*, ed. Muinuddin Nadvi, Azhar Ali Dihlawi and Imtiyaz Ali Arshi, Rampur, 1962, p.43.

[6] *Ā'īn-i Akbarī*, I, tr. H. Blochmann, rev. D.C. Phillott, Calcutta, 1927, p.49.

[7] See the separate description of *bārgāh* under *Ā'īn-i Farrāsh Khāna* in *Ā'īn-i-Akbarī*, ed. H. Blochmann, Calcutta, 1866-7, I, p.49. This shows that it was a hall made by a tented roof, so that '10,000 people or more could find shade under it'. The significance of *sargha* as mainmast appears from this passage and other occurrences of the word in the same chapter of the *Ā'īn*.

apart by curtain-walls. Ladies of the imperial harem find repose there.[8]

A 'wooden *rāwaṭī*' is duly described a little later in the *Ā'īn-i Farrāsh Khāna*:

The wooden *rāwaṭī*[9] is raised with ten pillars. A part of these is put into the ground, and all are equal in height, but those two,[10] on which the beam rests are slightly higher. The solidity is increased by [wooden] boards (*dāsa*) placed above and below [the resting beam], and some rafters are placed over the beam and board. All are attached to each other by iron covers with male and female fits (*huma rā āhan jāma ba-ṭarz-i nar-o-mādagī paiwand dahad*). The wall and roof are formed by woven bamboo. There are one or two doors, and they set up a [curtained] floor (*ṣuffa*) [in front of the door] according to the size of the lower board (*dāsa*). The interior is ornamented by brocade and velvet, and the exterior is girdled by broadcloth and silken tape.

Abū'l Faẓl goes on to describe the *do-āshyāna*, also mentioned in the initial passage on encampment:

The *do-āshyāna* is set up with eighteen pillars. Pillars of six *gaz* each are raised and wooden boards put over them. To them, by way of male and female fits (*ba-ṭarz-i nar-o-māda*), pillars of four *gaz* [in length] are attached, and so the upper room (*bālā-khāna*) is formed. Its interior and exterior are ornamented in the same way [as the wooden *rāwaṭī*]. In expeditions, it serves as the place of the emperor's bed-chamber.[11]

These extensive translations are offered to show that, as 'Arif Qandahārī says, much innovation went in to prepare posts and beams which could be used instantly to set up wooden structures, and not simply tents. A wood-and-bamboo palace, like the 'wooden *rāwaṭī*' and a double-storeyed structure, like the *Do-āshyāna*, could be set up and dismantled at each stage of journey. Blochmann's translation suggests that 'bolts and nuts' were put into use to attach the several

---

[8] *Ā'īn-i Akbarī*, ed. Blochmann, I, p.41.

[9] Abū'l Faẓl gives the letter-by-letter spelling of the word. It appears in John T. Platts, *Dictionary of Urdu, Classical Hindi and English*, reprint, New Delhi, 1977, p.584, given the same spelling, but with the pronunciation *rāoṭī*; it means a small rectangular tent. See also Henry Yule and A.C. Burnell, revised by William Crooke, *Hobson-Jobson*, reprint, Delhi, 1968, p.772 (*s.v.* rowtee). The *rāoṭī* was a tent of canvas or cloth; but Abū'l Faẓl has expressly described a 'wooden *rāvaṭī*'.

[10] Blochmann's ed. reads *magar do*, 'but two'; Br. Mus. Add. 7652, f.25a, *magar duzh*. *Duzh* means 'number', *daz/dazh*, 'gallery, balcony'. Nawal Kishor ed., 1893, I, p.32, reads *na-gardad*, which would make Abū'l Faẓl say that 'all pillars are *not* equal in height, for those...' But *na-gardad* seems an awkward reading here.

[11] *Ā'īn-i Akbarī*, ed. Blochmann, I, p.49.

parts.[12] If correct, this would be testimony to an early use of screw as an attachment, though even in Europe, the screw did not come into use in carpentry before the sixteenth century.[13] The words, *āhan jāma*, iron-cover, are, however, decisive in excluding the screw. Obviously, what we are told of are short iron-tubes that clothed the ends of masts and beams, with protrusions ('male') designed to fit into hollows ('female') of corresponding tubes fitted to other masts and beams, and *vice-versa*. These could extend both length-wise and at right-angles to the mast or beam. It is thus that modern iron scaffolding is often rigged up; and it would be interesting to see if there is any early evidence of the use of this device in timber construction in India. The general principle was known in ancient Iran, where *kārīz* clay pipes used to be fitted to each other this way, each being at one end 'male', and, at the other, 'female'. But I am not aware of its application there in any timber-construction.

Textiles

'Ārif Qandahārī is also our earliest source for Akbar's interest in textile technology. He says:

> His Majesty has such an eye for the finer things that he has introduced [lit.invented] silken clothes, brocade, tapestry and carpets of silk and brocade in India, and instructed highly skilled masters in that art, so that the work in India is now much better than the work of Persia and Europe. He has so well practised the making of designs (*ṭarrāhī*) that if Mānī [the great artist] was alive, he would bite his fingers in astonishment at such design-making and dyeing.[14]

This passage is important in showing that Abū'l Fazl did not invent Akbar's reputation for innovativeness in the realm of textile craft, and that this was widely recognized much before he began to write the *Ā'īn-i Akbarī*. Only, he offers more details:

> From the care bestowed by His Majesty different kinds of textiles (*qumāsh*)

[12] *Ā'īn-i Akbarī*, tr. Blochmann, rev. Phillott, 1927, I, p.56, lines 11 and 17.

[13] R.W. Symonds in Singer, *et al.* (ed.), *History of Technology*, II, p.242*n*. The terms 'male and female' (*nar mādagī*) are applied to the bolt of a lock in *Bahār-i 'Ajam*, the dictionary by Tek Chand 'Bahār', 1739, II, Delhi, A.H. 1283, p.682, *s.v. nar-mādagī*.

[14] *Tārīkh-i Akbarī*, p.45.

came forth, and Irani, European and Chinese textiles became common. Efficient masters and unique experts came and warmed up the work of instruction. In the imperial camp and the cities of Lahore, Agra, Fatehpur [Sikri], Ahmadabad and Gujarat different kinds of figures (*taṣvīr*), patterns (*naqsh*), and weaves [lit. knots (*girah*)] and wonderful designs (*ṭarḥ-hā*), gained currency, and world-travellers, able to recognize quality products, were wonderstruck. In a short while, the sagacious emperor obtained familiarity with all theoretical and practical aspects of that art, and, from his patronage, skilled masters of ready understanding belonging to this country also learnt it.[15]

The context makes it clear that here what was involved was the diffusion, under Akbar's patronage, of the pattern-weaves of Iran, China and Europe. Though experts could only have come from Iran, the use of the draw-loom was common to the weaving techniques in all three regions. It is tantalizing not to be certain whether Abū'l Faẓl is speaking of the introduction of this technique; but it is not unlikely.

Special attention needs to be paid to the words *ṭarrāḥī* in 'Ārif Qandahārī, and *ṭarḥ* in the passage from Abū'l Faẓl, quoted above. It is very possible that these also refer to the designs on the printing blocks for printed chintz. Ghanī Beg Asadābādī, who left 'Abdu'r Raḥīm Khānkhānān's service in 1592, is said to have 'endeavoured so much in the art of design-making (*ṭarrāḥī*) and inventing chintz-patterns (*ikhtirā'-i chīt*), that those who were experts in that art admired and imitated him.'[16] This is said of him during his stay at Sironj, the centre of printed chintz. His contemporary Āqā Muḥammad Shīrāzī 'made strange, wonderful inventions, and achieved much success in making designs for chintz (*ṭarrāḥī-i chīt*), which they make best in Sironj in all of India'.[17] While the technique of printing need not have come from Iran, the fact that both the chintz-designers in 'Abdu'r Raḥīm's service were Iranians seems to suggest that there was a tendency to transfer Persian designs in draw-loom weave over to printed chintz. If *ṭarḥ* and *ṭarrāḥī*, used in connection with Akbar's achievements in textile work, also include designs on printing blocks, one would more readily understand why the designs or patterns Akbar created should

[15] *Ā'īn-i Akbarī*, ed. Blochmann, I, p.101.

[16] 'Abdu'l Bāqī Nihāwandī, *Ma'āṣir-i Raḥīmī*, ed. M. Hidayet Hosain, Calcutta, 1910-31, III, pp.980, 986.

[17] Ibid., III, p.1659.

have had such a large admiring circle.

Printing-block designs would be connected closely with the application of colours, and Akbar's expertise in both is indeed praised by 'Ārif Qandahārī in the passage quoted. Abū'l Faẓl tells us of Akbar's experiments with the dyeing of shawl-wool. Until now *ṭūs*-wool had been used undyed, but Akbar set himself to dye it and found that it would not take red colour. Further, 'the white *alcha* also called *ṭarḥdār*, has natural colours. Its wool is either white or black in colour. It is woven in three ways: (all) white, (all) black or mixed. The first (white) in old times could take no more than three or four colours. But His Majesty has made it many-hued (*gūnāgūn*) [i.e. suceeded in applying many colours to it]'.[18] Clearly, then, there was much effort made and experimentation undertaken by Akbar to see what dye the wool would take.

Aircooling and Refrigeration

Abū'l Faẓl says that India used to be censured for 'the absence of cold water and the excess of heat', and so Akbar sought to remove the cause of the latter complaint by popularising *kh̲as*-frames:

> There is a fragrant root, very cool, which is called *kh̲as*. By His Majesty's command, it became common to make huts of bamboo frames (*nai-bast kh̲āna-hā*) stuffed with it. When water is thrown on it, winter seems to arrive in the midst of summer.[19]

It is to be investigated if before Akbar the practice of cooling houses or rooms through the wetting of *kh̲as*-frames was at all prevalent. It is not to be found in Bābur's description of India. 'Bahār' (1739) defines *kh̲as-kh̲āna* as something peculiar to India and illustrates it with a fair range of verses, but two of the three poets quoted are known to belong to the seventeenth and eighteenth centuries.[20] Abū'l Faẓl's ascription of the invention to Akbar may, therefore, be quite accurate.

[18] *Ā'īn-i Akbarī*, ed. Blochmann, I, pp.103-4. The sense is lost in Blochmann's rendering: 'His Majesty had given the order to dye it in various ways' (tr., I, p.97), as if it was a mere question of fashion. The verb is *barsāk̲h̲t*, 'made', not 'ordered'.

[19] *Ā'īn-i Akbarī*, ed. Blochmann, II, p.6.

[20] *Bahār-i 'Ajam*, I, Delhi, AH 1282, p.569, *s.v.kh̲askh̲āna*:'Hut made of *kh̲as* in which people sit in summer, and this fragrant *kh̲as* [or grass] and such hut are peculiar to India'. The poets quoted are: 'Qubūl', Ḥakīm Ṣādiq, and Mullā Abū'l

Of still greater interest is Akbar's device to cool water. This was through the use of saltpetre. Abū'l Faẓl quotes Akbar as claiming to have made the discovery;[21] and he himself more than once attributes the invention to Akbar without any qualification.[22] The *locus classicus* for the invention is the following passage:

His Majesty, out of the surge of far-seeing wisdom, made saltpetre, which creates such tumult in [the form of] gun-powder, the means of cooling water, so that both the poor and the rich were made happy thereby. It is a saltish-earth. They put it in a perforated pan and sprinkle some water on it. What drops [through the pan] is boiled, separated from ordinary earth and crystallized (*barbandand*). A *ser* of water is poured into a bottle made of pewter or silver or such metal and its mouth is closed. In a pan two and half *sers* of saltpetre are mixed with five *sers* of water, and the closed bottle is moved round and round within that mixture for the space of half a *gharī* [i.e. 12 minutes]. The water within the bottle gets very cold. For one rupee one can get three-quarters of a *man* to 4 *mans* (of saltpetre).[23]

Although Abū'l Faẓl does not explicitly date the invention, he says, immediately after the above passage, that Akbar's shift of headquarters to Lahore in 1585 enabled him to get snow to cool water. This suggests that the use of saltpetre for cooling water had been discovered when Akbar was at Fatehpur Sikri and Agra, i.e. well before 1585. No earlier description of the method exists, so that Abū'l Faẓl's claims for his master as the inventor seem justified. Subsequent descriptions, particularly of European travellers, are fairly numerous. These emphazise that it was a practice found only in India.[24] Akbar's invention, if made before

---

Barkat 'Munīr'. I have not been able to trace Ḥakīm Ṣādiq, but 'Qubūl' (Mirzā 'Abdu'l Ghanī Kashmīrī) died in A.H. 1139/A.D. 1726-7 and Abū'l Barkat 'Munīr' in A.H. 1054/A.D. 1644-5 (Āzād Bilgrāmī, *Sarv-i Āzād*, ed. Abdullah Khan and Abdul Haq, Lahore/Hyderabad Dn,1913, pp. 60, 198-9).

[21] In the collection of 'Heart-ravishing Sayings of His Majesty' at the end of the *Ā'īn-i Akbarī*, II, ed. Blochmann, p.241: 'When we experimented with saltpetre, it turned out that attachment to salt i.e. loyalty, is also to be found in water.'

[22] *Ā'īn-i Akbarī*, ed. Blochmann, I, p.51; II, p.6.

[23] Ibid., I, p.51. Blochmann's translation of this passage (tr., I, p.58) is accurate. One *man* of Akbar's time was equal to 55.32 lb. avdp.

[24] The earliest I have noted is Peter Mundy (1632) (*The Travels of Peter Mundy in Europe and Asia*, II, ed. R.C. Temple, London, 1914, p.77). See also François Bernier (1664), *Travels in the Mogul Empire, 1656-68*, tr. A. Constable, rev. V.A. Smith, London, 1916, pp.356-7, and John Marshall (1671), *John Marshall in India —Notes and Observations in Bengal, 1668-72*, ed. S.A. Khan, London, 1927, pp.428-9.

1585, had a clear precedence in time over chemical devices for refrigeration in Europe, which moreover required snow for initiating the process.[25]

Geared Waterlift

Babur had been greatly attracted by the device of gear-and-chain water-lift, to which Anglo-Indian usage later gave the name of 'Persian wheel'. He had apparently never seen it in Central Asia and Afghanistan and had the first sight of it at Bhera, West Panjab, in 1519.[26] In his account of India he provides us with the earliest scientific description of the device.[27] It is not surprising that Akbar should have been interested in these wheels, and it is certainly shown very frequently by his artists in the book illustrations that he commissioned.[28]

Abū'l Faẓl attributes to Akbar certain inventions here as well:

His Majesty made such water-wheels (*daulāb-hā*), and such (gear) wheels (*gardūn-hā*) were fixed thereon, that [I] water may be carried to a height from distant low-lying places; [II] two oxen may turn four wheels (*charkh*) simultaneously; and, [III] further, with one ox, turning two wheels, water may be brought up from two wells, and a water-mill be turned.[29]

Invention I is illustrated in two miniatures in the volume of Niẓāmī's *Khamsa*, written and illustrated for Akbar's library.[30] Here, while the ox remains on the ground, rotating a high vertical axle by going round and round with a drawbar, the axle caries at or near its top (in one illustration it seems to be attached to another post for stability; in the other it stands clear) a pin-drum, whose pins mesh with pegs of a vertical wheel.

[25] For these see R.J. Forbes, *Studies in Ancient Technology*, VI, Leiden, 1966, p.105. I drew attention to the precedence of Akbar's invention in 'Changes in Technology in Medieval India', *Studies in History*, New Delhi, II(i) (1980), p.38.

[26] *Bāburnāma*, 'Abdu'r Raḥīm's Persian transl., Br. Mus. Or. 3174, f.314b; tr. A.S. Beveridge, London, 1921, I, p.388.

[27] Ibid., Or.3174, ff.376b-377a; tr. A.S. Beveridge, II, pp.486-7.

[28] Cf. S.P. Verma, *Art and Material Culture in the Paintings of Akbar's Court*, New Delhi, 1978, p.109: the arrow indicating direction in diagram in Plate XLVII (Nos.14 and 15) needs to be reversed.

[29] *Āʾīn-i Akbarī*, ed. Blochmann, I, p.199.

[30] Br. Mus. Or. 12208, ff.65a, 99b.

The latter wheel in turn rotates the chain-of-pots wheel, placed on the same axle, and thus water is raised to a level much higher than that of the ox and drawbar. It was this invention which enabled water to be lifted to great heights through successive lifts at Fatehpur Sikri. As observed by Mundy in 1633

> The king's howse or Moholl stands on the highest hill... Also a little garden. The water to water it is also to fill the Tancks alofte, and for their use is drawne from the valley, first into one tancke and then from that into another higher, and soe into 4 or 5 until it came alofte, by that which wee in Spaine call Noraies [norias].[31]

The great wells, with provision for lifting water in successive stages, and the great network of viaducts are described in much detail by E.W. Smith in his survey of Fatehpur Sikri, but without any speculation as to the 'machinery' or the means by which the water could be lifted.[32] He could have seen it in the *Khamsa-i Niẕāmī* illustrations. In any case, the great water-works of Fatehpur Sikri make it certain that Invention I was in full use in the 1570s.

As for Inventions II and III, one can see that these could be made possible only by making the gearing more efficient. There is no evidence, as we shall also note below in the next section, that Akbar and his engineers knew of any alternative to pin-drum gearing. Given this limitation, improvements could come by better carpentry (making the mesh of pegs with pins more close and exact), the use of iron at places of contact, greater structural stability for the apparatus, and so on. But, unluckily, Abū'l Fazl does not inform us whether all or any of these were contemplated.

Other Applications of Gearing: Cart-mill & Gun-barrel Boring

In 1582 Mīr Fatḥu'llāh Shīrāzī, a renowned Iranian scholar, theologian and physician, came to Akbar's court, and immediately obtained high status among Akbar's main counsellors. Badāūnī reports that when the *nauroz* festival was celebrated on 20 March 1583, the emperor arranged a bazar where–

[31] Pater Mundy, *Travels,* II ('Travels in Asia, 1630-34'), ed. Sir R.C. Temple, London, 1914, p.228.

[32] Edmund W. Smith, *Moghul Architecture at Fatehpur Sikri*, Allahabad, 1896, Part II, pp.19, 32-1, 38-40.

as by previous custom, different shops were allotted to different nobles. In his own shop Shāh Fatḥu'llāh showed [products of] different kinds of skill, including load-moving machines (*jarr-i aṣqāl*) and fanciful devices.[33]

More precise information is offered by Shaikh Niẓāmuddin Aḥmad, who, writing in 1593, says of Fatḥu'llāh:

He was also skilled in the sciences of fanciful devices ('*ulūm-i gharība*), such as strange and magical works. Thus he invented a mill placed on a cart, which moved of its own and made flour; he made a mirror in which were seen strange figures from far and near; and by one wheel ten hand-guns had their heads fixed (*sar mī shud*).[34]

As M.A. Alvi and A. Rahman have pointed out, two of these inventions are classed among those attributed to Akbar by Abū'l Faẓl.[35] From this they draw the rather extreme conclusion that not only these, but practically all the other mechanical inventions attributed to Akbar in the *Ā'īn* were the work of Fatḥu'llāh Shīrāzī, though the latter was at Akbar's court for just seven years (1582-9).[36] Without entering into the debate as to how much should be ascribed to the Iranian scholar, it is best to understand the nature of these machines from Abū'l Faẓl's descriptions.

First, the cart-mill:

His Majesty, out of skill, invented a wonderful cart ('*arāba*), which became the means of comfort for the people of the world. During the time it is used for travel and transport, it mills various kinds of grain into flour.[37]

The statement that it milled 'various kinds of grain', surely suggests the presence of more than one or two mills carried by the cart. If we assume that it was a two-wheel cart, it would be necessary to imagine that an equal number of mills (say, two) must

[33] 'Abdu'l Qādir Badāūnī, *Muntakhabu't Tawārīkh*, ed. 'Alī, Aḥmad and Lees, Calcutta, 1864-9, II, p.321.

[34] *Ṭabaqāt-i Akbarī*, ed. B. De, Calcutta, 1913-5, II, p.457. The phrase, *sar mī shud*, should ordinarily be taken to mean 'fired', and this leads M.A. Alvi and A. Rahman, *Fatḥullāh Shīrāzī, a Sixteenth Century Indian Scientist*, New Delhi, 1968, pp.30-1 to conjecture that a 'wheel-lock' is here involved. A single wheel-lock could not fire ten guns at a time. Leaving this aside, if the guns were fired when placed around a big wheel, they would all point in different directions, which would be of no use.

[35] *Ā'īn-i Akbarī*, ed. Blochmann, I, pp.126, 199.

[36] M.A. Alvi and A. Rahman, esp. pp.4, 30-2.

[37] *Ā'īn-i Akbarī*, ed. Blochmann, I, p.199.

have been placed on either side of the axle to keep it in balance. Since no other mode of gearing than pin-drum is known to have been available to Akbar, we may suppose that the axle carried an elongated pin-drum, whose pins meshed with the vertical pegs placed on rims of horizontal wheels, one pair on either side and each wheel rotating a millstone. This would, of course, have enabled four different kinds of grain to be turned into flour simultaneously.[38] This invention must have been made in the 1580s during Fatḥu'llāh Shīrāzī's presence at Akbar's court. It has, therefore, precedence in time over the European wagon-mill, which in its first version (made *c.*1580 and described in 1607 by Zonca) did not mill when in transit, but had its mill-wheel rotated when it was itself stationery. Mills geared to cart-wheels and thus working as the cart moved are known in Europe only from the seventeenth century.[39]

Abū'l Fazl continues:

> Further, His Majesty invented a large cart (*saturg gardūne*), which an elephant pulls. It is so large that many chambers for hot bath are placed upon it; in it a hammam offers pleasure. Strange it is, that an ox can easily pull it. Also by camel and horse are these carts (*gardūn-hā*) moved, and give comfort to people. The more delicate cart is called *bahl* and on even ground many people can sit and convey themselves on it.[40]

The description leaves one in doubt as to the precise nature of the mechanical improvement. It is distantly possible that gearing was involved in fanning the fire for heating water, through wheel-driven bellows on the trip-hammer principle. On the other hand, Akbar may have done nothing more than merely multiplying the number of cart wheels (*gardūn*) to give greater length to the elephant-drawn carriage. There is no evidence that Fatḥu'llāh was involved in designing these carriages.

Finally, the machine for smoothening gun-barrels, which could be the same (or act on the same principle) as the machine said to

[38] The modern drawing, Fig.III, in Alvi and Rahman, p.8, shows a single mill and European-style toothed wheels. It is, therefore, hard to accept it as a plausible representation of the device.

[39] J. Needham, *Science and Civilization in China*, IV: 2, Cambridge, 1965, pp.255-7, where there is evidence offered also of a similar Chinese invention made 1300 years earlier, but then apparently forgotten.

[40] *Ā'īn-i Akbarī*, ed. Blochmann, I, p.199.

have been invented by Fatḥu'llāh Shīrāzī. Abū'l Faẓl's description is as follows:

The *Ā'īn* of Making *Barghū*

Formerly even a man of strong arms used to suffer great hardship in working with iron instruments till some smoothness (*ṣafā*) [within the hand-gun barrel] was achieved. His Majesty, out of wisdom, invented a wheel, which upon being turned by one ox, smoothened [the barrels of] sixteen hand-guns (*bandūq*) in a small amount of time. For the reader's information, a diagram is provided.[41]

The original diagram is preserved in many MSS and is reproduced with some deficiencies in Blochmann's translation.[42]

What the device did was not 'cleaning', as supposed by Blochmann.[43] While the term *ṣafā* can be applied to both cleaning and polishing (or smoothening) the gun, it is otherwise with the word *barghū* or *yàrghū* (as variously read in the MSS).[44] This word is not found in the dictionaries I have consulted, but its sense is made clear in the preceding chapter of the *Ā'īn*. After the barrel (*darāzī-i tufang*) had been made, without the 'hind part' (*tah*), it was sent to the imperial chambers. There, we are told,

The emperor determines the weight of the pellet, and according to this, the size of the hole [of the barrel] is given shape. In a long [handgun] the weight [of the pellet] does not exceed 25 *ṭānks*, [3.70 lb. avdp.] and in the smaller [gun], 15 *ṭānks* [2.202 lb.]. With such weights, only His Majesty has the boldness to fire. When the *barghū* is completed, the handgun is again sent to the imperial apartments [for approval].[45]

From this passage it is clear that *barghū* signified the gun-barrel

[41] Ibid., I, p.126.

[42] Upper diagram in Blochmann, Plate XV, facing p.18 of his translation. The lower drawing is a modern one and should be disregarded. The diagram is discussed further on in this article.

[43] *Ā'īn-i Akbarī*, tr. Blochmann, rev. Phillott, I, p.122. M.A. Alvi and A. Rahman, pp.4-7, so totally accept Blochmann's rendering that they speak even of 'rotating brushrods'! It speaks much for J. Needham's insight that while he had only Blochmann's translation to go upon, he could yet see that 'boring and cleaning' must have been the object of the machine (*Science and Civilization in China*, IV:2, Cambridge, 1965, p.88n.).

[44] Br. Mus. Add. 7652, which is one of the most accurate MSS of the *Ā'īn*, consistently reads *barghū*.

[45] *Ā'īn-i Akbarī*, ed. Blochmann, I, p.125. The *ṭānk* is said (ibid., p.60) to have been 1/5 *dām* in weight; and a *dām*-coin weighed 322.7 grains.

in its final shape after boring.[46] It was thus the hard work of grinding and boring the inside of the barrel which was sought to be lightened by using animal power to rotate the 'iron instrument' or drill within the barrel.

Abū'l Faẓl's diagram (which is best given in British Museum MS Add. 7652, with the heading 'Diagram of the *Bargh̲ū*-wheel', and with legends provided at various points) makes it clear that the ox (not actually figured, but its position at the end of the draw-bar indicated by the legend *taṣwīr-i gāu*, figure of ox) pulled a draw-bar around to rotate a large, horizontal pin-drum (*chark̲h̲-i 'aẓīm*) (figured, with pins shown on the rim), its axis (*mihwār*) clearly marked. On its circumference its pins meshed with pegs of eight vertical gear-wheels, shown as circles with triangular pegs on their circumference. The drills were formed by the axles of these wheels projecting on both sides, and thus each of the wheels could drill two barrels (*nāl*) pressed against their axle. The axle-drills would penetrate the mouths of the guns (*dahna-i bandūq*) and bore and smoothen the insides of the barrels. Straight lines, drawn across the outer ends of the outer barrels, and designated *qā'ima-i kamān* (supports of guns) in the diagram, probably indicate stakes and bars in which the barrels were fixed for stability. The technical completeness of the diagram strongly reinforces the supposition that here an actual, not an imaginary, machine is being described.[47]

Handguns and Cannon

Akbar's interest in handguns and artillery is emphasized in the *Ā'īn-i Akbarī*, and in a long passage we are told how the gun was again and again submitted to him by the imperial gunsmiths for testing and instructions at all stages of manufacture.[48]

[46] It therefore did not signify the geared contraption for smoothening the barrels, as supposed by Alvi and Rahman, pp.4-7.

[47] Add. 7652, has the diagram on f.55b. Some legends are not legible in the microfilm. The diagram in this MSS, as well as in British Museum MS. Add. 6552 (which like other MSS lacks the legends), differs from the one reproduced in Blochmann's translation (Plate XV) in showing large projections with inwardly bent ends emerging to the right out of the outer barrels, from near the latter's outer ends. Perhaps, these are handles by which the gunsmith kept the barrel in place while the drill bored it.

[48] *Ā'īn-i Akbarī*, ed. Blochmann, I, pp.125-6.

Abū'l Fazl assigns to Akbar the invention of a technique which led to the strengthening of the gun-barrel. He says:

His Majesty has great attachment to the handgun. He is one of the unique ones in making and firing it. [Under his patronage] they so make the gun that, filled to the brim with gun-powder, and fired, it does not break up. Formerly, they could not fill more than one-fourth [of the barrel]. Moreover, they used to flatten iron with hammer and anvil, and joined both edges of the flattened piece [to make the barrel]. Others, out of foresight, used to leave [part of the flattened sheet] over one side. Much injury used to result [from the weakness of such barrels], especially in the former case. His Majesty introduced an excellent method. Having flattened the iron, they twist it crookedly like a paper-roll (*ṯūmār*), so that with every twist, the roll gets longer. They do not join it edge to edge but pass one side over the other, and step by step strengthen it over the fire. Also, having fired and strengthened (*pukhta*) the iron-sheets, they draw them around an [iron] rod, and so a [barrel] hole is produced. Three or four pieces are used to make [a single gun barrel]; in the case of small guns mostly two pieces. The long [barrel] is nearly two *gaz* long, the small one is one and a quarter *gaz*.[In this state] it is called *damānak*.[49]

Akbar's arsenal thus claims to have introduced a new method of making the gun barrel, by (a) twisting a flat iron sheet, continuously fired, to fold round and round in an elongated fashion with its edges overlapping one another, and then (b) joining such twisted heated pieces over an iron rod to create a barrel. There would then be no weak joints in the barrel. Short of casting, this would appear to produce the greatest strength in the barrel and make it withstand high explosive pressure.

The passage we have discussed is followed by one which seems to be of great technological importance:

Further, from the expertness of His Majesty they have so made [handguns] that without the fire-match (*fatīla-i ātish*), with a little movement of the cock (*māsha*), explosion is produced and the pellet is expelled.[50]

In the subsequent description of the stages of hand-gun manufacture we are told that once the barrel and stock were fitted, then 'having brought in the *tah* (hind-part or priming pan?), they become responsible for setting right the cock, and the *gaz* (ramrod?) and *pargaz*(?).'[51] It is not clarified how the cock worked, and therefore

[49] Ibid.

[50] Ibid., p.125.

[51] Ibid., p.126. Jahāngīr, *Tuzuk*, ed. Syud Ahmud, p.199, uses the word *ātish-*

fore we do not learn how, without the match, it could have ignited the powder in the priming-pan.

I had initially suggested that a wheel-lock must have been employed, and then thought that a matchlock was meant after all, though the match-lock would still need to have a *fatila* or match.[52] Iqtidar Alam Khan is right to upbraid such inconsistency, and his very definitive study of the early history of handguns in India has narrowed the choice to the wheel-lock fairly closely;[53] but positive proof is yet to come.

Abū'l Faẓl in his short chapter on cannon-pieces (*Ā'īn-i top*), attributes to Akbar two inventions which need more than passing consideration. First, 'he had one [cannon-piece] made, which they can easily transport during expeditions by separating the parts. When it needs to be fired, it can be very well assembled together'.[54] Since we have no evidence of the use of fastening screws at Akbar's court, the only way in which such break-up and reassembling of gun-parts was possible must have been by shaping parts of the barrel on the principle of *kārīz* pipes: thicker on one side, thinner on the other. Thus the parts could be fitted one to another. The joints would still need to be strengthened with rings hammered into place over the joints, in order to prevent the barrel-pieces flying apart, when the cannon was fired. It will be seen that our reconstruction accords with the technique described for breaking up and reassembling wooden structures of the imperial camp.

The second invention was that 'he imparted to seventeen [cannon-pieces] such unison that one match can fire all of them'.[55] Unluckily, Abū'l Faẓl's brevity compels us to rely on speculation as to how this could have been done. There could surely not have been a single priming-pan connected with as many as seventeen barrels. The only likelihood is that the barrels along with their pans were laid so close to each other that when one pan had its explosion, there was not only a sympathetic explosion in its own

---

khāna, fire-chamber, for the priming pan.

[52] *IESHR*, XVII (1), p.17, and *Studies in History*, II (1), p.36.

[53] 'The Nature of Handguns in Mughal India', *Proceedings of the Indian History Congress, 52nd Session, New Delhi, 1991-92*, Delhi, 1992, pp.378-89, esp. pp.383-4 and p.386 *n*.21.

[54] *Ā'īn-i Akbarī*, ed. Blochmann, I, p.124.

[55] Ibid.

barrel, but also in the priming pan laid next to it. Presumably, the pans were made rectangular in shape to make such heat-transmission effective. The firing of the guns could not have been simultaneous, but in rapid succession, all the guns being fired the most quickly, if the pan in the middle was ignited first.[56]

Ship-Building

An aspect of Akbar's innovativeness that has received inadequate notice is his interest in construction of ocean-going ships, rather surprising in a ruler whose capital seats (Agra, Fatehpur Sikri and Lahore) were so far from the sea, and who had gone about on a boat in the sea only once (December 1572, at Cambay). The systematic and detailed description in the *Ā'īn-i Akbarī* of the duties and functions of the captain and crew of ocean-going ships, with even the wages specified, according to ports, strongly indicates imperial concern with sea-navigation.[57] Large imperial ships were built at the ports 'to become sources of comfort for those undertaking sea-travel'. But, what is still more interesting, 'ships were also built at Ilāhābās (Allahabad) and Lahore and conveyed to the sea [by river]'.[58]

Of the ships built at Allahabad we have no information, but we are better placed in respect of what was done at Lahore. It may be recalled that Sind was annexed to Akbar's empire only in 1591, so that the port of Thatta (with its outer port at Bandar Lahiri) now passed into his hands. Sind lacks timber, and so Akbar had the ingenious idea of building ships at Lahore, some 650 miles distant from Thatta as the crow flies, but linked to it by the Indus river-system. Lahore, in turn, had the advantage of proximity to Himalayan sources of timber.

According to Abū'l Faẓl,[59] the construction of the first great ship by the side of river Ravi at Lahore was completed in June 1594. The length of its keel ('the wooden beam on which this

[56] In a seventeen-piece contraption, the middle gun would have eight others on each side. The initial ignition of the middle pan would lead to successive ignitions of pans on either side, and so successive firing of guns simultaneously on both sides.

[57] *Ā'īn-i Akbarī*, ed. Blochmann, I, pp.202-3.

[58] Ibid., I, p.202.

[59] *Akbarnāma*, III, pp.651-2.

wooden structure is raised') was 35 *gaz-i ilāhī* (a little over 93 feet). It was made of 2936 large planks of *sal*-wood and pine-tree.[60] Iron, weighing 468 *mans*, 2 *sers*, i.e.11.56 tons of 2240 lb. avdp., was used up, indicating a very generous application of iron nails, strips, rings, etc., in joining the planks together. We are told that as many as 240 carpenters, ironsmiths and others were employed in the ship's construction. When it was completed, the emperor himself went to see it being launched. A thousand persons drew the ship with various ingenious devices; but it took ten days to put it into the river. It was obviously difficult to find enough water in the Ravi to accommodate a sea-going vessel. However, it ultimately reached Bandar Lahiri. Another contemporary narrator tells us that this ship was made and sent to 'the port of Sind' for undertaking voyages to Mecca, i.e., the Red Sea.[61]

Abū'l Faẓl says that the difficulty the first ship had experienced in drawing water in the Ravi led Akbar to try out the idea of building the next sea-going ship upon a big barge capable of carrying a burthen of 15,000 *mans* (370 tons in weight) or more. The ship began to be constructed around mid-July and was completed about mid-December 1596. It was 37 *gaz*, or nearly 99 feet long, but whether at the keel or at upper deck is not stated. A sum of Rs16,338 was spent on it. Carried by the barge, the ship was conveyed conveniently to Bandar Lahiri.[62] Apparently the barge, on which the vessel was built and carried, was there scuttled, enabling the vessel to enter sea water. This device anticipated the 'camel' (invented in Dutch dockyards in 1688), which was a barge that could be submerged to let a ship come over it and then be raised to carry the ship over shallows.[63]

[60] *Nākhūd* in the printed text must be a misreading of *najū*. In some MSS, as noted by the editor, the number of planks given is 9536.

[61] Ṭāhir Muḥammad Sabzwārī, *Rauẓat-u 'tṬāhirīn*, Br. Mus. Or.168, f.556a-b.

[62] *Akbarnāma*, III, pp.715-16. In his informative paper, 'Ship-building in Mughal India', *IESHR*, V(2), June 1928, p.160, A.J. Qaisar seems to misunderstand what was done by Akbar and speaks of his solving the problem by 'hauling the *jahāz* on to a large *kishtī* or craft'. Such 'hauling' or lifting of a ship, once constructed, would have been practically impossible; in any case, Abū'l Faẓl is clear in stating that the ship was to be built (*barsāzand*) upon the deck (*bar farāz*) of the barge.

[63] See Els M. Jacobs, *In Pursuit of Pepper and Tea: The story of the Dutch East India Company*, Amsterdam/Zutphen, 1991, p. 34; the date of the invention and the

Akbar was so interested in sea shipping that he even built a vessel, modelled after a sea-going ghurāb(small vessel, galley), to ply on the Jhelam river and the linked lakes in Kashmir. This is said to have caused general wonder among the beholders; and Akbar himself took a ride on it in July 1597.[64] One may conjecture that the vessel had sails along with space for rowers (on a lower deck?).

Fanciful Devices

Much of Arabic-Persian theoretical technology consisted of imagining diverse motions derived from water-flow, gearing, and levers and balances. Al-Jazarī provides the best illustration of this tradition. Making such devices in practice was a little more difficult, but we know that some, like water-clocks, were actually made.

Nūru'l Ḥaqq in his *Zubdatu't Tawārīkh* describes a 'magic machine' which Akbar saw in 1594-5 at Lahore and greatly enjoyed. Elliot selected and translated this passage, and I reproduce here part of his translation with some modifications based on a comparison with the text.

> One of the wonders of art which was exhibited during this year (A.H.1003) was the work of Saiyid Ḥusain Shīrāzī. He used to stand with a box in front of him, and when anyone gave him a rupee, he threw it into the box and it kept on rolling until it fell to the bottom. Upon this a parrot, which was placed above that box (*buq'a*), began to turn around and, then, two birds began to chirp at one another. Then a small window opened, and a panther put forward its head out of it, and a shell came out of its mouth to fall on a dish which was placed on the head of a tiger, and the shell came out of the tiger's mouth. ...[similar other motions and actions by toy animals and puppets follow; ultimately,] another window opened, and a puppet came forth with an ode from the *Dīwān* of Ḥāfiẓ in its hands, and when the ode was taken away, it retired, and the window closed. In short, whenever money was placed in his [Husain Shīrāzī's] hands, all these curious things took place. His Majesty first threw an *ashrafī* (gold coin) with his own hand and witnessed the sight. He then ordered those present to give a rupee each. The odes they received, they gave to Naqīb Khān, by whom they were read out. This entertainment continued for much of the night.[65]

---

inventor's name (Meeuwis Meendertsz Bekker) were kindly provided to me by Dr Jacobs in a personal communication (1 July 1993). The ship's camel was subsequently used in Peter the Great's shipyards (*OED*, s.v. camel, 2: a 1716 quotation).

[64] *Akbarnāma*, III, p.727-8; *Ā'īn-i Akbarī*, ed. Blochmann, I, pp.202-3. For ghurāb,

One can see that while the initial momentum came from the dropping of the coin, the further action derived from the displacement of successively heavier weights. The entire appratus needed only levers, balances and, perhaps, pulleys, to work as it did. No gears or springs were necessarily involved, and so no influence from European clockwork or mechanical devices can be predicated. It is, however, good to know that Akbar could enjoy a well-constructed magical device just like any one of us.

Akbar had a fascination for water works and architectural innovation. One can therefore understand how any fanciful device involving both would attract his interest. Badāūnī alleges that:

During this year [A.H. 986/1578-79] a *ḥakīm* (learned man) came to Fatehpur and said that a house can be built, which has water on all sides of it so that it can only be entered by going through the water, and yet water would not penetrate into it. For this reason His Majesty had a tank (*ḥauẓ*) constructed in the courtyard of the Palace, twenty *gaz* by twenty *gaz*, three *gaz* in depth. Within it was built a chamber of stone and over it a tall tower. On all the four sides of the chamber, bridges were laid out. But the claim of the *ḥakīm* were found to be false as is usual with claims for antidotes, and he fled away to some place.[66]

The only structure this could be identified with is the Anūp Talāo; but there are no traces of a chamber and tower on the Talāo's middle platform.

Badāūnī tells us that, seventeen years after this event, Ḥakīm 'Alī Gīlānī constructed at Lahore a tank of precisely this kind, in which he successfully demonstrated what the earlier pretender had failed to achieve. Badāūnī even gives a chronogram for its construction, viz. A.H. 1002/1593-4. Abūl' Faẓl reports the construction of this 'wonderful tank' under Urdībihisht 39 Ilāhī/ April-May 1594: 'A way through it led to a cell; and wonderful it was that the water from this reservoir did not enter that place'.[67]

Nūru'l Ḥaqq gives us more details of this structure. Putting its construction under the year 1003/1594-5, he tells us that Ḥakīm 'Alī

---

see Yule and Burnell, rev. Crooke, *Hobson-Jobson*, pp.391-2, *s.v.* 'grab'.

[65] H.M. Elliot and J. Dowson, *The History of India as told by its own Historians*, London, 1867-77, VI, p.192. I have checked with India Office MS. Ethe 290, f.189a-b, and considerably altered the rendering at places.

[66] Badāūnī, *Muntakhabu't Tawārīkh*, II, pp.264-5. (67) Ibid., p.265.

[67] *Akbarnāma*, III, p.650.

built an underground chamber (*tahkhāna*) of suitable width and length, and put a small door by which one could easily enter through the ceiling of that chamber. Above that ceiling he built a deep tank, filled with water. When any one desired to enter that house he had to wade through the water, reach that small door, when opened, and go that way into that chamber. Within the chamber were put all the needs of an assembly, such as carpets, books, etc. Water could not enter that chamber. It is said that one day His Majesty himself, along with his close counsellors, came through the ceiling (*kotah*) and held an assembly there. Having stayed there, he came out the same way through that small door.[68]

It is not stated how water was prevented from entering the chamber, if, as one has necessarily to presume, the small door was not above the level of the water in the tank. Mu'tamad Khān, who gives us practically the same particulars as Nūru'l Ḥaqq, assures us that 'air prevented the entry of water'.[69] The only conceivable way was to have an arrangement to drain away such water as entered through the door out of the chamber into a well, which could also be the source of water of the tank above. It is difficult, however, to be certain if this was what was done.

The range of Akbar's technological interests is undoubtedly impressive, from textiles to ship-building, and from cooling to gearing devices. Even if he was not the author of all the inventions which were made at his court, the spate of technological activity derived essentially from his interest and patronage. Such purposeful attention to technology had little precedent in our known history, and there came very little to match it in the subsequent period during which Europe advanced inexorably to its position of global technological supremacy.

[68] *Zubdatu't Tawārīkh*, I.O.MS, Ethe 290, f.190b.

[69] *Iqbālnāma-i Jahāngīrī*, Nawal Kishor, Lucknow, 1870, II, p.441. Nūru'l Ḥaqq's work has precedence in point of time over Mu'tamad Khān's, in which (II, p.479) the current date is given as Shahrīvar 15 R.Y. of Jahāngīr (August- September 1620).

12

Painting under Akbar as Narrative Art

SOM PRAKASH VERMA

Painting under Akbar, being largely connected with the art of book-illustration, may be described essentially as narrative art. As such its roots are traceable in both Persian and Indian art (sculpture as well as painting).

The Mughal school, which with its distinct style emerged by 1580, shows the imprint of the Safavid and Timurid art traditions and some influence of the classical Indian schools (the Ajanta and Western Indian Schools), especially in the case of manuscript painting: the best earliest testimony to this is provided by the illustrations of the *Ṭūṭīnāma* MS in the Cleveland Museum of Art, Cleveland (*c*.1565-70), the *Anwār-i Suhailī* MS in the School of Oriental and African Studies, London (1570), and the *Hamzanāma* (*c*.1565-80) fragments. A careful study shows that the various modes of visual narration found here continued later in the Mughal school, though with greater complexity. The Mughal pictorial tradition comes out in a variety of ways in the art of book-illustration.

The simplest of the modes of the artist's expression, in the Mughal narratives, is represented by the illustrations of the *Ṭūṭīnāma*. Here we find the selection of the key scene from the episode and a brief representation of it in one plane. Such scenes are pictured so as to enable the viewer to identify the episode. In this MS, while a single scene is intended for one episode, it helps the viewer little to narrate the story to himself, since earlier and later courses of the event do not form part of the artist's narration. Thus, representation of a single scene remains isolated, and there is no depiction of continuity of the event. Consequently, such visual narratives lack the concept of space and time. In them, only the key figures of an event appear in the scene, and the whole action revolves around them.

The *Ṭūṭīnāma* illustrations are thus characterized by 'single-scene' representation, e.g. an episode of the 'Thirty-first Night' (MS. folio 207r) is represented by how 'The donkey wearing the skin of a tiger, reveals his identity by braying'. The event is thus described:[1]

...He had a donkey but no money to buy hay for him. Because of the lack of fodder for the donkey, the merchant was losing business; and the donkey for the lack of oats headed for the storehouse of Judgement Day.

The merchant was a wise man of good deeds. He secured a lion's skin, and every night he put the skin on the donkey and let him wander in the nearby fields and gardens. He instructed him: 'If a watchman appears, bend your left knee and stand still in front of him. Move as much as your coat will allow, but keep him from discovering your real identity. Do not bray so that your disguise is not discovered and thereby your true nature can remain hidden'.

The donkey acted accordingly and fooled everyone.

In a few days the donkey recovered and in a short time gained some weight. Since the neighbours thought he was a lion, they abandoned their fields and gardens.

One night the donkey appeared in a certain field. The guards, scared of his claws,climbed up a tree. Just then a donkey nearby brayed. The merchant's donkey, as a donkey would, began to bray also by drawing his breath in and out, making a raucous noise which revealed what he was.

From this harsh sound, the guards discovered what he was and knew what he was not. They descended from the trees, tied the donkey to the tree, gave him a good beating and punished him for the scare and terror (he had spread). The animal's own voice had revealed his identity and was the cause of his disgrace.

The illustrative miniature, while it shows a donkey braying clad in tiger's skin [lion's skin in the text] amidst a field, and the guards hiding in the foliage of trees, alarmed at the animal's raucous noise, illustrates only the part of the story italicised in the above passage (Plate I).

The naivete seen in 'single-scene' representations is described by Douglas Barrett and Basil Gray as a result of their derivation from the Indian tradition.[2] This characteristic of the *Ṭūṭīnāma*

[1] Muhammad A. Simsar, ed. and tr., *The Cleveland Museum of Arts: Ṭūṭīnāma, Tales of Parrot by Ziāyuddīn Nakhshabī*, Austria, 1978, pp.198-9, colour pl. facing page 200.

[2] Douglas Barrett and Basil Gray, *Painting of India*, Cleveland, 1963, pp.82-3, colour pl. on p.85.

narratives tended gradually to disappear in the Mughal school since the art of visual narration led from simple to complex. In 'single-scene' representations the narrative movements of the text are almost discarded and, thus, there are always limited possibilities of pictorial action. In such examples, the dramatic aspect of the illustration is the only force which stimulates the viewer to relate it to the story. Even in some cases like the illustrations on folios 37v, 43r, 51v, 102v, 223v, 282v and 316r, the illustrations neither unfold a story, nor even depict a part of it.[3] Their purpose appears didactic and purely decorative. Of course, in these cases, visual recounting of a scene does not appear to have been aimed at by the artist (Plate II).

The compositions representing continuous narration of an event are sometimes seen in the *Anwār-i Suhailī*, which is contemporaneous with the *Ṭūṭīnāma*. Otherwise, in general, this manuscript also contains 'one-scene' representations. In it, within one picture plane more than one phase of an event or story is represented. Of course, the phases selected for representation form normally the end/climax of the story. But the artist does not demarcate the two phases and depicts them in a single visual field. The only indication for identifying these courses is the repetition of the main figure in different spaces plotted by the artist in the composition. These phases of an event relate the successive movements of the story, and are suggestive of both space and time in painting. The miniature on folio 232r in the *Anwār-i Suhailī* illustrates the story of an old farmer's unfaithful young wife who eloped with a prince. On their way, while they rested by a spring, a lion suddenly attacked the woman and the prince galloped away in terror. In the illustration, the figures of the main characters, the prince and woman, are repeated twice.[4] In the composition, in the right hand corner (below), the prince and the woman are shown seated by a spring; and the left hand corner depicts the woman being mauled by the lion and the prince galloping away (Plate III). Thus, these two successive stages of an event are presented

[3] For their reproductions, see Pramod Chandra and Daniel J. Ehnbom, *The Cleveland Ṭūṭīnāma Manuscript and the Origins of Mughal Painting*, Chicago, 1976, pls.12, 21-5.

[4] See John Seyller, 'The School of Oriental and African Studies *Anvār-i Suhaylī*: the illustration of a de luxe Mughal Manuscript', *Archives of Asian Art*, Vol.38, New York, 1985, p.124, fig.12.

in a single visual field so as to suggest the continuity of the event taking place at different times. The repetition of figures of the main characters in Mughal narrative painting is, however, rather rare: it is also unknown in Persian book-illustration. In Indian art its earliest evidence is found in the Gandhara and Mathura sculpture (Plates IV-V).[5] An example of this narrative method is seen at the Stupas of Sanchi (second half of the first century B.C.) and in Ajanta paintings (Plate VI).[6]

Continuous narration in the Mughal school appears in the *Hamzanāma* illustrations, which show multiple phases of an event depicted within a single visual field. These phases (units of an event) revolve around the central theme and make the representation of the event more elaborate and descriptive. In such instances, the main figures are not repeated. Rather, the picture plane is divided into small units which contain action related to the main theme. In the division of the visual field, use is freely made of the receptacles comprising hillocks, mounds of earth, stream, vegetation, architectural columns, etc. — a technique well known to the Ajanta painter,[7] but equally in vogue in Persian MS painting (Plate VII).

In general, in 15th-16th century Persian narrative art, the trend of breaking up a visual field into two or more units was in vogue, but these units remained isolated in the absence of the artist's effort to show some kind of relationship between them. As a result, cohesive effect in the narration suffered. Mughal artists rectified this shortcoming and succeeded in connecting the units through

[5] Madeleine Hallade, *The Gandhara Style and the Evolution of Buddhist Art*, London, 1968, p.133, pl.97. The Gandhara bas-relief (British Museum, London) depicts two episodes from the scene 'Conversion of Nanda' (*c.*200 A.D.). In the centre, Nanda is about to carry a bowl of food to the Buddha; on the left, Nanda offers the bowl to the Buddha. Thus, the panel shows the main figure being repeated to fulfil the demand of continuous narration. See also ibid., p.100, pl.72.

The bas-relief from Mathura (Sarnath School, Gupta style, 5th-century) lodged in National Museum, New Delhi, shows 'The Departure of Bodhisattva; Bodhisattva shaves his head; his ritual immersion in the river Nairanjana; food being offered to him by Sujāta; and the Buddha in meditation' in one visual field with no demarcation between these phases of the life of the Buddha (ibid., pp.201-2, pl.162).

[6] Vidya Dehejia, 'Narraive Modes in Ajanta Cave 17: A Preliminary Study', *South Asian Studies*, Vol.7, London, 1991, pp.48-9, Fig.4.

[7] Lubor Hajek, *Indian Miniatures of the Mughal School*, Prague, 1960, p.31: 'In the Ajanta Paintings the group of figures are held together by the receptacles; and the contact between the figures was emphasized by the overcrowding of these restricted spaces.'

rhythmic movements, gestures and facial expressions. In their work, there appeared something free, bold and more vigorous in effect than the Persian painters had ever expressed.[8] The rhythmic movement not only established a relationship between the figures but also promoted naturalism. Barrett and Gray have defined this relationship between the figures as 'psychological', in contrast to the almost entirely formal relationship seen in Iranian painting.[9] In the narratives of the *Ṭūṭīnāma* also there is an emphasis on establishing a psychological relationship between the figures. Pramod Chandra and Daniel J. Ehnbom hold that the vitality, inner coherence and unity seen in the *Hamzanāma* illustrations are obviously the result of indigenous elements at work in the formation of the Mughal style.[10]

Such compositions emerged in their most mature form in the illustrations of the *Tārīkh-i Khāndān-i Timūriya*, *c.*1584-7 (Khuda Bakhsh Oriental Public Library, Patna), the *Jāmi'-ut Tawārīkh*, dated 1597-8 (Imperial Library, Teheran) and the *Akbarnāma*, *c.*1602-5 (Victoria and Albert Museum, London) where we find the visual field in a single illustration accommodating three to five units containing successive details of an event. An outstanding example of such an arrangement is an illustration of 'Daughters of Sulṭān Muḥammad being married' in the *Tārīkh-i Khāndān-i Timūriya*.[11] In it, the visual field accommodates four units. The upper half, divided diagonally, represents the emperor and the nobles (the latter wishing him on the occasion) and the princess being attended upon by their maids. The lower half accommodates musical parties in two separate groups. First of all, there comes the group of female musicians and dancers; and thereafter, outside the palace, the musicians of the *naqqārkhāna* are shown giving performances, while the attendants stand with gifts, etc., in their hands (Plate VIII). Here the units are separated by architectural features (mainly walls) and are set in a series of ascending diagonals in a zigzag order.

In another instance, 'Rejoicing at the birth of Akbar's second

[8] Karl Khandalavala, 'The Mughal School and its Ramifications', in *The Development of Style in Indian Painting*, Delhi, 1974, p.70.

[9] Barrett and Gray, p.81.

[10] Pramod Chandra and D.J. Ehnbom, p.11.

[11] Som Prakash Verma, *Art and Material Culture in the Paintings of Akbar's Court*, New Delhi, 1978, p.18, pl.XIV.

son at Fatehpur-Sikri', the visual field comprises five units: the unit on the top right shows the queen with her new-born baby attended by maids; the unit adjoining it on the extreme top right shows female attendants engaged in some work; the units just below the above two units depict female musicians and dancers, while a group of astrologers are busy preparing the horoscope. And, lastly, the unit at the bottom contains the depiction of the musicians of the *naqqārkhāna* with the accompaniment of the male dancers outside the palace (Plate IX).[12]

The above narrative modes remained in practice at Akbar's atelier simultaneously, with the exception of the second category of the narration where the main figure is repeated. This statement is equally true in the case of narrative paintings of Jahāngīr's and Shāh Jahān's reigns as well.

Mughal painters lacked the technical ability to represent three-dimensional reality on a two-dimensional plane. Therefore, in compositions intended to represent continuous narration, they often composed various phases of an event in a vertical format, that is, in an ascending order. In such narratives, units of an episode are represented one upon the other without firm demarcation between them, though the receptacles placed in the visual field help the viewer to distinguish them.

In the vertical order, objects are shown simultaneously at eye-levels (direct-view) and from above (bird's eye-view). Hajek observes that this narrative mode seen at Ajanta was improved by Buddhist artists by making use of hierarchical perspective in addition to the direct view and bird's eye-view.[13] Kramrisch has called this complexity of views 'multiple perspective'.[14] Vidya Dehejia notes continuous narrative in a vertical format from Cave 17 at Ajanta: 'Buddha's descent from the heavens.'[15] This narrative mode shows a definite shift away from the strict Persian convention, the earliest examples of which shift in Akbar's atelier appear in the *Hamzanāma* miniatures containing typical treatment of the picture-space with an arrangement of plane behind plane, i.e.,

[12] Ibid., pp.17-8, pl.XIII. [13] Hajek, p.28.

[14] Ibid.

[15] Vidya Dehejia, p.49: 'Continuous narrative in a vertical format is effectively utilized to portray the Buddha's descent from the heavens at Sankissa. At the top-most level, the Buddha preaches in the heavens to his mother and to the gods; the middle portion refers to the descent; while the lowest level depicts him on earth, preaching to monks and lay worshippers.'

subsidiary scenes set in the background — an expression fundamentally Indian, and not Persian.[16] In this context, Ettinghausen's observations on 'Abdu-ṣ Ṣamad's miniature, 'Akbar presenting a miniature to his father Humayun' (datable before 1559), is important: 'the hustle and bustle of the subject, the realistic approach of the painter, and the way of showing the attendants and servants outside the wall with the main scene behind, that is higher up in the painting, betray an Indian style.'[17]

It was the ingenuity of the Mughal painters that in the continuous narratives they made the fullest use of receptacles to create rhythm. A zigzag placement of small units in a single visual field, suggesting movement, also enhanced depth in the picture. Similarly, the diagonal setting of objects (main characters) well suited action-filled narratives.

Walter M. Spink and Deborah Levine observe that the visual narratives mainly marked by violent physical action and excitement seen in the *Akbarnāma* show that artists considered that a diagonal emphasis was more vital than a vertical or horizontal one. Their remarks on the narratives 'Retainers watching elephant chase across the bridge of boats' and 'Bullocks dragging siege-gun during attack on Ranthambhor' are worth quoting.[18]

> The diagonal pull of the thundering elephants seems about to topple the composition, as it threatens to upset the flimsy pontoon bridge. The fleeing Ran Bagh even crosses the picture frame to give further tension to the whole. We find this bold diagonal axis repeated in other illustrations from the *Akbarnāma*. It appears to have been a favourite compositional device.
>
> In this scene, one of the two illustrations on facing pages from the Victoria and Albert manuscript, the adjoining ascent is dramatically depicted. The artist Miskin has employed two bold diagonal axes, one jutting off at a sharp angle from the other, which conveys brilliantly the sense of a precipitous and rocky terrain, and the strain on men and bullocks as they force their way foot by foot up the almost vertical path. ...This painting is certainly one of the most powerfully conceived and executed in the entire *Akbarnāma* manuscript.

[16] Basil Gray, in Leigh Ashton, ed., *The Art of India and Pakistan*, London, 1940, p.93.

[17] Richard Ettinghausen, 'Abd-uṣ-Ṣamad', *Encyclopedia of World Art*, New York, Vol.I, p.19, pl.16.

[18] Walter M. Spink and Deborah Levine, *Akbarnāma: Catalogue*, New York, no date, pls. and text, Nos.3-4 and 15-16.

In other instances from the same manuscript, a series of ascending diagonals can be seen in the 'Building of the Fort at Agra' and 'Trained elephants executing Khan Zamān's followers.'[19]

The figures shown, though in a very casual manner, extending beyond the picture frame — a marked characteristic of the Safavid and Timurid miniatures — appear complementary to the mode of continuous narration. Similarly, the objects shown only in part on the extreme outer margin of the visual field, some portion of them being cut out of vision, are also suggestive of continuity of the scene beyond the picture frame. The artists have used the picture frame to cut the scene, implying that the viewer is confronted with only part of the whole. This mode undoubtedly imparted breadth to the visual field.

Though at present it is not our purpose to evaluate the historicity of the Mughal narratives, a brief discussion of it is necessary since it relates to the selection of certain passages of an event and the choice of descriptive details.

In spite of the limitations of the narrative styles, there was always a great variety in the artist's mode of expression even in the depiction of narratives on similar themes. The artist seems to have enjoyed considerable freedom in the selection of descriptive details related to the main event. A comparison of four miniatures from the various copies of the *Baburnāma* in the British Museum, London; National Museum, New Delhi; Museum of Oriental Cultures, Moscow; and Fogg Art Museum, Boston, representing one and the same event ('Bird-trapping') would confirm that the pictures differed in details of the objects.[20] One finds that the British Museum miniature is more elaborate when it represents bird-trappers in action with a variety of devices used in trapping. As against this, the illustrations from the National Museum (Delhi) and Moscow collections are comparatively simple in detail as well as in composition. Thus the number of the objects introduced in a visual field and other details comprising the background always varied in narratives of identical themes. Nevertheless, an identity of the miniature with the related text always remained. Further, in the selection of the passage of an event, too, the artist had a choice.

[19] Ibid., pls. and text, Nos.7-8 and 21. Also see No.22.

[20] For their reproductions see, Hamid Suleiman, *Miniatures of Bābur-nāma*, Tashkent, 1970, colour pl. 27; S.I. Tyulayev, *Miniatures of Babur Nāmah*, Moscow,

It becomes clear after a comparison of the miniatures illustrating one and the same event and the appreciation of their content in the light of the literal demands of the text. One such example is 'Akbar on his way to Pak Patan hunting wild asses' illustrated in the *Tārīkh-i Khāndān-i Timūriya* (*c.*1584-7) and *Akbarnāma* (*c.* 1602-05).[21] This particular event is thus described by Abū'l Faẓl:[22]

On the way a strange thing occurred on the borders of Rāi 'Alā'ud-dīn's Talwandī near the Sutlej, which is there called the Harharī. The brief account of this is that the scouts reported that there was a herd of wild asses (gorkhar). The sovereign proceeded to hunt them, attended by three or four special huntsmen. When he came near the plain he dismounted and proceeded on foot. At the first shot he hit an ass, and the rest of the herd fled far away at the report of the gun. That Divine world-hero took his piece in his hand and proceeded rapidly on foot over the burning sand, attended by the same three or four huntsmen. He soon traversed the plain and came up with the herd and killed one after the other with his gun. He continued to follow them up, and on that day he shot thirteen wild asses. Whenever he killed one the others went further off than at first. At this time he became consumed by thirst. There was no sign of water. As he had decided to follow the prey on foot, those attached to the hunt thought that H.M. was near at hand, and so kept in view the place where the game was and did not leave their place. When the lord of the world had traversed some *kos*, his attendants, though they searched, could get no news of the water-carriers, nor any trace of water. A strange condition supervened, and the weakness from thirst increased to such a degree that he lost the power of speech.

The miniature in the former MS, showing Akbar on foot engaged in hunting wild-asses with his matchlock, is a visual narration of the first part of the event (Plate X). The second and concluding phase of the event is the choice of the *Akbarnāma* artists Mahesh and Kesav. They represent Akbar seated and exhausted after the hunt, his matchlock resting on his shoulder and the attendants enquiring about the strange condition of the emperor (Plate XI).

1960, pl.15; M.S. Randhawa, *Paintings of the Bāburnāma*, New Delhi, 1984, colour pl.VIII; S.C. Welch, *Art of Mughal India: Painting and Precious Objects*, New York, 1963, pl.9. See also Som Prakash Verma, 'Treatment of similar themes: a study based on the illustrations of *Tuzuk-i Bāburī*', *Proceedings of Indian History Congress*, Chandigarh, 1973, pp.293-4.

[21] The miniature on folio 331a in *Tārīkh* MS is not published. For the reproduction of the *Akbarnāma* miniature see Geeti Sen, *Paintings from the Akbarnāma*, New Delhi, 1984, p.137, colour pl.60.

[22] Abū'l Faẓl, *Akbarnāma*, ed. text, Vol.II, 359-60; tr., Vol.II, p.522.

Thus, while the event remains the same, the choice varied in the selection of the part of an episode to be presented in the visual field. Of course, the selection was always related to the crucial part of the episode which enabled the viewer to relate to the story.

Often, to lay emphasis on a particular event, the visual-field is enlarged by making the composition into a 'double-page' illustration. The theme 'Battle between the rival groups of *sanyāsīs* at Thanesar' forms a one-page illustration in the *Tārīkh-i Khāndān-i Timūriya* (*c.*1584-7) and represents the main characters in the middle of the visual field, and the battle-scene on the right hand corner (Plate XII).[23] A double-page illustration of the same event, executed during 1602-5 in the *Akbarnāma* (V&A), is clearly much richer in descriptive details.[24] The location of the battle in both the visual narratives is identical, that is, the huge banyan tree is depicted in both of them in the middle of the masonry platform by the side of a large tank, besides which the whole action is shown as taking place (Plates XIII-XIV). The *Akbarnāma* illustration contains more details in conformity with the text of the event as described by Abū'l Faẓl:[25]

> While he was encamped at Thanesar, a dispute arose among the Sanyāsīs which ended in bloodshed ...
>
> The leader Kisū Pūrī came to Ambala and did homage, and made a claim for justice... After that the Pūrīs attacked the Kūrs with stones... They came up with their Pīr and head, who was called Ānand Kūr, and slew the miserable creature.

The *Akbarnāma* illustration shows Akbar's men joining one group (*Pūrīs*) of the *sanyāsīs* in their attack on the rival group (*Kūrs*), and Ānand Kūr, the chief of the latter group, being slain. Thus, one finds that the above two historical illustrations though executed in a different space and time, adhered to the text in its essence. This characteristic of visual narrations also confirms their historical nature.

Double-page illustrations appear first in 1584-7 in the MS *Razmnāma* of the Sawai Man Singh II Museum, Jaipur.[26] In general,

[23] The miniature on folio 322a in *Tārīkh* MS is not published.

[24] For reproduction, Sen, pp.105-9, colour pls.43-4.

[25] *Akbarnāma*, ed. text, Vol.II, pp.286-7, tr., Vol.II, pp.422-4.

[26] See T.H. Hendley, *Razmnāmah* (*Memorial of Jeypore Exhibition-1883*), IV, Jaipur, pls.xlvii-xlviii, lxi-lxii, lxiv-lxv, lxxii-lxxiii, cxxvi-xxxvii, cxxxii-cxxxiii, cxxxix-cxl.

the compositions running on two pages were preferred for narratives dealing with feasts and festivities and battle and hunting scenes.

In some cases, the emphasis given to a certain event is explained by treating various phases of the event as the subject of separate visual fields.[27] But, in such instances, the quality and spirit of the continuous narration is lost.

The visual narrative styles and methods discussed above were not innovations of the Mughals, since these were in practice earlier, both in sculpture and painting in India and Persia. Their ingenuity lies in treating the visual field, even when it comprised multiple views, so as to offer an integrated and compact picture of an event filled with action. The elaborate visual field containing more than two or three units of an episode, held within receptacles, yet remains unified so as to unfold the story and its various phases coherently.

The Mughal visual narratives are manifestly at variance with their counterparts in pre-Mughal Indian art; and there is a clear departure from the traditional didactic function of the illustrations, as seen in the the illustrated MSS of the Western Indian School (and also in early Mughal MS *Ṭūṭīnāma*), where incorporation of the illustrations seems decorative and simply serves as a vehicle for increasing the appeal of the text. At the Mughal atelier, representation of actual narrative details became the mainstay of an artist's work. He always seems particular about the accuracy and truthful depiction of the objects related to the descriptive details in the portrayal of a scene or event. As such, his visual narratives are well recognized for the faithful depiction of material culture and natural history. While looking at them today, one finds oneself transported into the past. Of course, in the case of past events the artist had no opportunity to formulate a direct visual contact with the textual details, as it was possible for him in the portrayal of contemporary episodes and events from day-to-day life. In such narratives, the descriptive details in the visual field are expanded by the artist by drawing upon his experience though imagination, too, played a part. Further, his pictorial narratives are imbued with naturalism — a characteristic which enlivens

[27] T.W. Arnold and J.V.S. Wilkinson, *Library of Chester Beatty, A Catalogue of the Indian Miniatures*, Vol.II, London, 1936, plates 39a-b, 43a-b, 44a-b.

the scene. By placing the main characters of an event in their appropriate surroundings, the Mughal artist creates drama in the visual field to meet the literal illustrative demand of the text. Barrett and Gray detect realism in Mughal narrative art at an early date, 1570, when they observe it especially in the representation of figure drawings and architecture, with the application of shading and modelling.[28] Eletr says that with the emergence of Indian ideals in the Mughal School, the Persian traditions and methods weakened.[29] However, the Mughal artist's originality was in shaping naturalism to explore objective characteristics of the material world. His deep interest in the subject matter left little scope for spiritual and emotional aspects in his narratives — an element in conflict with Indian tradition. The reality as understood from the Mughal painter's work is well described by Hajek: 'It is non-symbolic; it does not imply any reality that it does not portray.'[30]

[28] Barrett and Gray, p.81.

[29] M.R. Eletr, 'Birds and Animals in Mughal Painting', *Bulletin of the College of Arts*, Vol.I, Baghdad, 1959, p.16.

[30] Hajek, p.23.

Plate I. Donkey wearing a tiger-skin reveals its identity by braying. *Ṭūṭīnāma*, Cleveland Museum of Art, Cleveland, f.207.

Plate II. Parrot addresses Khujasta. *Ṭūṭīnāma*, Cleveland Museum of Art, Cleveland, f.282.

Plate III. Conversion of Nanda (c. 500 A.D.), Gandhara School.
British Museum, London.

Plate IV. Old farmer's unfaithful wife, and her end. *Anwār-i-Suhailī*, School of Oriental and African Studies, London, f.232.

Plate V. Departure of the Bodhisattva (*c*.500 A.D.), Mathura (Sarnath School). National Museum, New Delhi.

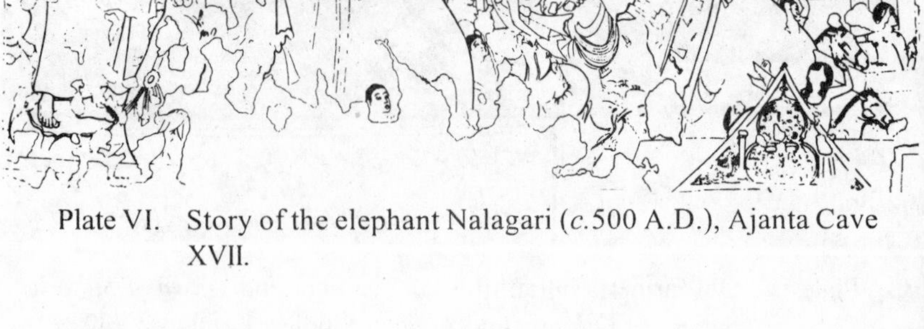

Plate VI. Story of the elephant Nalagari (*c*.500 A.D.), Ajanta Cave XVII.

Plate VII. Folio from a copy of the *Hamzanāma*. Victoria and Albert Museum, London.

Plate VIII. Daughters of Sulṭān Muḥammad being married. *Tārīkh-i Khāndān-i Tīmūrīa*, Khuda Bakhsh Oriental Public Library, Patna, f.40.

Plate IX. Rejoicing at the birth of Akbar's second son. *Akbarnama*, Victoria and Albert Museum, London, No.80/117.

Plate X. Akbar hunts wild asses. *Tārīkh-i Khāndān-i Tīmūrīa*, Khuda Bakhsh Oriental Public Library, Patna, f.331.

Plate XI. Akbar lost after hunting. *Akbarnāma*, Victoria and Albert Museum, London, No.84/117.

Plate XII. Akbar present at armed combat of ascetics. *Tārīkh-i Khāndān-i Tīmūrīa*, Khuda Bakhsh Oriental Public Library, Patna, f.322.

Plate XIII. Akbar present at armed combat of ascetics. *Akbarnāma*, Victoria and Albert Museum, London, No.61/117 (first part of double-page illustration).

Plate XIV. Second part (No.62/117) of the illustration on Plate XIII.

13

Revisiting Fatehpur Sikri An Interpretation of Certain Buildings

S. ALI NADEEM REZAVI

Since the monumental work of E.W. Smith in four volumes, much has been written about Fatehpur Sikri, the imperial city of Akbar. Apart from a large number of papers and articles published in various journals, a number of books have also appeared.[1] A perplexing problem has been the nomenclature of buildings, with various authors using different names for the same buildings. Then again there is the problem of the popular attributions circulated sometime in the previous century and accepted by archaeologists and historians. A recent work broadly divided the monuments into two categories: those that have been mentioned in the Persian sources and those that have not.[2] Another controversy regarding this city is of a more recent origin: Is Fatehpur a planned city, like the later Shahjahanabad laid out by Akbar's grandson, or did it evolve gradually. A. Petruccioli tries to persuade us to the former view,[3] although a reading of the sources leads to a contrary conclusion. Much may be learnt in time by careful archaeologicalwork. In the 1970s a joint team of archaeologists of the Archaeological

[1] Eg.,S.K.Banerji,'Buland Darwāza of Fatehpur Sikri', *London Historical Quarterly*, XIII, 1937; idem,'A Historical Outline of Akbar's Darul Khilāfat, Fatehpur Sikri', *Journal of Indian History*, XXI, 1942; Fr. Heras, 'The Palace of Akbar at Fatehpur Sikri', *JIH*, 1925; Ashraf Ḥusain, *A Guide to Fatehpur Sikri*, Delhi, 1947; A.B.M. Husain, *Fatehpur Sikri and its Architecture*, Dacca,1970; Muḥammad Sayeed Marahravi, *Tārīkh-i Fatehpur* (Urdu), 1905; S.A.A.Rizvi, *Fatehpur Sikri*, New Delhi, 1972; S.A.A. Rizvi & V.J.A. Flynn, *Fatehpur Sikri*, Bombay, 1975;Michael Brand and Glenn D. Lowry (ed.), *Fatehpur Sikri: A Source Book*, Massachusetts, 1985.

[2] Michael Brand and Glenn D. Lowery (ed.), op. cit.

[3] Atilio Petruccioli, *La Citta' Del Sole & Delle Acque Fatehpur Sikri*, Rome, 1988.

Survey of India and the Department of History, Aligarh Muslim University, excavated a number of sites around the palace complex pertaining to 'nobles' complexes, bazar, stables, harem, etc.', a detailed report of which is yet to be published.[4]

The present paper is an attempt to identify certain structures which have so far escaped the eye of scholars, despite the fact that some of the so-called unidentified structures might, after all, have been mentioned by contemporary chroniclers. An attempt is also made to present in summary the results of a survey of the remains at Fatehpur Sikri which was undertaken by me first in May1989 and then, subsequently, on different occasions till the first week of October 1992.[5]

The most detailed contemporary description of Fatehpur Sikri is given by Father Monserrate, who visited the court in 1580 along with Fr. Acquiviva and Fr. Henriques. He writes:

Unlike the palaces built by other Indian kings, they are lofty; for an Indian palace is generally as low and humble as an idol-temple. Their total circuit is so large that it easily embraces *four great royal dwellings*, of which the King's own palace is the largest and the finest. The second palace belongs to the queens, and the third to the royal princes, whilst the fourth is used as a store house and magazine.[6]

The 'King's own palace' was divided into two parts, the *daulatkh̲ānа* and the '*dīwānkh̲āna-i 'ām*'. Describing the latter, which he calls *daulatkh̲āna-i'ām*, Badāūnī informs us that it consists of '114 *aiwāns* (porticos)'.[7] This structure, where the Emperor gave public audience, had four gateways, apart from the king's own personal entrance, which was secured by a guard each. To quote Monserrate:

...various kinds of chains, manacles, hand-cuffs and other irons are hung

[4] The Aligarh team worked under the directorship of Professor R.C. Gaur, who subsequently presented in his Presidential Address at the Indian Archaeological Society, a preliminary report on 'The Archaeology of Urban Mughal India: Excavations at Fatehpur Sikri', Santiniketan, Dec. 1988.

[5] Please see Plan at end of this paper, which incorporates the identifications of the buildings of the Palace complex here made. The author is beholden to Mr Zameer Aḥmad of the Archaeology Section, Deptt. of History, AMU, and his colleagues the late Mr Rajiv Sharma and Dr Jabir Raza for accompanying him.

[6] Monserrate,Fr. Anthony, *The Commentary of Father Monserrate,S.J.*, tr. J.S. Hoyland, London, 1922, p.199.

[7] Badāūnī, *Muntakh̲abu-t Tawārīkh̲*, ed. M.A. Alvi, Calcutta,Vol.II, 1869, p.365.

up on one of the palace gateways, which is guarded by the aforementioned chief executioner. The other three gateways are guarded by the chief doorkeeper, the chief trainer of gladiators, and the chief despatch-runner respectively.[8]

Presumably, the chief doorkeeper stood at the gate which opens into the *daulatkhāna-i khāṣ*, in front of the hall with the Lotus Pillar. The chief despatch-runner might have stood near the gate which connects the building with the road leading to the Agra Gate, through the *Chahārsūq* Bazar, this being the shortest route out of the city. The gate opening towards the *hauẓ-i shīrīn* appears to have been the main door through which ceremonial entrance was provided to the nobility along with their retinue. Here possibly stood the chief executioner to instil awe and fear in their hearts. The chief trainer of the gladiators guarded the gate opening towards the south. A miniature depicts the entry of *bāzīgars* (tumblers) along with their animals through this gate.[9]

The *daulatkhāna-i khāṣ* appears to have been divided into two parts, namely the *daulatkhāna* and the *daulatkhāna-i anūptalāu*.[10] Entry to this area was restricted to only a few and those whom the emperor personally invited. It is in this area of *daulatkhāna-i anūptalāu* that the *khilwatkada-i khāṣ*(the imperial chambers) and the *khwābgāh* (resting quarters) of Akbar are located. The area got its name from Anūp Talāu, a *ḥauẓ* (water tank) constructed in this area. However, Fr. Monserrate and Jahāngīr give the nameof the tank as Kapūrtalāu.[11] Badāūnī mentions the existence of a structure which he calls the *ḥujra-i Anūptalāu* (the room of the Anūptalāu) where the emperor used sometimes to hold religious discussions.[12] Fr. Monserrate in one of his letters to the Provincial, Fr. Rue Vicente, speaks more explicitly about this place when he writes:

[On] Saturday, the day set aside for hearing the things of God, all three of us [Frs. Acquaviva, Henrique and Monserrate]went to the palace 'Darigtiana' (*daulatkhāna*), and when it was time, the King having himself

[8] Monserrate, p.211. [9] See Plate I.

[10] Badāūnī, II, p.215. At another place Badāūnī calls it the '*imārat* (building) of Anūptalāu', ibid., II, p.201.

[11] Monserrate, p.28; *Tuzuk-i Jahāngīrī*, Ghazipur & Aligarh, 1863-4, p.260. Qandhārī, like Badāūnī, refers to Anūptalāu (*Tārīkh-i Akbarī*, Rampur, 1962, p.151).

[12] Badāūnī, II, p.208.

six of his mullahs of the most knowledgeable, he sent for us and we went up to a *veranda* where he is wont to speak at other times ...[13]

... he [Akbar] was listening out of courtesy, for while not a point escaped him and he asked somethings in order to understand better what was being read, he was nodding, making believe that he was sleeping, and on the other hand he cast his very bright eyes all about the *room* taking stock of the persons with the dissimulation of a very prudent and wise man.[14]

This evidence explicitly indicates that the so-called 'Turkish Sulṭāna's chamber' and the cloistered verandah around it are the structures which Badāūnī calls by the name of *ḥujra-i Anūptalāu*. The cloisters, apart from being used to seat the people called for interview by the emperor,[15] also shielded the area of the *daulatkhāna-i Anūptalāu* from the *daulat-khāna-i khāṣ*. To the west of the *ḥujra-i Anūptalāu*, and connected through the cloistered double passage with it, is a structure which is sometimes erroneously called a 'girls' school'.[16] Athar Abbas Rizvi appears to be correct in calling it the 'Abdārkhāna and Fruit Store', where food and beverages for the emperor were stored.[17] The *Khilwatkadah-i khāṣ* and the *Khwābgāh* are also situated in this area.[18]

To the east of the *Khilwatkada-i-khāṣ* and the *Khwābgāh* structure are two rooms which have traditionally been assigned various purposes. One is situated at the back, and provided with a raised platform: this has been identified as the *Dīwān-khana-i-khāṣ* by Athar Abbās Rizvi,[19] whereas the one situated in the front has variously been identified as the 'pantry' or the 'library'. Rizvi, on the other hand, finds several uses for it. He writes that it 'was used as Akbar's private library, for informal chats with distinguished guests, and a dining hall.'[20] We are informed that there was a *khizāna-i Anūptalāu* or the treasury of Anūp Talāu.[21] Possibly this

[13] *Letters from the Mughal Court: The First Jesuit Mission to Akbar (1580-1583)*, ed. John Correia-Afonso, Bombay, 1980, p.72.

[14] Ibid., p.74.

[15] Ibid., p.83.

[16] S.K. Banerji,'Akbar's Dāru'l Khilāfat, Fateḥpur-Sikri', *Journal of Indian History*, 1942, p.211.

[17] S.A.A. Rizvi & V.J.A. Flyn, *Fatehpur Sikri*, Bombay, 1975, p.35.

[18] For details on this, see ibid., pp.28-9.

[19] Rizvi, op.cit., p.26.

[20] Ibid., p.26. Fr. Heras, 'The Palace of Akbar at Fatehpur Sikri', *Journal of Indian History*, 1925, pp.61-2, erroneously calls it the dining hall.

[21] Abū'l Faẓl, *Akbarnāma*, III, p.246.

building would more appropriately have performed this purpose. The hollow walls with sliding panels would be more suited for this purpose than any other.

Beyond the *Abdārkhāna* is the courtyard of the *daulat-khāna-i khāṣ* with the famous Panch Mahal, the so-called 'Treasury of Gold and Silver' (Ānkh Michaulī) and 'the Jewel House' (the lotus-pillar chamber). It is generally believed that the contemporary Persian sources are totally silent regarding them. But a perusal of the account of 'Ārīf Qandhārī puts to rest this contention. Describing the courtyard of the *daulat-khāna* Qandhārī writes:

On one side of the *ṣaḥn* (courtyard) of that '*imārat* with sky-like roof, they have raised a *chahārkhāna*, *chahārṣuffā* and an *aiwān-khāna,* all carved out of red stone. Their *abvāb* (doors) and *shibāk* (screens) have been wrought in such a way that the keeper of the eight-doored heaven cannot enter a claim of equality...[22]

The *Chahārkhāna* is a square chamber with openings on all its four sides. This is a clear reference to the hall of the lotus-pillar, which is situated on the northern side of the courtyard, and is a perfect square. To the north-west of the courtyard is the Panch Mahal, which is a four-storeyed structure surmounted with a cupola: *Chahārṣuffā* means a structure with four platforms or floors. Between these two structures stands the so-called Treasury, which comprises three large porticos or *aiwāns*; thus the term *aiwānkhāna*. Interestingly, all the three were once provided with perforated screens (*shibāk*).

Badāūnī mentions that in AH 985/1577 Akbar ordered the construction of a square *ḥauẓ* (tank) with each side measuring 20 yards and a depth of 3 yards. In the middle of it was constructed *ḥujra* (room), on the top of which was raised *mīnāra-i buland* (a high tower). On all the four sides of the room were placed cause-ways (*pul*).[23] Abu'l Fazl also gives the same dimensions.[24] Badāūnī mentions that this *ḥauẓ,* which was constructed in 1577, was 'filled with *zar-i siyāh* (copper coins) to an amount of 20 kror'. Qandhārī says that the *talāu* (tank) 'placed in that *ṣaḥn* (courtyard)' was in 986 AH/ 1578-9 emptied of water and filled with 'copper, silver and gold *tankas*'.[25] Abū'l Faẓl gives the same information for the

[22] Qandhārī, p.151. [23] Badāūnī, II, pp.264-5.
[24] Abū'l Faẓl, *Akbarnāma*, Calcutta, 1887, III, pp.141-2.
[25] Qandhārī, p.152.

same year.[26]

Jahāngīr, on the other hand, mentions a *ḥauẓ* in the courtyard, which he calls 'Kapūr Talāu' and gives its measurement as 36 yards square and 4½ yards deep.This was also filled with copper coins up to the brim.[27]

The question arises whether this tank was the same as *ḥauẓ-i Anūptalāu* if one goes by the latter's dimensions given by Abū'l Faẓl. Like the *Anūptalāu*, this tank too had causeways. But then Badāūnī mentions the year of construction of the *Anūptalāu* as 1575-6 (AH 983)[28] — i.e. two years before he mentions the construction of this second tank. Secondly, the latter tank is said to have been surmounted with a high tower, which unfortunately is missing now. The statement of Badāūnī regarding the existence of this tower is authenticated by two *Akbarnāma* paintings, in both of which a tower is depicted somewhere behind the *dīwān-i 'ām*.[29] Thus one can safely say that the *daulatkhāna* once had two tanks: the *Anūptalāu* and a second one. Is it, then, the one which Jahāngīr mentions as 'Kapūrtalāu'?

Another problem relating to the 'first palace' of Akbar, as mentioned by Monserrate, is about the location of the emperor's dining hall. If it was not located near the *Khilwat-kada* and the *dīwānkhāna-i khāṣ*, then where was it? An answer to this problem is given by Monserrate himself. While describing the private dining chamber the Father writes:

> In his dining-hall he had pictures of Christ, Mary, Moses and Muḥammad; when naming them he showed his true sentiments by putting Muḥammad last; for he would say, 'This is the picture of Christ, this of Mary, this of Moses and that of Muhammad'...[30]

Further on he writes:

> His table is very sumptuous, generally consisting of more than forty courses served in great dishes. These are brought into the royal dining-hall covered and wrapped in linen cloths...They are carried by youths to the door of the dining-hall, other servants walking ahead and the master-of-the-household following. Here they are taken over by eunuchs, who hand them to the serving girls who wait on the royal table. He is accustomed to dine in private, except on the occasion of a public banquet...[31]

[26] *Akbarnāma*, III, p.246.
[27] *Tuzuk*, p.260.
[28] Badāūnī, II, pp.200-1.
[29] See Plates 1 & 2.
[30] Monserrate, p.29.
[31] Ibid., p.199.

The second quotation points to the location of the dining-hall which must have been at a place where the men were not allowed to enter. To the west of the cloisters of the *daulatkhāna-i Anūptalāu*, not very far from the *ābdārkhāna*, where the food is supposed to have been laid out, is a private door which opens towards what now appears to be the *ḥaramsarā* or ladies' quarters. This door leads one from the *daulatkhāna* to a structure which is popularly known as 'Sunahra Makān' or 'Maryam's quarters', which in turn was originally screened off from the rest of the *ḥaramsarā* with the help of walls, towards the Ḥaramsarā offices, and the gate of the Principal *Ḥaramsarā* ('Jodhbai's Palace'). Another wall screened off this structure towards the *Ḥaramsarā* garden. Thus, in other words, 'Maryam's house', although outside the *daulatkhāna*, was yet not a part of the *ḥaramsarā*. This building could easily be visited by occupants of both the palaces. Its central chamber is provided with *ṭāqs* (niches) on which some traces of portraits can still be discerned. On one of the *ṭāqs* (the south-east) of the central chamber is depicted a portrait of a woman in European fashion.[32] The eastern and western facades of this building depict winged personages, who to Smith appeared to be angels.[33] Wall paintings are profuse in this building, depicting a court scene, elephant fights, and floral patterns which might well be scenes from the *Hamzanāmah* or some such other work.[34]

These paintings might have misled Monserrate, as they did Smith, into believing that they depicted Christian themes. The lady in the *ṭāq* might well be thought to have represented Mary.

If it was the quarters of a woman, howsoever exalted she might have been, the numerous hunting, battle and siege scenes would be quite out of place. It would thus appear that this building is the 'dining-hall' of Akbar described by Monserrate.

Another structure which has been mentioned in the sources but has so far defied proper identification is the School for the Princes. Monserrate makes it clear that this 'school' was inside the palace itself:

Friday morning I went to the palace, and when I reached it, the King was entering the place where we teach and, when I had greeted him, he made

[32] See plate 3. [33] See plates 4 & 5.
[34] For a detailed description see Rizvi, pp.53-5.

a sign that I should enter within...[35]

A closer look at the so-called 'ḥaramsarā guest-house' reveals that it is connected with the *daulatkhāna* through a passage near the structure which we have defined as the *Aiwānkhāna*. This is definitely separated from the *ḥaramsarā* with the help of a huge gateway which opens towards the *ḥaramsarā* garden. The central chamber of this so-called 'guest house' is also well suited for a prince to study under the eyes of occupants of both the main palace and the *ḥaramsarā*. Was this the school or nursery of the young imperial princes whom the Jesuits taught?

As far as the 'second palace' of Monserrate is concerned, much has been written about it by authorities like Rizvi and Petruccioli.[36] But what about the 'third palace', the prince's quarters? Rizvi maintains that the area near the so-called Tānsen's *bāradarī*, in front of Curzon's Dak Bungalow, was the area of Prince Salīm's quarters.[37] But subsequent excavations in that area have brought to light only some 'nobles' structures'. The only place where a person of Prince Salīm's stature could have resided can be the so-called 'Ḥakīm's quarters', which although separated from the imperial quarters are yet the nearest and grandest. No noble could have been allowed to live in an area so close to the *Khwābgāh* and the waterworks which supplied the required water to the imperial baths and the Anūptalāu.

As far as the *kārkhānas* are concerned, they were also within the palace or very near it. Monserrate in one of his letters says: 'The King is a mechanic and has all sorts of craftsmen within the palace enclosure...'[38] He further writes that Akbar used to walk from the *dīwān-i 'ām* to the 'gun-maker's workshop' situated nearby.[39] In his *Commentaries*, he explains:

...he has built a workshop near the palace, where also are studios and workrooms for the finer and more reputable arts, such as painting, goldsmith-work, tapestry-making, carpet and curtain-making, and the manufacture of arms.[40]

[35] *Jesuit Letters*,p.85.

[36] Rizvi, *op.cit.*; A. Petruccioli, *La Citta' Del Sole & Delle Acque Fatehpur Sikri*, Rome, 1988.

[37] Rizvi, p.24.

[38] *Jesuit Letters*, p.37, also 81.

[39] Ibid., pp.35-6.

[40] Monserrate, p.201.

It appears that the area from the imperial workshop ('Mint') mentioned about the Hathipol was given to *Yatash-khānas* or offices-cum-residences of the various officials. Adjoining the northern wall of the *Dīwān-i 'Ām* is situated the kitchen establishment, along with the *Yatashkhāna* of the Superintendent of Kitchen Establishment, Muḥammad Bāqir. Further on, below the *Ḥauẓ-i shīrīn,* is the house of the Superintendent of Animals. This *Yatashkhāna* adjoins the *chītah-khāna*, *fīlkhāna,* etc, which have been recently excavated. This series of offices and officers' residences continues till beyond the Hathipol, behind which on the ridge stands the house which is directly connected with steps to the so-called *farrāsh-khāna* or *sarāi* near the Hiran Mīnār. Architecturally, the structure of this 'sarai' appears to be the same as that of other Akbarī buildings. Qandhārī writes in the plural (*sarā-hā*) when he mentions the construction of sarais at Fatehpur Sikri by Akbar.[41] But then Wāriṣ informs us that in AH 1064/1655 Shāhjahān ordered the construction of a palace (*Daulatkhāna*) overlooking the lake.[42]

R.C. Gaur, in his presidential address above cited,[43] mentions a massive structure situated between the 'Samosa Maḥal', the Chishti quarters, the Jāmi' Mosque and the house of the Superintendent of the 'sarāi' of Hiran Mīnār. He identified it as the 'Minor Ḥaramsarā'. The mere location rulers it out as the residence of any women of the reigning emperor, for they could never have been allowed to reside in an area containing bureaucratic establishments. Yet the structure is on such a massive scale that it can also not be identified as a nobleman's house. It consists of two hammams, a *chahār-bāgh*, an underground water reservoir and an open tank, apart from a large number of rooms. The walls of this structure and its hammams are profusely painted with floral patterns of a shining maroon colour. The plan as drawn by Gaur fails to show any opening or entrance into the structure. But closer observation revealed a massive door which, during some late renovations, was converted into a room. This gate opened on the road leading from the Hāthīpol to the Chishti quarters and Rang Maḥal. To its north is a breathtaking view of the lake. Thus, instead of the *Minor*

[41] Qandhārī, p.150.

[42] Wāriṣ, *Badhshāhnāma*, transcript of Rampur MS in Department of History, AMU, II, pp.244,284.

[43] R.C. Gaur, op.cit.

ḥaramsarā, this magnificent building appears to have been the palace built by Shāhjahān when the palace complex of Akbar and the bureaucratic quarters had both been abandoned.[44]

Although profusely written about, Fatehpur Sikri appears to be an inexhaustible quarry for information regarding the age of Akbar. The shops from the *hiran mīnār* to the Ajmer darwāza, the Indarawali area along with its platforms, buildings, wells, tanks and *bāolīs*, the area around Bīrpol, Gwalior darwāza and the structures on the ridge, all need detailed studies to unravel the mysteries of this city built by so unique a genius.

[44] See my mimeographed paper, 'Post-Akbar Fatehpur Sikri' presented at the 8th session of U.P. History Congress, Varanasi, Feb.1994.

DAULAT KHANA (PALACE), FATEHPUR SIKRI

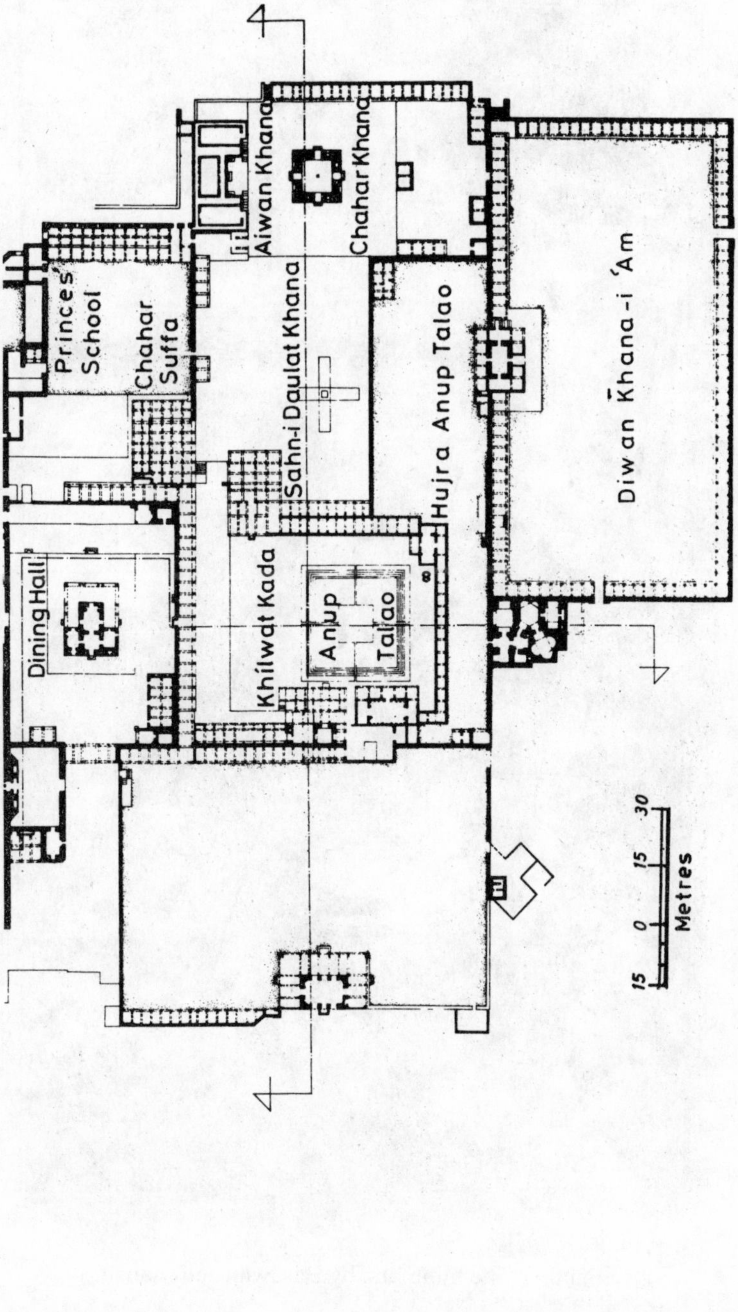

Plan based on Petruccioli

Plate 1. The tumblers, by Basāwan and Manṣūr.

Plate 2. Court scene by Ḥusain Naqqāsh and Kesav.

Plate 3. Wall-painting of woman in European dress in 'Maryam's House'.

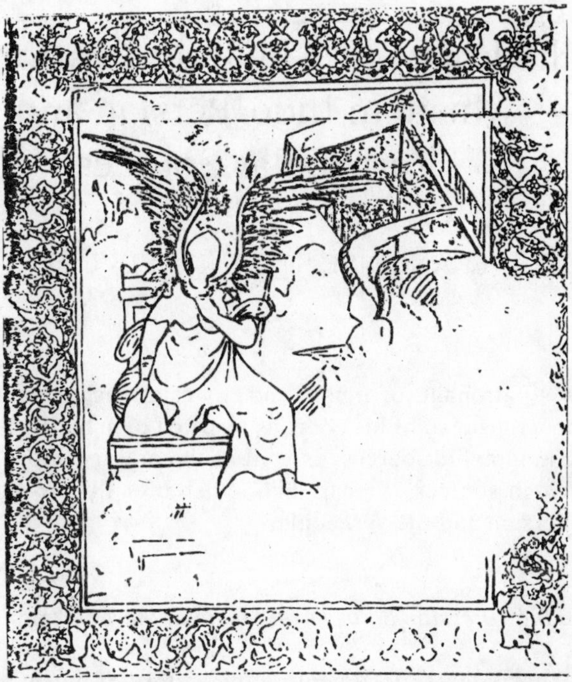

Plate 4. Winged angels in wall-paintings in 'Maryam's house'.

Plate 5. Winged angels in wall-paintings in 'Maryam's House'.

14

The Image of Akbar as a Patron of Music in Indo-Persian and Vernacular Sources

FRANÇOISE 'NALINI' DELVOYE

Akbar's patronage of music and his relationship with Tānsen, foremost musician of his court, is testified to in numerous written and iconographic sources, as well as the oral tradition. Amongst the written sources, we can distinguish broadly two groups, the Indo-Persian and the vernacular.

A. The Indo-Persian Sources on Music at the Court of Akbar

Indo-Persian texts[1] documenting the history of music patronized by Akbar may be sub-divided into documents contemporary to the emperor, and later chronicles. Indo-Persian texts of a more musicological character generally provide theoretical and technical information, as well as biographical accounts of musicians and their patrons. Earlier texts, normally, naturally command a greater degree of authenticity than later sources.

The main contemporary sources are the *Akbarnāma* of Abū'l Fazl[2] and the *Muntakhab al-Tawārīkh* of Mullā 'Abd al-Qādir Badā'ūnī.[3]

[1] See Françoise 'Nalini' Delvoye, 'Indo-Persian Literature on Art-Music: Some Historical and Technical Aspects', *Confluence of Cultures. French Contributions to Indo-Persian Studies*, ed. F. Delvoye, New Delhi, 1994, pp.93-130.

[2] See Abū'l Fazl, *Akbarnāma* (henceforth *AN*), Persian edn. by Āghā Aḥmad 'Alī and Maulavī 'Abd al-Raḥīm, 3 Vols. Calcutta, Asiatic Society of Bengal, (Bibliotheca Indica), 1873-86; English tr. by H. Beveridge, 3 Vols., Calcutta, Asiatic Society of Bengal (Bibliotheca Indica), 1873-1939; Reprint, Delhi, 1972-3.

[3] See 'Abd al-Qādir Badā'ūnī, *Muntakhab al-Tawārīkh*, Persian edn. by Kabīr al-dīn Aḥmad, Aḥmad 'Alī and W.N. Lees, 3 Vols., Calcutta, Asiatic Society of Bengal (Bibliotheca Indica), 1864-9. See also the English tr. in 3 Vols., by G. Ranking (Vol.I), W.H. Lowe (Vol.II) and T.W. Haig (Vol. III), Calcutta, Asiatic Society of Bengal (Bibliotheca Indica), 1884-1925.

Later sources include some brief references in the *Tūzuk-i Jahāngīrī*,[4] the *Pādshāhnāma* of 'Abd al-Ḥamīd Lāhaurī,[5] the *Ma'aṣir al-Umarā* of Ṣamṣām al-Daula Shāh Nawāz K̲h̲ān,[6] the anonymous preface in Persian to the *Hazār Dhurpad* or *Sahasrās*, a collection of one thousand songs attributed to Nāyak Bak̲h̲shū, compiled in Shāh Jahān's court,[7] and texts of a musicological nature from the latter half of the seventeenth century onwards like Saif K̲h̲ān Faqīrullāh's *Rāg Darpan*.[8] The texts of the last category, that is from the late seventeenth and eighteenth centuries, usually repeat the same information with minor variations, and are thus of limited value for history, though they are valuable in documenting the musical history of their own period.

1. Akbar as a Musician and a Keen Listener

From the Indo-Persian sources we can gather details of different aspects of Akbar's relationship with music: as a music-composer,

---

[4] See Jahāngīr, *Tūzuk-i-i Jahāngīrī*, Persian edn. by Syed Aḥmad K̲h̲ān, Aligarh, 1864; English tr., *Tūzuk-i-i Jahāngīrī* or *Memoirs of Jahāngīr*, by A. Rogers, rev. and annotated by H. Beveridge, Reprint, New Delhi, 1978.

[5] See 'Abd al-Ḥamīd Lāhaurī, *Padshāhnāma*, Persian edn. by Kabīr al-dīn Aḥmad, 'Abd al-Raḥīm and W.N. Lees, 2 Vols., Calcutta, Asiatic Society of Bengal (Bibliotheca Indica), 1866-72.

[6] See Ṣamṣām al-Daula Shāh Nawāz K̲h̲ān, *Ma'āṣir al-Umarā*, revised and enlarged by his son 'Abd al-Ḥayy 'Ṣārim' Aurangābādī, 3 Vols., Calcutta, Asiatic Society of Bengal (Bibliotheca Indica), 1888-91; English Tr. by H. Beveridge, Calcutta, Asiatic Society of Bengal (Bibliotheca Indica), 1911, Text, Vol.II, pp.134-35; tr., Vol.II, p.581.

[7] See the critical edition of the anonymous preface of *Hazār Dhrupad*, from MSS in the India Office Library, London, and the Bibliotheque Nationale, Paris, by Sharif Husain Qasemi (*Qand-e Pārsī*, New Delhi, Vol.VIII, 1994). See also the Devanāgarī transliteration and Hindi tr. of the same by P.L. Sarma, *Sangīt Nāṭak Akādemi, Nāyak Bak̲h̲su ke dhrupadom̐ kā saṁgrah*, New Delhi, 1972, Part II, pp.3-13.

[8] Among many MSS kept in India and abroad, see Saïf K̲h̲ān 'Faqīrullāh', *Rāg Darpan*, MS N⁰ 1937, dated A.H. 1196/1782, in the India Office Library, London, described in Hermann Ethe, *Catalogue of Persian Manuscripts in the Library of the India Office*, Oxford, 1903, Vol.I, Notice N⁰ 2017, pp.1120-1. An important MS of the *Rāg Darpan*, with Faqīrullāh's seal, is kept at the Maulana Azad Library, Aligarh Muslim University, Lytton Collection, *Fārsīya 'ulūm*, N⁰ 41. See also the Persian edn. by N.H. Anṣārī, and Sh. Shukla, 'Rāga Darpana' and 'Ṣaut al-Nāqaus' of Muḥammad 'Uṣmān Qais, *Persian Research Journal Special Number*, Delhi, Dept. of Persian, University of Delhi, 1981.

a musician and a keen listener, but also as a patron of theoreticians of music and musicians, with the remarkable example of Tānsen, the premier musician in his court (1562-89).

a) Predisposition to Music: Among various horoscopes of Akbar cast from the Greek and Indian astrological systems, four are presented by Abū'l Faẓl in the *Akbarnāma*. All allegedly reveal exceptional qualities in all fields.[9] According to the Indian court-astrologer Jotik Rāi, who cast Akbar's horoscope probably many years after his birth, 'he will be acute and discriminating in musical notes, in subtle harmonies and in the secrets of melody.'[10]

According to Abū'l Faẓl's account, Akbar's birth was celebrated with Persian vocal and instrumental music, which is attested to by the *Akbarnāma* and some of its illustrations and also by a remarkable painting in the *Tārīkh-i Khāndān-i Tīmūriya* (c.1584).[11]

b) Akbar as a Musician and a Composer of Tunes: Mentions can be found - especially in Abū'l Faẓl's writings - of Akbar being himself a musician (who played the *Naqāra*). In the *Ā'īn-i Akbarī*, among the 'Ensigns of Royalty' (*shukoh-i salṭanat*), Abū'l Faẓl describes the military band,[12] and the instruments and tunes played in the *Naqāra-Khāna,* according to some fixed timing.[13] He avers: 'His Majesty has such a knowledge of the science of music [*ilm-i mūsīqī*] as trained musicians [*ṣāḥibān-i īn fan*] do not possess; and he is likewise an excellent hand in performing especially on the *naqāra.*'[14]

[9] See Abū'l Faẓl, *AN*, Text, Vol.I, pp.23-43; Tr., Vol.I, pp.69-125.

[10] Ibid., Vol.I, p.30; Tr., Vol.I, p.94.

[11] Ibid., Vol.I, p.21; Tr., Vol.I, p.63 and the illustrated MS of the *Akbarnāma* in the British Museum (Or. 12988, fols. 20b-21a and fol.22a), and another MS in the Chester Beatty Library, Dublin (Ind. Ms. N°3). See the *Tārīkh-i Khāndān-i Tīmūriya* MS of the Khuda Bakhsh Library, Patna, fol.284a, painted by Khem and La'l. See also Geeti Sen, 'Music and Musical Instruments in the Paintings of the *Akbarnāma*', *Quarterly Journal of the National Centre for the Performing Arts*, Vol.VIII, N°4, Dec. 1979, pp.1-7, especially pp.4-5.

[12] Since the Sassanids, the military band (*nauba*) is an important institution of the royalty; see H.G. Farmer, *A History of Arabian Music to the XIIIth Century*, (1929), London, 2nd edn., 1973, pp.206-8 and by the same author '*Ṭabl Khāna*', *Encyclopaedia of Islam*, Leiden, E.J. Brill, Suppl., 1938, pp.217-22.

[13] See Abū'l Faẓl, *Ā'īn-i Akbarī* (henceforth *Ā'īn*), Persian edn. by H. Blochmann, 2 Vols., Calcutta, Asiatic Society of Bengal (Bibliotheca Indica), 1877; English tr. in 3 Vols., by H. Blochmann, (Vol.I) and H.S. Jarrett, (Vols. II and III), Calcutta, Asiatic Society of Bengal (Bibliotheca Indica), 1867-77, Reprint, New Delhi, 1977-8; Text, Vol.I, pp.45-7; Tr., Vol.I, pp.52-4.

[14] Ibid., Text, Vol.I, p.47; Tr., Vol.I, p.54. Henceforth Persian terms in square brackets have been reintroduced from the edn. cit. by the present author.

The playing of old Khwārizmian tunes is part of the *Naqāra-Khāna* performance: 'Of these his Majesty has composed more than two hundred, which are the delight of young and old, especially the tunes *Jalālshāhī*, *Mahāmīr karkat* (?) and the *Nawrozī*.'[15]

A certain confusion remains about the instruments played at the *Naqāra-Khāna* and in the audience-hall of the imperial court.[16] The question persists about the genre of music which was played according to the occasion, and marking the daily routine of the court, the arrival and the departure of the emperor, the nobles and the guests of honour; so also the celebration of happy events, such as princely births and festivals, and when accompanying the army to the battle-field. Iconographic data provide some information about instruments played in different settings, implying that the music performed by the *naubat* band, with a heavy use of trumpets and like instruments, and a variety of drums, could not be the Persian or the Indian art-music performed by a singer, or by a limited number of solo or accompanying instruments, such as in Western chamber-music.

c) Akbar, a Knowledgeable Listener of Music: 'His Majesty has a considerable knowledge of the principles explained in the *Sangita* and other works, and what serves as an occasion to induce a lethargic sleep in other mortals, becomes to him a source of exceeding vigilance'.[17]

In this flattering statement, Abū'l Fazl epitomizes Akbar's knowledge of music. Elsewhere, introducing the account of the circumstances leading to Tānsen's arrival at Akbar's court, he indicates that music from Persia and India was one of the sciences known to Akbar, in its theoretical and practical aspects.[18]

Another source on Akbar's interest in music is provided by

[15] Ibid., Text, Vol.I, p.47; Tr., Vol.I, p.53.

[16] See G. Sen, *op.cit.*; Andrew J. Greig, 'Musical Instruments of Akbar's Court', *Journal of Asian Culture*, Vol.IV, Spring, 1980, pp.154-77, and 'Indian Music in the 16th Century', Ph.D. Thesis, University of California, Los Angeles, 1989 (not published), Chapter VI; S.P. Verma, *Art and Material Culture in the Paintings of Akbar's Court*, New Delhi, 1978, Chapter VI on musical instruments, pp.60-70, and by the same author, *The Life of Akbar as Illustrated in Contemporary Miniatures*, Exhibition Catalogue, Seminar 'Akbar and His Age', Aligarh, October 1992.

[17] See Abū'l Fazl, *Ā'īn*, Text Vol.II, p.144; Tr., Vol.III, p.273.

[18] See Abū'l Fazl, *AN*, Text, Vol.II, p.181; Tr., Vol.II, p.279.

the account given by Asad Beg Qazwīnī of his first trip to Bijapur, in 1603-4, recorded in the *Waqā'i'-i Asad Beg* (1602-5).[19] During the farewell party for the Mughal envoy, Ibrāhīm 'Ādil Shāh II, the Sulṭān of Bijapur (r. 1580–1627), inquired about Akbar's interest in music and whether Tānsen sang standing or sitting in the imperial presence. Asad Beg replied that the emperor did sometimes listen to music and that if he stood, the singers would stand, but if he sat, the musicians would be allowed to sit, especially in great festivals and concerts, and when the emperor was busy conversing with his courtiers or entertaining them with banquets.[20]

Akbar's curiosity extended not only to Persian and Indian music, but also to European music, which is attested by Badā'ūnī, who says that Akbar expressed curiosity about a European musical instrument, an organ (*orghanum*) displayed in Fatehpur Sikri, in 1581.[21]

2. Akbar as a Patron of Theoreticians of Music

The Indian system of music is described in a methodical way in the portion of the *Ā'īn-i Akbarī* devoted to the culture and the intellectual life of Hindūstān.[22] One section is entitled 'Sangita', lit. 'the art of singing, accompanied by music and dancing';[23] another, 'On the Classes of Singers' (*shumāra-ye naghma-sarāyān*);[24] and a third deals with 'Akhāra', 'an entertainment held at night by the nobles of this country, some of whose (female) domestic servants are taught to sing and play...'[25] The treatment of Indian music in seven

[19] See the MS of the British Library, Or. 1996. See also P.M. Joshi, 'Asad Beg's Mission to Bījāpūr, 1603-1604', *Mahāmahōpādhyāy Prof. D.V. Potdar Sixty-First Birthday Commemoration Volume*, ed. Surendra Nāth Sen, Poona, published by D.K. Sathe, 1950, pp.184-96.

[20] See Asad Beg, *op.cit.*, MS. British Library, Or. 1996, fol. 16a; P.M. Joshi, *op.cit.*, p.193; Nazir Ahmad, *Kitāb-i-Nauras by 'Adil Shāh II*, New Delhi, 1956, pp.48-9.

[21] For a description of the instrument and the astonishing way it was played, see 'Abd al-Qādir Badā'ūnī, *Muntakhab al-Tawārīkh*, Text, Vol.II, pp.290-1; Tr., Vol.II, p.299.

[22] See Abū'l Fazl, *A'in*, Text, Vol.II, pp.134-44; Tr., Vol.III, pp.260-73.

[23] Ibid., Vol.II, 134-42; Tr., Vol.III, pp.260-71.

[24] Ibid., Text, Vol.II, pp.142-43; Tr., Vol.III, pp.271-3.

[25] Ibid., Text, Vol.II, p.144; Tr., Vol.III, p.273.

'chapters' (*adhyāya*) reminds us of Sanskrit treatises on music, such as the *Saṁgīta Ratnākāra* composed by Śārṅgadeva in the first half of the thirteenth century, often referred to as 'Saptādhyāyī', lit. 'which has seven chapters', but also of their translations and commentaries in Persian, such as the *Lahjat-i Sikandar Shāhi* of Yaḥyā al-Kābulī.[26] In the first chapter (*Svarādhyāya*), Abū'l Faẓl gives a number of technical definitions. The second chapter (*Rāga-vivekādhyāya*) gives classifications of *Rāga*, and a list of the obsolete and current musical genres, with interesting details about their characteristics, but also the region in which each of them was prevalent and a brief historical survey of their origin, development and current practice. In so doing Abū'l Faẓl illustrates one common feature of most Indo-Persian writers on music, i.e. the presentation of music in its theory and practice. The third chapter (*Prakirnādhyāya*) is a brief presentation of the improvised and composed parts of a *Rāga*. The fourth chapter (*Prabandhādhyāya*) deals with the structure of a musical composition. The rhythmic system is just referred to in the fifth chāpter (*Tālādhyāya*), without any exposition of the various rhythmic cycles of the past or those still in use, which is also a common shortcoming in many other Indo-Persian texts on music. The sixth chapter on musical instruments (*Vādyādhyāya*) gives an interesting account of Persian and Indian instruments, presented according to the traditional Indian classification and presumably used in the court, though no precise mention is made about the kind of music played on each of them. Nor is it specified which ones may be played together, a matter of some interest, since they are shown in rather arbitrary combinations in some miniatures. The seventh chapter on dance (*nrityādhyāya*) is only referred to. The next section on the categories of musicians provides first-hand information on the geographical and social origins of male and female musicians and acrobats, mimics and conjurers, which is of particular interest for the socio-cultural history of medieval music.

[26] See the *Saṁgītaratnākara* of Śārṅgadeva, with the *Kalānidhi* of Kallinatha and the *Saṁgītasudhākara* of Siṁhabhupala, ed. S. Subrahmanya Sastri, 4 Vols., Madras, 1943-53. For the *Laḥjat-i Sikandar Shāhī* of Yaḥyā al-Kābulī, see C.A. Storey, *Persian Literature, A Bio-Bibliographical Survey*, Vol.II, Part 3, G., Arts and Crafts, Leiden, E.J. Brill, 1977, Notice N° 705, p.414. See also N., Ahmed, 'The Lahjat-i Sikandar Shāhī, A Unique Book on Indian Music of the Time of Sikandar Lodī (1489-1517)', *Islamic Culture*, Vol.XXVIII, N° 3, July 1954, pp.410-17.

The last section on Indian music is about the *akhāra*, which has been referred to above. Such an exposition of Indian music, in its classical as well as folk aspects, reveals the didactic spirit of its author, and hence probably the orientation of his patron, Akbar.

One may also mention two texts on Persian music dedicated to Akbar, indicating at the least that their authors were aware of Akbar's interest in music theory. According to C.A. Storey's description,[27] the *Kashf al-autār* by Qāsim, b. Dōst-'Alī al-Bukhārī, is 'a short treatise dedicated to Akbar... on the divisions of the strings in musical instruments, being an exposition of the sixth *maqām* of the work entitled *Duwāzdah maqām*, which was dedicated to Humāyūn ... by Darwīsh Ḥaidar Tuniyānī'.[28] The *Tuḥfat al-adwār* by 'Ināyat Allah, b. Mīr Ḥājj al-Harawī, is 'a short tract, partly in prose and partly in verse, dedicated to Akbar...' in order to facilitate the study of music.[29]

3. Akbar as a Patron of Musicians. The Case of Tānsen

'His Majesty pays much attention to music, and is the patron of all who practise this enchanting art...'[30]

The Indo-Persian sources also shed light on Akbar as a patron of musicians, and especially the sub-chapter of the *Ā'īn*, which deals with the 'Imperial musicians'(*Khunyagarān*).[31]

After an hyperbolic description of the magical power of music, Abū'l Faẓl indicates that the numerous male and female court-musicians (Hindus, Irānīs, Tūrānīs and Kashmiris) are arranged in seven divisions, one for each day in the week: 'When his Majesty gives the order, they let the wine of harmony flow.'[32] Judging the

[27] See C.A. Storey, *op.cit.*, Vol.II, Part 3, G., Arts and Crafts, Notice N° 707, pp.414-15.

[28] See C. Rieu, *Supplement to the Catalogue of the Persian Manuscripts in the British Museum*, London, British Museum, 1895, Notice N° 162 (4) (MS dated A.H. 1073-5 / 1662-64).

[29] See C.A. Storey, *op.cit.*, Vol.II, Part 3, G., Arts and Crafts, Notice N° 708, p.415 referring to a MS (dated A.H. 1077/1666) kept in the Bodleian Library. Cf. E. Sachau and H. Ethe, *Catalogue of the Persian, Turkish, Hindūstānī and Pushtu Manuscripts in the Bodleian Library*, Oxford 1889, Part I, Notice N° 1845, pp.1063-4.

[30] See Abū'l Faẓl, *Ā'īn*, Text, Vol.I, p.263; Tr., Vol.I, p.681.

[31] Ibid., Text, Vol.I, pp.262-4; Tr., I, pp.680-2.

[32] Ibid., Text, Vol.I, 263; Tr., Vol.I, p.681.

description of this class of people too difficult Abū'l Faẓl only gives a list of the thirty-six principal musicians, with their names, the places where they came from, and their musical specialities, whether as singers (*goyanda*), reciters (*khwāninda*) or instrumentalists.[33] A brief comment is added for a few musicians like Tānsen and Bāz Bahādur, and the family ties are mentioned for some. Though fragmentary, the few details available from the imperial musicians' list are significant. They reveal that the Mughal ruler was interested both in music from Iran, Khurāsān and Central Asia, and in music from India. The first type of music tended to be largely instrumental in character, while the latter was for the most part vocal, with a number of singers coming from the region of Gwalior, and more generally the Madhyadesh, also known as Sudesh, a remarkable artistic and literary region still remembered by later Indo-Persian writers such as Saïf Khān Faqīrullāh'(1666).[34]

a) Tānsen's Arrival at the Mughal Court: First in the list of imperial musicians given by Abū'l Faẓl, and the most famous recipient of Akbar's patronage, was 'Miyān Tānsen Gwālyarī: his equal has not appeared in a thousand years'.[35]

Akbar was only twenty when he acquired him from Rājā Rāmachandra Baghela, in 1562. Tānsen - whose early life is obscure - was already very famous at the Baghela court of Rewa, as testified to by the *Vīrabhānudaya Kāvya*, in Sanskrit, composed *c.*1555 by Mādhava, a scholar and court-poet of the Baghela kings, to whom this encomium is dedicated.[36] The Xth Canto of the *Vīrabhānudaya Kāvya* deals with the reign of the king, Rāmachandra. In one verse, the poet reports that the king 'presented the artist named Tānsen, who was the true incarnation of music, a

[33] Ibid., Text, Vol.I, pp.263-4; Tr., Vol.I, pp.681-2.

[34] See 'Faqīrullāh', *Rāg Darpan*, p.34.

[35] See Abū'l Faẓl, *Ā'īn*, Text, Vol.I, p.263; Tr., Vol.I, p.681; my translation. For bibliographical references and comments on books on Tānsen, see F. Delvoye, 'Tānsen et la tradition des chants dhrupad en langue braj, du XVIe siecle a nos jours', D. Litt. Thesis, Sorbonne University, Paris, 1990, *passim*; Abstract in English, 'Tānsen and the Tradition of Dhrupad Songs in the Braj Language, from the 16th century to the Present Day', *Dhrupad Annual*, Vol.VIII, Varanasi, 1993, pp.37-44.

[36] See Mādhava, *Vīrabhānūdaya Kāvyam*, ed. K.K. Lele and H.S. Upadhyaya, with a critical analysis by Hiranand Shastri, Rewa, Rewa Darbar, 1938. See also P.K. Gode, 'A Contemporary Sanskrit Tribute to the Musical Talents of Tānasena, the Greatest Musician of Akbar's Court, and its Historical Perspective', *P.K. Gode Studies in Indian Literary History*, Vol.III, Poona, 1956, pp.188-95.

crore of silver coins (*śaoṣāṅkao* and *taṅka*) for each musical mode (*rāga*), for each series of notes (*tāna*), and for each *dhrupada* he performed'.[37] This is followed by a description of Tānsen's musical talents, with an emphasis on his literary merits, as a poet-composer of Dhrupad.[38]

Both Abū'l Faẓl and Badā'ūnī give details, although conflicting ones, of the way in which Tānsen came to the Mughal court, in 1562. To make the comparison with Badā'ūnī's 'version' easier, the full account is given below, as in H. Beveridge's English translation of the *Akbarnāma*:[39]

Among the occurrences was the coming of Tānsen to the holy court. The brief account is as follows. Inasmuch as the holy personality of H.M. the Shāhinshāh is a congeries of degrees, spiritual and temporal, and a collection of divine and terrestrial excellences, so that when matters are discussed the master of each science imagines that the holy personality has devoted his whole attention to his particular subject, and that all his intellect has been expended on it, the knowledge which H.M. has of the niceties of music, as of other sciences, is, whether of the melodies of Persia, or the various songs of India both as regards theory and execution, unique for all-time. As the fame of Tānsen, who was the foremost of the age among the kalāwants of Gwāliar came to the royal hearing and it was reported that he meditated going into retirement and that he was spending his days in attendance on Rām Chand the Rājah of Pannah, H.M. ordered that he should be enrolled among the court-musicians. Jalāl Khān Qūrchī, who was a favourite servant, was sent with a gracious order to the Rājah for the purpose of bringing Tānsen. The Rājah received the royal message and recognised the sending of an envoy as an honour, and sent back with him suitable presents of elephants of fame and valuable jewels, and he gave also Tānsen suitable instruments and made him the cheek-mole of his gifts. In this year Tānsen did homage and received exaltation. H.M. the Shāhinshāh was pleased and poured gifts of money into the lap of his hopes. His cap of honour was exalted above all others. As he had an upright nature and an acceptable disposition he was cherished by a long service and association with H.M., and great developments were made by him in music and in compositions.

Badā'ūnī mentions Tānsen several times in his *Muntakhab al-Tawārīkh* among a number of references to music and musical eventswhich the orthodox author did not appreciate much, or even

[37] See Mādhava, *op.cit.*, verse 26; Sanskrit text and the English rendering in P.K. Gode, *op.cit.*, pp.190-1; this is my translation.

[38] Ibid., verses 27-31.

[39] See Abū'l Faẓl, *AN*, Text, Vol.II, p.181; Tr., Vol.II, p.279-80.

condemned. While referring to Rājā Rāmachandra's submission to the Mughal power, and his lavish presents to Akbar, Badā'ūnī recalls the Rājā's generosity:

This Rām Chand in his natural disposition was of such high spirit, that he has none equal in our days. And among his presents was this: he gave in one day a *kror* of gold pieces to Miyān Tānsingh (*sic*) the musician [*Miyān Tānsen kalāvant*]. And I have mentioned above how he gave to Ibrāhīm Sūr the ensigns of royalty. Miyān Tānsingh did not wish to leave him. Finally came Jalāl Khān Qūrchī, and brought him back to his sense of duty.[40]

Badā'ūnī's remark about the genuine reluctance of Rāja Rāmachandra to part with Tānsen and his helplessness indicates the author's realistic appreciation of the situation, which is not to be found in the account given by the official chronicler.

Other sources of the period of Shāh Jahān also pick up this incident for comment, such as the *Pādshāhnāma* of 'Abd al-Ḥamīd Lāhaurī.[41] Later texts often refer to the fact that Tānsen was a court-musician of Rājā Rāmachandra, before joining the imperial court, as we see from the *Risāla-i zikr-i mughanniyān-i Hindūstān* of 'Ināyat Khān 'Rāsikh' (b.1701).[42]

In the notice on Rājā Rām Chand Baghela, in the biographical compendium *Ma'āṣir al-Umarā* (1780), the author, Shāh Nawāz Khān, depicts the arrival of Tānsen at Akbar's court in a way rather close to Abū'l Fazl. He precisely states the amount of money given by Akbar to Tānsen: 'When Tānsen arrived, the Emperor on the first day presented him two *krors* of *dāms*, equal to two lacs of current rupees, and became enamoured of his performances. His compositions [*taṣānīf*], many of which bear Emperor Akbar's name, are current even today.'[43] The final remark is corroborated by the fact that many song-texts with the 'signature' (*chāp*) of Tānsen addressed to Akbar are found in late-seventeenth-century

[40] Badā'ūnī, *op.cit.*, Text, Vol.II, p.335; Tr., Vol.II, p.345. On Rājā Rāmachandra's defeat and submission in 1563, see also Abū'l Fazl, *AN*, Text, Vol.I, pp.181-3; tr., Vol.I, pp.281-3.

[41] See 'Abd al-Ḥamīd Lāhaurī, *Padshāhnāma*, edn. cit., Vol.I, p.7.

[42] See 'Ināyat Khān, *Risāla-i zikr-i mughanniyān-i Hindūstān*, Persian edn. by Sayyid 'Alī Ḥaider, (based on MS Nº 1734-35, Khuda Bakhsh Library, Patna), Patna, 1961, pp.12-13, and the introduction to the edited text by S.A. Haider, pp.25-2.

[43] See Ṣamṣām al-Daula Shāh Nawāz Khān, *Ma'āṣir al-Umarā*, *op.cit.*, Text, Vol.II, pp.134-38; Tr., Vol.II, pp.581-4.

court-musicians' repertoires, as will be touched upon below.[44]

Oral tradition - probably inspired by later vernacular hagiographies - is rich in several tales reflecting Rājā Rāmachandra's powerlessness and his attachment to his favourite musician. Rājā Rāmachandra is said to have substituted himself as one of the bearers of the palanquin in which Tānsen was sitting, while going to Agra. Tānsen recognized him when they stopped for water *en route*. Another story recalls Tānsen's promise of not using his right hand to accept any imperial present, as a mark of his reluctance to leave the Baghela ruler, thus contravening the rigorous etiquette of the Mughal court.[45]

b) Competition between Court-musicians: In spite of Abū'l Faẓl's laudatory remarks about Tānsen, one may presume that there were many good artistes - singers, poet-composers and instrumentalists - competing with one another to win Akbar's favours. One such happening is mentioned by Badā'ūnī, while describing the square pond (*ḥauẓ*), built in 1577 in Fatehpur Sikri, with a central platform connected to the courtyard by four bridges in front of Akbar's apartments and known today as Anūp Talāo. Akbar had the tank filled to the brim with copper coins, up to twenty crores.

One day he [i.e. Akbar] had an interview with one Shai<u>kh</u> Banj'hū by name, a singer [*qauvāl*] with a sweet voice [*<u>kh</u>ūsh <u>kh</u>wānī*], and of Ṣūfī tendencies, one of the disciples of Shai<u>kh</u> Adhan of Jaunpūr (whose name gives the date of his death [A.H. 970]), and had a very agreeable time of it. Then he sent for Miyān Tānsīn, and other unequalled singers of Hind; but he preferred him to any of them, and ordered that Shai<u>kh</u> Banj'hū should carry off the whole of that sum of money. But his strength was unequal to carrying it, so he asked for a little gold instead. The Emperor, accordingly, presented him with nearly 1,000 rupees in exchange. And the rest of the money the Emperor in the course of three years, more or less, got rid of by means of various expenses. About this time he received from Shai<u>kh</u> Mubārak [father of Abū'l Faẓl] a lecture on his extravagant expenditure. Before that, at the time of the (musical) exhibitions, Shai<u>kh</u> Faiẓī [brother of Abū'l Faẓl] had said: 'Our Shai<u>kh</u> [Mubārak] is not much of a courtier'. 'No', replied the Emperor, 'he has left all those fopperies to you.' He sent Shai<u>kh</u> Banj'hū and Miyān Tānsīn, and all the musicians to the Shai<u>kh</u> [Mubārak] that he might tell him what they were worth as musicians. He said to Miyān Tānsīn: 'I have heard that you can sing a bit'.

[44] See *infra* pp.41-6.

[45] See Hariharnivas Dvivedi, *Tānsen, jīvanī, vyaktitva tathā krtitva*, Gwalior, 1986, p.41, and personal communication, Dec 1985.

At last he compared his singing to the noise of beasts, and allowed it no superiority over it.[46]

Besides the documentary aspect of this account, it indicates the strong link between court-musicians and Ṣūfī musicians, despite Badā'ūnī's desire to make fun of Shaikh Mubārak as a critic of music. Given the lack of any contemporary data on Tānsen's actual music at that time, which contrasts with the number of laudatory remarks on his poetical talents, the derogatory comments about Tānsen's voice may also be explained by the age of the singer, who thought of retirement when he was asked to join the court in 1562.

c) The Death of Tānsen: Another important historical fact found in the *Akbarnāma* relates to Tānsen's death:

On the 15th do [Ardibihisht 997; 26 April 1589] Miyān Tānsen died, and by H.M.'s orders, all the musicians and singers accompanied his body to the grave, making melodies as at a marriage. The joy of the Age was overcast, and H.M. said that his death was the annihilation of melody. It seems that, in a thousand years, few have equalled him for sweetness and art![47]

To my knowledge, no other contemporary Indo-Persian document refers to Tānsen's death, its stirring effect on Akbar's mind and the subsequent arrangements which he ordered to be made for his funeral. The *Akbarnāma's* account raises a number of questions which are left unanswered, such as the place where the death of Tānsen occurred. Today popular accounts refer to this event as happening in Agra or Fatehpur Sikri. But at that time Akbar was in Lahore, starting upon his first trip to Kashmir.[48] The date given by Abū'l Faẓl is precise and the emperor seems to have witnessed the event. The text refers to the bier (*na'sh*) on which the corpse of Tānsen was laid, before being buried. The Persian text uses unambiguous terms and the indication of a burial — hence a tomb — leads us to another controversial aspect of Tānsen's biography, namely his faith and the authenticity of his tomb in Gwalior, close to the mausoleum of Shaikh Muḥammad Ghauṣ, who may have been Tānsen's spiritual mentor.[49] Written references to the tomb

[46] See Badā'ūnī, *op.cit.*, Text, Vol.II, p.265; Tr., Vol.II, pp.272-3.
[47] See Abū'l Faẓl, *AN,* Text, Vol.III, pp.536-7; Tr., Vol.III, p.816.
[48] Ibid., Text, Vol.III, p.537; Tr., Vol.III, p.817.
[49] See Badā'ūnī, *op.cit.*, Text, Vol.III, pp.4-6; Tr., Vol.III, pp.6-10. See also R.

of Tānsen in Gwalior are rather late. To my knowledge the first mention occurs in the *Tuḥfat al-Hind* (1675), the encyclopaedic work of Mīrzā Khān in which a full chapter deals with Indian and Persian music.[50] Mīrzā Khān traces the career of Tānsen with the 'Rāja' (i.e. Rājā Rāmachandra of Rewa) before he joined Akbar's court. Being a protégé of Shaikh Muḥammad Ghauṣ Gwāliārī he lies buried in the same funeral garden (*rauẓa*).[51] Another graphic description of both the tombs, with a hagiographical account of Tānsen, is found in the account of James Forbes, who was at Gwalior in May 1785.[52]

The dispute about Tānsen's religion, raised by musicians and music-historians, is regularly revived on the occasion of the yearly celebration of his death (*'urs*) in Gwalior, marked by the offering of a new *chādar* (grave-sheet) on his tomb and followed by an important music festival. However a further discussion on the current controversy is beyond the scope of this paper.

As testified to by Mādhava's Sanskrit text as well as Indo-Persian sources, Tānsen was not merely a musician. He was also a poet-composer (*Vāggeyakāra*) whose lyrics were largely produced in *madhyadeśīya bhāṣā*, later known as Braj Bhāṣā.[53] The fact that Akbar patronized him and others like him suggests that the emperor was familiar with the vernacular languages in which the song-texts were composed, and could appreciate its imagery and aesthetic values, which were quite different from those of Persian poetry.[54]

Nath, 'The Tomb of Shaikh Muḥammad Ghauṭh at Gwalior', *Islamic Architecture and Culture in India*, Delhi, 1982, pp.79-86.

[50] See Mīrzā Khān, *Tuḥfat al-Hind*, Persian edn. by N.H. Anṣārī, Tehran, 1976, especially the fifth chapter on music (*dar 'ilm-i sangīt ya'ni 'ilm-i mūsīqī*), pp.322-456.

[51] Ibid., p.361.

[52] See James Forbes, *Oriental Memoirs Selected From a Series of Familiar Letters Written During Seventeen Years Residence in India*, 4 Vols. London, 1831; 2nd rev. edn., London, 1834; Reprint, with a new introduction by W.H. Siddiqi, Delhi, 1988, Vol.IV, pp.31-3.

[53] See *supra*, note 35. On Tānsen as a poet see also Suniti Kumar Chatterji, 'Tānsen as a Poet', *Acharya Śrī P.C. Ray Commemoration Volume*, Calcutta, 1932. pp.45-65; see also F. Delvoye, 'The Thematic Range of Dhrupad Songs attributed to Tānsen, Foremost Court-Musician of the Mughal Emperor Akbar', *Studies in South Asian Devotional Literature*, Research Papers 1988-91 presented at the Fifth Conference on Devotional Literature in New Indo-Aryan Languages, held at Paris-EFEO, 9-12 July 1991, eds., Alan W. Entwistle and Françoise Mallison, New Delhi, and Paris, 1994, pp.406-27.

[54] See F. Delvoye, 'Les chants dhrupad en langue braj des poetes-musiciens de

d) Other Court-musicians: Nothing much is known from other sources, about the musicians and poet-composers mentioned by Abū'l Faẓl. However, among other poet-composers patronized by Akbar, Bāz Bahādur, the ruler of Malwa, before his surrender to the Mughal emperor, is mentioned as 'a singer without rival' by Abū'l Faẓl. He is an interesting political figure, whose romantic story with Rūpmati, more than his actual contribution to music and dance, has inspired a number of legendary accounts and recent choreographic performances.[55] He deserves a more correct evaluation based on Indo-Persian sources, vernacular literature and iconographic documents. In a more unassuming manner, the court poet-musician Dhondhī, many of whose several lyrics are found in late-seventeenth-century repertoires, is also an important devotee- poet (*bhakta-kavi*) of the *Puṣṭi Sampradāy*, the Vaishnava sect of Vallabhāchārya, which had strong links with the Mughal court.[56]

4. The Indo-Persian Sources: An Overview

The information collected from Indo-Persian texts documents both the Persian and Indian forms of music patronized at Akbar's court. The geographical and cultural origins of many musicians imply diversified musical performance patronized by a single patron, who might have had his personal preferences set according to various occasions and his own frame of mind. The coexistence of the two main trends of art-music and the presence of some folk-oriented forms referred to by Abū'l Faẓl and later writers like Saīf Khān 'Faqīrullāh', as well as the mobility of court musicians, imply an interaction which is difficult to evaluate through the contemporary written sources available so far.

Was the court of Akbar then a forum for experimentation in a composite musical style, which has survived in today's Hindūstānī

l'Inde Moghole', *Litteratures medievales de l'Inde du Nord, contributions de Charlotte Vaudeville et de ses eleves*, ed., F. Mallison, Paris, 1991, pp.139-85.

55 See Ṣamṣām al-Daula Shāh Nawāz Khān, *Ma'āṣir al-Umarā*, *op.cit.*, Text, Vol.I, pp.387-91; Tr., Vol.I, pp.394-6.

56 See Alan W. Entwistle, *Braj, Centre of Krishṇa Pilgrimage*, Groningen, 1985, pp.157-62. See also Dīndayālū Gupta, *Aṣṭachāp aur Vallabha-Sampradāy ek gaveṣṇātmak adhyāyan*, 2 Vols., 2nd edn., Prayag, 1970, Vol.I, p.32.

music? Was there any 'Indo-Persian' musical practice by Persian and Indian musicians, encouraged by Akbar, who manifested elsewhere his interest in cultural experimentation by patronizing synthesis and innovation in architecture and painting ?

B. Vernacular Sources on Akbar as a Patron of Music

Literature produced in vernaculars, especially Braj Bhāshā, from the sixteenth century onwards in the region of Agra-Gwalior, or Madhyadesh, constitutes a rich corpus of written sources documenting socio-cultural aspects of Mughal history. Braj poetic and prose works concerning Akbar as a patron of music may be divided into two broad categories. The first set of sources are the Vaishnava hagiographical accounts (*vārtā* and similar literature), and the second the lyrics sung in art-music, in which Akbar appears as a patron or even as a poet-composer.

1. Evidence of Hagiographies

Parallel to its popular appeal, the Vaishnava and more precisely the Krishnaite 'renaissance' that emerged from the 'rediscovery' of the ancient sacred character of the Braj area, inspired a vast devotional literature still extant in the written and oral traditions.[57] The first category of texts relevant to the image of Akbar includes works in prose and verse composed from the seventeenth century onwards under the impulse of the Bhakti revival. Being hagiographical accounts of the great saints of the past or exemplary biographies of the founders and followers of various sectarian movements, these texts are meant to edify readers and a wider audience through the oral tradition. Vallabhāchārya (1479-1531), the founder of the *Puṣṭi Mārg*, 'the Way of fulfilment through Divine Grace (*Puṣṭi*)', and his son and successor, Viṭṭhalnāth (c. 1515-86), who organized the cult and expanded the sect, are preeminent among religious leaders who personally contributed to or inspired or patronized a rich literature composed mostly in Braj

[57] See Charlotte Vaudeville, 'Braj, Lost and Found', *Indo-Iranian Journal*, N° 18, 1976, pp.195-213.

Bhāshā.[58] The Vallabhite hagiologies are known as *vārtā*. The main *vārtā* are the *Caurāsī vaiṣṇavan kī vārtā* and the *Do sau bāvan vaiṣṇavan kī vārtā*, which describe respectively the legendary life of 84 disciples of Vallabha and of 252 disciples of Viṭṭhalnāth.[59] Both are texts for which no critical edition exists, and are ascribed to Gokulnāth (*c.*1551-1647?), a son of Viṭṭhalnāth, but Harīrāy, a disciple of Gokulnāth and the author of a commentary on the *vārtā (Bhāvaprakāśa)*, is often understood as being the original compiler.

Akbar often appears episodically, together with Tānsen. One recurring theme in these texts is as follows. A musician, often Tānsen, sings a composition of a Vaishnava saint-poet (*bhakta kavi*) at Akbar's court. Akbar expresses curiosity about the song's composer, and is taken to the saint-poet. There, the emperor is tested in some way, and a moral emerges from the episode. The theme has many variants, but shows the central image of Akbar as a patron of music - especially Indian vocal music - and a connoisseur of vernacular lyrics. It also emphasizes his curiosity and eclecticism regarding religious experience.

Some examples selected from Braj sources present various episodes illustrating the musical interest Akbar manifested for the songs composed by the saint-poets Sūrdās, Kumbhandās and Nanddās, and also by the ascetic musician Swāmī Haridās. In three cases Tānsen is shown as the 'middleman', who sang thecaptivating lyrics before Akbar.

a) Sūrdās: The biography of Sūrdās has inspired a good number of scholarly works, using sparse and controversial 'historical' elements, Vaishnava (Vallabhite as well as non-sectarian) hagiographical sources and the literary work attributed to him, which is in the process of being critically edited.[60] In the *Caurāsī vaiṣṇavan*

[58] See A.W. Entwistle, *op.cit.*, pp.141-3, 151-4 and *passim*. See also Richard Barz, *The Bhakti Sect of Vallabhācārya*, Faridabad, 1976, Reprint, New Delhi, 1992.

[59] See *Caurāsī vaiṣṇavan kī vārtā*, edited from a MS dated 1695, by Dvārkādās Parīkh, 2nd edn., Mathura, Śrī Bajrang Pustakalay, 1970. See two editions of *Do sau bāvan vaiṣṇavan kī vārtā*, by Brajbhūśan Śarmā and Dvarkadās Parīkh, 3 Vols., Kankroli, 1951-3 and by N.D. Śarmā Gaur, 2nd edn., Mathura, 1972.

[60] See Ch. Vaudeville, *Pastorales par Sour-dās*, Paris, N.R.F., Gallimard, 1971; Kenneth E. Bryant, *Poems to the Child-God*, Berkeley and Los Angeles, 1978, pp.VIII, 1-6; John Stratton Hawley, 'The Sectarian Logic of the *Sūr Dās kī vārtā*', *Bhakti in Current Research*, 1979-82, ed. M. Thiel-Horstmann, Berlin, 1983, pp.157-69 and by the same author, *Sūr Dās: Poet, Singer, Saint*, Seattle, 1984, and Delhi, 1984.

kī vārtā, the Sūrdās his meeting with Vallabhācārya and, at his Gurū's instance, the exclusive dedication of his poetical work to the *Puṣṭi Mārg*, which is obviously a later sectarian appropriation. The third section (*prāsaṁg*) of the *vārtā* stresses the large number of lyrics composed by Sūrdās which were learnt and sung by everybody. The following incident, involving Akbar and Tānsen, is summarized here from Richard Barz's translation.[61] 'Once Akbar heard a lyric (*pad*) composed by Sūrdās and sung by Tānsen. The emperor immediately gave orders to summon Sūrdās who used to sing for Shrī Nāthjī on Govardhan Hill in Braj. After some difficulties, the devotee-poet was brought to Akbar who respectfully asked him to sing some of his compositions in honour of Vishṇu, which he greatly appreciated.[62] Then the emperor provoked Sūrdās by asking him to sing his glory. Sūrdās sang a *pad*, but it was in praise of Krishṇa and not of Akbar.[63] Impressed by the poet's spirituality, Akbar questioned him about the dual meaning of a certain verse, and even wanted to give him a reward which was however bluntly refused. Sūrdās then told him not to try to meet him again'. One episode dilates further on Akbar's interest, not only in the performing aspect of music, but also in the lyrics sung by his court-musicians. The emperor offered gold and silver coins for lyrics composed by Sūrdās and read them in their Persian translation.

The sectarian account is eloquent as an image of the emperor Akbar and his desire for knowledge about Hindu culture. It is interesting to note the mention of Akbar getting Sūrdās's compositions translated into Persian, though the prior account makes it clear that the emperor could understand instantly the meaning of the lyric which was sung for him by Sūrdās and to which he reacted on the spot.

b) Kumbhandās: The *vārtā* of Kumbhandās,[64] a saint-poet disciple

[61] See the *vārtā* of Sūrdās in *Caurāsī vaiṣṇavan kī vārtā*, edn. cit., N° 81, pp.400-41, especially pp.417-19 and the English translation by R. Barz, *op.cit.*, pp.105-39, especially pp.121-3.

[62] See *Caurāsī vaiṣṇavan kī vārtā*, edn. cit., pp.414-15; R. Barz, *op.cit.*, pp.120-1, does not give the translation of the *pada* '*yaha saba jāno bhakta ke lacchana*', in *rāga* Nat.

[63] See *Caurāsī vaiṣṇavan kī vārtā*, edn. cit., p.417; R. Barz, *op.cit.*, p.121, does not give the translation of the *pada* '*nāhina rahyo mana meṁ ṭhaura*' in *rāga* Kedāro.

[64] See the *vārtā* of Kumbhandās in *Caurāsī vaiṣṇavan kī vārtā*, edn. cit., pp.476-90; Tr. pp.165-206.

of Vallabha, in the *Caurāsī vaiṣṇavan kī vārtā* presents another account of Akbar and a musician (*kalāvat*) who is not named, and who sang a composition by Kumbhandās to the emperor at Fatehpur Sikri. The devotee poet was pressed by Akbar's men to come to the court, which he did - on foot as he refused to travel by the vehicle sent by the emperor - very reluctantly and cursing himself for leaving his familiar Braj and having come to hell (*naraka*). Finally Kumbhandās composed a *pada* which he sang to Akbar:

Now I must pay homage to one whose very face brings sorrow; Kumbhanadāsa says, 'without Lāla Giridhara this whole palace is only a sham'.[65] First Akbar was angry and then he realised Kumbhandās's devotion and said to the saint: 'Bābā Shāhib, I will carry out any order that you deign to give me'. Kumbhandās replied, 'from this day on, you must never call me here again'... Upon hearing Kumbhanadās's words, Akbar dismissed him.[66]

Other references to Akbar's interest in music are found in some *vārtā* of the *Do sau bāvan vaiṣṇavan kī vārtā*, which mention Tānsen. Another incident is recorded in the *vārtā* of Govindsvāmī: Akbar who heard of Govindsvāmī came in disguise to listen to his music. Filled with wonder the emperor could not repress an appreciative '*vahvavahva*' (*sic*) (Wāh! Wāh!), which made Govindsvāmī furious. As a consequence, the musician decided not to sing *rāga* Bhairav any more, as it had been polluted![67]

c) Nanddās: Like Sūrdās, the great poet Nanddās is one of the *Aṣṭachāp* or 'Eight Seals', the main saint-poets of the Vallabhita sect. His *vārtā* is presented in the *Do sau bāvan vaiṣṇavan kī vārtā*, and also with important variants in the *Aṣṭachāp kī vārtā*, a less known Vallabhite hagiology.[68] In one episode of the *Aṣṭachāp kī vārtā*, Tānsen sings a beautiful *kīrtān* (*sic*) of Nanddās to Akbar who is so impressed by the description of Krishṇa in the *rās* dance that he is keen to meet its author, who is summoned to the court by Bīrbal. When, finally, Akbar meets Nanddās in Mānasī Gaṅgā,

[65] Ibid., *prāsaṁg 3*, pp.486-90; Tr., pp.176-7.

[66] Ibid.

[67] See the vārtā of Govindsvāmī Sanoḍiyā Brahman, in *Do sau bāvan vaiṣṇavan kī vārtā*, *op.cit* (edn. N.D. Śarmā Gaur, Mathura), pp.1-11, especially the *prāsaṁg 5*, pp.8-9.

[68] See *Do sau bāvan vaiṣṇavan kī vārtā*, *op.cit*. (edn. B. Śarmā and D. Parīkh, Kankroli), Vol.III, pp.356 ff.; *Aṣṭachāp kī vārtā*, edition (based on two MSS dated 1640 and 1695) by K.M. Sastri, Kankroli, 1952, pp.525-92.

he asks him the meaning of a certain line of the poem, which the poet is reluctant to give; instead he suggests to the emperor that he ask a particular woman in his court; leaving Bīrbal with Tānsen, Akbar goes back to the court and asks the woman, who faints and dies instantly. Then Akbar runs back to Nanddās, who at once 'left his body and entered the divine play (*līlā*)'. Bīrbal explains to the puzzled emperor that both as true devotees had to keep the meaning secret and instead preferred to die.[69]

d) Svāmī Haridās: In the late hagiographical literature from the eighteenth century onwards, and in today's oral tradition of musicians and popular belief, the famous saint-musician Svāmī Haridās of Vrindaban is often presented as the Gurū of Tānsen. His poetical work is well known but many aspects of his biography are still obscure; these questions cannot be gone into here.[70]

i. Hagiographic Evidence: The first account mentioning Tānsen, Akbar and Svāmī Haridās seems to be the *Pad-prāsaṁg-mālā* attributed to Nāgaridās (1699–1764), who, as Savant Siṁh, was the former ruler of Kishangarh (from 1744), and retired to Vrindaban in 1757, where he was known as 'Nāgaridās'.[71] The *Pad- prāsaṁg-mālā* is not dated but is extant in various manuscripts, one of which is dated *saṁvat* 1748 (AD 1691). The account starts with Akbar's query to Tānsen on who taught him and who could sing better than him. Tānsen answered that he was the disciple in vocal music of a Vaishnava by the name of 'Haridās-jū' who lived in Vrindaban. As in the previous stories, Akbar and Tānsen go immediately to meet 'Swāmījī' in Vrindaban. Tānsen sings first and then requests the 'Mahārāj' to sing something. 'Śrī Haridās-jū starts with *rāgā* Malār and though it is the month of Caitra-Vaiśākh (March-May), clouds gather and peacocks start singing.' Then he begins singing a *bisṇupada*, 'the season is such that peacocks

[69] See *Aṣṭachāp kī vārtā*, *op. cit.*, pp.587-92.

[70] Among many publications on Svāmī Haridās, see Richard Dale Haynes, Svāmī Haridās and the Haridāsī Sampradāy, Ph.D. Dissertation in South Asia Regional Studies, University of Pennsylvania, Philadelphia, 1974; Gopal Datta, *Svāmī Haridāsjī kā Sampradāy aur uskā vānī sāhitya*, New Delhi, 1977, and Chail Bihari Upādhyāya, *Haridās tatva jijñāsā, aitihāsik, sāhityik sākṣyoṁ ke ādhār par*, Vrindaban, Manipara, 1983.

[71] On Nāgarīdās and his work, see R.S. McGregor, *Hindī Literature from its Beginnings to the Nineteenth Century*, Wiesbaden, 1984, pp.158-9 and 210 (description of *Pad-prāsaṁg-mālā*); see also A.W. Entwistle, *op.cit.*, pp.270-1 and R.D., Haynes, *op.cit.*, pp.102-8.

go on singing,' which he has just composed, and instantly it starts raining.[72] This brief anecdote follows the pattern of the Vallabhite accounts with an added magic dimension given by the power of Svāmī Haridās's music.

In the *Nijmat Siddhānt*, attributed to Kiśordās (1763?), Tānsen is mentioned as a disciple of Svāmī Haridās, who in this text is related to the Nimbarka sect.[73] Tānsen appears in one episode - still famous today - in which he sings the *rāga* Dīpak, whose burning effect, if performed perfectly, is well known, and which eventually happens to Tānsen. The incident occurs in this version at the court of Rāmachandra Baghela (and not at the Mughal court, as in modern versions). Rāmachandra could not see any remedy, other than getting someone to sing *rāga* Mālār as an antidote to the burning, but no musician of the court could sing it properly. Looking for such a singer, Tānsen started for Orcha, where a woman diagnosed his 'illness', and taught him *rāga* Mālār. Following her suggestion, Tānsen went to Vrindaban, where he learned the same *rāga* from 'Svāmīji' (i.e. Svāmī Haridās, on whom the text is focused) and became his devotee (*dās*). From there he came to Agra, where Akbar heard about him and invited him to sing. Then Akbar asked him why he could not sing as well as Svāmī Haridās. Tānsen answered that he was singing for the lord of the world, and Svāmī Haridās was singing for himself.[74] Modern versions would give a more dignified answer, suggesting that God was Svāmī Haridās's patron.[75]

A second episode goes that one day Akbar rewarded Tānsen for his virtuosity by giving him two costly pearls. Later on the emperor became furious when he heard that Tānsen had given them away to two servants. Akbar asked for them back. Tānsen went to Rāmachandra Baghela for help. The king saved him by presenting him with a fan inlaid with pearls, the value of which

[72] See *Pad-prasaṁg-mālā*, attributed to Nāgarīdās, edited by K. Gupta, *Nāgarīdās granthāvalī*, 2 Vols. Varanasi, 1965.

[73] On Kiśordas and *Nijmat Siddhānt*, see R.S. McGregor, *op.cit.*, p.165 and A.W. Entwistle, *op.cit.*, pp.156 and 194. *Nijmat Siddhānt* has been published by the Taṭṭī Sthān (the sect of Svāmī Haridās), 4 Vols., Vrindaban, 1911-15.

[74] See *Nijmat Siddhānt*, *op.cit.*, *Madhya khāṇḍ*, pp.89-91. Summary from the text given in Ch.B. Upādhyāya, *op.cit.*, p.13-14. The summary is mine.

[75] A different version of this legend is given (without reference) by K. Khandalavala and M. Chandra, eds., 'A Contemporary Portrait of Tānsen', *Lalit Kalā*, Nos 1-2 (April 1955-March 1956), p.15.

was three hundred times that of Akbar's gift. Rāmachandra also requested Tānsen to greet Swāmī Haridās on his behalf. Akbar was filled with wonder. Later on Tānsen went to Vrindaban to convey Rāmachandra's greetings, etc.[76]

A similar spirit animates the *Bhaktasindhu* of Lakṣman Dās, a later work in Braj, the original text of which is lost, but which has been translated into English by F.S. Growse (1882).[77] The translation of the *Bhaktasindhu* constitutes the main part of the chapter on Svāmī Haridās. Based on some earlier hagiologies, the text provides a few 'new' elements on the Vaishnava version of the Akbar-Tānsen-Haridās relationship.[78]

Late hagiographical literature inspiring a rich oral tradition, provides some colourful elements which help us follow the development of Tānsen as a legendary personage. In the process the image of Akbar as a patron of Indian music is also gilded.

However, some nineteenth-century texts in Hindī on music based on hagiologies and the oral tradition present derogatory accounts of Mughal musicians, hence of the low standard of music patronized by Akbar. One strikīng example is the *Nād-binod-graṁth* of Pannālāl Gosvāmī, published in Delhi in 1896.[79] One of the first works in Hindi on the theory of music and instrumental practice, with hundreds of lyrics illustrating rāga, this book was commissioned by Śrī Kisor Siddhajī, Commander-in-Chief of the Rājā of Marwar. Eight pages of the introduction deal with Svāmī Haridās.[80]

References to Gosvāmī's account are many, often without acknowledgement, in later secondary sources and manuals on music and musicology recommended to students.[81] Akbar is always mentioned in twentieth-century writings about Svāmī Haridās. Recent articles and pamphlets published for the celebrations of the

[76] See *Nijmat Siddhānt*, *op.cit.*, *Madhya khāṇḍ*, 96-9.

[77] See F.S. Growse, *Mathura: A District Memoir* (1882), Reprint of the 3rd rev. edn. (1883), Ahmedabad, 1978, pp.219-20.

[78] See also R.D. Haynes, *op.cit.*, pp.55-63.

[79] See Pannālāl Gosvāmī, *Nād-binod-graṁth*, Delhi, 1896.

[80] Ibid., pp.43-50.

[81] One example in which the *Nād-binod-graṁth* is duly mentioned is the first volume of the *Saṁgīt-Kāvya-sudhā* (Ahmedabad, 1937), a book on vocal music in Gujarati. The authors C.Ch. Nāyak and R.C. Nāyak give a brief biography of Svāmī Haridās, pp.73-4, followed by a notice of Tānsen, pp.74-7. In both cases, they refer by name to the *Nād-binod-graṁth* of Pannālāl Gosvāmī.

ii. Some Iconographic Evidence: Iconography also 'confirms' the meeting of Akbar, Tānsen and Svāmī Haridās described in late vernacular sources. A series of paintings representing the 'event' seem to have been inspired by a famous miniature painting produced in Kishangarh about 1760, displayed in the National Museum, New Delhi.[83] In Karl Khandalavala and Moti Chandra's words:

> The scene is laid in a beautiful landscape with flowering trees swarming with buds. On the right, Haridās, a lean and thin person with clean shaven head, is playing on a *vīṇā*. On the left, Tānsen is seated in Persian fashion and behind him stands Akbar with folded hands. The black clouds overcast the sky. The painting breathes an atmosphere of pious quietude providing a proper background to the grand music of the master and his disciple. Tānsen is depicted as a younger man than seen in the National Museum portrait, but the facial resemblance is unmistakable.[84]

K. Khandalavala and M. Chandra refer to a standing portrait of Tānsen (*c*.1585-90) in the National Museum, New Delhi, which shows the musician in his old age, but with similar features, like a sharp nose and a dark complexion.[85] Rather improbably, Akbar looks older than the other figures. Inscriptions in Devanāgarī identifythe three personages as 'Svāmī Haridāsajī', 'Mīyā Tānase-mina', and 'Pātasāha Akabara'. It is interesting to note that this

[82] See Ācārya Śrīgopal Gosvāmī, 'Rāsikh-sakhī-Sampradāyācārya, Śrī Svāmī Haridās', *Indian Philosophy and Culture Quarterly Journal of the Institute of Oriental Philosophy*, Vrindaban, Vol.XIX, N° 3, Sept. 1974, pp.183-94.

[83] The painting N° 48-14/61 has been often reproduced; see for instance K. Khandalavala and M. Chandra, *op.cit.*, Plate I, fig.1, described p.20; see also G. Datta, *op.cit.*, pp.104-8 and K. Chaitanya, *A History of Indian Painting, Manuscript Moghul and Deccani Tradition*, New Delhi, 1979, N° 47 (though the author dates it back to the period of Akbar). See also F. Brunel, *The Splendour of Indian Miniatures*, bilingual edn., Boulogne and New Delhi, nd, Plate 55 (in double page), though surprisingly the author did not identify the characters (precisely named) of such a celebrated painting and describes (p.151) the scene as 'The Prince's music lesson', ignoring the figure of Akbar. See also some comments by Rāy Ānand Kṛṣṇa, 'Svar Samrāt Tānsen kī śabīheṁ', *Dhrupad Annual*, Vol. III, 1988, pp.3 and 5 (English Summary, pp.7-8 and 9). The painting could have been copied from two similar miniatures probably from the early seventeenth century (?) kept in the Vrindaban Research Institute, see C.B. Gupta, 'A Note on the Preservation of Miniature Paintings of VRI (Vrindavan Research Institute)', *Journal of the Vrindavan Research Institute*, Vol.II, Sept. 1977, pp.57-61.

[84] See K. Khandalavala and M. Chandra, *op.cit.*, p.20. The instrument played by Svāmī Haridās is not a *vīṇā* but a drone-instrument (*tampūrā*).

[85] See the painting N° 50.14/28 in the National Museum, New Delhi, described in K. Khandalavala and M. Chandra, *op.cit.*, p.16 and reproduced in colour, Plate A.

painting is contemporary to the reign of Sāvant Siṁh, the kīng of Kishangarh, from 1744 till his 'spiritual retirement' in Vrindaban in 1757. Sāvant Siṁh patronized the famous painter Nihal Chand, author of 'The Barge of Love', also conserved in the National Museum, New Delhi.

The same subject has been painted many times and reproduced in recent publications, indicating the popularity of the theme, which is still commented upon in the written and oral tradition.[86]

e) The Hagiographical Sources: an Overview: Indo-Persian sources on music and musicians contemporary to Akbar or slightly later, do not mention any link between Akbar and Svāmī Haridās. Only later sectarian literature refers to the emperor's meeting with the saint-musician, through Tānsen (represented as a performer and not as a poet-composer-singer), illustrated by some fictitious 'iconographic evidence'. The most unlikely meeting between the three seems to stand as one more multi-faceted illustration of the traditional archetypal visit kings pay to saints, here under the impulse of some mystical verses sung in wonderful music, with all its stylized context: precipitate travel, unusual disguise, and fabulous imperial rewards rejected by the saint or even provokīng angry reactions, which only holy men can afford to display in front of mighty rulers! Such apocryphal data do not constitute historical evidence, but contribute to the composite 'image' of an unconventional ruler.[87]

2. Akbar as a Patron of Music in Braj Lyrics

Was Akbar himself a poet in Persian and Hindi? Or was he familiar enough with the Indian vernacular poetical language to appreciate the lyrics sung by his Indian court-musicians? Abū'l Faẓl says:

> The inspired nature of his Majesty is strongly drawn to the composing of Hindi and Persian poetry and is critical and hair-splitting in the niceties of poetic diction. Among books of poetry, he recites off-hand the Maulavi's Maṣnavī [of Rūmī] and the Dīwān of the 'mystic tongue' [Hāfiẓ], and takes delight in their verities and beauties... He has also strung glorious thoughts in the Hindi language, which may be regarded

[86] See references to other paintings on this theme in Delvoye, D. Litt. Thesis, *op.cit.*, pp.227-9.

[87] A more detailed and analytical study on the appropriation of Tānsen by

as masterpieces in this kind.[88]

Akbar's patronage of great Persian poets is well known,[89] and the protection he extended to poets composing in vernacular languages is also well attested.[90] Nevertheless his own proficiency as a poet in the vernacular language is hard to confirm. A number of metrical and unmetrical poems are found with the name of Akbar, given as a 'signature' or mentioned as the addressee, found in manuscript, lithographic and printed collections of lyrics.[91] Their authenticity is however doubtful and as difficult to establish as for other poets and poet-composers whose independent poems (*muktaka*) or lyrics (*geya pada*) are scattered in various collections.[92]

Jahāngīr mentions in his Memoirs that L'al Kalāwant, who, from his childhood grew up in the service of Akbar, 'had taught him every breathing and sound that appertains to the Hindī language...'[93] One may presume that L'al Kalāwant, being a singer, must have taught Akbar some poetical form of 'Hindī', or more precisely Braj, in which most of the lyrics sung in the vocal art-music of the period were composed.[94] Akbar must have benefited from this linguistic and probably literary training, for understanding the poetry read out to him by his close court-poets such as Kavi Gaṅg and 'Abdu-Raḥīm Khān-i Khānān, and sung by his court vocalists, among whom Tānsen was the most illustrious.

In lyric anthologies and court-musicians' repertoires of the seventeenth-eighteenth centuries, Tānsen is particularly prominent,

---

Vaishnava sectarian traditions is in preparation by the present author.

[88] See Abū'l Faẓl, *AN*, Text, Vol.I, p.271; Tr., Vol.I, p.520.

[89] See M. 'Abdu'l Ghanī, *A History of Persian Language and Literature at the Mughal Court, with a Brief Survey of the Growth of Urdu Language*, Allahabad, 1930; Reprint, Westmead, 1972, Part III.

[90] See R.S. McGregor, *op.cit*, pp.118-22; see also Sarayu Prasād Agravāl, *Akbarī darbār ke Hindi kavi*, Lucknow, 1950.

[91] For further bibliographical references, see for instance R.S. McGregor, *op.cit.*, pp.120-1.

[92] See Prem Latā Śarmā, 'Dhrupad ke padoṁ meṁ 'chāp' aur usse udbhūt samasyāeṁ', *Dhrupad Annual* (henceforth *DA*) (Varanasi), Vol.II, 1987, pp.84-98 and the Summary in English, 'Signature in Dhrupad Song-Texts and the Problems Arising Therefrom', pp.99-101. See also F. Delvoye, 'Problems and Prospects of Critical Studies of Lyrical Texts', *Saṁgīt meṁ anusandhān kī samasyāeṁ aur kṣetra - Problems & Areas of Research in Music*, ed. S. Chaudhary, Ajmer, 1988, pp.149-80, especially pp.161-3.

[93] See Jahāngīr, *Tūzuk-i Jahāngīrī*, *op.cit.*, Tr., Part I, p.150.

[94] See Suniti Kumar Chatterjee, *Indo-Aryan and Hindi*, Calcutta, Firma K.L. Mukhopadhyay, 2nd rev. and enlarged edn. 1960, p.200: '...if any Indo-Aryan language

which is an indication of his poetical talent, already noticed by Indo-Persian writers who mentioned him.[95]

The fact that Tānsen was the favourite musician of Akbar and was known as a Dhrupad composer and performer implies the emperor's interest in that particular form of art-music. Dhrupad was the main genre of vocal music in the sixteenth century;[96] lyrics meant to be sung in that genre were generally composed in Braj by poet-composers (*Vāggeyakāra*) who used to be court-singers or were attached to a Vaishnava temple or both.[97] Transmitted by means of oral tradition and occasionally compiled in lyric anthologies and court-musicians' repertoires extant even today, *dhrupad* songs remain a rich literary source for the cultural history of medieval India.[98]

Dhrupad is presented in Abū'l Faẓl's survey of Indian Music, as the pre-eminent vocal form of the region of Agra, Gwalior and Bari. After giving a brief history of its origin at the court of Rājā Mān Singh Tomar of Gwalior (r. 1486–1516), Abū'l Faẓl describes Dhrupad as:

.... a form [of singing] liked by the common man and favoured by the elite..... Dhrupad is made up of four rhyming lines and the equality of their words and syllables is not indispensable. It deals with the magic of love and the wondrous affairs of the heart.[99]

---

could be labelled as a *Bādšāhī Bolī* in North India, it was certainly Braj bhākhā'.

[95] See F. Delvoye, D. Litt. Thesis, *op.cit.*, *passim*.

[96] Ibid., See K.C. Bṛhaspati, *Dhruvapada aur uskā vikās*, Patna, 1976 and Indu Rāma Śrīvastava, *Dhrupada, A Study of its Origin, Historical Development, Structure and Present State*, Delhi, 1980. For bibliographical references on Dhrupad, see F. Delvoye, 'Bibliography on Dhrupad', *DA*, Vol.I, 1986, pp.95-115; *DA*, Vol.II, 1987, pp.119-21; *DA*, Vol.III, 1988, pp.98-102; *DA*, Vol.IV, 1989, pp.105-7; *DA*, Vol.V, 1990, pp.117-20; *DA*, Vol.VI, 1991, pp.30-3; *DA*, Vol.VII, 1992, pp.112-15; *DA*, Vol.VIII, 1993, pp.86-90; *DA*, Vol.IX, 1994, pp.56-60 and F. Delvoye, '*Les chants dhrupad en langue braj...*', *op.cit.*, pp.140-1, 180-5.

[97] See Campaklāl Chabīldās Nāyak, *Aṣṭachāpīya Bhakti Saṁgīt (Havelī Saṁgīt), Udbhav aur Vikās*, Ahmedabad, Vol.I, 1983, Vol.II, 1985. Besides the established association between Akbar's court-musicians and the Vaishnava music tradition, a link between court-music and the Ṣūfī music (*samā'*) performed in *dargāhs* by professional musicians is indicated by the *Haqā'iq Hindī* (1566) of Mīr 'Abdul Wāḥid Bilgrāmī, ed. and tr. into Hindī by S.A.A. Rizvi, Varanasi, 1957. Scattered information found in Indo-Persian texts corroborate this relationship, which is worth further investigation.

[98] See F. Delvoye, 'La transmission des repertoires dans la musique vocale Hindūstānī. L'exemple des chants *dhrupad* attribues a Tānsen, premier musicien de la cour d'Akbar', *Purusartha* (Paris) (forthcoming).

[99] See Abū'l Faẓl, *Ā'īn*, Text, Vol.II, p.138; Tr., Vol.III, pp.265-6. My translation.

Besides numerous temple lyric compilations (*padāvalī* and *pad-saṅgrah*) from the late sixteenth century, used in the Vaishnava liturgy, which include *dhrupad* songs, court-musicians' repertoires constitute the major sources of lyrics which should be considered as a valid literary source for medieval cultural history. Sometimes *dhrupad* songs were used to illustrate theoretical treatises like the late-seventeenth-century musicological texts in Sanskrit of Bhāvabhaṭṭa, at the court of Rājā Anūp Singh of Bikaner (r.1669–98), an officer of Aurangzeb known for his culture and artistic patronage.[100] Bhāvabhaṭṭa illustrates his exposition of many *rāgas* with hundreds of compositions in vernacular languages, probably gathered from his father, Janardhana Bhaṭṭa, a court-musician of Shāh Jahān and Aurangzeb.[101]

Many compositions found in repertoires compiled or even patronized by royal courts include the name of a ruler, such as Sulṭān 'Alāal-dīn, Sulṭān Salīm, Shāh Bahādur, Bāz Bahādur, Rājā Rām, Akbar, Jahāngīr, Shāh Jahān, Aurangzeb, etc., Akbar being the best represented.[102]

Devotional and secular lyrics composed in vernacular languages often bear the 'signature'(*bhanitā* or *chāp*) of the presumed author. Similarly, in many *dhrupad* song-texts, which are generally non-metrical compositions noted down or memorized through the oral tradition, the fourth line (*ābhoga*) includes the 'signature' of a poet-musician. Nevertheless such mention is hardly a guarantee of the authorship, a point which has been ignored by most of the scholars who have published hundreds of these song-texts under one author's name.[103]

In the course of collecting and editing a large number of such lyrics with the *chāp* of Tānsen, I have found many where Akbar

[100] On Mahārājā Anūp Singh, see P.W. Powlett, *Gazetteer of the Bikaner State (1874)*, Reprint, Bikaner, 1908, 2nd Reprint, 1932, pp.38-45; Gaurishankar Hirachand Ojha, *The History of Rajputana*, Vol.V, Part 1, *History of the Bikaner State*, Ajmer, 1939, pp.253-91; Dīnānāth Khatrī, *Bīkāner rājya kā sankṣipta itihās*, Bikaner, 1978, pp.47-52; Hermann Goetz, *The Art and Architecture of Bīkāner State*, Oxford, Bruno Cassirer (for the Government of Bikaner State and the Royal India and Pakistan Society), 1950, *passim*.

[101] On Bhāvabhaṭṭa see Ādināth Upādhyāy, 'Bhavabhaṭṭa ke granth aur un-meṁ dhruvapada' *DA*, Vol.I, 1986, pp.69-92; see also G.H. Ojha, *op.cit.*, p.285 and H. Goetz, *op.cit.*, p.47.

[102] See also some examples of *dhrupads* addressed to Akbar on various subjects, given with the text in Braj and the translation into French, in F. Delvoye, 'Les chants *dhrupad* en langue Braj...', *op.cit.*, pp.176-9.

[103] See *supra*, note 92.

appears as the patron, or is referred to by name or at times can even appear as himself being the poet-composer (that is, the *chāp* being of Akbar and not of Tānsen), as has been already noted above.[104] Like other *dhrupad* texts composed in honour of kings, these too are often mediocre from the literary point of view.

Conclusion

Taking all these diverse materials, we can attempt to reconstruct one aspect of Akbar's life, but also one facet of the legend of Akbar for posterity. In medieval Indian history the rulers who encouraged belles-lettres, architecture, painting and performing arts like music and dance, of both Indo-Persian and Indian inspiration, Akbar represents the archetype of the perfect patron, whose endless curiosity appealed to the imagination of artists from various walks of life. Among them, talented poet-composers responded in plentiful vernacular lyrics compiled in repertoires which are the extant artifacts of their prolific creativity, enduring in the memory of living musicians. For the most gifted ones, the extraordinary power of their music and their close association with the emperor carved out a place for them in the cultural history of India.

[104] See for instance the remarks in the *Ma'āṣir al-Umarā*, *op.cit.*, Text, Vol.II, pp.134-8; Tr. Vol.II, pp.581-4.

15

The Perception of India in Akbar and Abu'l Fazl

M. ATHAR ALI

For much more than a century, the status of India as a concept has repeatedly been under discussion. Is it really just a 'geographical expression', a half-ring of high mountain ranges guarding it in the north, and the ocean embracing the rest of it as an inverted cone in the south? Its limits formed the ideal 'scientific frontiers' for the British Indian empire and suggested a continued tradition of ambitions of supremacy over land enclosed by them, which the Raj claimed consciously to be its inheritance. Whether there was still anything beyond a territory imagined for political convenience as India, was something on which spokesmen of British imperialism allowed themselves to be of two minds. V.A. Smith would assert,[1] while the Simon Commission would deny,[2] a 'unity in diversity'. More recently, partly under the influence of works like Anderson's *Imagined Communities*,[3] there has been a criticism among subaltern and/or post-modern circles of the concept of the Indian nation. As Professor Partha Chatterji tells us, 'the very singularity of the idea of a national history of India' tends to divide 'Indians' further[4] – though one naturally wonders where these 'Indians' could have arisen from, if there was no India.

There should be no two opinions, therefore, that the case for the study of a history of the concept of India is strong, both for those who assert its present or past reality, as did the spokesmen of the National Movement, and for those who deny it in the footsteps of Lord Simon. To this study, the present paper, touching on the perception of India in the minds of Akbar and his advisors – admittedly a most elite group – is a modest contribution.

[1] *Oxford History of India*, London, 1919, pp.ix-x.

[2] See the critique of its views in R.P. Dutt, *India Today*, Bombay, 1947, pp.237-39.

[3] Benedict Anderson, *Imagined Communities: Reflections on the Origin and Spread of Nationalism*, London, 1983.

[4] *Subaltern Studies*, VIII, New Delhi, 1994, p.49.

One has to begin with, the Arabic-Persian tradition in which Akbar's background especially lay.India had two names, the Arabic 'Hind' from Ancient Iranian 'Hindu' (the Avestan variant of Vedic 'Sindhu'), whence the Greek 'India' also came; and the late Iranian 'Hindostān', created by the Iranian tendency of adding '-stān' as a suffix to territorial names (Tukhāristān, Sijistān, Gurjistān, etc.). As outsiders, the Iranians were prone to consider India to cover all territory east of the Indus, whence the two names. In the eleventh century the scientist Abū Raiḥān al-Bīrūnī, in his celebrated *Kitāb al-Hind* (1035) was able to offer a precise geographical definition of the country of al-Hind: 'limited in the south by the above mentioned Indian ocean, and on all three other sides by the lofty mountains, the waters of which flow down to it.'[5] By his study of Sanskrit scientific and sacred texts, al-Bīrūnī is aware also of a problem in the perception of the territory. The inhabitable world extending southwards from Himavant is Bhārata-varsha, which is the centre of Jambu-dvipa. Al-Bīrūnī says that there was an assumption that Bhārata-varsha comprises the entire inhabitable world, while in actual fact, the parts named and ascribed to it are located in al-Hind alone.[6] To al-Bīrūnī, the 'Hindus' as inhabitants of this country, had an identifiable single higher culture, with Sanskrit as its language, which he made it his business to study and interpret, critically and without bias. He thus saw a firm cultural unity, reflected in an arrogant insularity on the part of the Hindus, which he regretted characteristically on account of the obstruction it raised to the study of their culture by an outsider.[7]

Once the Ghorian conquest and the establishment of the Sultanate, had implanted over a large part of India another culture in parallel existence with the Brahmanical, the clear-cut all-exclusive identification of the Brahmanical culture and India, so natural for al-Bīrūnī, could no longer be sustained. Yet the concept of Hindostān for the same limits as in al-Bīrūnī survived, sometimes with culturally neutral qualities. This is most visible in 'Iṣāmī's ode to India (1350), which begins:

Blessed the splendour of the country of Hindostān,
For Heaven itself is envious of this scented garden.

[5] Edward C. Sachau (tr.), *Alberuni's India*, London, 1910, I, p.198.
[6] Ibid., I, pp.294-98. [7] Ibid., I, pp.22-24.

What is acclaimed in this ode is its climate, its rivers, its fertility, its life-strengthening environment, attracting all immigrants to settle in it. Cultural specifity plays no part here.[8] In fact, 'Iṣāmī cearly uses the word '*Hindīān*' or 'Hindīs' for natives of India, including Muslims,[9] so that the distinction between 'Hindūs' as followers of a religion and 'Hindīs' as Indians was by now established.

But already in 1318 Amīr Khusrau in his metrical work *Nuh Sipihr* found other more profound qualities beyond these purely natural or physical ones, to attribute to India. He stridently proclaimed his patriotism: 'Hind was the land of his birth, where he lived, his native place'; 'the love of one's native land (*waṭan*) is part of one's faith (*īmān*)'.[10] He too thought that India (for which he uses the name 'Hind' throughout) was paradise-like in the fertility of its soil and pleasant climate.[11] To this he adds the achievements of Hindu learning and beliefs. Like Greece (Rūm), the Hindūs had sciences, and their higher minds believe in one God.[12] Here is an echo from al-Bīrūnī. But then Amīr Khusrau begins to speak in the first person plural. We, the 'people of Hind', are able to speak foreign languages; but the Chinese, Mongols, Turks, and Arabs are unable to speak 'our Hindī tongue'.[13] Indians do not go to other countries to seek knowledge; others have to come here.[14] India has given the world the numerals, the *Panchatantra* tales, and chess.[15] He goes on to associate India with certain languages that had currency in it. 'The Ghorians and Turks' had brought with them Persian, which was now learnt by all levels of people; then there were the regional languages (*Hindawī*'s), of which Khusrau lists twelve (including Tamil, and Kannada), and, finally, Sanskrit, the language of the learned Brahmans.[16] He takes special pride in this wealth of languages. Clearly, with Khusrau, India has an entity that is not defined merely by Brahmanical high culture, though it is an essential part of it. Already, we see a tendency

[8] 'Isami, *Futūhu's-Salātīn*, ed. A.S. Usha, Madras, 1948, pp.604-5. 'Iṣāmī was writing at Daulatabad in the Deccan and thus understood the whole of India by 'Hindostān'.

[9] Ibid., p.465. 'Iṣāmī is here speaking of Muḥammad Tughluq's army confronting the Mongol troops of Tarmāshīrīn.

[10] *Nuh Sipihr*, ed. Mohammad Wahid Mizra, London, 1950, p.150.

[11] Ibid., pp.151-61.

[12] Ibid., pp.162-66.

[13] Ibid., pp.166-67.

[14] Ibid., pp.167-68.

[15] Ibid., pp.168-170.

to envision India as a country with a composite culture specific to itself, to which a member of a Turkish Muslim immigrant family like Amīr Khusrau can proudly proclaim his allegiance, and which has adopted Persian as one of its own languages.

A noteworthy development which was bound to affect the perception of India as a country with cultural and social institutions of its own, was the growth of a Muslim community within India, distinct from the Muslim communities of other countries. The orthodox theologian and historian 'Abdu'l Qādir Badāūnī, in his work on ethics written in 1590-91, acknowledges with manifest regret that marriages for limited periods and speedy divorces (by the husband) are permitted by Muslim law and sanctified by precedent, but then comments: 'What good custom have the people of India that they shun this practice and regard it (divorce) as the worst word of abuse, so much so that if some one is called '*ṭalāqī*' (divorcer), he, out of folly, would be ready to fight to death'.[17] Clearly, Badāūnī thought that Muslims in India had a way of life different from Muslims of other countries, one example of it being their thinking very ill of any one divorcing his wife. Whether this outlook was influenced by the absolute permanence of marriage in Hindu law cannot be said for certain; but the recognised existence of a distinct Indian Muslim custom is unmistakable here.

Almost simultaneously came the recognition of India as an entity for historical purposes. It began with Badāūnī's friend, Niẓām'uddīn Ahmad, who in 1593-94 completed his *Ṭabaqāt-i Akbarī*, designed to give the annals separately for nine regions of India (Delhi, Deccan, Gujarat, Malwa, Bengal, Jaunpur, Kashmir, Sind and Multan). Such a departure from dynastic history in favour of a general history of India is something for which Niẓām'uddīn has surely not received adequate credit. He inspired a series of works including Badāūnī's history, but notably Muḥammad Qāsim Firishta's celebrated *Gulshan-i Ibrāhīmī* (1609-10), where the attempt is extended to reconstruct even the pre-Islamic history of the country. Even if the conception of history is rather narrow here, calling for little more than a grouping of separate dynastic histories (laboriously compiled), the constant underlying assumption of the

[16] Ibid., pp.178-181. Was Amir Khusrau, then, India's first patriotic poet? A.B. Keith commented long ago on Sanskrit writers not 'much moved by patriotism' in the classical period (*A History of Sanskrit Literature*, London, 1920, p.345).

[17] *Nijāt al-Rashīd*, ed. Sayyid Muinu'l Haqq, Lahore, 1972, p.427.

historical unity of India is remarkable.[18]

The concept of India had thus gone much beyond a purely geographical one in the Indo-Muslim tradition with which Akbar obtained familiarity first. Though born in India (1542), Akbar's boyhood was spent in Afghanistan, until 1555, and he himself spoke later of his 'arrival in India ('Hind')'.[19] But he developed an increasing interest in the language and customs of his subjects. In 1563 confronting Adham Khān, he used a Hindi word of abuse still living with us.[20] He composed verses in Hindi, containing, in the words of the official biographer, 'colourful conceits'.[21] Imitating 'the loyal Indians', he let grow his hair, rather than cut it short;[22] and he never grew a beard. His love for Indian tales made him commission the translation of *Singhāsan Battīsī* even before 1571-72.[23] But it is in October 1578 that, for the first time, we find him referring with affection and pride to the people of India ('Hind'). In an assembly at the Court Akbar 'praised the truth-based nature of the people of India, whose women, however hard the life they might have borne (with their husbands), show the greatest affection and love for their husbands once they are dead', and went on to refer to the self-sacrifice offered by Indian women as *sati*. At the same time Akbar condemned the pusillanimity of men of 'Hindostān' who allowed or encouraged such acts by their women.[24] Since Muslims did not practise anything remotely resembling *sati*, the identification of Indians and India largely with Hindus and Hinduism both in the friendly and censorious aspects is unmistakable.

A similar identification tended to occur when Akbar began to acquire familiarity with the religious beliefs of the various schools of Hinduism. In 1578, again, two Brahmans, Purushuttam and

[18] There is a faint earlier glimmer of it, though, in 'Iṣāmī, who says that 'Alā'uddīn Khaljī enriched, while Muḥammad Tughluq ravaged, 'Hindostān' (*Futūḥ- u's Salāṭīn*, p.605).

[19] Abū'l Faẓl, *Ā'īn-i Akbarī*, ed. Naval Kishore, Lucknow, 1892, III, p.188: 'When we arrived in India, our heart was attracted to the elephants'.

[20] Bāyazīd Bayāt, *Tazkira-i Humāyūn wa Akbar*, ed. M. Hidayat Hosain, Calcutta, 1941, pp.251-2.

[21] Abū'l Faẓl, *Akbarnāma*, ed. Ahmad Ali, Calcutta, 1873-87, pp.270-1.

[22] First version of *Akbarnāma*, B.L.: Add. 27,247, f.294a.

[23] Badāūnī, *Muntakhab-u't Tawārīkh*, Calcutta, 1865-69, II, pp.177-8.

[24] *Akbarnāma*, first version, B.L.: Add. 27,247, ff.295b-296a. A stronger condemnation of the men's behaviour by Akbar is quoted by Abū'l Faẓl among the 'sayings of Akbar' towards the end of *Ā'īn-i Akbarī*, III, p.190.

Devi(?), introduced him to these complexities, leading him to believe that transmigration of souls was an essential element of Hinduism.[25] In his sayings, as reported by Abū'l Faẓl, Akbar shows a grasp of the doctrine of transmigration of souls, and the consequence which such a belief led to in India: divine incarnation not prophethood. Thus he observed: 'In India ('Hind'), no one set forth a claim to Prophethood: this is because the claim to Divinity has had precedence here'.[26]

We see in these statements a pride in India tempered with a critical spirit. If India is to be identified by the currency of certain customs and beliefs, it is not necessary that these be accepted. Akbar thus adds a new component to the vision of India, that of reform. His prohibition of *sati*, and of pre-puberty marriages, his demand for equal inheritance for the daughter, his condemnation of slavery and slave trade,[27] all suggest the rejection of some of the burdens of the past. From India seen as a cultural unity, and then as a cultural diversity undergoing synthesis, we have with Akbar the first vision of India undergoing moral or social improvement. It was linked to a bold rejection of traditionalism. He is reported as saying:

> The pursuit of reason ('*aql*) and rejection of traditionalism (*taqlīd*) are so brilliantly patent as to be above the need of argument. If traditionalism was proper, the prophets would merely have followed their own elders (and not come with new messages).[28]

One could almost say that with Akbar we begin to have in a rudimentary form a pre-modern vision of modernization of India, a patriotism without revivalism. But for what, in greater detail and depth, India meant to Akbar and his circle we have to go to his principal spokesman, Abū'l Faẓl.

There is no doubt that Abū'l Faẓl was more conscious of the geography of India than any previous writer. In the north he considered the great mountain ranges to separate India from Tūrān

[25] Badāūnī, *Muntakhab-u't Tawārīkh*, II, pp.398-400.

[26] *Ā'īn-i Akbarī*, III, 185.

[27] Cf. Irfan Habib, 'Akbar and Social Inequities: A Study of the Evolution of his Ideas', *Proceedings of the Indian History Congress, Warangal (1992-93) Session*, Delhi, 1993, pp.300-310. He sees in Akbar, 'the early flickers of that critique of traditional India, which would later turn into flame in the 19th-century Indian Renaissance'.

[28] Akbar's sayings in *Ā'īn-i Akbarī*, III, p.179.

(Central Asia) and Iran, on one side, and China ('Chīn and Māchīn'), on the other.[29] The following passage from his pen was to serve long as an aid to the arguments of those British strategists who would place the 'scientific frontier' of the Raj across the heart of Afghanistan:

Intelligent men of the past have considered Kabul and Qandahar as the twin gates of Hindostan, one (Qandahar) for the passage to Iran, and the other for that to Tūrān. By guarding these two places, Hindostān obtains peace from the alien (raider) and global traffic by these two routes can prosper.[30]

It is significant that Abū'l Faẓl considers India to be a peninsula, for he says that the sea borders Hindostān 'on the east, west and south'. He, however, claims that Hindostān also included 'Sarāndīp (Sri Lanka), Achīn (in Sumatra), Malūk (Malaya), Malāgha (Malacca) and many islands', so that 'the sea cannot really demarcate its limits'.[31] This too is a rather expansive concept of India – anticipating the 'Greater India' concept of later days – which one can hardly endorse. But probably Abū'l Faẓl meant no more than that the sea could not prevent Indian cultural influences from reaching certain oversea territories; and this in itself was an interesting statement for him to make.

Abū'l Faẓl displays his patriotism by showering unqualified priase on the people of India:

The people of this country, are God-seeking, generous-hearted, friendly to strangers, pleasant-faced, of broad forehead, patrons of learning, lovers of asceticism, inclined to justice, contented, hard-working and efficient, true to salt, truth-seeing and attached to loyalty.[32]

These qualities, it is worth noting, are assigned to inhabitants of the territory, and not to the followers of any one religious persuasion. But since the majority of Indians were Hindus, Abū'l Faẓl claims that 'all' (that is, including the Hindus) 'acclaim the oneness of God'. Though some of them revere images, he argues, this is not really idol-worship, since images are used merely to assist in the worship of God.[33] We are not concerned here with the

[29] Ibid., p.4.

[30] Ibid., II, 192. See the citation of this passage in V.A. Smith, *Oxford History of India*, p.755, in a discussion of the 'scientific' frontier.

[31] *Ā'īn-i Akbarī*, III, p.4.

[32] Ibid., p.5.

[33] Ibid.

veracity of this defence, but with the fact that Abū'l Faẓl needed to make it: his praise of Indians as God-seekers covered the Hindus as well.

The recognition of India as the birth-place of an important culture, which found its major expression in the Indian ('Hindī') language (i.e. Sanskrit), forms the starting point of a long and accurate survey of it in the latter portion of the *Ā'in-i Akbarī*, entitled 'Account of Hindostān'(*Aḥwāl-i Hindostān*). There is no indication that he intended the culture to be considered in a sectarian colour: It is characteristic of modern biases that when Abū'l Faẓl begins by stating his intention 'to describe a little of the conditions of this country and survey the opinions of the Indian (*Hindī-nazād*) sages',[34] the translator renders the last phrase as 'the opinions professed by the majority of the learned among the Hindus'.[35] In fact, Abū'l Faẓl does not begin with religion at all, but with the Indian beliefs in the spheres of astronomy and geography. His attitude in this respect is very similar to that of al-Bīrūnī, who too was concerned with the entire range of Indian learning. At the conclusion of his survey, Abū'l Faẓl regrets that he did not have time to compare the opinions of the learned of India with those of Greece and Persia.[36] This again suggests, that beyond this regret, ât not having been able to proceed as al-Bīrūnī had done, lay an essentially secular or non-sectarian perception of Indian culture.

There is no doubt that Abū'l Faẓl's description of Indian culture running to about 150 pages of the large folio edition in Persian is an outstanding achievement in detail and accuracy, covering secular learning, religion, ritual and ethnography. The account is largely independent of al-Bīrūnī and from the point of view purely of information adds much to his account. Abū'l Faẓl professedly derived his knowledge from a large number of Indian texts, through the medium of numerous learned interpreters and translators,[37] but

[34] *Ā'īn-i Akbarī*, III, p.2.

[35] *Ā'īn-i Akbarī*, III, tr. H.S. Jarrett, ed., Jadunath Sarkar, Calcutta, 1948, p.1. It is also not clear where Jarrett gets his 'majority' from. With similar inaccuracy, though less unjustly, Jarrett and Sarkar render 'Hindī' as Sanskrit, without letting the reader know that the original has 'Hindī', not 'Sanskrit' here.

[36] *Ā'īn-i Akbarī*, ed. Naval Kishore, III, p.177. In respect of astronomy and geography, Abū'l Faẓl does indeed make extensive references to Greek views and findings.

[37] Ibid., III, p.2.

the care and precision he exercised in setting out the information is very greatly to his credit. The survey needs to be analysed, despite Sarkar's rather disparaging remarks,[38] since it tells us how, with what points of emphasis, various beliefs and opinions were held or expressed in India at the time (c.1595).

Abū'l Faẓl has a particular interest in presenting to the Persian-knowing reader the essentials of Indian culture, which is seen, despite its diversities, as a unity. He looks forward to a larger unity so that 'the inner and external conflict should turn into amity, the thorn-bush of enmity and hostility into the garden of friendship and the sounds of reasoned argument should come forth and an informed assemblage be arranged'.[39] He is too scientific and too scornful of 'tradition-bound imitators'[40] to approve of the various Indian beliefs and opinions he surveys. He says, on one occasion, in obvious deprecation of the Indian and Greek views on the habitable world that 'today the truth-inclined learned consider the south [below the Equator] to be inhabited just like the north'.[41]

In other words, Abū'l Faẓl was looking to much beyond a parallel coexistence of cultures or a composite traditional Indian culture, a mere synthesis of traditions. He made his own bow to the cultural compositeness of India, by giving us notices of foreigners arriving in India ('Hindostān') from Adam to Humāyūn,[42] and then of the more noted Muslim divines and saints of India,[43] as if these constituted streams that too belonged to India. But such streams had to join together, purified by reason, before the higher unity could be achieved. For this higher ground to be reached, Abū'l Faẓl saw an essential role to vest with the sovereign.

Humāyūn's arrival in India after so many travails was to be celebrated, because it led to Akbar's accession, and it was under the aegis of Akbar's justice and judgement of men that 'Hindostān has become the concourse of good men of the seven climes and every one in different ways attains his objects'.[44] The key instrument of the sovereign was the enforcement of *Ṣulḥ-i Kul*, absolute

---

[38] *Ā'īn-i Akbarī*, III, tr. Jarrett, ed. Sarkar, p.iv.

[39] *Ā'īn-i Akbarī*, ed. Naval Kishore, III, p.2.

[40] Ibid., p.30.　　　　　　　　[41] Ibid., p.22.

[42] Ibid., p.152-63.

[43] Ibid., pp.163-177. In this Abū'l Faẓl had a very orthodox scholar preceding him by a few years. 'Abdu'l Haqq of Delhi completed in 1591 the *Akhbāru-'l Akhyār*, a collection of biographical notices of 255 Indian Muslim saints.

[44] *Ā'īn- Akbarī*, ed. Nawal Kishore, III, p.163.

peace, a means of relief for individuals like Abū'l Fazl himself,[45] as well as for the people at large. For the sovereign is 'father to humanity. All kinds of people seek comfort from him, and no dust of duality rises forth from the variety of religions believed in by men.' But at the same time, the sovereign 'should not seek popularity among people through opposing Reason'.[46] In other words, tolerance of existing beliefs is only one part of the sovereign's duty; persuasion to follow reason, and so reject traditionalism is a necessary and complementary one.

We can now see that Abū'l Fazl reaches a conclusion which justifies Akbar's promotion of both rationalism and social reform, in order to construct a 'Hindostān' that could stand out in the world. Is this view still so singular that it must be summarily thrown out of court as some scholars are now suggesting?

[45] Ibid., III, pp.177-78.
[46] Ibid., I, p.3.

16

Middle Bengali Literature: A Source for the Study of Bengal in the Age of Akbar

ANIRUDDHA RAY

The sixteenth century in Bengal proved to be a century of turmoil and transformation. While the Portuguese had appeared on the scene at the end of the second decade of the century, the conquest of Gaur first by Sher Shāh and then by Humāyūn in the third and the fourth decades ushered in a long struggle between the Afghans and the Mughals, in which the kings of Orissa also became involved. The struggle was temporarily won by Akbar's general Mun'im Khān who captured Gaur in 1575. Yet the final pacification came only in the second decade of the seventeenth century.

Along with the arrival of the conquistadors, we have the appearance of the religious reformer Chaitanya, whose brief and meteoric career greatly affected the cultural fabric of Bengal. It would be our endeavour here to analyse in the light of Bengali sources the operation of socio-economic forces which preceded the age of Akbar in Bengal, and the transformation which, as will be argued, took place here in the course of the sixteenth century.

Some scholars had long back accepted middle Bengali literature as a source of the medieval history of Bengal. In 1964[1] Asutosh Bhattacharyya drew attention to the rich material in the Mangal poems. Others like Tapan Raychaudhuri,[2] Abdul Karim,[3] Sukhomoy Mukhopadhyay[4] and lately Anil Chandra Banerjee[5] utilized these

[1] Asutosh Bhattacharyya, *Bangla Mangal Kavyer Itihās*, Calcutta, 1964.

[2] Tapan Raychaudhuri, *Bengal Under Akbar and Jahāngīr*, New Delhi, 1969 (2nd ed).

[3] Abdul Karim, *Banglar Itihās: Sulṭānī Amal*, Dhaka, 1987, 2nd ed.; 1st ed.,1979.

[4] Sukhomoy Mukhopadhyay, *Bangla Sahityer Prachin Kavider Parichaya o Samāj*, Calcutta, 1987: also, his *Musalman Adhikarer Adi Parba*, Calcutta.

[5] Anil Chandra Bandopadhyay, *Madhyayuger Bangla o Bangali*, Calcutta, 1986.

sources to study both the Sultanate and Mughal Bengal. Yet there is need to go to these sources afresh to review the nature and impact of the new forces gradually emerging in Bengal. For reasons of uniformity of the sources we have concentrated on those of the Bhagirathi belt ('Rarh' region) excluding the rich and varied Bengali sources of Chittagong and Arakan. Even then, the contemporary Bengali sources in the Rarh region differ in their approaches, content and style, which we would now consider.

II

Middle Bengali literature generally falls under two broad categories based on religious affiliations.[6] One genre comprised the Vaishnava poems from the middle of the sixteenth century after the death of Chaitanya. The second type was the Śākta group of poems, which can be subdivided further into three sub-groups, namely, *Manasā Maṅgal* (worship of the Snake Goddess), *Chaṇḍi Maṅgal* (worship of the Goddess Chaṇḍi) and *Dharma Maṅgal* (worship of the God Dharma). The earliest was *Manasā Maṅgal* and the latest, the *Dharma Maṅgal,* which actually began from the late seventeenth century and flourished in the eighteenth century. It was limited to only one region of Bengal. Sukumar Sen considers that Manasā or Chaṇḍi worship was a continuation of a pre-Vedic tradition and was deeply rooted in the psyche of the ordinary people of Bengal.[7]

Interestingly, the first two groups of Maṅgal poems (Manasā and Chaṇḍi) always weave the story around the difficulties of the merchants journeying across the sea for trade. The favour of the goddess to enable the merchant to recover his fortune is the central theme. Among these, the story of Chānd Saudāgar remained the most consistent. It has been asserted that the story originated probably from Pataliputra and migrated to Bengal some time after the fourteenth century.[8]

[6] Asutosh Bhattacharyya, *Bais Kavir Manasā Maṅgal*, Calcutta University, 1962 (to be referred henceforth as *Bais Kavi*).

[7] Sukumar Sen, *Bangla Sahityer Itihās*, I, Calcutta, 1978 (1st ed., 1940), 12-14.

[8] *Bais Kavi*, Introduction, 25-7.

It is interesting that Bengal also became independent and came under one administrative system from the middle of the fourteenth century, with the conquest of the Sonargaon region by Sulṭān Ilyās Shāh in 1351-2.

Vaishnava poems referred to here belonged to the second half of the sixteenth and early seventeenth centuries. Since Chaitanya mainly worked in small towns, we get from this genre of literature a picture of these towns on both banks of the Bhagirathi. In the process, we can look at the world of artisans and trade, as gleaned from this literature. This would bring us to the introduction of Mughal rule in Bengal and the transformation of society and economy occurring in the Bhagirathi belt during the sixteenth century. Mughal rule shattered the existing political framework and inaugurated a long and bloody war, particularly in the upper Bhagirathi, that saw the fall of Gaur, then the biggest city in eastern India, with attendant consequences.

III

Hari Datt, perhaps the originator of the Maṇgal poems in its present form, lived at the end of the fourteenth century.[9] His work was about a merchant who returned from trading with his fourteen ships full of treasure. Interestingly the manuscripts of the work, all late copies, have been found from the coastal area of Bengal, in the present district of Bakerganj.[10] The area was known as Bāklā and is so referred to by Abū'l Faẓl,[11] and was the base for mercantile activities from the twelfth century onwards.[12] The next poet, Nārāyaṇ Dev, had left his ancestral house in the Bhagirathi belt and come to eastern Bengal. The dating of his manuscript has created some uncertainties and current theory puts him at the end of the fifteenth century.[13] Since there is no mention of Chaitanya in his *Padmā Purāṇ*, this early date had

[9] Ibid., 28. [10] Ibid., 29.

[11] Abū'l Faẓl, *Ā'īn-i Akbarī*, tr. by Jarrett and annotated by J. Sarkar, Calcutta, 1978, II, 154.

[12] This was part of the kingdom of the later Sena dynasty. For a full discussion, see Nihar Ranjan Ray, *Bangalir Itihās*, Calcutta, 1949, 364-80.

[13] *Bais Kavi*, 32-6.

gained acceptance. The story centres around the trials and difficulties of a merchant called Chānd Saudāgar.

Vijay Gupta, who finished writing his *Padmā Purāṇ* in 1484-5 during the reign of Sulṭān Jalālu'ddīn Fatḥ Shāh of Bengal (1481-7),[14] gave this genre of poems wide popularity. His manuscript was also found from the Bāklā region, in the village of Gaila-Phullasri, where his descendants were to be found till the time of the Partition.[15]

From our point of view the information on mercantile activities, such as types of boats, route to the sea, the towns on both banks and the commodities exchanged, form the most interesting parts. Till the end of the fifteenth century, the number of ships taken by the merchant Chānd to the sea was fourteen. By the early sixteenth century, this had been reduced to seven, the number fourteen being regarded as perhaps much too large for a merchant. Either this was a concession to realism or indicates the gradually dwindling mercantile activities of Bengali merchants.

Vijay Gupta gave details of the commodities taken by the merchant for trading at Dakshin Patan in his fourteen Dingas. The commodities included rice, textiles, various types of precious stones brought from south India, including coral and pearls, various types of grain, betel, betel-nut and flower vases. Later, 700 horses and spices are mentioned, in exchange for which gold was brought.[16] The poet perhaps had in mind the city of Patan in Gujarat which was important as a port in an earlier period. In any case, it was coastal trade he was speaking of, and not commerce with the kingdoms of south-east Asia.

A description of boat construction comes to us from the writing of Jīvan Maitra,[17] of North Bengal, belonging to the middle of the eighteenth century. He wrote that a *dinga* was 100 yards in length and 50 yards in breadth with a special kind of wood (named poetically as *Delight of the Mind*) collected from an island in the middle of the sea. Interestingly, there were masts

[14] Sukhomoy Mukhopadhyay, *Bangla Sahityer Tathya o Kalakram*, Calcutta, 1988 (2nd ed.), 1-4.

[15] Vijay Gupta, *Padma Purāṇ* (ed. by J.K. Dasgupta), Calcutta University, 1962, 238-42.

[16] Ibid., 238-42.

[17] *Bais Kavi*, 129-32. Maitra had mentioned 14 *dingas*.

and various paintings, including those of animals. There was a ritual of boat construction. The Adhikārī or master carpenter began it. Before that various animals were sacrificed to the accompaniment of music. The familiarity of the poet with such rituals is clear, and this ritual had been handed over from centuries. It is similar to the worship of the Goddess Chaṇḍi or Kāli, which usually starts from September-October onwards to continue till the middle of November. This is the period of the south-west monsoon which would bring ships from the west. That would be the period to go further east, with the wind, to the kingdoms of south-east Asia. However, we do not have accounts of such journeys in this literature. Also, the *zamīndār* is the merchant in the story of Manasā, although in later periods we get the names of other merchants.[18]

At the end of the sixteenth century, Mukundarām Chakravartī from the Rarh region[19] gave the description of the boat called Dinga. Since the boat was constructed by the god Viśwakarma, he did not give any details of its construction. The size of the boat was 100 yards in length and 20 yards in breadth, thus smaller than was usual in the eighteenth century. No artisan is mentioned.

It was from the end of the fifteenth century that we find a clear description of the route to the sea by the Bhagirathi river. By then the number of Chānd's vessels had been reduced to seven. The merchant in the poem of Vipradās, ascribed to the end of the fifteenth century,[20] stopped at Guptipara, Mirzapur and Triveni but not at Saptagram. But he had gone on to Saptagram by land from Triveni to make purchases. Obviously the Saraswati river had ceased to be navigable and the Bhagirathi channel, as it stands today, was flowing past Triveni. The city of Saptagram had extended up to Triveni, a holy city, due to the confluence of three rivers, and serving as a port linked with Saptagram. The bridge linking Saptagram and Triveni was constructed by 'Alāu'ddīn Ḥusain Shāh in 1506,[21] thus fulfilling

[18] Ibid: Dwija Bansidās, *Manasā Maṅgal*. He completed it in 1575, although Bhattacharyya assigns it to the end of the 17th century. He gives names of merchants.

[19] Mukundarām Chakravartī, *Kavi Kankan Chaṇḍī*, Allahabad, 1921 (2nd ed.), 227-9.

[20] *Bais Kavi*, 147-50.

[21] Shamsuddin Ahmed, *Inscriptions of Bengal*, Rajshahi, 1960, 173-6.

the need to connect Saptagram and Triveni overland with the main channel of the Bhagirathi.

The description found in Vipradās is perhaps the earliest Bengali description of the port city. Referring to the existence of 36 castes and their liberty to worship, a tract written within a century later by a visiting Frenchman[22] described the working of the Hindus at Saptagram and the existence of the Mughals and the Pathāns in this city. Vipradās also described the rows of houses, with each house shining like glass with silver strings. The wealth of the city dazzled the writer.[23] Yet he did not mention even once the Saraswati river.

Interestingly, Vipradās refers to Kalikatta,[24] which is mentioned too by Abū'l Faẓl a century later.[25] But the reference of Vipradās to Bettore, where goods were unloaded from the big Portuguese ships in the 1530s, seems to suggest that it had existed prior to the arrival of the Portuguese, who merely followed the practice of anchoring the big ships at Bettore and forwarding the goods to Saptagram.[26]

The Bengali concept of the sea, given by Vipradās[27] as well as by others in the next two centuries,[28] suggests that the authors were not in touch with the mercantile world, particularly with merchants who sailed to distant places. This is also seen by the reference to the boat, which remains basically a riverine or coastal vessel, having been constructed inside the Rarh region and brought to the sea through several rivers. The difference between the rivers and the sea, as visualized by Vipradās and later writers, was set by the space of water and the turbulence in the sea, where the fears of imaginary devils and animals of the sea tormented the merchants and crew. The trading was only to Ceylon and Orissa, which are mentioned, and perhaps to more distant Gujarat, although its memory by then seems strangely to have faded. The life of the merchant seemed to be easy and the domination of the Brahmin in society undisturbed.[29]

[22] Sr. Vincent Le Blanc, *Les Voyages Fameux*, 1948, 126-9.

[23] *Bais Kavi*, 148-9.

[24] Ibid., 150.

[25] *Ā'īn*, II, 154.

[26] Caeser Fredricki, between 1573 to 1581 (*Purchas his Pilgrimes*, Maclehose edn., Edinburgh, V, 410).

[27] *Bais Kavi*, 153.

[28] Among others, see Ketakadās Khemānanda, ibid., 159.

[29] Vijay Gupta, among others, refers to worship of the Brahminical gods and

IV

The Vaishnava group of poems started from the middle of the sixteenth century. They were of different nature and portray a different but far more mundane world. The earliest of them was Chuḍāmaṇi Dās, who finished his writing by 1548-9.[30] By that time south Rarh, the lower part of the Bhagirathi, had been considerably affected by the Chaitanya movement. Small towns like Nabadwip or Nadia, Katwa, Santipur, Khardaha, Fulia and Saptagram, were now Vaishnava strongholds.

Since the invasion of Bengal by Sher Shāh in 1538, followed by the brief occupation of Gaur by Humāyūn, the upper part of the Bhagirathi, called Barindri, was involved in the Mughal–Pathan and often Pathan–Oriya struggles. While Gaur was under severe strain, the linkage between Saptagram and Gaur was sorely tested. While the central structure of Bengal, independent since the middle of the fourteenth century, was being weakened due to this struggle, the small towns on the lower Bhagirathi belt continued to flourish. This could be best seen in the growth of both the towns of Nabadwip and Santipur. By mid-seventeenth century, Nabadwip had become a large town.[31]

With the political unification of Bengal in the middle of the fourteenth century, the Chittagong–Sonargaon complex developed, with the capital located at Pandua in the upper part of the Bhgirathi. The description of Chinese visitors to Bengal and particularly to Pandua by the Chittagong–Sonargaon route leaves us with an impression of flourishing production and foreign trade.[32] Perhaps due to the Arakan conflicts around Chittagong, from the middle of the fifteenth century the Bhagirathi route came increasingly under use. Thus we see the coincidence of the composition of the Maṅgal poems describing this route, the rise of Saptagram as a port with its connection up to Triveni and the establishment of the capital at Gaur located

animal sacrifices before departure (*op. cit.*, 238-9).

[30] Chuḍāmaṇi Dās, *Gauranga Vijaya*, Calcutta.

[31] P.C. Bagchi, 'Political Relations between Bengal and China in the Pathan period' in *Viswa-Bharati Annals*, 1945, I, 96-134.

[32] Jayānanda, *Chaitanya Maṅgala*, Calcutta, 1971, 10-11; VrindāvanDās, *Chaitanya Bhagavat*, Nabadwip, 3rd ed., 161.

on the Bhagirathi, although big ships could not reach there. By the end of the fifteenth century, certain areas in the lower Bhagirathi belt were being urbanized. Nabadwip, for example, was gradually filled up by immigrants, particularly from Chittagong and Sylhet, from where among others Chaitanya's wealthy parents had come.[33] Nabadwip, by the beginning of the sixteenth century, became a small university town with emphasis on Brahminical teaching, where the teachers were dependent on the fees of a large number of students.[34] The emergence of the middle class, to which these teachers belonged, also included poets, all of whom were not neccessarily Brahmins. As a matter of fact, a broader span of the Hindu middle class had emerged from the middle of the fourteenth century, dominated by educated Kayasthas employed in the government and zamīndārī offices. The middle-class character of the town of Nabadwip was confronted by Chaitanya when he brought the lower classes, including service people, into his movement, thereby endangering the strict observance of caste rules and the domination of the Brahmins.

Unlike the Maṅgal poets, the Vaishnava poets did not dwell much on the journey of the zamīndār-merchant on the Bhagirathi for trading. Instead, the Vaishnava poets dwelt on the activities of Chaitanya in these small towns. Yet till the middle of the sixteenth century Nabadwip had not developed much. The description of Chuḍāmaṇi Dās showed that open fields lay behind the Barkona ghat of Nabadwip. This was filled up by houses within a span of twenty years. There were now artisans too. Among the inhabitants of Nabadwip Vrindāvan Dās refers to the Kavirājas, Vaishyas (generally merchants), and the betel worker, oil presser, weaver, gardener, barber, goldsmith and ironsmith as well as musicians.[35] There is no mention of conch-shell workers, nor is there any mention of the division of the town into *mahallas* (mohullas).

Curiously, there is no mention of the Portuguese, despite the fact that the Portuguese had begun trading in the Bhagirathi belt through Bettore at least from the 1530s.[36] While the upper

[33] Vrindāvan Dās *Chaitanya Maṅgala,* Calcutta, 1971, 10-11.

[34] Ibid., 11.

[35] Ibid., 230-41.

[36] J.J.A. Campos placed the first arrival of the Portuguese at Satgaon in 1535,

part of the Bhagirathi belt, from Saptagram, was being devastated in the political conflict, these smaller towns along its lower course continued to thrive. This was the period when Chaitanya's teaching began to confront the Brahmin-dominated Nadadwip, which was then in the *sarkār* of Saptagram (Satgaon). At Nabadwip, the Qāẓī appeared to be the only authority and there were many Muslims living in Mollāpara, the only exclusive area of the town mentioned in the sources.

Chaitanya's victory over the Qāẓī is too well known to be recounted here. Chaitanya converted people of the low castes, as well as mercantile communities of the nearby towns on the lower Bhagirathi. Obviously the service groups and mercantile communities wanted to be liberated from orthodox caste rules. Thus we see a conjunction of forces in Bengal on the eve of Akbar's reign. The increased use of the Bhagirathi route, the emergence of small towns, the appearance of the Portuguese and the gradual spread of a new ideology all worked for a closer connection between the artisan and the merchant and at least partly freed them from the rigid rules of caste.

The growth of Nabadwip could be seen best in the writing of another Vaishnav writer, Jayānanda, writing in 1560. Describing Nabadwip as a large town, Jayānanda referred to many decorated temples and to the freedom of worship enjoyed there. There were brick houses, walls and lofty gateways. Goods were brought from far-off places to be sold there, including those of Kanchipuram and Kashmir. Even merchants were settling at Nabadwip.[37]

Other towns on the lower Bhagirathi were developing at the same time. Most of them were built of bricks,[38] and had temples. These were also the centres of textile manufacture, perhaps supplying the markets of Saptagram.

V

The legendary merchant, Chānd Saudāgar, in the poem of Dwija

---

although he did not mention trading (*History of the Portuguese in Bengal*, Indian ed., Patna, 1979, 37).

[37] Jayānanda, *op. cit.*, 11-12.

[38] Hari Charan Dās, *Adwait Maṅgal*, Burdwan University, 1966.

Bansidās (written around 1575), was a zamīndār, mahājan and merchant rolled into one.[39] That this type was not a figment of the imagination could be seen from the commercial treaty of 30 April 1559 between the Portuguese and the *zamīndār* of Bāklā.[40] In the poem of Bansidās there is no mention of Saptagram nor of the construction of boats. Instead, one finds a picture of communal confrontation between the Qāẓī and the Hindus, with details of the oppression of the Qāẓī, who seems to be the principal man in authority and who had called upon all the Muslims to convert the Brahmins.

Such religious overtones are absent in another Maṅgal poem of the period, written by Mukundarām Chakravartī between 1594 and 1624. Mukundarām was a well-to-do farmer of Damunya village in Arambagh pargana of the district of Hughly. During the governorship of Rājā Mān Singh,[41] he had to leave his ancestral village and cross the river to go west.

Dihidār Māmud Sarif (Maḥmūd Sharīf) of Mukundarām's village had begun to measure the land. It is clear that such measurement (15 cottas to a bīgha) was introduced to produce a smaller *bīgha* without reducing the rate, which naturally ruined the peasants, including Mukundarām. Perhaps the *ta'luqdār* (in Bengal he was lower in position than his counterpart in Awadh) Gopīnāth Nandī resisted it and was arrested. The value of the rupee fell to ten annas and the Poddar (moneylender) of the village began to charge two and a half annas on each rupee (*ṭākā*) paid,[42] which was considered intolerably high by Mukundarām. It is clear that the market economy, in which cash transactions were a concommitant feature, had entered the villages of Bengal. The problem arose perhaps because of the fact that the Mughals tried to introduce the Ẓabṭ system, in which measurement of land was an essential feature.

That the measurement of land was not in vogue could be seen from another passage of Mukundarām. The poet describes

[39] *Bais Kavi*, 58-85.

[40] Jadunath Sarkar (ed), *History of Bengal*, Dacca University, 1972, 2nd ed. (1st ed. in 1948), II, 358.

[41] For a discussion of the date of the flight of Mukundarām and the date of his writing, see Sukhomoy Mukhopadhya, *Bangla Sahityer*, *op. cit.*, 150-68.

[42] Mukundarām, 4-5.

the establishment of a city (significantly called Gujarāt) by clearing the jungle. To induce the peasants to settle there, the authorities levied no revenue for the first three years, which was the usual Mughal practice for new settlement. There would not be any measurement; the revenue when levied would be one *ṭanka* per plough.[43]

The contrast in the two pictures given by the same poet is worth close observation. The earlier picture was of fleeing peasants forcibly stopped by the *piyādas* (foot-men) of *Dihidār* Maḥmūd Sharīf, who even began to record fallow land as revenue-paying.[44] With the fall of the value of the rupee, there was nobody to buy paddy or cows. The collection of revenue was stopped; there is no mention of such collection by force; and there was scarcity of liquid cash in the village.

In the other picture, we see the settlement of a city in which, as per the usual Mughal practice, a certain area of land would be attached. Anyone could till the land and Balarām Mandal, the new settler, would give pattas to the peasants. Even cash would be advanced to the peasants to construct houses, and buy cows and ropes. There would not be any *salāmī* (salutation-payment) for the settlement and no tax would be charged for the sale of paddy. Kāyasthas would be allowed to settle and their land would be demarcated.[45] This might have been necessary in order to limit the land of the Kāyasthas, as we know from an early seventeenth-century source that Kāyasthas had influence since they usually were in government service and were reputedly very greedy.[46] This would not mean that the entire land would be measured or that measurement was in vogue.

Here perhaps one could take issue with Tapan Raychaudhuri, who has used this poem in some detail.[47] He makes elaborate comparison with two seventeenth-century sources, namely the *Bahāristān-i Ghaybī* and *Fatḥiya 'Ibriya*. On the basis of these sources, Raychaudhuri suggests that measurement of land

[43] Ibid., 85-91.
[44] Ibid.
[45] Ibid.
[46] Krishṇadās Kavirāj, *Śrī Chaitanya Charitāmrita*, Basumati ed. (9th impression), 200-1.
[47] Tapan Raychaudhuri, 'Revenue Administration of Bengal in the early days of Mughal rule', *JASB*, XVII (1), 1951, 51-61.

was in vogue in Bengal before the Mughal conquest.[48] This cannot be accepted in view of the image of the greedy nature of the Kāyasthas current in Bengal and in view of Mukundarām's opinion, wherein he blamed the introduction of measurement under Mān Singh as the root cause of the trouble. He clearly stated that in his dream city there would be no measurement.[49]

Mukundarām's contribution to the history of late-sixteenth century Bengal is important from another point of view. In the poem, there was no particular mention of merchants among the people coming to settle in the legendary city of Gujarāt. The people he mentionned were Vaishyas, who were mahājans and Vaishnavas.[50] Most of them were also peasants and some were wanderers, selling precious stones. Through buying and selling, the Vaishnavas of 'Gujarāt' were very happy. That the days of the overseas mercantile activities of Bengali merchants were over could be seen from another comment by Mukundarām. He says that the merchants of Saptagram do not go anywhere but get all their profit sitting at home.[51] At another place, he comments that although Saptagram is a beautiful city, the area of Rarh, in which the city is situated, is full of bandits.[52] This is not an exaggeraton or the expression of his personal dislike. A contemporary traveller described the area between Saptagram and Gaur as full of robbers living in dense forests.[53] Obviously the link between Saptagram and Gaur had been cut, while Gaur was being abandoned.

Among the contemporary Maṅgal poets, Mukundarām has given us much information on the merchants, although he did not make much distinction between Saudāgar, Baṅik and Bepārī. For the *sradh* ceremony of the father of Dhanapat Saudāgar the merchants had been invited, of whom Mukundarām gives a list which included Dhus Datt (bania) from Burdwan; Chānd Saudāgar from Champainagar; Lakshmi Saudāgar, who came on horseback; Nilambar Dās; Binod Naskar (with his eight brothers); Sanātan

[48] Ibid., 58.

[49] Mukundarām, 85.

[50] Ibid., 88.

[51] Ibid., 201, for description of Saptagram where merchants from all over India and abroad come with their ships.

[52] Ibid., 73.

[53] Ralph Fitch in Foster (ed.), *Early Travels in India*, Indian ed., 1985, 25. Fitch mentions Tanda and not Gaur (p.24).

Chānda from Ganeshpur (along with his two brothers, Gopāl and Govind); Basula from Dasghara; Sridhar Hazra from Saptagram; Sankha Datt, Bishnu Datt (with seven brothers, who came in palanquins); Jadabendra Dās from Kaiti; Raghu Datt from Jaugram; Gopāl Datt (bania) from Teghara; Rām Rāy from Triveni (with nine brothers); Rām Datt from Lauga; Chaṇḍīdās Khān from Langan; Rām Daw (a bania), from Satghara; Bhagyabanta Khān (bania) from Bishnupur; Basu Datt from Khandaghosa; Madhu Datt (with four brothers) from Getan; and Lakshmipati, father-in-law of Dhanapati. Seven hundred Baniks also came.[54] Obviously in a Hindu religious ceremony Muslim merchants were not invited. Yet it is implied in the poem that the Muslims were mostly traders and had dealings in different weekly markets.[55] Strangely enough, Mukundarām refers to the city of Gaur on several occasions, although by the time he was writing Gaur was probably abandoned. Dhanapati, the merchant, had gone to Gaur to get a bird's cage manufactured there.[56] Obviously, artisans had not abandoned Gaur. Even the life led by Dhanapti at Gaur did not suggest that an epidemic had visited the city a few years earlier.[57] In that case, one may have to revise the current view regarding the actual condition of the city of Gaur. While the capital was transferred, the city might not have been totally abandoned. However, there is no trader from the city of Gaur in Mukundarām's list of merchants. There is no one from eastern Bengal either.

From the point of view of the route of the Bhagirathi, it may be recalled that the poem was written close to 1594. Bhagirathi, in Mukundarām, had taken a turn towards the east from Purbasthali, where Mān Singh had anchored his boats, as was done by the merchant hero of Mukundarām.[58] The river had thus not changed its course since the days of Chuḍāmaṇī Dās.

The wealth of Saptagram is described by Mukundarām while his legendary merchant is shown anchoring his boat at Triveni on the Bhagirathi. Singificantly, Mukundarām does not mention the Saraswati river, nor does he mention Hughly, estab-

[54] Mukundarām, 179. [55] Ibid., 181.
[56] Ibid., 134.
[57] He had spent one year playing chess there (ibid., 134).
[58] Ibid., 200.

lished recently by the Portuguese armed with a *farmān* of Akbar, although he mentions Garifa on the opposite bank. Opposite Triveni Mukundarām mentions Halishahr.[59]

Triveni had become a well populated town with 'lakhs of people' since it was considered a holy place due to the confluence of three rivers. It became important for its link with Saptagram, as explained earlier. The merchant of Mukundarām had stayed two days at Triveni on the Bhagirathi and made his purchases at Saptagram.[60] Evidently, despite the silting of the Saraswati, which meant the shifting of the channel from west to east, Saptagram attracted merchants from all over India, including Vijayanagar, and from as far as Malaya.[61] This conflicts with the map of Joa de Barros (published in 1615) which showed a Saraswati channel beside the Bhagirathi.[62]

Mukundarām's description of the route seems to suggest that the Bhagirathi was following the old course (not the present one) on which stood Kalighat, Bettore and Chitrabhog. There is the mention of Kalikatta,[63] which was obviously a village then. It was becoming important, as Abū'l Faẓl mentions it in his *Ā'īn*.[64] Such well-marked stations on the route seem to suggest that the route was used frequently by merchants for quite some time. The only difference with earlier poems is that many new stations had come up in the lower Bhagirathi, whose origin could be seen in the poem of Vipradās, referring to Chitpore, Kalikatta and Kalighat.

The other difference from the earlier poems is that Mukundarām on more than one occasion refers to Portuguese pirates (he calls them *harmada*, obviously from armada). However, Mukundarām placed them more towards the side of Orissa than exactly on the mouth of the Bhagirathi.[65] Since no description

[59] Ibid., 201, Irfan Habib puts this in his map as Ḥavelīshahr (*Atlas of the Mughal Empire*, Delhi, 1982, Sheet 11 A).

[60] Mukundarām, 201. [61] Ibid.

[62] See the map printed in Susan Gole, *India Within the Ganges*, New Delhi, 1983, 117.

[63] Mukundarām, 201. Jayānanda, writing around 1560, does not mention Kalikatta. Around the end of the 17th century, in *Sitala Maṅgal*, there is mention of Dihi Kalikatta (Satyarayan Bhattacharyya, *Kavi Krishnarām Daser Granthabali*, Calcutta University, 1958, 267).

[64] *Ā'īn*, II, 154.

[65] Mukundarām, 205. He crossed the river to go to Dravida country.

has been given, one may assume that Mukundarām had no personal encounter of any kind with them. Excepting the presence of the *Harmadas*, there was not much disturbance in the route to the sea; but in the case of upper parts of the Bhagirathi, Mukundarām mentioned such disturbance. There was no difference regarding the type of vessel used since the days of Vipradās. Mukundarām also used the term *dinga* for coastal craft.

In Mukundarām's imaginary city of Gujarāt, he enumerates the different Muslim and Hindu artisans and service people, a description ably utilized by Abdul Karim.[66] What is interesting is that Mukundarām shows the operation of two parallel sets of forces in Bengal at the time. The existence of a market economy, based on cash nexus and exchange, is evident here.[67] The location of different occupational groups of his city of Gujarāt, without an encompassing wall, is put in the suburbs. This picture is similar to the picture of contemporary Gaur as gleaned from a contemporary Portuguese source.[68] On a small scale, this was similar to the picture of Nabadwip seen from Vaishnav sources. Interestingly, Mukundarām does not provide any ideology for the solace of the artisans, with whom he was not concerned. Nor does he try to show the desire of the artisans to be free from rigorous Brahminical rules, which, in this city of Gujarāt, remain transcendent. That the prostitutes, who were allowed to settle on one side of the city, were part of the cosmic (market) order, can be seen in Mukundarām's plan of the city.[69]

The occupations in this city are given in detail. There were weekly markets (called *hat*) within the city where people earned their living by buying and selling. Even for crossing the river, the boatman would collect royal taxes. The grass-cutter would cut the grass for a few cowries, while the tailors, settled in one side of the city, would work for a salary. The point about salary

[66] Abdul Karim, *Social History of the Muslims in Bengal*, Chittagong, 2nd ed., 1985.

[67] This has been accepted by Tapan Raychaudhuri in the Introduction to the second edition of his book (*op. cit.*, 32-3).

[68] G. Bouchon and L.P. Thomaz, ed., *Voyage dans les Deltas du Gange et del'Irraoudy, 1521*, Paris, 1986, containing the description by the interpreter of Britto.

[69] Mukundarām, 91.

remains unclear unless we think of big households where the tailor was working on fixed wages; but such households do not otherwise appear.

The sweetmeat manufacturer would himself hawk sweatmeats from door to door.[70] Evidently the artisanal system of production with much peddling was operative in this market economy. These artisans were generally settled in the suburbs, though well within the city. But some of the occupational groups remained outside the city for reasons that are not very clear. The *malangīs* (called here *mal*) lived outside and earned their living by selling salt. Perhaps their association with the Chaṇḍāls forced them to live outside. Some of the occupational groups also manufactured certain other things for extra income. The Dom, who collected wood for cremation, also manufactured the straw hats generally used by peasants.

Mukundarām seems to have disliked certain groups. Regarding the Subarnabaniks, who traded in gold ornaments, he wrote that they bought and sold little but drained away the wealth of men. But the physicians were the worst: they fled on a pretext if they saw the serious condition of the patient.[71] It would thus be evident that the middle class had emerged as an important element in the city of Gujarāt.[72] The arrival of the Kāyasthas, who were all educated, clearly confirms this.

Another social phenomenon to be noted was the system of *Jajmānī* still prevalent in the city of Gujarāt. Mukundarām described the arrival of different groups of Brahmins and their students (numbering 700 Brahmins). Another stray reference would confirm that the legendary merchant used to live in Gaur country (not in Gaur city), that is Barindri. Some of these Brahmins, after learning the ritual of worship, as most of them were ignorant in these matters, performed jajmānī (i.e. rituals for clients) within the city and got various commodities like rice, sweetmeats, curds and oil as fee.[73] Apart from the fact that this might suggest the process of de-urbanization after the decay of Gaur, it showed the extent of the Jajmānī system existing in the

[70] Ibid., 90-1. [71] Ibid., 88-91.

[72] See a brief discussion in Raychaudhuri, *op. cit.*, 196, in which he accepted the existence of the middle class in Bengal during this period, which was 'different in character from its modern counterpart'.

[73] Mukundarām, 87.

network of the market economy. Although these two forces were often mutually contradictory, the contradiction is quite in conformity with the all-India situation where the cash nexus, money economy and middle class were emerging during this period.[74]

This development was neither uniform nor spread all over Bengal. As a result, some of the skills had remained localized only in certain cities. For example, Mukundarām relates how Srimanta could not find a bird's cage in Rarh areas and had to go to Gaur city, where the artisans made one for him.[75]

Mukundarām's enunciation of the Muslim groups, including their occupations, does not indicate any animosity towards Muslims, as is seen in the writings of early Vaishnava or Maṅgal poets. Vrindāvan Dās had referred to the violent conflict between the Qāẓī of Nabadwip and Chaitanya, which resulted in the burning of the Qāẓī's outer house.[76] Vijay Gupta also referred to such trouble with the Qāẓī, easily the man most hated among the Hindus.[77] By the time we come to Krishṇadās Kavirāj[78] in the early seventeenth century, the confrontation between the Qāẓī and Chaitanya had mellowed to a mere verbal duel. The Qāẓī had affectionately called Chaitanya his nephew in view of the fact that they had come from the same village. The absence of such confrontation as we move towards the end of Akbar's reign would suggest a closer integration of the various strata in a growing economy. The growth of Bengali culture, so ably documented by Tapan Raychaudhuri and Abdul Karim among others, along with the growth of the Bengali language mixed with Arabic and Persian words — later gradually incorporating a Portuguese vocabulary — represents the emergence of an integrative culture. Evidently, the religious animosity that one notices at the end of the Sultanate period in Bengal was part of a political and economic crisis. In the political field, the conquests of Sher Shāh and the Mughal-Afghan struggle created an anarchic situation, of which the deurbanization in the upper part of the Bhagirathi was the result. In the economic

[74] Iqtidar Alam Khan, Presidential Address, Medieval India section, *Proceedings of the Indian History Congress, Aligarh, 1975*, 113-41.

[75] Mukundarām, 134.

[76] Vrindāvan Dās, *op. cit.*, 802-5.

[77] Vijay Gupta, *op. cit.*, 121-5.

[78] Krishṇadās Kavirāj, *op. cit.*, 71-3.

field, the dominance of the Portuguese over the Bay of Bengal and the Indian ocean put a severe check upon maritime activities of the Bengali merchants. Within a span of another fifty years, by the end of Akbar's reign, Indian merchants had largely managed to elude the Portuguese net. Although Bengali merchants did not resume their mercantile activities till the middle of the seventeenth century, merchants from other parts of India had begun to trade extensively in Bengal. The merchants of Mukundarām and Vipradās belonged to the groups of Gandhabanik, who had gone to Sri Lanka, Orissa and possibly Gujarāt. They took with them mainly spices, fruits and in some cases, sheep and horses as well as textiles, which had not become the major item of export as yet. In exchange they brought back precious stones, particularly pearls from Sri Lanka, horses and various kinds of spices. They were not bringing back bullion, while some of the imported items were again re-exported from Saptagram. It was the coastal trade that managed to keep Bengali merchants afloat. Mukundarām, therefore, could see the merchants of Saptagram sitting at home and selling products to overseas merchants.

The central authority of Bengal, weakened by the long struggle, had given place by the 1570s to semi-autonomous zamīndārs in eastern Bengal, who flourished with the help of Portuguese mercenaries on the trade of rice, textiles and spices.[79] The 'Moorish' towns of Saptagram and Gaur were replaced by the small towns on the lower Bhagirathi. It was therefore the age of contrasts, of transformation, of the culmination of certain forces, often in conflict with each other. The middle class Bengali, like Mukundarām, was not unhappy as he sang the praises of Mān Singh,[80] while another Hindu poet sang in praise of Akbar.[81]

[79] Tapan Raychaudhuri's view of the zamīndār was limited to the role of mahājan (*op. cit.*, 32-4). It appears that the zamīndārs of eastern Bengal, immediately after the fall of Dāūd Karrānī, acted differently from of their counterparts in Western Bengal (see my article on the pattern of urbanisation and social transformation in Bengal at the end of the 16th century, in A. Ray and R. Chatterjee, ed.: *Madhyayuger Bangali Samāj o Sanskriti*, Calcutta, 1992, 61-86).

[80] Mukundarām, 2-3.

[81] Dwija Mādhav, before 1600, in S. Mukhopadhyay: *Madhyayuger Bangla*, *op. cit.*, 158.

17

The Sikh Movement During the Reign of Akbar

J.S. GREWAL

It is generally believed that the socio-religious community founded by Gurū Nanak became 'a state within the state' by the end of Akbar's reign. However, the question whether or not there was any connection between this development and the Mughal state established by Akbar, has not been discussed seriously by the historians of the Sikhs. They have tended to look upon the situation in terms of personal relations between the emperor and the Gurūs, without postulating the possibility that the empire established by Akbar could have impersonal or unintentional bearing on the development of the Sikh panth.

Indubhusan Banerjee, for example, refers to Akbar's visit to Gurū Amar Dās at Goindwal. Very much impressed by the saintliness of his character and the purity of all around him, Akbar requested the Gurū to accept a favour. The Gurū, however, politely declined to accept any favour. Eventually, however, a grant of several villages in and around the present city of Amritsar was accepted in the name of the Gurū's daughter, which was a great material gain. Furthermore, the emperor's visit enormously increased the fame and prestige of Gurū Amar Dās. The new faith was further raised in the general estimation of the people when Akbar visited Gurū Arjan, and on his request remitted the revenues of the Punajb for one year. According to Banerjee, Akbar's friendliness towards the Gurūs was of help to them also in neutralizing the complaints brought against them by their enemies.[1]

For a fresh look at the bearing of the Mughal state under Akbar on the development of the Sikh panth, we may first turn to that development itself. For this, we have to take into account not only the work of the Gurūs who were contemporary with Akbar but also the work of their predecessors till the beginning of Akbar's reign. In the ideology of Gurū Nānak, the most important single feature was probably his concept of God and man's relation with

[1] *Evolution of the Khalsa*, 2nd ed., Calcutta, 1963, pp.171,213-4.

Him. In the compositions of Gurū Angad, the first successor of Gurū Nānak, the unity, omnipotence, omnipresence, omniscience and immanence of God are taken for granted, like some of the other ideas: God's will or order (*hukm*, *razā*, *farmān*), His grace (*nadar*, *kirpa*, *prasad*), and man's self-centredness (*haumai*). Devotion is to be addressed to God with love and dedication, in trust and fear, in misery and comfort. The first successor of Gurū Nānak remains within the parameters set by Gurū Nānak: the compositions of Gurū Rām Dās read like annotations on the compositions of Gurū Nānak. In both of them God figures in this attributeless state. His revelation through the Word, tell of the divine order, the divine Preceptor, His grace, His transcendence and immanence, the *māyā* and *haumai* and the true path of devotion. However, there are also significant shifts of emphasis and connotation. The idea that every cosmic age has its appropriate faith becomes important: the dispensation peculiar to the present age is that of the Name. In the compositions of Gurū Arjan, God is given some new attributes. He is free from anxiety (*achinta*): He is the remover of misery (*dukh-bhanjan*): and He is the destroyer of the enemy (*satr-dahan*). As we shall see later, these new attributes of God were intimately connected with the historical situation in which Gurū Arjan was composing the hymns in which these epithets occur.

The concept of the Gurū underwent more significant change than the conception of God in the compositions of Gurū Nānak's successors. For Gurū Angad, not only God and the *shabad* (as in the compositions of Gurū Nānak) but also Nānak becomes important as the Gurū. Therefore, the connotation of the statements with a bearing on the Gurū begins to change. 'The Gurū holds the key to salvation'; 'there is utter darkness without the Gurū'. Such statements become as much applicable to Gurū Nānak as to the divine Preceptor. For Gurū Amar Dās, there is no *gurū* but the true Gurū. Those who do not serve the true Gurū remain in misery throughout the four cosmic ages. One should do as the Gurū says, and conform to his wishes (*bhaṇa*). The importance of the Gurū increases further in the compositions of Gurū Rām Dās. He is the father and the mother; he is the friend and the relation. He is the honour of those who possess no honour on their own. He provides the common bond between the Sikhs. In the compositions of Gurū Arjan, the Gurū is the true king, the king of kings; his Sikhs deem it a great boon to sit with him even for a moment. His court is the most high, he is the source of all gifts. His sight removes all sins. His service is always well-rewarded. The Sikhs are expected to remember the Gurū all the time. Indeed, the Gurū is God (*Parbrahm*, *Niranjan*). Gurū Arjan, like his predecessors, carried an aura of divinity for his Sikhs.

Like the Gurū the connotation of the Word (*shabad*) and the name (*nām*) underwent a significant change. In the compositions of Gurū Nānak, the Name is the object and the Word is the medium of divine self-expression. In the compositions of Gurū Angad the Word and the Name get equated also with the sacred compositions of Gurū Nānak himself. There is only one true *shabad*, the nectar-like *bāṇī* of Gurū Nānak. In the compositions of Gurū Amar Dās, the *bāṇī* of the true Gurū is true. It is the sweet nectar of immortality. The *bāṇī* is God: 'Gurmukh *bāṇī* is Brahm'. Any composition other than the composition of the true Gurū is unripe. What is conveyed by unripe compositions is unripe. Gurū Amar Dās prepared two volumes of the true *bāṇī*, consisting mostly of the compositions of Gurū Nānak, Gurū Angad and Gurū Amar Dās himself. Included in these two volumes was the *bāṇī* of *sants* and *bhaktas* like Kabīr and Nāmdev. In the compositions of Gurū Rām Dās, the *bāṇī* of the Gurū is the embodiment of truth: there is no other true *bāṇī*. For Gurū Arjan, the *bāṇī* of the Gurū is a shower of rain for those who are thirsty in spirit. He found 'priceless gems' and an 'inexhaustible treasure' in which it had been preserved by his predecessors. To the two volumes compiled by Gurū Amar Dās, he added his own compositions and the compositions of Gurū Rām Dās, besides the compositions of some more *bhaktas*. A book was compiled in 1604, marked by an unusually systematic arrangement and a complex but generally consistent pattern of division and sub-division. It is now popularly known as *Gurū Granth Sāhib* to indicate that it enjoys the status of the Gurū. Already for Gurū Arjan, it was 'the abode of God'.

Just as the *Granth* came into parallel prominence with the Gurū, so did the Sikhs. In the compositions of Gurū Nānak, Gurmukh is a person oriented towards God. In the compositions of Gurū Angad, Gurmukh gets equated with the followers of Gurū Nānak, and by implication with his own followers. Gurū Angad shows a deep regard for his followers. He is the slave of those who recognize the *shabad*; they are like God to him. He is the slave of those who recognize the unity of God and the secret of His Divinity; they are like God to him. Only those who have turned to the Gurū know that in the outside world of *kaliyug* the king is really a pauper and the learned pandit is really a fool. The 'Gurmukh' thus stands distinguished from the rest of his contemporaries. Gurū Amar Dās underlines the importance of true association (*sat-sangat*) in his compositions. This was the association of his followers who came to the abode of the Gurū (*gurduār*) for singing the *shabad* of the Gurū and to listen to the *bāṇī* sung by the minstrels appointed by the Gurū for this purpose. This true association of 'brothers-in-faith' and 'friends-in-faith' is a source of 'understanding': it opens the door to salvation. Access to the *sangat* is a gift of the Gurū. He who fails to turn to the Gurū and to recognize the *shabad* is self-oriented (*manmukh*). The *sangat* becomes the collective body of the Sikhs in the compositions of Gurū Rām Dās. The *sangat* of the Gurū is dear to God. The food, dress and possessions of those who have appropriated the name are sanctified. They who entertain the Sikhs, their houses and mansions are sanctified. The caparisoned horses which the Sikhs ride are sanctified. They who have God's name on their lips, their actions and affairs are sanctified. They who bring offering to the Gurū, acquire the true merit of charity. The Sikh of the Gurū (*gursikh*) is like the Gurū himself; the true Gurū dwells in him. To meet a *gursikh* is the sign of God's grace.

II

Gurū Nānak had left for his successors the legacy not only of a set of ideas but also of a concrete institution consisting of three distinct but inter-related activities: a place for worship (*dharmsāl*), congregational worship (*sangat*), and community meal (*langar*). This institution was maintained by all his successors not only at the places of their residence but, in due course, also at other places. In contemporary writings, there are references to sweet pudding of rice boiled in milk being served in the community kitchen of Gurū Angad. Similarly, the community kitchen of Gurū Amar Dās was known for the plenty of its fine flour and clarified butter. During the time of Gurū Amar Dās centres for congregational worship and community kitchen were established at places other than Goindwal. A representative of the Gurū was appointed at each of these places. He was expected to cater to the needs of the local congregations and to serve as an intermediary between the Sikhs and the Gurū.

With the proliferation of local congregations arose the need of general congregations at the centre. Gurū Amar Dās encouraged his followers to come to Goindwal at the time of the Baisākhī and the Dīwālī every year. He constructed a stepwell at Goindwal which came to serve the purpose of ritual bathing. Consequently, Goindwal became the first centre of Sikh pilgrimage. The better known centre of Sikh pilgrimage was established in the present city of Amritsar by Gurū Rām Dās and Gurū Arjan. A pool was constructed for ritual bathing, and in its midst was constructed the place of worship called the Harmandir. Around this pilgrimage centre arose the town of Ramdaspur. A few other towns too were founded by Gurū Arjan, like Tarn Taran and Hargobindpur in the Bari Doab and Kartarpur in the Jalandhar Doab. Whereas in the time of Gurū Amar Dās his representatives were expected to collect offerings from the Sikhs and to bring them to the Gurū, in the time of Gurū Arjan his representatives called *masands* used to move from place to place to collect funds for the Gurū, so that the projects undertaken by him could be completed.

The number of Sikhs increased considerably in the time of Gurū Amar Dās. Instead of a few individuals here and there in the countryside, some villages came to have a large number of Sikhs. For the propagation of his faith he visited Kurukshetra and some of the sacred places on the Jamuna and the Ganges. It is not unlikely that some of the Khatri followers of Gurū Amar Dās had started their trading activity outside the province of Lahore. In the compositions of Gurū Rām Dās there is a good deal of insistence on the merit of offerings to the Gurū: 'Give your wealth and riches to him who enables you to meet the Friend'. The followers are asked to send corn and cloth. All their wishes are fulfilled who serve the Gurū with devotion. Whatever they wish, all they wish for, is given: true faith, earthly riches, pleasures and salvation (*dharma, artha, kāma, moksha*).

While Khatris and Brahmans were ignored by God, Nāmdev was drawn close. There were other low-caste devotees of God who attained to salvation through their devotion, like Kabīr, Jaidev, Tarlochan, Ravidās, Dhannā and Sen. Appreciation for the low-caste *Sants* and *Bhaktas* may be treated as an indication of the presence of the low castes among the Sikhs. Gurū Rām Dās is aware of the presence of the cultivators among the Sikhs. He feels concerned about drought and gratified about timely rainfall; he is also aware of wells with the Persian wheel to irrigate the fields. Then there were shopkeepers, petty traders, artisans and craftsmen among the Sikhs, besides the wealthy merchants and traders. The community was never much short of women, but in the compositions of Gurū Rām Dās their presence is as palpable as that of men. He contributed much to the Sikh awareness of a distinct identity by separating them clearly from 'the others' in his compositions. The 'noseless' *manmukh* stands dishonoured: he is a 'nameless' bastard born to a prostitute.

There is no doubt that the number of Sikhs increased considerably in the Punjab during the pontificate of Gurū Arjan. There were many Sikhs in Lahore. Similarly, Sultanpur Lodhi was known as a great centre of Sikhism. There were Sikhs in the smaller towns like Patti Haibatpur, and there were Sikhs in many villages. There were certainly some Brahmans among the Sikhs and some of the out-caste. The trading communities, the cultivators, the artisans and craftsmen were well represented. Among the trading communities, there was a clear preponderance of the Khatris; and among the cultivators, that of the Jats. There was one Mīān Jamāl among the eminent Sikhs who remained present with the Gurū. Furthermore, the Sikhs were not confined to the Punjab. There were Sikhs in Kashmir and Kabul, and in Delhi and Agra. It is most likely indeed that Sikhs could be found now in all the provinces of Akbar's empire.

However, all was not well with the affairs of the Sikh Panth. The law of the state could be invoked by the legal heirs of Gurū Nānak to claim Kartarpur as a matter of right. Therefore, Gurū Angad voluntarily moved to Khadur (in the Amritsar district), leaving Kartarpur in the hands of Sri Chand and Lakhmi Chand, the sons of Gurū Nānak. Sri Chand built in fact a structure over the spot where Gurū Nānak was cremated, and refused to recognize Gurū Angad as the Gurū. Some people were taken in by his claim to succession. The followers of Guru Angad were not thus the only followers of Gurū Nānak. In the compositions of Gurū Angad, the presence of the 'others' is assumed.

Gurū Amar Dās had to leave Khadur because it was claimed

by Dasu and Datu, the sons of Gurū Angad, as their inheritance. They set themselves up as Gurū Angad's spiritual heirs. Gurū Amar Dās founded a new centre a few miles away on the right bank of the river Beas, on the route from Lahore to Delhi, which developed into a township known as Goindwal. There are detractors (*nindak*) too, and there are deserters who have turned away (*bemukh*). The Gurū does not regard anyone as his enemy, and his Sikhs are safe under the protection of the all-powerful God. Their enemies do not know that He is the only true king: His worshippers cannot come to any harm at the hands of the agents of the earthly kings. There are indications, thus, that the opponents of the Gurū were seeking help from the local administrators. Opposition to the Gurū may be taken as a measure of his increasing success in propagating his faith. The principle of nomination was upheld by Gurū Amar Dās rather vehementhly. 'God Himself is the Gurū and He Himself is the disciple (*chelā*)'. This could be applied to Gurū Nānak and Gurū Angad as well. In any case, it is a part of the divine order that the Gurū can raise another to the status of the Gurū.

In the compositions of Gurū Rām Dās, the opponents of the nominated successors do not realize that the treasure of *bhakti* had been bestowed upon the true devotees of God from the very beginning. The opponents had been cursed by Gurū Nānak and by Gurū Angad. The third Gurū had thought that they possessed no power to harm. The fourth Gurū forgave the detractors and their associates. But the detractors persist in their folly and suffer ignominy. They seek the support of local administrators and *chaudharīs*. This combination presented a threat which Gurū Rām Dās could not fail to notice. He advises his followers not to retaliate, and to leave things to God. The *dīwāns* of God, the Sikhs, need not be afraid of the earthly *dīwān*, the administrators of the empire. All the emperors and kings, *k͟hāns* and *amīrs* and *shiqdārs* are subject to the power of God and they only do what. He wills for them. Since the Sikhs belong to the 'faction' of God they need not fear an earthly faction (*dharā*). Gurū Rām Dās invokes myth and legend to reassure the Sikhs that God is their protector.

If the idea of Gurū Rām Dās was to enable his successor to have legal claims over Ramdaspur as one of his heirs, and thereby to enable him to remain in control of the headquarters, it was eminently successful. Gurū Arjan was the first successor of Gurū

Nānak, who succeeded to the missionary centre of his immediate predecessor. However, he was also the son of his predecessor, and the other heirs could claim a share in the property. Gurū Arjan's eldest brother, Prithi Chand, approached the local administrators probably to claim the position of his father but he had to be content with a share in the income from Ramdaspur. Gurū Arjan was only eighteen years old at the time of his nomination, and he had no son. Prithi Chand ḅided his time, remaining unreconciled to the elevated position of his younger brother. After the birth of Gurū Arjan's son Hargobind in 1595, Prithi Chand's hostility was sharpened and he tried to harm Hargobind.

There were other detractors too. Gurū Arjan refers to them rather frequently in his compositions. They are generally foiled in their attempt to harm the Gurū's interests. If one of them submitted an affidavit signed by a number of persons (*maḥẓar*) to the *qāẓī* against the Gurū, it turned out to be false and the author of this falsehood met an ignominious end. If another tried to poison the child Hargobind, he was himself killed. An inveterate enemy of Gurū Arjan was one Sulhi; he got axed to death before his evil intentions got clothed in action. The faces of the detractors were 'blackened' when they made a representation against the Gurū to a high dignitary of state who found their charges baseless and allowed the Gurū safely to return home. It is most likely that Akbar's attitude towards Gurū Arjan had a sheltering effect. To cope with the feeling of insecurity, Gurū Arjan exhorted his followers to cultivate profound faith and trust in God. He who remembers God gets rid of fear. The *shabad* of the Gurū acts like a protective garrison all around. The 'wealth of God' is the antidote for anxiety. The Name makes one fearless. They who take refuge in God have nothing to fear.

III

To sum up, at the time of Akbar's death in 1605 the Sikhs were living in many cities of the Mughal empire, with a clear concentration in the towns and the villages of the province of Lahore. Accredited representatives (*masands*) of the Gurū looked after the distant congregations (*sangats*) and brought their offerings to

Ramdaspur (Amritsar) at least once a year. Included among the Sikhs were members of the trading communities of merchants and shopkeepers, and of the producing communities of culivators and craftsmen. Themselves self-reliant, they provided the economic backbone for the organization evolved by the Gurus to enable them to undertake large projects without financial dependence on outside agencies.

The religious ideology of Gurū Nānak was reinforced by his successors in a manner that added new dimensions without minimizing the importance of his basic ideas. With reference to the nomination of Angad as the Gurū in the lifetime of Gurū Nānak, the successors were brought into equal prominence with the founder; the idea of the unity of Gurūship was adumbrated and upheld; the office of the Gurū became more important than the person of the Gurū; and his decisions became as legitimate as the decisions of the founder. Thus, the pontificates of the successors became an extension of the mission of the founder, and the work of his successors became an extension of his work. With reference to the reversal of the position of the disciple with the Gurū, the individual Sikh was given great consideration by the Gurū, and the collective body of the congregation (*sangat*) was given even greater importance. With reference to the *shabad* as the medium of divine revelation, and the *bāṇī* of Gurū Nānak as a part of that revelation, the composition of the Gurūs were brought into parallel prominence with the Gurū. Though neither an incarnation of God nor His prophet, the Gurū was so closely allied to Him that his followers regarded him as the *locus* of divinity.

The religious ideology of the Sikhs, which informed their attitudes to life, was embodied in the *Granth* compiled by Gurū Arjan. The Sikhs were now becoming more and more conscious that their scripture was tangibly distinct from the Veda and the Qurān. Incorporating the ideas contained in the compositions of *sants*, *bhaktas* and *ṣūfīs*, which had the greatest affinity with the ideas of the Gurūs themselves, the Sikh scripture thus contained ideas becoming current in much of the Indian subcontinent. Composed in a language that was easily understood by common people over a large part of northern India, it was written out in a script that was easily the simplest of all the scripts known to India. It became the only authentic source of the characteristically Sikh ideas which were distinct from much in the contemporary systems of religious belief and practice. Copies could be made of the entire *Granth*, or a significant selection could be made, for use in distant places. To listen to *gurbāṇī*, in any case, was to hear the voice of the Gurū himself.

The distinctive Sikh identity, based initially on religious ideology, was reinforced by the adoption of distinct ceremonies on the occasions of birth, marriage and death. The Sikhs were free to maintain the old horizontal links of castes and sub-castes for matrimonial purposes, but there was nothing in the teachings of the Gurū that could be invoked in support of such links. The ideal of equality was openly demonstrated in the institutions of congregational worship and community meals. Ramdaspur (Amritsar) as the place of pilgrimage was open to all Sikhs from far and near, and large crowds used to come to the festivals of Baisākhī and Dīwālī. The bi-annual convergence of Sikh pligrims to the town of Gurū Rām Dās gave them a feeling of spiritual elation; it gave them also a sense of belonging to a large brotherhood.

The Sikh Panth was a distinct entity within the Mughal empire at the death of Akbar, but one that had its opponents and enemies whose presence was continuously felt by the successors of Gurū Nānak. The enemies were becoming more numerous, and their intrigues were on the increase. If the law of the state enabled some of them to approach the administrators with plausible claims over the property and wealth of the Gurūs, the cupidity of the administrators induced them to entertain those claims. Akbar's catholicity could protect the Gurūs and their followers against open violence, but it could not obviate all the designs of their enemies. The removal of a protecting umbrella could fuel the heat of hostility for the Gurū and his followers. It was not entirely fortuitous that within eight months of Akbar's death in October 1605, Gurū Arjan died the death of a martyr, tortured by the new emperor's underlings at Lahore.

We are now in a position to say something about the bearing which the Mughal state under Akbar had on the development of the Sikh Panth. Akbar adopted several measures which modified the character of the state. He made an extensive and effective use of suzerain-vassal polity by which a large number of non-Muslim chiefs became politically subordinate to him. He tried to induct the willing vassals into the *mansabdārī* system as an important component of his general policy. He abolished the discriminatory *jizya* and the pilgrimage tax. He discouraged cow slaughter and forcible conversion from one faith to another. He extended state patronage to non-Muslim institutions and individuals. His concessions and measures for conciliation resulted in peace and security in his vast dominions.

The establishment of relative peace and security became an important condition for the growth of prosperity. Extension of agriculture was an important objective of Akbar's revenue policy. There are clear indications that more and more land was brought under cultivation during the late sixteenth century. Cash crops were sown for the market and agricultural produce was used for manufactures. Standardization of weights, measures and currency was conducive to economic development. To encourage trade, Akbar abolished many internal imposts. Routes were protected for caravans and trade became a pretty safe proposition. Akbar's reign was marked by revival of trade on a large scale. The increase in the size and the number of urban centres in the dominions of Akbar during the late sixteenth century was an indication of increase in the volume of trade and manufactures as well as in agricultural production.

The province of Lahore was among the advanced provinces of Akbar's empire in terms of agriculture, manufactures and trade, with Lahore as one of the largest cities of the Mughal empire. Abū'l Faẓl observed that most of the province was irrigated by wells. This artificial means of irrigation enabled the peasants to grow high-quality or cash crops. Well known for its rock-salt, the province was reputed also for its exports of sugar, textiles, shawls and carpets. The city of Lahore was on the trade route from Delhi to Kabul. The economic development of the Punjab provided good opportunities for enterprising traders and cultivators.

The prosperity of Khatri and Jat Sikhs, who brought generous offerings to their Gurūs to enable them to undertake large-scale projects, was itself made possible by developments in the Mughal empire under Akbar. Ironically, the increasing wealth and resources of the Gurūs made their rivals increasingly vehement in their opposition to the nominated successors. In this situation, the support received by the Gurūs from the authorities of the state was extremely helpful. Nevertheless, continued opposition profoundly influenced the development of Sikh ideas and attitudes.

The compilation of the *Granth*, which included the compositions of *Sants*, *Bhaktas* and *Ṣūfīs*, was not unconnected with the atmosphere of rivalry and dissension within what would be broadly seen as the Sikh-fold. Emphatic insistence on the importance of the Gurū and the unity of Gurūship was linked up with the same situation. The importance of the individual Sikh and the collective body of the Sikhs was part of the same process. Some of the new epithets for God were clearly a product of tension within the Sikh community.

If the prosperity of the state was reflected in the material wealth and financial independence of the Gurūs, the dissensions arising out of the concern to control material resources were giving a particular kind of shift and emphasis to Sikh ideology in its bearing on the conception of God, the concept of Gurūship, the importance of the Sikhs and the compilation of the *Granth*. These precisely were the developments which gave to the Sikh Panth the character of a state within the state. The reaction of Gurū Hargobind to the death of Gurū Arjan was only a logical step from the position at the time of Akbar's death. As Bhāī Gurdās put it, the successor of Gurū Arjan decided to erect the hedge of the hardly *kikar* tree around the orchard of the Sikh faith to make it safe against the strong winds of opposition from wherever direction they might come. This may be regarded as the most appropriate metaphor for the smooth transition from the peaceful development of the Sikh Panth to what is generally referred to as its militarization.

SELECT BIBLIOGRAPHY

Ādi Srī Gurū Granth Sāhib Jī (Sri Damdami Bir, various printed editions, standard pagination).

Banerjee, Indubhusan, *Evolution of the Khalsa*, Vol.I, A. 3 Mukherjee & Co., Calcutta, 1963 (2nd ed.).

Cunningham, J.D., *A History of the Sikhs*, London, 1849.

Ganda Singh (ed), *Mākhiz-i-Tawārīkh-i Sikhān*, Amritsar, 1949.

Gopal Singh, *Sri Guru Granth Sahib* (Eng. tr.), Delhi, 1962.

Grewal, J.S., *Guru Nanak in History*, Chandigarh, 1979 (2nd ed.).

———, *From Guru Nanak to Maharaja Ranjit Singh*, Amritsar, 1982 (2nd ed.).

———, *The Sikhs of the Punjab* (II.3 of *The New Cambridge History of India*), Cambridge, 1990.

Irfan Habib, *The Agrarian System of Mughal India*, Bombay, 1963.

Khan, Ahsan Raza, *Chieftains in the Mughal Empire During the Reign of Akbar*, Shimla, 1977.

McLeod, W.H., *Guru Nanak and the Sikh Religion*, Oxford, 1968.

———, *The Evolution of the Sikh Community*, Oxford, 1975.

———, *Early Sikh Tradition: A Study of the Janam-Sakhis*, Oxford, 1980.

———, *Textual Sources for the Study of Sikhism*, Manchester, 1984.

Nurul Hasan, *Thoughts on Argarian Relations in Mughal India*, New Delhi, 1973.

Ray, Niharranjan, *The Sikh Gurus and Sikh Society: A Study in Social Analysis*, Patiala, 1970.

Raychaudhuri, Tapan, and Irfan Habib (eds.), *Cambridge Economic History of India*, Cambridge, 1984.

Sabdārth Srī Gurū Granth Sāhib Jī (text and commentary, 1936-1941).

Shireen Moosvi, *The Economy of the Mughal Empire*, New Delhi, 1987.

Teja Singh, *Sikhism: Its Ideals and Institutions*, Bombay, 1937.

18

Akbar and Portuguese Maritime Dominance

K.S. MATHEW

By1556 when Akbar ascended the throne, the Portuguese had established themselves firmly on the Western coast of India and had set up a large number of fortresses and factories there, with a few settlements on the Eastern coast. Navigation in the Indian Ocean was restricted to a large extent by the introduction and enforcement of the Portuguese system of *cartazes*. Merchants, the nobility and the rulers of the subcontinent were constrained to purchase passes from the Portuguese and to abide by the terms and conditions of these passes at risk of confiscation of their vessels and cargo. In the words of 'Abdu'l 'Azīz, writing in the last quarter of the sixteenth century, certain commodities like pepper which were produced by the Indians had to be purchased from the Portuguese. He added: 'Whoever wanted a corn of pepper for soup (the Portuguese gave it) powdered and packed in a piece of cloth.' The complaint of Abdu'l 'Azīz, the brother of Shaikh Zain-ud-din of Ponnani (Kerala), could be considered as representative of the feeling of the common folk of the country. The resentment of the nobility was shown in the concerted effort made by Khwāja Safar, the merchant governor of Surat in the 1540s, to oust the Portuguese from Gujarat and the Indian Seas. The alliance he made with the rulers of West Asia to drive them away speaks clearly of the attitude of the nobility involved in maritime trade. Upon his conquest of Gujarat (1572), Akbar not only achieved his first access to the sea, but also came to confront the problems the Portuguese presence posed to Indian trade and maritime activities.

Gujarat, one of the most commercialised regions of India during the medieval period, provided a very congenial rendezvous for people of diverse nationalities. Malik Ayāz, originally a Christian from Russia established himself on a firm footing at Diu and became one of the chief governors of the sultanate of Gujarat. With a view to keeping the Portuguese traders at bay he constructed a bastion in the sea, called *Sankal Koth* and connected Diu to the shore by means of an iron chain to prevent the ships of the *Firangīs* from forcing a passage.[1] Khwāja Safar who was the governor of Surat and commanded great respect among the nobility, was an Albanian who took refuge in Diu with 300,000 *cruzados*, 600 Turkish soldiers, a few pieces of artillery, jewels and his women. Subsequently around 1527 he entered the service of Bahādur Shāh simultaneously involving himself in trade with a capital of 600,000 *cruzados* invested in Diu.[2] Diu, which was one of the important ports of coastal Gujarat, was regarded by the Portuguese as the gateway to India and right from the very beginning of their overseas enterprise, they fixed their eyes on it, ultimately acquiring it in 1535.

The relations between Akbar and the Portuguese could be studied on the basis of trade and navigation as well as religious contacts. Much has been written on the latter aspect while very little attention has till now has been paid to the former. A better understanding of the problem will be possible against the backdrop of the maritime supremacy claimed by the Portuguese in the sixteenth century. Akbar himself consented to take a *cartaz* from the Portuguese for the Imperial ships leaving the Gujarat coast every year for the Red Sea and the Gulf. In this he was merely following precedent.

The origin of the issue of *cartazes* could be traced to 1502 when Vasco da Gama insisted that all ships plying in the Indian Ocean that wanted to be escape the violent hands of the Portuguese mariners, must take a pass signed by the Portugue sea-captain.[3] This obligation was accepted by the merchants, the nobility as well as several rulers in various parts of the subcontinent under

[1] Sikandar Muḥammad, alias Manjhu Gujarātī, *Mir'āt-i Sikandarī*, translated by Fazlullah Lutfullah Faridi, Delhi (reprint), 1990, p.84.

[2] MSS. Archive Nacional da Torre do Tombo (hereafter ANTT.), Lisbon, 'Cartas dos Vicereis', maco unico No.24; K.S. Mathew, 'Khwāja Saffar, the Merchant Governor of Surat and the Indo-Portuguese Trade in the Early Sixteenth Centurys' in *Vice-Almirante A. Teixeira Da Moto in Memoriam*, I, Lisboa, 1987, pp.319-28.

[3] Gaspar Correa, *Lendas da India*, I, Coimbra, 1922, p.298.

the threat of confiscation of their men and material. Except for the Portuguese, all the parties were put to a loss thereby; the Indian rulers, the Arabs, the Egyptians and the Venetians put up a stiff fight in the first decade of the sixteenth century, but did not meet with any great success. In almost all the diplomatic engagements signed between the Portuguese and the Indian rulers, it was agreed that the ships leaving Indian coasts would take passes signed by the Portuguese officials against a nominal payment and would return to the stipulated port for the payment of customs duties. Bahādur Shāh, the Sulṭān of Gujarat, concluded a treaty with Nuno da Cunha, the Governor of Portuguese India, on 23 December 1534; while surrendering Bassein to the Portuguese. He took upon himself the responsibility to see that the vessels leaving any part of Gujarat to West Asia or any other regions outside India as well as those coming to India would carry the Portuguese pass.[4] The same ruler signed another treaty on 25 October 1535 accepting the obligation of taking *cartazes* from the Portuguese. This was done at the time of the surrender of Diu to the Portuguese for building a fortress.[5] The vessels violating the terms and conditions under which passes were issued were confiscated by the Portuguese. A situation of this nature was odious to the Indians, but the Portuguese naval power could not be effectively challenged. The change of situation since the time of Malik Ayāz is clearly brought out by contemporary writers who recalled that during the time of Malik Ayāz no Portuguese vessel dared to come to coastal Gujarat while after the death of Ayāz no Indian ship could leave the Gujarat coast without a pass from the Portuguese.[6] Khwāja Safar, the governor of Surat organised a naval battle in 1546 as a representative of all those who were humiliated by the Portuguese, but he could not achieve much.[7]

[4] Simao Botelho, 'O Tombo do Estado da India', in Rodrigo Jose de Lima Felner (ed.), *Subsidios para a Historia da India Portgueza,* Lisboa, 1988, pp.134-8.

[5] Ibid., folio 180v.

[6] Manjhu writes: 'During the government of the Malik, the *Firangī* was unable to enter the Gujarat ports. Now, however, by degrees, things have come to such a pass that without a permit from the *Firangī*, a vessel dare not leave any of the ports of Gujarat, except Surat, and this also is owing solely to the gallantry and bravery of those entrusted with the government of the city of Surat'. (*Mir'āt-i Sikandarī*, pp.84-85).

[7] For detailed information on this naval confrontation see Diogo de Teive, *Com-*

Chroniclers of the period of Akbar were fully aware of the premeditated murder of Bahādur Shāh in February 1537 by the Portuguese and their efforts to control movement of the ships in the Indian Ocean[8] Some of them were of the opinion that Khudāwand Khān built the fortress at Surat, later repaired under the orders of Akbar, for the purpose of preventing the Portuguese from seizing ships leaving Surat for West Asia.[9]

Intent on bringing Gujarat under his control Akbar besieged Surat, where he met the Portuguese for the first time.[10] This friendly gesture was probably judged necessary by Akbar to facilitate the pilgrimage to Mecca and avoid any harm to the vessels carrying pilgrims by the Portuguese mariners. Akbar, after having established friendly contacts with the Portuguese at Surat, left for the north probably on 8 March 1573, marching to Ahmedabad via Broach, and Cambay. It is recorded by a contemporary Portuguese writer that the relations between Akbar and the Portuguese turned out to be so friendly that he took to wearing Portuguese dress obtained from Portuguese merchants at Cambay. As Akbar went on occupying the port-cities of Surat, Broach, and Cambay, the fifty to sixty Portuguese merchants at Cambay sought from him the special favour of exempting them from the obligation of paying custom duties for the commodities imported into Cambay by them. The Emperor granted the request as a mark of favour towards the Portuguese. It was reported that

mentarius de rebus a Lusitanis in India apud Dium gestis anno salutis nostrae MDXLVI, Coimbra, 1548, Goert (ed.), Lisboa, 1973.

[8] Abū'l-Faẓl, *Akbarnāma*, Vol.I, translated by H. Bever idge, New Delhi, 1977, pp.322-324; Badāūnī, *Muntakhabu-t Tawārīkh*, I, p.458.

[9] 'Abdu-l-Qadīr Badāūnī, *Muntakhabu-t-Tawārīkh*, I, translated and edited by George S.A. Ranking, New Delhi, n.d., p.150.

[10] It is supposed by the contemporary Persian chroniclers that the Portuguese came to Surat at the invitation of the Mirzās to fight against Akbar. But on realising that Akbar had an invincible army, they resorted to diplomacy and the Portuguese Governor sent an ambassador to Akbar for establishing peace and friendship. It is also opined by some other chroniclers that Akbar himself had sent an envoy to Goa asking the Portuguese Governor to send some persons to meet him at Surat. This attempt on the part of Akbar to send his envoys to the Viceroy at Goa could be on account of the projected pilgrimage of the members of his harem as well as his mother and other relations to Mecca. Probably the 'mother' referred to by Diogo do Couto, the Portuguese chronicler, could be Ḥājī Begam, the step-mother of Akbar, who, went along with Mariam Makānī, his own mother, and Gulbadan Begum. See Abū'l-Faẓl, *Akbarnāma*, III, p.37; Diogo de Couto, *Da Asia*, decada IX, Lisboa, 1786, pp.64-87.

an amount of 300,000 *cruzados* was paid every year by the Portuguese as duties to the captain of Cambay.[11] Subsequent to the establishment of friendly relations, Akbar issued a *farmān* on March 18, 1573 presumably at Broach, instructing his captains, governors, administrators and other officials working especially in Surat, Broach, Nausari and Velodra (Vadodara) in the province of Gujarat not to disturb the Portuguese in their possessions like Daman. He added that the Portuguese viceroy Dom Antonio de Noronha had sent his envoy Antonio Cabral to him offering friendship. It was further enjoined that they should not favour the Malabar pirates, but on the contrary should extend help to the Portuguese. In case slaves belonging to the Portuguese took refuge in any part of the Mughal territory of Gujarat, they were to be judged according to their law and returned to their masters.[12]

The Portuguese on their side showed their goodwill by issuing passes to the members of the family of Akbar to go on pilgrimage to Mecca. In view of the request made by the officials of the Emperor, Antonio Cabral provided their vessel with *cartaz* (*salvo conducto*). Antonio Cabral was requested to make special mention in the pass (*cartaz*) about the extraordinary attention to be paid to this particular vessel and the important persons travelling to Mocha, the Red Sea port, which was done readily by him. It was further agreed that every year a free *cartaz* would be issued to a ship leaving for Mocha from Surat according to the desire of the Emperor and the ship equipped with the pass would be exempted from custom-duties on its return to the Gujarat coast. This practice continued even after the death of Akbar so much so that Jahāngīr and his successors were regularly given the free *cartaz* and mention was made in such passes that this was done according to the custom in vogue.[13]

[11] Diogo do Couto, op. cit., pp.66-7.

[12] Diogo do Couto, who was later appointed by Dom Philip, the King of Portugal, as the first keeper of the Archives (Torre do Tombo) in Goa obtained the *farmān* issued by Akbar from some one in Goa and showed it to the Viceroy (Dom Francisco Mascarenhas ?). Later it was deposited in the Archives. Couto says that this *farmān* was written on paper of high quality and sealed by the hanging seal of Akbar. He expresses his surprise as to how this document reached the hands of a private individual in Goa. He, however, did not know the name of the person. The full text of the *farmān* in Portuguese translation is provided by Couto, Decada X, pp.82-4.

[13] In the *cartaz* issued to Bhimji Parekh under the orders of Jahāngīr for the

A *cartaz* thus issued contained a reference to the circumstance in which it was given. The name and the tonnage of the ship, the age and the name of its captain, the port of embarkation as well as disembarkation, and the approximate date of the departure were also indicated in the *cartaz*. Mention was also made of the arms and ammunition carried in the ship and the items that were prohibited to be transported were also stated. Lastly, the names of the writers and of the issuing authority were given along with the date of issue.

The financial implications of a *cartaz* of this nature annually given to Emperor Akbar by the Portuguese are worth noting. According to the prevailing terms and conditions agreed upon both by the Sulṭāns of Gujarat and the Portuguese authorities, all vessels leaving or heading for the Gujarat coast were obliged to report at the customs house at Diu for paying customs. The revenues of the customs house at Diu were farmed out to the highest bidder. Therefore, the revenue farmers of the port, being aware of the free *cartaz* issued to Emperor Akbar, demanded a reduction of 18,000 *pardaos* from the amount due from them per annum. They justified their demand showing the details from the books of the customs house at Diu. So the finances of Portuguese India suffered a loss of 18,000 *pardaos* solely because of the free pass issued. It is calculated that the effects of the loss were aggravated by another decrease of 5,000 *cruzados* per year in the income of the Portuguese.

The residents of Cambay who used to proceed to Mocha in their own vessels numbering between twelve to fifteen were obliged to reach Diu every year on their return voyage to pay the custom duties. In view of the fact that Akbar's ship returning from Mocha was exempted from paying custom duties, these merchants from Cambay began to load rich cargoes of gold, silver, brocade, coral and other commodities into this ship at Mocha. This was hardly to Portuguese interest, since the customs house at Diu used to get large revenues from

ship called *Mubārakshāhī* on 18 May 1620, special reference is made to the tradition of issuing a free *cartaz* every year, and it is added that the present issuance was in conformity with this as well as on account of the ties of friendship between the Portuguese and the Mughal Emperor Jahāngīr (MSS. Historical Archives of Goa, Codex No.1043, fl.50).

such costly items. A great loss in revenue was thus inflicted on the customs house and subsequently on the finances of Portuguese India. But the Portuguese could do little about it, being bound by the agreement made with Akbar in 1573.[14]

Occasionally the cargo brought from the Red Sea to Gujarat by ships equipped with free *cartaz* issued by the Portuguese in view of the understanding since 1573 cost much more than what was calculated. Five ships loaded with commodities from Jidda in the Red Sea reached Goga in the month of August, 1577(?). The Portuguese authorities on account of information given by the farmers of revenue at Diu, who would be losing their income, decided to chase these ships and capture them, whether they carried *cartaz* or not.[15] Later, another vessel belonging to the Emperor too was sighted at Goga and was captured by the Portuguese. Fernao Miranda was ordered by the Viceroy to proceed to Goga to deal with the matter. This ship was carrying the pass issued by Portuguese, though the revenue farmers of Diu expressed suspicion about its genuineness. The vessel, returning from Jidda, was taken to the channel at Goga escorted by Portuguese vessels. The revenue farmers insisted that the ship should be sent to the customs house at Diu arguing that the customs duties from the cargo of the ship belonged to them in view of the terms and conditions of the contract signed by them. Caught in such a situation, Braz de Azevedo decided to await the decision of the Viceroy. In the meantime a certain Rāo who was the governor of the Mughals in Gujarat sent his envoys to the Portuguese Viceroy pleading justice in the name of Akbar for the captured ship. At the same time he made preparations to send a few vessels from Surat to extend help to the Imperial ship. The Viceroy sent Francisco Paes to bring the ship with its cargo to Goa. At last the ship laden with commodities from Jidda was returned to the Emperor's agents after detailed negotiations. This ship, according to the log book kept in it carried gold and silver worth 600,000 *cruzados,* besides coral, brocade and other items.[16]

The news that the Portuguese were capturing Gujarati ships returning from Mocha reached various parts of India. It was reported by Shai<u>kh</u> Zainuddīn of Ponnani on the Malabar coast,

[14] Diogo do Couto, Decada IX, pp.86-87.
[15] Ibid., Decada X, part 1, pp.287-88.
[16] Ibid., pp.300-04.

who, writing in the last quarter of the sixteenth century, narrates that several Gujarati ships were captured, by the Portuguese in 1577. A few ships belonging to Akbar were among those captured, and they had very rich cargo. On account of this the relations between the Portuguese and the Emperor were temporarily strained, though peace was re-established and the seized cargo restored. Every one interested in trade and commerce and the freedom of the sea earnestly wished that Akbar should oust the Portuguese from Indian ports.[17]

Despite the friendly relations existing between Akbar and the Portuguese, rumours were spread that the latter would continue to hinder the movement of ships from Surat to West Asia. When the Emperor was passing through Udaipur, he was told that the passengers due to leave Surat aboard ship were frightened over the possible threat from the Portuguese. Immediately, Qulij Khān, one of the powerful administrators of Gujarat, was asked to ensure their departure and safe voyage from Surat. The fact that the passengers set sail in two ships, the *Salīmī* and *Ilāhī*, even before Qulij Khān reached the port, proved the rumour to be baseless.[18] However, it still points to the general anxiety in the minds of the people about Portuguese intentions.

Akbar appointed Quṭbu-d-dīn Khān in February 1580 to initiate military action against the Portuguese with the help of the officers in Malwa and Gujarat. The rulers of the Deccan too were urged to join in the common cause of ousting the Portuguese from India. They were told that this would be an opportunity to show their loyalty to the Emperor and that their subjects would thereby be saved from the attacks of the imperial army.[19]

[17] David Lopes, ed., *Historia dos Portugueses no Malabar por Zinadim: Manuscripto Arabe do Seculo XVI*, Lisboa, 1898, p.83. The way in which vessels and merchants without *cartaz* issued by the Portgeuse were treated and the humiliation inflicted on the Indians are graphically described in the Arabic *Urjuza:Fatḥul-Mubiyin* of 'Abdu'l 'Azīz. This work was explicitly composed by him to prompt kings and emperors to wage war against the Portuguese and bring to their notice the misery of the Indians on account of the supremacy imposed by the Portuguese on the Indian Ocean. The original manuscript in Arabic is found under Or.No.1044, Section no.vi fols.152-173 of the India Office Library. The translation of the same is provided by M.A. Muid Khan, in P.M. Joshi and M.A. Nayeem (eds.), *Studies in the Foreign Relations of India from the earliest times to 1947*, Hyderabad, 1975, pp.169-183.

[18] Abū'l Faẓl, *Akbarnāma*, III, p.275.

[19] Ibid., pp.409-410.

Akbar was of the opinion that the *Feringīs*, who turned out to be a great threat to the pilgrimage to Mecca as well as to trade, should be driven away from the Indian Ocean.[20] It was considered quite humiliating for so powerful an emperor as Akbar to ask for passes from the Portuguese, it being held by the people that the obligation of taking passes for the ships of the Emperor was an infringement of his dignity.[21] The sense of resentment was so great that Akbar is reported to have forbidden the pilgrims from going to Mecca altogether.[22] It was reported that under the orders of the Emperor, a *fatwā* prohibiting the Ḥaj pilgrimage was issued by one of the jurists, on the ground that while passage through Persia caused much harassment at the hands of Shiites (*Qizilbāshīs*), the sea voyage involved the necessity of carrying the passes issued by the Portuguese, which were stamped with pictures of Jesus and Mary considered by the Muslims to be acts of idolatry.[23]

Though Akbar had instructed his officials in Malwa and Gujarat to take necessary steps to drive away the Portuguese with the assistance of Deccan rulers, there is no record of any effective expedition against the Portuguese. On the contrary, even Akbar's successors like Jahāngīr sent their men for the *cartazes* from the Portuguese, who, quoting long-standing practice, issued the passes.[24] This implies that the arrangement in vogue from 1573 when Akbar made a formal compact with the Portuguese and agreed to take *cartazes*, was not discontinued during his lifetime and afterwards, however odious it might have been thought to be.

It may be concluded that Akbar kept friendly relations with the Portuguese during his reign, and he did not seek any serious confrontation with them or challenge their naval supremacy. It

[20] Ibid., p.757. [21] David Lopes, op.cit., p.96.

[22] Ibid.

[23] Badāūnī, op.cit., vol.2, p.206; David Lopes, op.cit., p.96. Blochmann denies the fact that Akbar prohibited pilgrimages to Mecca before A.H. 990 and states that the extract given by Elliot on page 244 is misleading. (Abū'l Faẓl, *Ā'īn-i-Akbarī*, Delhi, 1977, vol.1, p.181 f.n.). It is, stated by Abū'l Faẓl that actually the Emperor did not prohibit pilgrimage at this time, it being only a story propagated by Khān Jahān who wanted to escape from the alms he was bound to pay on his wealth. It is added by Badāūnī that Makhdūm-ul-Mulk propagated the story with a view to avoiding legal alms. Badāūnī, op.cit, II, p.206.

[24] See reference in footnote 13.

is not easy to affirm with certainty that the weakness of Akbar on the naval front compelled him to adopt an attitude of this nature. A ruler of his stature could have developed the required naval force if he considered it essential. Presumably, in the general framework of his dealings with various religious denominations, he did not want to take any serious step that was directed towards creating animosity towards the Portuguese, who were Catholics, though one might as well argue that he entertained the Portuguese missionaries with a view to avoiding any damage to his ships. The complications in the Deccan also must have contributed to shift the scales in favour of amicable relations with the Portuguese.

DOCUMENTS

1

A Farmān of Akbar (1558) from the Period of the Regency

SAIYID ZAHEER HUSAIN JAFRI

Recently the National Archives of India have acquired a set of family documents from Begum Amina, wife of Professor Abu Bakar, Jamia Millia Islamia, New Delhi, whose ancestors enjoyed the office of *qāẓī* and *khaṭīb* in *pargana* Chandpur, *sarkār* Sambhal, *ṣūba* Delhi for a considerable period during Mughal rule.[1] These documents cover a period of three centuries, and mainly relate to property disputes, the division of the *madad-i ma'āsh* holdings among heirs, and initial and confirmatory *farmāns* and *parwānas* for land-grants. There are a few papers from the reign of Akbar which shed light on important aspects of the revenue administration during the period of the *karorī* experiment (beginning, 1574-75). Certain insights are also provided into the problems faced by the grantees (*a'immadārs*) during this period, which ultimately necessitated the concentration of the *madad-i ma āsh* lands in the certain (*a'imma*) villages in each *pargana*.

In the present note I only wish to draw attention to the earliest of these documents, a *farmān* of Akbar dated the month of Ṣafar 966, corresponding to 13 November-11 December 1558.

I first give a translation of this *farmān*, which now bears the number 2719/1 at the National Archives.

[Invocation:] 'He is without need' (*Huwa al-Ghanī*)
[Ṭughrā:] *Farmān* of Jalālu'ddīn Muḥammad Akbar Pādshāh Ghāzī.
[Round Seal on the right against the top two half-lines:]
[Legend in middle of Seal:] Jalālu'ddīn Muḥammad Akbar Pādshāh Ghāzī, son of Muḥammad Humāyūn Pādshāh Ghāzī.
[Names of ancestors up to Amīr Timūr on the rim]

[Text:]

Let the *wajhdārs* [officers holding *wajh*, or territorial assignments in lieu of salary] of *pargana* Chāndpūr know that Maulānā Aḥmad, *Khaṭīb* [sermon-reader], has come to the Imperial Court and petitioned that in respect

[1] Chandpur and Sambhal are well-known towns respectively in the Districts of Bijnor and Moradabad, Uttar Pradesh.

of the hereditary land (*zamīn-i maurūṣī*), which he holds in the limits of the *qaṣba* (township) of the said *pargana*, there had been a dispute between the petitioner and Wajīhu'd-dīn, and the said dispute had been placed for adjudication before the *qāẓīs* of Islam and the reputed scholars of the *khiṭṭa* of Sambhal and [of] the said *pargana*, who gave the petitioner's share to him; but now the said Wajīhu'd-dīn is deviating from that settlement (*dastūr*). Should what has been represented be true, it IS incumbent on them [the addressed officials] to act according to the settlement arrived at before the *qāẓīs* of Islam and the reputed scholars of that place, in which behalf he (the petitioner) holds a public statement (*maḥẓar*), and not to allow the said person [Wajīhu'd-dīn] to deviate from that settlement (*dastūr*). Written on the date Ṣafar 966.

The *ẓimn* (reverse) has two seals, of two scholars Shaikh Anẓar, son of Shaikh Khiẓr, and Shaikh Mīr 'Īsā Bābā, son of 'Abdullāh. Unfortunately, the xeroxed copy taken before the document was acquired by the National Archives is not good enough for reproduction. But there are no great problems in deciphering the main text.

The purport of the text is clear enough. The following points, however, deserve attention.

1. *Pargana* Chāndpūr was then a part of the *Khiṭṭa* (region) of Sambhal. This accords with the important position assigned to Sambhat by Bābur as a *sarkār*;[2] it later became a *sarkār* of Akbar's *ṣūba* of Delhi.[3]
2. The officials to whom the *farmān* is addressed are termed *wajhdārs*, perhaps a unique instance among the surviving *farmāns* from Akbar's time. This term reminds us of its use in the *Bāburnāma*, in the sense of officials holding *wajh*, or territorial assignments in lieu of salary.[4] The term *wajh* in this sense has a history traceable to the latter half of the fourteenth centurty.[5] In Akbar's early years the sense of *wajhdār* came to be carried by the term *jāgīrdār/jāygīrdār*,[6]

[2] *Bāburnāma*, Turki text, ed. Eiji Mano, Kyoto, 1995, p.470; Eng. trans. A.S. Beveridge, II, p.521.

[3] Chāndpūr appears as a *pargana* of the *sarkār* of Sambhal in the *Ā'īn-i Akbarī*. It was important enough to be the headquarters of a *dastūr* circle within that *sarkār*. See Irfan Habib, *Atlas of the Mughal Empire*, Delhi, 1982, Sheet 8A, 29+78+.

[4] *Bāburnāma*, ed. Mano, p.553. Beveridge's rendering 'stipendiaries' (trans., II, p.617) is hardly apt. See also Iqtidar A. Khan, 'The Mughal Assignment System', *Medieval India-1*, ed. Irfan Habib, Bombay, 1992, pp.67-8.

[5] Cf. Irfan Habib in *Cambridge Economic History of India*, I, Cambridge, 1982, pp.73-4.

[6] Irfan Habib in *The Indian Economic and Social History Review*, IV (3) (1967),

and we may, therefore, infer from the occurrence of the former term in this *farmān* that the term *jāgīrdār* had still not become universal in 1558, nor was *wajhdār* entirely obsolete as yet.

3. Although the dispute between Maulānā Aḥmad and Wajīhu'ddīn is stated to be over 'hereditary land', there is little doubt that the land was attached to the office of *khaṭīb*, which too was shared with the other party in the dispute, Wajīhu'ddīn. This is shown by an agreement reached on 15 Rabī' II 982/4 August 1574 between Saiyid Wajīhu'ddīn and Shaikh Aḥmad regarding the division of the duties of the *khaṭīb* (*qawā'id-i khiṭābat*). It was agreed that the '*Īd al-fiṭr* sermon would be delivered by Saiyid Wajīhu'ddīn, and '*Īd al-aẓḥā* sermon by the father of Shaikh Aḥmad. The Friday sermons were to continue to be shared between the parties in accordance with earlier practice. Similarly, 200 *bīghas* of land pertaining to the office (*a'imma-i khiṭābat*) was now divided equally between the two claimants.[7]

4. The way the dispute between Shaikh Aḥmad and Wajīhu'd-dīn was decided, some time before the present *farmān*, is not without interest. The case was carried for decision not before secular authorities but before an assemblage of the *qāẓīs* and scholars of Sambhal and Chandpur. It was, therefore, possibly an informal body that arranged the settlement, which is given here the designation *dastūr*, not generally used for ordinary judgements by the *qāẓīs*. In subsequent times such informal procedures came to be replaced by more formal adjudications, so that resort to the former in or before 1558 may be indicative of a lack of administrative control by the central authorities.

5. The *farmān* is written in the semi-cursive *dīwānī* mode of writing usual in Akbar's early *farmāns*, and there is no identifiable seal of an official or legible official endorsement on the back (*ẓimn*). Thus the case does not seem to have been processed by the *Ṣadr* (minister for revenue grants) as it would have been in later times.

6. This *farmān* was issued during Bairam Khān's regency, when the Regent as *Wakīl* of the Emperor was at the height of his authority.

---

p.209, notices a *farmān* of Akbar of 1563-4, as the earliest document containing the term.

[7] See NAI 2919/2.

Yet the *farmān* nowhere has his name. This seems to show that Bairam Khān's authority was not formally reflected in actual Imperial orders. Such lack of formal recognition may partly, perhaps, explain why in the later confrontation with the young Akbar the Regent's position was so quickly undermined.

2

Three Early *Farmāns* of Akbar, in Favour of Rāmdās, the Master Dyer

IRFAN HABIB

In January 1996, my friend Professor Abul Fazl Usmani, former Dean of the Faculty of Social Sciences, Aligarh Muslim University, kindly gave me xerox copies of three *farmāns* of Akbar, the originals of which, he said, were in possession of a businessman of Feṛozabad, District Agra, who did not wish to part with them. Copies of the xerox reproductions were also kindly donated by Professor Usmani to the library of the Centre of Advanced Study in History, Aligarh. Upon closer examination, I found that there must have been a fourth *farmān* also; of this unfortunately only a strip survives containing the title (*tughrā*) and a minute portion of the first line of the text.

The three *farmāns* which are fairly well preserved (except for the earliest, which has portions torn away on the left side and bottom) are of very great interest, both because of their early dates (1561, 1562 and 1569), and the nature of their contents.

Translations of all the three *farmāns* are provided at the end of this paper, along with reproductions of the frontal portions of the documents.

All the three *farmāns* were issued to favour a single person, Rāmdās, who belonged apparently to the *pargana* of Chanwār, a place situated on the left bank of the Yamuna near the town of Ferozabad in Agra District, Uttar Pradesh.[1] The way Rāmdās is referred to in *Farman* II (1562), *'Ustād* Rāmdās *Rangrez'*, shows that he was a master dyer, the term *ustād* very closely signifying what 'master' has meant in English craft tradition; the reference to his *'alūfa* or salary in *Farmān* I (1561) implies that at that time he was in the Emperor's service. One may

[1] Chanwār appears as Chandwār in the Survey of India's One-Inch Sheet 54 I/8, First Edition (based on 1921-22 survey), situated 2.75 miles (4.45 km) in straight distance, south tending west, from Ferozabad railway station on the Delhi-Kanpur main line. The ruins at Chandwar are noticed in A. Fuhrer, *The Monumental Antiquities and Inscriptions in the North-Western Provinces and Oudh*, Allahabad, 1891, p.74.

recall here Abū'l Fazl's remarks about Akbar's great interest in the dyeing of textiles.[2] This interest possibly explains, in part, the extraordinary attention Rāmdās as a craftsman received from him while in his service. By 1569 we find Rāmdās in retirement, and possibly in a state of senility, for he could now be accused of 'insanity' (*junūn*) by a person with whom he was entangled in litigation over a claim for recovery of loan. But *Farmān* III, from whose contents these facts transpire, shows that the artisan's imperial master remembered him still and gave him the relief he was seeking.

We may now pass on to the examination of the contents of the individual *farmāns*.

II

For Mughal administrative history, *Farmān* I is of singular interest. So far as our present knowledge goes, it is the earliest surviving order of *jāgīr* assignment. Though the year at the end of the document is lost, the *farmān* can be dated from the reference to 'the beginning of *rabī*', *takhāqoī īl*'. The Turkish year *takhāqoī īl* corresponded to the seasons of *rabī'* and *kharīf*, October 1560 to September 1561, as is shown by *Farmān* II, dated 20 Ramazān 969/24 May 1562, which refers to the *rabī'* and *kharīf* of the succeeding Turkish year, *īt īl*. The *hijrī* year that is lost in the date of *Farmān* I must, therefore, have been 968, so that, its date and month being given as 21 Rajab, it is to be presumed that it was issued on 7 April 1561. It may be noted that two seals on the back of the *farmān* bear the year 968, and another (9)62, so that, otherwise too, 968/1561 is the likely year of issue.

The *farmān* assigns the village of Hamīrpūr in the *tappa* of Jāmān within *pargana* Chanwār, carrying the *jama'-i raqamī* of 5000 *tanka murādī* 'in assignment of salary' (*dar wajh-i 'alūfa*) to Rāmdās. Neither Jāmān nor Hamīrpūr are traceable on the old 1-inch survey maps of the area; but one must assume that both were not far from Chanwār. The term *jama'-i raqamī* appears in Abū'l Fazl, as signifying the estimated revenue-income of a particular area assigned for payment of salary in the early years of Akbar.[3] The present *farmān* shows that the term was in actual use in Mughal administration in 1561, though

[2] *Ā'īn-i Akbarī*, ed. H. Blochmann, I, Calcutta, 1866-67, pp.101-04.

[3] *Akbarnāma*, Bib. Ind., Calcutta, 1873-87, II, p.270; *Ā'īn-i Akbarī*, I, p.347.

there is a still earlier occurrence of it in Bābur's *farmān* of 13 Zīqa'd 933/11 August 1527, where it is stated of a village in *pargana* Vatāla (Batāla in the Panjab) that 'its *jama 'i raqamī* is 2,000 *tanka-i siyāh*'.[4]

One may stay here a moment over the currencies in which the *jama'-i raqamī* is given in Bābur's *farmān* and our *Farmān* I. By *tanka-i siyāh*, or 'black *tanka*', in the former is obviously meant the billon *tanka* of Lodī times. So far as I have been able to determine, the earliest occurrence of *tanka-i murādī* so far known was in Akbar's *farmān* of 29 Rabī' I, 975/3 October 1567;[5] the present *farmān* pushes it six years earlier. It also occurs in a *farmān* which can be dated either 975/1568 or 985/1577.[6] It is possible that the term *murādī* (lit. desired) was especially coined (by Akbar?) for the pure copper *tanka*, which, introduced under the Sūrs, Akbar continued to mint, and whose coppery appearance was in contrast to the dark visage of its billon predecessor. According to the rate prevailing in Akbar's later years (1 Rupee = 20 *tankas*), 5000 *tankas* should have been worth Rs 250.

Formally, then, Rāmdās was supposed to have an annual salary (*'alūfa*) of 5000 *tankas*, which he was given the right to realise by collecting the revenue (*wājibī*) from the village of Hamīrpūr, whose *jama'-i raqamī* amounted to this figure. Since, however, the *raqamī* figures were widely known to be inflated,[7] the actual revenue-realization must have been far less.

The *farmān* is among those early documents of Akbar which use for the holder of such assignment the term *jāigīrdār*. The term already occurs in Akbar's *farmān* of 1 Rabī' I, 967/1 December 1559.[8] Our *Farmān* I of 7 April 1561 is the immediately next document in which it is used.

Iqtidar Husain Siddiqui had in 1961 suggested that 'terms such as *jāgīr* and *jāgīrdār* were adopted [only] during Akbar's reign'.[9] And

[4] India Office, London: I.O. 4438(1). Some later hand has tried to change 2000 into 5000.

[5] *Farmān* relating to *madad-i ma'āsh* in *pargana* Jalandhar: Display-case, Maulana Azad Library, Aligarh.

[6] *Farmān* dated Sha'bān..5, relating to the Ajmer shrine, in Qāẓī Sayyid Imāmu'ddīn, *Mu'īnu'l Auliyā*, Ajmer, 1312/1894, pp.66-7, reprinted in Bashīruddīn Aḥmad, *Farāmīn-i Salāṭīn*, Delhi, 1344/1926, pp.2-3. The reference to 'Abdu'n Nabī as *Ṣadr* (appointed 972/1565) rules out any date earlier than 1565 for this *farmān*.

[7] Cf. Irfan Habib, *Agrarian System of Mughal India*, Bombay, 1963, pp.261-2 & 262*n*.

[8] Xerox of photograph in the Farangi Mahal Collection of documents in Library of Centre of Advanced Study in History, Aligarh.

[9] 'Iqta System under the Lodis', *Proceedings of the Indian History Congress, Delhi (24th) Session (1961)*, Calcutta, 1963, pp.145, & 148-9 (*n*.6).

now our *Farmān* I and other documents from the early years of Akbar's reign enable us to reconstruct how the two terms might have come into vogue.

It is noteworthy that the early documents do not use the term *jāgīr*, but only *jā(i)gīrdār*. The latter term can only be a shortened form of **jāi-gīr-o-dār* (lit. one who takes and holds a place). It is clearly spelt *jāigīrdār* (with the letter *yā* in *jāi-* clearly indicated) in the *farmān* of 1559, above cited, as also in our *Farmān* I (1561) and the *farmān* in favour of Gopāldās of Vrindavan (5 Jumāda II 972/8 January 1565).[10] Only in a *farmān* in favour of certain land-holders of Bilgram (Jumāda I, 971/17 December 1563 to 15 January 1564) do we get the still shorter spelling *jāgīrdār*.[11]

Farmān I calls upon 'the *muqaddamān* (headmen), *ri'āyā* (peasants), and *muzāri'ān* (cultivators) of the said village' to recognise him as their *jāigīrdār*. Since the document does not itself call the assignment *jāgīr*, but *wajh-i 'alūfa*, we may infer that the word *jāgīr* was not yet in official use, despite the fact that the holder of a territorial revenue assignment was now called *jāigīrdār*. This form could well have emerged in popular use first, for it is difficult to think of deliberate official application of this word, proper for a person, not for a strip of territory.

The genesis of the term *jāgīr* out of *jā(i)gīrdār* in popular use, however, would seem natural, the moment folk etymology forgot that in *jā(i)gīrdār*, the components *gīr* and *dār* are synonyms, and took *jāgīrdār* to mean the holder of *jāgīr*, which thereby came to mean the territory, and not the person, of the revenue-assignee. There may be earlier occurrences of the term, but in the tell-tale spelling *jāgīr* it definitely occurs in 'Ārif Qandhārī's account of Akbar's resumption of *jāgīrs* in 1574-75, and 'Ārif was probably writing this portion of his work no later than 988/1580-81.[12] About the same time in his letters written in 989/1581, Abū'l Fatḥ Gīlānī was freely using the term *jāgīr* (so spelt) in its standard territorial sense.[13] It is, therefore, likely that during the 1570s the new word became well established in administrative circles.

[10] Madan Mohan Collection, No.50 (photograph sent to me by the late Dr Tarapada Mukherji).

[11] Bilgram Docs. no.7, Library of CAS in History, Aligarh.

[12] *Tārīkh-i Akbarī*, ed. Muinuddīn Nadwi, Azhar Ali Dihlawi and Imtiyaz Ali Arshi, Rampur, 1962, pp.197-8.

[13] *Ruq'āt-i Abū'l Fatḥ Gīlānī*, ed. Muhammad Bashir Husain, Lahore, 1968, pp.26,27,34,38. On the occurrence of the term *jāgīr* and its significance in the early years of Akbar's reign, see also Iqtidar A. Khan, 'The Mughal Assignment System', *Medieval India-1*, ed. Irfan Habib, Delhi, 1992, pp.66-7.

III

How long Rāmdās continued to enjoy his '*jāgīr*' – to anticipate later terminology – cannot be known for certain. According to *Farmān* II, issued in his favour the very next year (20 Ramaẓān 969/24 May 1562), he received as *in'ām* a hundred *bīghas* of cultivated land in another village, Tātiya or Tānth (untraced) in the same *tappa* Jāmān, *pargana* Chanwār, to be effective from the beginning of *kharīf, īt īl* (April 1562). It is possible that this was designed to replace his '*jāgīr*'-assignment, though this fact is nowhere stated in the *farmān*.

The *farmān* entitled Rāmdās to collect the due revenue (*wājibī*) from that land measuring a hundred *bīghas*, from the beginning of *kharīf, īt īl*, year after year in assignment (*dar wajh*) of his *in'ām*, and render the service required of him by the Central *Dīwān*. The formula exempting Rāmdās from all fiscal claims over his grant was routine, though the list of the claims is rather short. What is rather out of the common is the concession given to him through the placing of his entire grant at its initial conferment within cultivated land, which must have been paying revenue already. The normal rule was to place only half of the original grant within cultivated land, and this principle can be seen being applied in a grant of Sher Shāh as well as in Akbar's grant to Gopāldās of Vrindavan, 8 January 1565, already cited.[14] Since the *bigha* of that time was about 10.5 per cent smaller than the later *ilāhī bīgha*, the cultivated area made over to Rāmdās in *in'ām* must have measured 89.5 *ilāhī bīghas* (21.73 hectares).[15] Given Abū'l Faẓl's estimate in the *Ā'in* that grantees could draw a minimum annual income (*hāṣil*) of one Rupee (20 *tankas*) from each *bīgha ilāhī*,[16] Rāmdās's possible income from his grant should have been about 1790 *tankas*. This may look rather small in comparison with the *jama'-i raqamī* of 5000 *tankas* carried by Rāmdās's '*jāgīr*'-assignment, now probably terminated; but since, as Abū'l Faẓl admitted, the *jama'-i raqamī* tended to be grossly inflated, the difference in real income from the two sources might not have been so large.

The *farmān* goes on to make a further concession to Rāmdās. It recites that Rāmdās already had 37 *bīghas* of land in that village, as 'his own cultivation' (*zirā'at-i khāṣa*), which was apparently to be in-

[14] Cf. Irfan Habib, *Agrarian System of Mughal India*, p.302&n.

[15] Based on equivalents worked out in ibid., pp.352-63. See also Shireen Moosvi, *The Economy of the Mughal Empire, c.1595 - a Statistical Study*, Delhi, 1987, pp.97-99.

[16] *Ā'īn-i Akbarī*, I, p.199.

cluded within the area of his *in'ām* grant. But on this particular area, he was allowed to keep the land-revenue from the beginning of *rabī'*, *īt īl* (October 1561). We thus see that the Master Dyer already held some 8.16 hectares of land on which he paid revenue. We are not told how he came by this large area of land; nor are we perhaps entitled to impart a strict construction to *zirā'at-i khāṣa* and insist that the whole of it was 'cultivated' by him personally through wage-labourers. It is possible that no more was intended than to say that Rāmdās paid revenue on these 37 *bīghas* (perhaps on some concessional rates), deriving his profit from the difference between this amount and his gross income gained through his renting out the land to share-croppers or cultivating it through wage-labourers. In any case, a heavy degree of differentiation and the existence of property-rights within the village of Tātiya/Tānth are firmly attested here.

IV

Farmān III issued to Rāi Kālā, *shiqqdār* of *pargana* Chanwār, Shawwāl 976/19 March - 16 April 1569 seeks to enforce the repayment of a loan advanced by Rāmdās. The amount involved was Rupees 13: the shift from *tanka* to rupee as a medium of transactions may be noted. The borrower was one Darayyā – the spelling established by a careful placing of the *tashdīd* (for repetition of a consonant) and the vowel-sign, to distinguish it from Daryā. It recites that Darayyā, by making accusations of insanity (*junūn*) against Rāmdās, had evaded the examination of lawful proof through denying Rāmdās's entitlement to be heard before the *Qāẓī*. Rāmdās had, therefore, gone to the Imperial Court, and on his petition it was ordered that the *shiqqdār* should (a) recover the amount of the loan from Darayyā and pay it over to Rāmdās, after the lawful proof had been furnished; and (b) take Darayyā to the Qāẓī (*ḥuzūr-i shar'-i sharīf*), to ensure that he would henceforth not harass Rāmdās through any legal proceedings.

The *farmān* not only brings out the access Rāmdās had, even now in his retirement, to the Emperor's ear, but also helps us to draw certain inferences about the judicial system. The recovery of a loan could normally be enforced only through a *Qāẓī's* decision, even if both parties were Hindus. In the present case, it needed the Emperor's intervention to by-pass the judicial process, which Darayyā had stalled, and have the loan recovered through the authority of the revenue-collector, himself a Hindu. The *farmān* goes on to convey to the *qāẓī*, through this official, that Rāmdās was to be deemed exempt from any legal proceedings resorted to by Darayyā. For a favoured servant one could clearly close one's eyes to the freedom of the judiciary!

Incidentally, the *farmān* reminds us that in these years the designation of *shiqqdār* was borne by a fairly important officer, responsible at the *pargana* level for both revenue-collection and maintenance of law and order. Subsequently, as the term *karorī* came into vogue for the imperial revenue-collector, *shiqqdār* became the designation of a much lowlier official.[17]

V

These *farmāns* of fairly early dates (the first being issued barely one year after Akbar's gaining control of authority from Bairam Khān) also illumine one of the sources of Akbar's later religious policy. Importance is very properly attached to the admission of Rāja Bhāramal of Amber into the Mughal nobility by Akbar in early 1562.[18] But our *Farmān* I shows Akbar in April 1561 assigning a '*jāgīr*' to a Hindu master artisan of his establishment, so that his characteristic attitude of tolerance of (or indifference to) the religious beliefs of those who served him, seems to have been already formed. Incidentally, *Farmān* II, of 24 May 1562, is still the earliest known revenue grant given to a Hindu by Akbar.

Akbar's tendency towards a non-formal attitude to religion is borne out by the legend of the seal he selected for *farmāns* issued on judicial or quasi-judicial matters. It occurs on the seal on a *farmān* issued in favour of some land-holders of *pargana* Bilgram, in December 1563-January 1564, but the impression is rather faint.[19] Our *Farmān* III, issued March - April 1569, has an exceptionally clear impression of the legend, and enables us to improve the reading so far made from other impressions.[20]

[17] Cf. Irfan Habib, *Agrarian System of Mughal India*, pp.274-6&nn.

[18] *Akbarnāma*, II, 155-6: 'The Rāja, from the rectitude of his thought and exalted good fortune, so designed that he should come out of the ranks of the *zamīndārs* and make himself one of the select of this Court'.

[19] Bilgram Coll. No.7, Library of CAS in History, Aligarh.

[20] Cf. S.A.I. Tirmizi, *Mughal Documents (1526-1627)*, New Delhi, 1989, p.17.

Rāstī mūjib-i raẓā-i Khudā'st
Kas nadīdam ki gum shud az mard-i rāst.[21]
Just conduct wins the approval of God:
I saw no one being led astray by a just man.

Whether deliberately so designed, this is a general declaration in favour of fair or just conduct (*rāstī*), with no appeal to Islam, or even mention of the *Sharī'at*. That it was already put on imperial orders as early as January 1564 may fairly be seen as yet another indication of Akbar's very early gropings towards a non-sectarian basis for his sovereignty.[22]

VI

The script, seals and endorsements of our three *farmāns* shed some light on the practices of the Mughal chancery in the 1560s. Unfortunately, except for *Farmān* I, the invocation and the title (*ṭughrā*) are lost, though the small surviving fragment of the fourth practically comprises its *ṭughrā* only. As in the case of *farmāns* relating to revenue matters issued in the early phase of Akbar's reign (and by his predecessors like Bābur)[23] the invocation is *Huwa al-Ghanī*. 'He [God] is Rich', a modest attribution of all wealth to Him. The *ṭughrā* is written with little flourish and is far less stylised than came to be fashionable in later days when the scribes turned it into an absolute rectangle or square.[24]

The imperial seals on the three *farmāns* are all different from each other. That *Farmān* III, which relates to a semi-judicial matter, should have a seal different from that on the other two, is understandable; and, as we have just seen, the couplet on it also is apt for a *farmān* of a judicial nature. But why the seals on *Farmāns* I and II should differ is not clear. *Farmān* I has the round seal with Akbar's name in the middle, along with his father Humāyūn's, his ancestors up to Tīmūr

[21] Not *rāh-i rāst*, as in Tirmizi, op.cit., which in any case would deprive the second hemistich of much meaning. A different couplet, but with the same metre and rhyme, occurs in Sharafu'uddīn 'Alī Yazdī, *Ẓafarnāma,* Asiatic Soc. Bengal, Calcutta, 1888, II, p.21.

[22] This seal appears to have been replaced by a pyramidal one by 1572, to judge from the seal on a *farman* of 979/1572 relating to Bilgram on a similar judicial matter (Subhanullah Coll: *Faramin* (1), Maulana Azad Library, Aligarh).

[23] See Bābur's *farmān* of 933/1527 in India Office Library, I.O. 4438:(1).

[24] The *ṭughrā* is similarly simple in Bābur's *farmān* (I.O. 4438:(1), op.cit.) and in other early *farmāns* of Akbar cited in this paper.

being listed around the rim of the circle; *Farmān* II has just a short legend, 'Jalālu'ddīn Muḥammad Akbar Pādshāh Ghāzī, 967'. This seal, with the same year 967/1559-60, was stamped as late as 6 October 1568 on a *farmān* issued in favour of Jīv Gosāin of Vrindavan.[25] Yet during the years in between, the larger, year-less seal, with names of Akbar and his ancestors, can be seen on *farmāns* issued in connection with land-revenue grants, in 972/1565 and 975/1567.[26]

As with most of Akbar's *farmāns*, and all of his earlier ones, our three *farmāns* are written not in standard *nasta'līq*, but in a cursive hand, there being a notable similarity (though the scribes are obviously different) between *Farmāns* I and II, and an obvious difference between the writing style of these and of *Farmān* III. The style of writing of *Farmān* III matches that of the *farmān* issued 971/1563-64 in favour of certain land-holders of Bilgram.[27] Since both these *farmāns* concern quasi-judicial matters, of no concern to the Finance Ministry, it may be inferred that while the writing style of *Farmāns* I and II is that of *farmāns* prepared in the *Dīwānī*, *Farmān* III and the *farmān* relating to Bilgram are written in the style current in the offices concerned with judicial matters.

The first two lines of the text are half-lines in all our three *farmāns*, in conformity with the strict Mughal convention with regard to the writing of *farmāns*.

VII

It is obvious that the practice of stating on the back (*ẓimn*) all the major facts on the basis of which the *farmān* came to be issued, comprising a veritable recapitulation of the 'file' along with such details as could not appear in the *farmān* itself, had not developed by the time our three *farmāns* were issued. In fact, on *Farmān* I a clarification is put on the bottom of the right margin of the face of the *farmān* itself: it states that whatever revenue had been collected by officials for part of the period since the beginning of the term of assignment of Rāmdās should now be paid over to him by the *Dīwān* of Chanwār, but the treasury's claims on the arrears relating to previous years were not to be waived. Clearly, this is a clarification from some official of the

[25] Vrindavan Research Institute, Vrindavan, *Farmāns*. Acc. No.1.

[26] Madan Mohan 50; Akbar's *farmān* of 975 on display, Maulana Azad Library, Aligarh.

[27] Bilgram Coll. No.7, CAS in History Library, Aligarh.

Finance Ministry, of a kind which in later years would have appeared either on the *ẓimn* or in a separate *parwāna* (official's letter or order).

The *ẓimns* of our three *farmāns* contain the seals and office endorsements of such nobles and officials as were expected to see the *farmāns*, and record their contents in their registers (so the endorsements: *ṣibt shud, qalmī shud*, 'recorded' with the date). In *Farmāns* I and II, the endorsements add *'fī at-tārīkh'*, '[same] date', which suggests that the *farmāns* were inspected and their contents recorded in the various registers on the same date as that of issue of the *farmān*. Later on, the dates tend to vary, showing the leisurely pace at which the *farmān* went from one office to another.

The numerous seals on the *ẓimns* of *Farmāns* I and II include those of some well-known nobles of Akbar. Since these were issued within fourteen months of each other it is not surprising that some officers are represented by their seals on both *farmāns*. Thus we have the seal of 'the Slave [of God], Mun'im, son of Mīram, son of Nāṣir' – that is, Mun'im Khān, Khān-i Khānān, who was the *Wakīlu's Salṭanat*, the 'Regent' or highest minister at this time.[28] Then we have 'the Slave [of God], Shihābu'ddīn Aḥmad Khān al-Ḥusainī'. He was a high official at this time, and as such was a witness to the murder of Atka Khān by Adham Khān on 16 May 1562; Shihābu'ddīn was then sitting with Mun'im Khān and Atka Khān in the royal palace (*daulat-khāna-i pādshāhī*) on the working day of the finance ministry (*roz-i dīwān*), busy transacting government business.[29] It is interesting that only eight days after that unsettling event, they were affixing their seals (in a joint session, presumably) on documents like our *Farmān* II, issued on 24 May.[30]

Two other well-known officials' seals appear on the *ẓimn* of *Farmān* II: Muẓaffar Khān Turbatī and Ṣādiq Khān. At this time, the first had not attained the title of Khān and so had to style himself Muẓaffar-i Khāqānī ('Muẓaffar, servant of the Emperor'). But he was due to

[28] Cf. Iqtidar A. Khan, *The Political Biography of a Mughal Noble: Mun'im Khān, Khān-i Khānān*, New Delhi, 1973, pp.59ff. The mention of the name of the grandfather, Nāṣir, on the seal establishes the identification of Mun'im Khān's father with Mīram-i Nāṣir, with whom Iqtidar A. Khan, *op. cit.*, p.1&n., has already sought to identify him, but without definitive proof.

[29] *Akbarnāma*, II, p.174.

[30] Both Mun'im Khān and Shihābu'ddīn Aḥmad Khān had left Agra after the murder, fearing Akbar's anger at their suspected complicity in the crime; they were persuaded to return, yet they fled again in June 1562 (Iqtidar A. Khan, *op.cit.*, p.67).

receive the title 'Khān' and appointment as *Vazīr* (Finance Minister) the very next year (1563).[31] The legend is therefore different in his seal on the *ẓimn* of *Farmān* III, issued in 1569, where the decipherable words are 'Muẓaffar Khān Tūchī(?) Turbatī'. Ṣādiq Khān was an important officer of Akbar already by 1562, having been assigned the duty of giving a confidential report to Akbar on Adham Khān's doings in Malwa.[32] There is, however, no reference in our sources to his performing any particular duty in the central administration during 1562.

Another officer identified from the seal of *Farmān* I is Kamālu'ddīn Ḥusain-i 'Alī. This must be Kamālu'ddīn Ḥusain, who came to India in 1555-56 as *dīwān* in the retinue of Prince Akbar; his father Maqṣūd 'Alī had been the *dīwān* of Mirzā Kāmrān.[33]

On the *ẓimn* of *Farmān* III, beside the seal of Muẓaffar Khān, there is another seal whose legend is difficult to decipher; but the words Qāẓī-u'l Islām appear to be clear, and there is a possibility that the seal also contains the name 'Abdu'n Nabī. 'Abdu'n Nabī was appointed *Ṣadr* in 1565, at the recommendation of Muẓaffar Khān;[34] and he could have been involved in the processing of a judicial document in 1569. But his later seals read differently; and he is known to have borne the title of 'Shaikhu'l Islām', not 'Qāẓī-u'l Islām'.[35]

TRANSLATION

FARMĀN I

Note: An asterisk marks (*) space of text lost through wear and tear of paper. [Upper portion containing Invocation and *Ṭughrā* lost]

[Round Seal:]
[In the centre:]

[31] *Akbarnāma*, II, p.197.

[32] Ibid., I, p.140.

[33] Bāyāzīd Biyāt, *Tazkira-i Humāyūn o Akbar*, ed. M. Hidayat Hosain, Calcutta, 1941, pp.184-5. Kamālu'ddīn Ḥusain's seal appears also on the *ẓimn* of a *farmān* of Akbar, 4 Rabi' II 983/13 July 1575 (transcript in CAS in History Library, Aligarh).

[34] *Akbarnāma*, II, pp.247-8.

[35] The legend on his seal in two *farmāns* of 983/1575 runs: *'Abdu'n Nabī ibn Aḥmad al-Ḥanafī, khādim-i 'ilm-i ḥadīṣ-i nabawī*. (Transcript in CAS in History, Aligarh, op.cit; U.P. Record Office, Allahabad, No.II, 23.) The designation *Shaikhu'l Islām* occurs after 'Abdu'n Nabī's name in *ẓimn*-endorsements on a *farmān* of 14 Rabi' II 976/6 October 1568 (Vrindavan Research Institute, *Farmān* No.1) and of 983 (transcript in Library of CAS in History, Aligarh, *op.cit.*)

Jalālu'ddīn Muḥammad Akbar Pādshāh
Ghāzī, son of Muḥammad Humāyūn
Pādshāh Ghāzī
[On the rim:]
son of Ẓahīru'ddīn Muḥammad Bābur
Pādshāh Ghāzī, son of 'Umar Shaikh,
son of Sulṭān Abū Sa'īd, son of Sulṭān
Muḥammad, son of Mīrān Shāh, son of
Amīr Tīmūr.

[Text:]

At this time the exalted obedience-requiring *farmān* has been issued [to the effect that]* from the beginning of the *Rabī'* [harvest], Takhāqoī Īl, the village of Hamirpur in *tappa* [Jāmān, belonging to]* *pargana* Chanwār, the *jama'-i raqamī* of which [village] is twenty-five thousand *tanka murādī* [is hereby assigned]* in assignment (*dar wajh*) of the salary ('*alufa*) of Obedient-to-Islam[36] Rāmdās. [It is requisite that]* the high officers, the central [lit. great] finance ministry officials and the revenue-collectors and those in control of matters and affairs in the said *sarkār*,[37] should, deeming it [the assignment] to be settled as above recorded, not allow any transfer or change therein. [It is necessary that]* the headmen (*muqaddamān*), peasants (*ri'āyā*) and cultivators (*muzāri'ān*) of the said village should, recognising him as their *jāigīrdār*, [pay]* their due revenue *(wājibi)*, every year in the rescribed two harvests, [and]* be answerable to him, [and]* not prove deficient or defiant in anything. [The prescribed duty for all is that]* acting in accordance with this exalted *farmān*, they should not deviate from what has been ordered. Written on the 21st of the month of Rajab....*

[Endorsement on right margin, upside down:]

...*Endorsement (*sharḥ*): Whatever of the revenue (*ḥāṣil*) of the village has been collected, the *dīwān* of Chanwār, having determined it, should pay it to the above named [Rāmdās]. The *dīwānī* officers of the *sarkār* should [however] realise the [arrears of] revenues of the [previous] years (*sanwāt hāṣil*) of this village, [with reductions for?][38]... and calamity.

[Reverse (*Ẓimn*):]

[36] *Muṭī'u'l Islām*, normal designation for a Hindu officer or person of substance; a form later abandoned by Akbar's chancery.

[37] But the *sarkār* (of Agra presumably) is not mentioned earlier in this *farman*; it should have followed the first mention of *pargana* Chanwār.

[38] Words undeciphered.

	[Round Seal:] The slave Mun'im, son of Mīram, son of Nāṣir	
[Round Seal:] The slave Muḥammad Muḥsin 968...	[Small round seal:] ...'Alī son of 62	[Round Seal:] The slave Shihābu'ddīn Aḥmad Khān al-Ḥusainī
[Round Seal:] The slave 'Alī.....	[Round Seal:] ...... Muḥammad Ḥusaini 968	[Round Seal:] Muḥammad Kamālu'ddīn Husain 'Alī. Trust... [self] to God.
		[Endorsements:]
[Pyramidal seal:] Muhammad		[1] Recorded (?) [2] Recorded, [same] date [3] Have been informed, [same] date [4] Recorded, [same] date

[Five other seals undecipherable]

FARMĀN II

[Invocation:] He (God) is Rich

[Ṭughrā:] *Farmān* of Jalālu'ddīn Muḥammad Akbar Pādshāh Ghāzī

[Round Seal:]

Jalālu'ddīn Muḥammad Akbar Pādshāh Ghāzī, [A.H.] 967

At this time the exalted, obedience-requiring *farmān* has been issued [that][39] one hundred *bīghas* of cultivated land, from village Tātiya [or Tānth], in *pargana* Chanwār, in *tappa* Jāmān, under the jurisdiction of the Capital Agra should vest with Obedient-to-Islām, Master (*Ustād*) Rāmdās the Dyer (*Rangrez*), so that he may, realising the due revenue (*wājibī*) of that [land] from the beginning of Kharīf, Īt Īl, year after year, in assignment (*dar wajh*) of his *in'ām*, render the service that may be prescribed in return by the Central Finance Ministry (*Dīwān-i A'lā*). It is requisite that the high officers, central (lit.

[39] Part of text torn and lost.

great) finance ministry officials, the revenue-collectors in charge of administration and persons in control of matters and affairs of the finances (*dīwānī*) of the territories of Hindostān,[40] especially the superintendent (*darogha*) and officials in charge of the administration (lit. important affairs) of the said *pargana*, should deem [the said grant] settled as above recorded, not allow any transfer, and, having measured and delimited (*chak-basta*) the land, deliver it into his possession; and not trouble him or his agents (*gumāshta-hā*) and cultivators (*muzāri'ān*) with the demand for land revenue and other cesses (*māl-o-jihāt*) or insistence upon cultivation (*takrār-i zirā'at*) or the measurer's levy (*ẓābiṭāna*) or the survey-charge (*jarībāna*) and all expense-recoveries (*sā'ir ikhrājāt*); and, recognising him to be exempt and relieved from all charges (*ḥawālāt*), never try to levy these for any reason. Mindful of this duty, they should not deviate from what has been ordered and should not demand a fresh *farmān* or official order (*parwāncha*) every year. It is further settled that whereas thirty-seven *bīghas* of land in that village are in his own personal cultivation (*zirā'at-i khāṣa*), whatever amount of revenue (*māl*) falls due on that land during the *rabī'* harvest of Īt Īl, should not be claimed [from him]. They should obtain an acknowledgement of receipt (*qabẓ-i waṣūl*) [of the amount], so that in accordance with the receipt, they shall have proof of [the payment under the head of] expenditure (*kharj*).[41] Written on the 20th of the month of Ramaẓān, Year 969.

[Reverse (*Ẓimn*)]

[Round Seal:]
Having gained knowledge
in the Universe....
Mīrān-i Turbatī
Muẓaffar, servant
of the Khāqān (Emperor)

[Round Seal:]
The devoted
[servant]......
Ṣādīq Khān
Khān-i Sāmān(?)

[Endorsement:]
Recorded, (same) date

[Endorsement:]
Informed

[Endorsement:]
Recorded

[Small seal:]
The Slave Darī(?)
son of Muḥammad
[A.H.] 968

[Round Seal:]
The slave Mun'im
son of Mīram ...

[Pyramidal Seal:]
(Illegible)

[Round Seal:]
The Slave

[40] This identification of Akbar's empire with Hindostān (Northern India/India) already in 1562 may be noted.

[41] This translation assumes that *khwāhad dāsht* is slip for *khwāhand dāsht*.

Shihābu'ddīn Aḥmad Khān
Al-Ḥusainī

[Endorsement:]
Recorded, [same] date

[Round Seal:]
Muẓaffar 'Alī,
son of 'Abdullāh...
[Endorsement:]
Informed.

[Pyramidal Seal:]
.... 'Ali... God

[Seal]
[Endorsement:]
Informed,

[Endorsement:]
Recorded
[same] date

[Endorsement:]
Recorded, [same] date
[On left margin, a vertical line reading:]
Parwāncha of the highest of servants, the perfect of the chief of... [undecipherable]

FARMĀN III

[Top portion containing Invocation and *Ṭughrā* lost]
[Square Seal:]
Jalālu'ddīn Muḥammad Akbar Pādshāh Ghāzī
[Couplet on seal:]
Just conduct wins the approval of God: I saw no-one being led astray by a just man.

Obedient to Islām, Rāi Kālā, *Shiqqdār* of *pargana* Chanwār, should know [that][42] Rāmdās, having come to the Imperial Court, petitioned that he having given the sum of thirteen rupees to Darayyā, the said person does not repay it, and, by accusing him of insanity (*junūn*) before [consideration of] the legal (*shar'ī*) proof [of his debt], harasses the petitioner and evades any questioning.[43] It is [therefore] requisite that he [the *Shiqqdār*] should, after the legal proof is established, realise the debt of the said person and pay it to the petitioner. He is to summon the said Darayyā to the presence of the Qāẓī (*Shar'-i Sharīf*) and ensure that hereafter he [Darayyā] should not on any legal pretext harass the petitioner. Deeming this his duty, he [the said official] is not to question [these orders]. Written in the month of Shawwāl, Year 976.

[Reverse (*Ẓimn*):]

[Round Seal:]
... Muẓaffar Khān
Tūchī, [Tur]batī

[No endorsements]

[Round Seal:]
The slave...
Qāẓīu'l Islam
'Abdu'n Nabī(?)
...God.

[Third round seal, too faint to be deciphered.]

[42] Small portion of text lost at the end of first line.
[43] *Az suwāl hech(?) bāshad.*

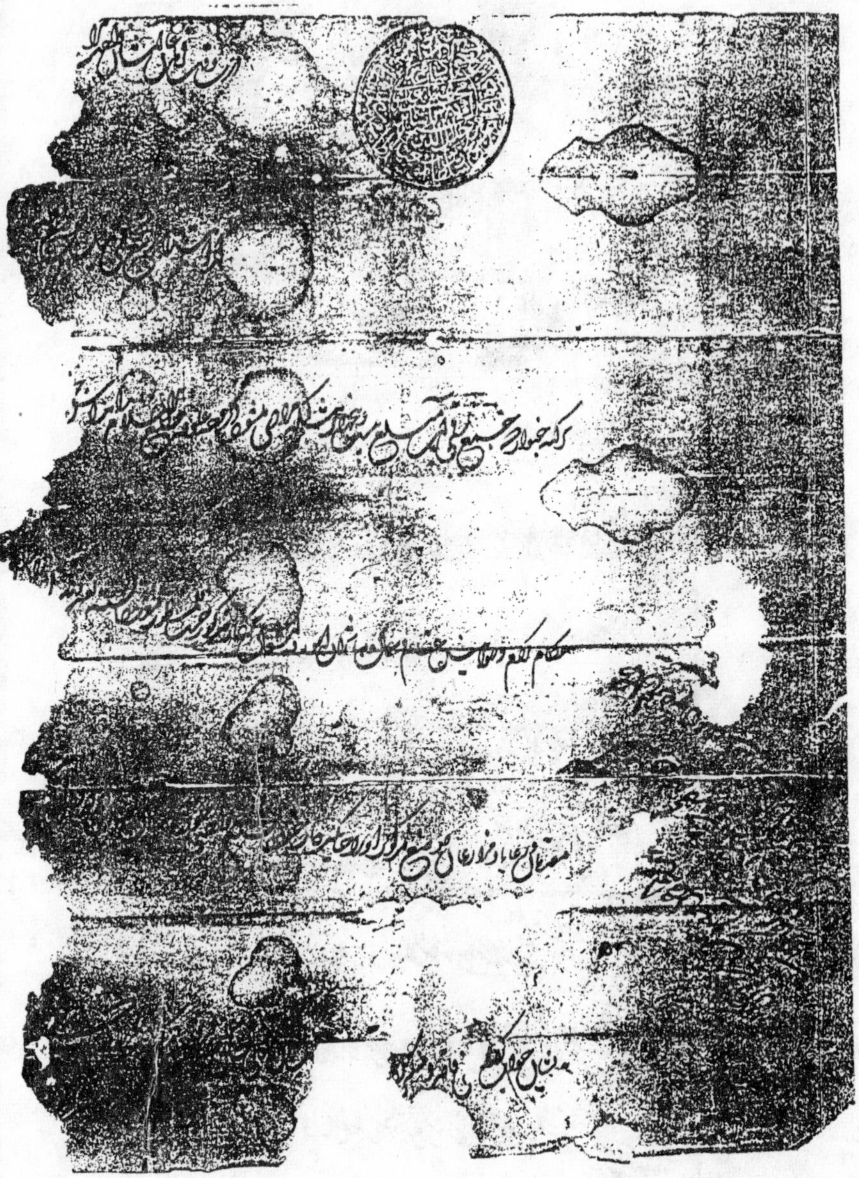

Farmān I

Farmān II

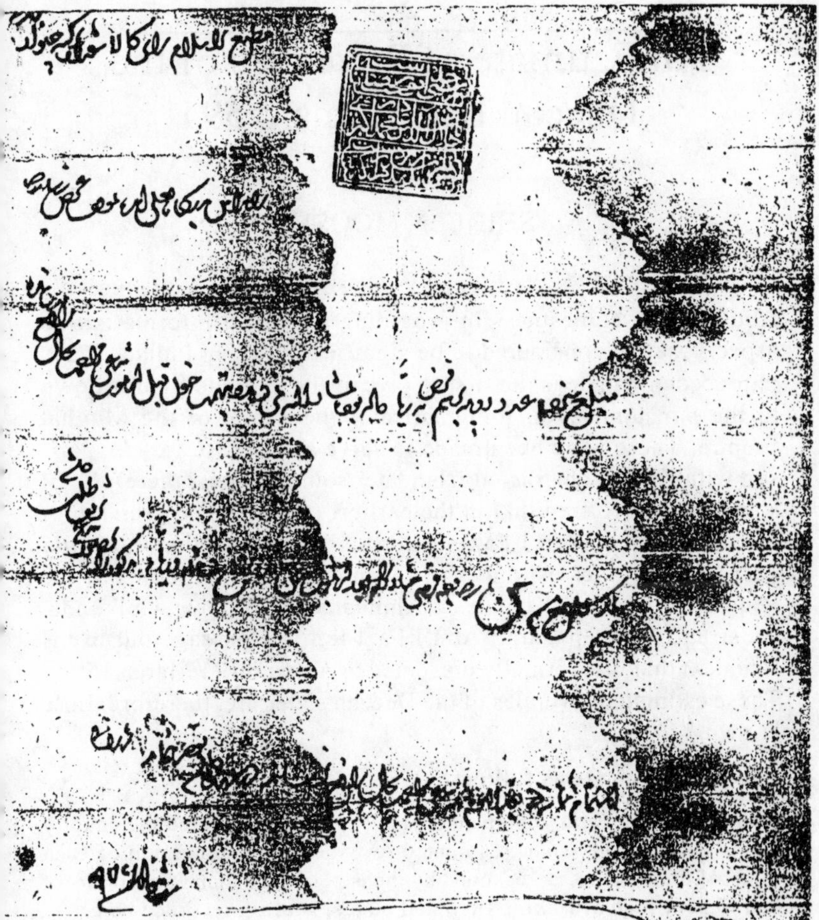

Farmān III

3

An Estimate of Revenues of the Deccan Kingdoms, 1591

SHIREEN MOOSVI

Abū'l Faẓl's earnestness in providing statistical information on aspects that he considered to be significant was, in India at least, unprecedented. He is the first to give us the revenue figures down to the *pargana* level, for practically the whole of the Mughal Empire. These have been made to serve as the base for comparison with figures abstracted from later sources.[1] It is, therefore, of some interest to find that in the earliest (unpublished) version of the *Akbarnāma*, Abū'l Faẓl, under his account of the 36th *Ilāhī* year (1591), gives estimates of revenues of the kingdoms of the Peninsula, namely, Khandesh, Ahmadnagar, Bijapur, Golkunda, Bidar and Vijayanagara.[2] Abū'l Faẓl left this passage out in his final text that was formally presented to Akbar on 21 March 1598.[3] These estimated revenues of the Deccan states are, therefore, little known.[4]

The passage reads as follows:

Although the Imperial commanders have not yet subjugated the country of the Deccan, the *jama*' (estimated revenue) of the dominion of each ruler[5] of the Deccan, as reckoned by the experienced men of accounts of that region, such as Ḥakīm Misrī and others, is being recorded here.

One *tanka* of the Deccan is the equivalent of eight *tankas* of the whole of Hindostān, which comes to sixteen *dāms*. In terms of this money [*tanka*

[1] E.g. in E. Thomas, *Revenue Resources of the Mughal Empire*, printed at end of *The Chronicles of the Pathan Kings of Delhi*, London, 1871, pp.52-54; Jadunath Sarkar, *India of Aurangzeb*, Calcutta, 1901, p.xxxii; and Irfan Habib, *Agrarian System of Mughal India*, Bombay, 1963, pp.328, 399-409.

[2] Br. Lib., Add. 27,247, ff384Aa-b. The original scribe renumbers folios after 390 as 381, 382, etc., again, so that these folios up to 390 have to be treated as 381A, 382A, etc.

[3] S. Moosvi, *Economy of the Mughal Empire c.1595*, New Delhi, 1987, pp.4-9.

[4] H. Beveridge in his translation notes these figures, *Akbarnāma* (tr.), Calcutta, 1897, pp.890-91 *n.*; but this seems to have been missed by almost all students of Mughal revenue statistics, including the writer.

[5] The text reads *harāwalī* instead of *har wālī*, an obvious slip by the scribe.

of the Deccan], the *jama*ʻ (revenue) of the country of Khandesh is two and a half crores, which amounts to forty crore *dāms*. Niẓām'ul-Mulk of Ahmadnagar[6] possesses that country; the revenue of that territory is nine crore *tankas* of that place, which amounts to one hundred and fortyfour crore *dams*: ʻĀdil Khān, who is in possession of Bijapur and those territories — the *jama*ʻ (revenue) of which is twelve crore *tankas* of that region equal to one hundred and ninety crore *dāms*. Quṭb'ul-Mulk is in possession of Golkunda and its territory — the *jama*ʻ of his territories (*maḥals*) is three and a half crore *tankas* of that place, which amounts to fiftysix crore *dāms* of these [Imperial] territories. The territory of Barid [ruler of Bidar] yields half a crore *tankas*, which comes to eight crore *dams*. [The *jama*ʻ of] the dominious of Rām Rāja yields four crores of *tankas* of that place, amounting to sixtyfour crore *dāms*.

Abū'l Faẓl enters figures of the revenues of the Deccan immediately after mentioning the report of the despatch of the Imperial emissaries to the rulers of Khandesh, Ahmadnagar, Bijapur and Golkunda on 14 Shahrīwar [36 Ilāhī], said to correspond to Friday, 17 Zīqaʻd [999], or 6 September 1591.

Little information is forthcoming about the career of the Ḥakīm Miṣrī, the only expert from the Deccan named by Abū'l Faẓl as a source for the figures. Such information as is available on him is given here Ḥakīm Miṣrī is mentioned in the *Āʼīn-i Akbarī* among the *manṣabdārs* of 400.[7] He was a physician of repute,[8] first mentioned in the final text of the *Akbarnāma* when he is said to have come to the court at Lahore, on 19 March 1591, from the Deccan, and successfully treated Abū'l Faẓl for stone in the bladder.[9] He seems to have remained at the court, since, a little later, the Emperor deputed him along with some others to select a suitable site at the bank of the river Chenab for laying the foundations of a city.[10] On 18 Amardād 41st Ilāhī (August 1596) he was still at the court when he treated Akbar for an injury received in a deer hunt.[11] n April 1599 he was despatched from Agra to Burhanpur to treat Prince Murād, who however died on 2 May 1599 before the physician could reach him.[12] Ḥakīm Miṣrī returned to Agra, but his asso-

6 ʻAhmadānagaraʼ in the MS. Why Abū'l Faẓl uses this spelling here is not clear: it does not seem to be due to a slip by the scribe.

7 Abū'l Faẓl, *Āʼīn-i Akbarī*, I, ed. Blochmann, Calcutta, 1866- 7, p.230.

8 Badāūnī, *Muntakhab'ut Tawārīkh*, III, ed. Ahmad Ali, Calcutta, 1869, p.165.

9 *Akbarnāma*, III, ed. Ahmad Ali, Calcutta, 1873, p.586.

10 Ibid., pp.600-01.

11 Ibid., p.712.

12 Ibid., p.753.

ciaion with the Deccan is underscored by the fact that in the 45th Ilāhī (1600-01), he was back again to the Deccan where he died on 16 Bahman 45 R.Y. (4 February 1601).[13]

The revenue estimates for the territories of the Deccan should actually relate to a little before 1591 because by the middle of March Ḥakīm Miṣrī had already reached Lahore after being imprisoned, for some time by Amīr Khān Ghaurī, on his way from the Deccan.[14]

These estimated *jama*ʻ figures for the states of the Deccan gain special interest because estimates of the revenues of those territories prior to their conquest by the Mughals have not been traced so far. At the same time owing to the frequent changes in the boundaries of these kingdoms and the Mughal provinces carved out of them, one has to be very careful in comparing these *jama*ʻ estimates with later figures. Nevertheless, one can venture some comparisons.

Khandesh was taken over by Akbar in 1600,[15] and was made a *sūba* in 1601. Its boundaries remained more or less unaltered till 1632, when Galna was added to it. In 1633 the *sarkār* of Nandurbar, Bijagarh and portions of *sarkār* Handia were transferred from Malwa to Khandesh, and in 1635 Baglana was annexed to it.[16] The *jama*ʻ estimate given in Add.27,247 thus remains comparable with later figures for the *ṣūba* till only 1632; thereafter it has to be compared with the *jama*ʻ of *sarkār* Burhanpur only, representing the old *ṣūba* of Khandesh.

*Jama*ʻ in *dāms*	year[17]	Reference
40,00,00,000	1591	Add. 27, 247, f.384 Ab.
30,32,03,112	1601	*Āʼīn*, I, p.478.
29,70,18,561	1605	Muʻtamad Khān, *Iqbālnāma-i Jahāngīrī*, II, Or.1834, f.232b.

[13] Ibid., p.783. Faiẓī Sirhindī gives 1 Shaʻbān 1009 as the date of his death, Br. Lib., Or 619, f.274a. Badāūnī, who brings his narrative down to 1598, reports his death in his biographical volume, and adds that he was buried at Burhanpur (*Muntakhabu't Tawārīkh*, Bib. Ind., III, p.165). This detail shows that Badāūnī was alive at least until 1601.

[14] Add. 27,247, f.483Ab.

[15] *Akbarnāma*, III, p.779.

[16] For details of alterations in the boundaries see Irfan Habib, *Atlas of the Mughal Empire*, New Delhi, 1952, Notes to Sheets 9A,14-16A.

[17] I have generally accepted the dates to which Irfan Habib assigns these figures in *Agrarian System*, p.397.

29,70,16,586	1628-33	*Bayāẓ-i Khwushbūī*, I.O.828, f.181.
33,69,30,000	1658	*Dastūr-ul 'Amal-i·'Ālamgīrī*, Add. 6598, f.118b.

The *jama'* stated in local *tankas* in the *Ā'īn* for the entire *ṣūba* 1601 was 1,26,47,062 and the totals of the figures stated for each of its *parganas* was 1,26,33,463 *tankas*. This figure, it will be seen, is far less than that of 2½ crores of local *tankas* given on the basis of the reports received in 1591. If the *tanka* was equal to 16 *dāms* the stated *jama'* in the *Ā'īn* should have amounted to 20,23,52,992 *dāms* only. But Abū'l Faẓl says that after the capture of Asirgarh in 1601, Akbar increased the *jama'* of Khandesh by 50 percent by reckoning the *tanka* at 24 *dāms*, instead of 16 *dāms*.[18] His editor gives the enhanced *jama'* as 45,52,94,232 *dāms*, but this is exactly what one gets if one converts the *jama'* into *dāms* not at 24 *dāms* to the *tanka* but at 36 *dāms* (1.5 × 24) to the *tanka*. This double enhancement seems to be due to a simple calculation error.[19] Converting the *jama'* of Khandesh stated in *tankas* in the *Ā'īn* at the rate of 24 *dāms* to a *tanka*, the figure works out at 30,32,03,112 *dāms*, which matches rather well with the figures in the *Iqbālnāma* (1605) and *Bayāẓ-i-Khwushbūī* (1628–33), as well as with the *jama'* of *sarkār* Khandesh (Burhanpur) c. 1658. The *jama'* stated for Khandesh in 1591 thus appears clearly inflated being about 33 per cent higher than the true *jama'* in the *Ā'īn* and later sources.

The *jama'* for Ahmadnagar kingdom in the 1591 report should include the *jama'* of Berar, since Berar was annexed by Murtaẓā Niẓām Shāh in 1573-4.[20] The *jama'* of Ahmadnagar reported in 1591 is then comparable with the sum of the figures for Ahmadnagar and Berar in later statistics.

Jama' in *dāms*	Year	Reference
1,44,00,00,000	1591	Add 27,247 f.384Ab.
80,37,97,986	1605	*Iqbālnāma*, or. 1834, f.119a.
95,37,97,369	1628-33	*Bayāẓ-i Khwushbūī*, I.828. f.182.
1,10,00,00,000	1646-7	Lāhorī, *Pādshāhnāma*, II, pp.710-11.
1,14,49,12,000	1658	Add.6596, ff.119a-b.

[18] *Ā'īn*, I, p.474.

[19] Cf. *Agrarian System*, p.406*n*; and *Economy of the Mughal Empire*, pp.29-30*n*.

[20] Abū'l Qāsim 'Firishta', *Gulshan-i Ibrāhīmī*, Nawal Kishore, Kanpur, 1874, p.176.

Note: Since the *Ā'īn* gives the *jama'* for the *ṣūba* Berar but not for Ahmadnagar its *jama'* statistics cannot be used here.

For Ahmadnagar and Berar the *jama'* of 1591 is found to be even more inflated than that of Khandesh. It is nearly 56 percent higher than the total of *jama'* for Ahmadnagar and Berar in 1605 and 66 percent higher than the *jama'* of these provinces in c.1628-33. In 1636 the southern parts of Ahmadnagar were aded to Bijapur so that the last two figures in the above table are not really comparable with the three earlier ones.

For the revenues (*maḥṣūl*) of the kingdom of Bidar we have an estimate in Firishta (1606), viz. 4,00,000 gold *hūns*.[21] Assuming a *hūn* to be equal to 4 rupees as it was in the 1630s,[22] and taking 40 *dāms* to the rupee, the revenues of Bidar according to this estimate should have been equal to 6,40,00,000 *dāms*. This figure is again distinctly lower than the *jama'* of 8,00,00,000 *dāms* reported to Akbar's court in 1591.

For Bijapur and Golkunda that came under the Mughal control in 1686 and 1687, and where many alterations in the boundaries took place, any comparison of the other *jama'* figures for either kingdom or *ṣūba* (after annexations to the Mughal Empire in the 1680s) would be far too risky.

The 1591 report as quoted by Abū'l Faẓl mentions the Vijayanagara Empire under the designation of 'dominions of Rām Rāja' owing to the great repute of its Regent and Emperor of that name, who fell at the battle of Raksas Tagdi in 1565. In 1591 the ruler of the Vijayanagara Empire was actually Venkatapatideva Rāya II (1585-1614). Unfortunately, there is no information, at least amidst the large amount of material presented by Heras, about the revenues of the empire under that ruler to compare with our 1591 figure.[23]

Under such circumstances one can only add up the 1591 figures for Golkunda, Bijapur and Vijayanagara and compare these with the *jama'* figures for the *ṣūbas* of Bijapur and Haidrabad in Aurangzeb's later days, when these two *ṣūbas* had also come to include the bulk of the Vijayanagara Empire. The result is as follows:

[21] Ibid., II, p.177.

[22] Lahori, *Pādshāhnāma*, I(a), p.178.

[23] I follow the reconstruction of the events of his reign in Rev. Henry Heras, *The Aravidu Dynasty of Vijayanagara*, I, Madras, 1927, pp.300-40, 494-512.

Jama' (*dāms*)	Year	Reference
3,12,00,00,000	1591	Add. 27, 247, f.384 Ab.
3,10,00,00,000	1687-91	*Ẓawābiṭ-i Ālamgīrī*, Add.6598, ff.130b-132a.
3,30,30,20,000	1687	Fraser 86, ff.57b-61b.
3,34,61,52,140	1687	*Intikhāb-i Dastūr-ul 'Amal-i Pādshāhī*. Edinburgh, No.224 ff.1b-3b.
3,46,68,00,000	1709	Jagjīvandās, *Muntakhabu-t Tawārīkh*, Add.26,253. ff.51a-54a.

The estimated *jama'* for the territories of Bijapur, Golkunda and Vijayanagara, in 1591 was thus only around 7% lower than the *jama'* of that territory in c.1687 and a little over 11 percent lower than that of 1709. These figures suggest that the report given to Akbar of the revenues of these kingdoms of the Deccan overstated the true position, since we have to take into account the rise in prices during the seventeenth century to the extent of about 30 percent.[24] The *jama'* of the Mughal Empire excluding the Deccan itself registered an increase of over 44 percent between 1595 and 1700.[25]

It is thus obvious that the *jama'* estimates of the Deccan for 1591 were greatly inflated. This may be the possible reason for Abu'l Fazl deciding not to include them in the final version of the *Akbarnāma*. Our enquiry on the passage thus is partly negative in its result, since, owing to the degree of overestimation, its evidence is not likely to be of much use for statisticians of the fiscal resources of sixteenth-century Deccan. But these would nevertheless be of use in indicating the comparative fiscal strenghts of the Deccan states. By 1591 Bijapur was in this respect deemed to be the best placed. It was assigned the revenues of 12 crore Deccan *tankas,* as against 9 crore *tankas* for Ahmadnagar and only 4 crore *tankas* for Vijayanagara. Perhaps, this was a reflection of the large extension of the Bijapur kingdom at the expense of Vijayanagara by this time.

[24] S. Moosvi, 'The Silver Influx, Money Supply, Prices and Revenue-Extraction in Mughal India', *Journal of the Economic and Social History of the Orient*, vol.XXX, p.90.

[25] Ibid., p.89. My figures are different from those of Irfan Habib, *Agrarian System*, p.328, owing to the difference in the total *jama'* calculated for 1595.

4

A Dutch Memoir of 1603 on Indian Textiles

ISHRAT ALAM

The importance of textile production in the Mughal period was well underlined by Moreland.[1] This is especially true of silk, cotton and wool industries. Textiles had few rivals among other industries, none of which could compete with them in terms either of their contribution to the national product or of geographical diffusion.

It is, then, of some interest that there exists a Dutch 'Memorie', dated November 1603, prepared by Stalpaert van der Wiele, on the kinds of textile products, especially such as were expected to find a market in South-east Asia on the basis of exchange with spices.[2]

The Memoir lists the following commodities:

(1) 'Cayn Tourias' (Kain Turia), coarse printed/dyed cotton cloth. Generally, these had a length of 3 fathoms and width of 4 spans. Some times they were dyed with red or green stripes, roses or round 'daalders'. The red were known as 'Tourias Meera' in Malaya and were much in demand. The green coloured were called 'Tourias Itchu' and were purchased for 3 or 4 Rials per corge (i.e.

1 W.H. Moreland, *India at the death of Akbar, An Economic Study*, London, 1920, pp.171-184; W.H. Moreland, *From Akbar to Aurangzeb, A Study in Indian Economic History*, London, 1923, pp.53-58.

2 *Memorie van November 1603 over den toenmaligen handel, voornamelyk met lijnwaden, in Voor Indie, uitgezonderd Cambay en Chaul (Tjasel), op. het Maleische Schiereiland, en in den Maleischen Archipel*. The original is to be found under 'Kamer van Zeeland 41 G' in the Algemeen Rijksarchief, 's-Gravenhage, The Netherlands. On the parchment is written, 'Artikelen ende Instructien op de Schepen'. The whole 'Memorie' has been carefully reproduced in G.P. Rouffaer and H.H. Juynboll, *De batikkunst in Nederlandsch-Indie en haar geschiedenis*, Utrecht, 1914, Bijlage III, pp.xi-xxv. This was partly published by J.K.J. de Jonge, ed., *De Opkomst van het Nederlandsch Gezag in Oost Indie, 1595-1610*, III, 's-Gravenhage/Amsterdam, 1875, p.149. F.W. Stapel has used this 'Memorie' in explaining some textile terms in Dr F.W. Stapel, ed., Pieter van Dam, *Beschryvinge van de Oostindische Compagnie*, 's-Gravenhage (relevant volumes). Tapan Raychaudhuri, *Jan Company in Coromandel, 1605-1690, A Study in the Interrelations*

20 pieces) and were sold in Banda for 150 to 200 'catti' nutmegs.[3] (2) 'Baftas' (*bāftas*), purchased for 3/4 to 5/4 Rial per piece and in Banda fetching 40 to 80 'catti' nutmegs. (3) 'Carycam', red and blue cloths: red were much in demand, 20 pieces being sold for 8 to 10 Rials, and blue for 7 to 8. In Banda they fetched 10 to 20 'catti' nutmegs. (4) 'Osinani' ('Osmani') (*āsmānī*), a coarse cloth: could be purchased for 3-4 Rials. (5)'Camykyn'('Canykyn') (Kannekin), white cotton cloth, length 7 & 8 fathoms, sold for 1¼ to 1½ Rials; could procure 30 to 35 'catti' nutmegs in Banda.[4] (6) 'Mecanis', finer than 'Canikins', but slightly more expensive. (7) 'Tjauanis' (Chaveni), white cotton cloth but smooth, 5 fathoms long and 2 spans wide and sold for 4 to 6 Rials per 20 pieces; fetched in Banda 25 to 40 'catti' nutmegs. (8) 'Tschyndes' (*Chindis*) (Chintz), a multi-coloured ('Bonte') silk cloth, sold in Banda for 40-50 'catti' nutmegs per piece. These were sent to Arabia and Persia to be sold in exchange for silver and gold.

Since St. Thome and Mylapore were under Portuguese control, the Dutch procured their supplies of cloth from places like Calliture and Armagon, the procurements being controlled from Paleacat. The sorts listed are as follows: (9) 'Dragons', with two colours either red and white, red and green or red and blue. They were sold for 130 and 150 Rials per 'basta' which consisted of 160 pieces. (10) 'Pattas', also called 'Tschermalleyas'. This was woven red or green for about half fathom, and further in the middle had red or blue stripes. It was sold for 13 to 16 Rials per corge, and fetched 30 to 45 'catti' of nutmegs in Banda. (11) 'Tapisarassi' (Tapi Sarassa), painted cloths with figures of foliage or birds and purchased for 10 to 13 Rials per corge, 25 to 30 'catti' of nutmegs (in Banda). (12) 'Sarasses tsechramalais', the best and smoothest, and fetched 60 to 70 Rials per corge. The lesser quality could fetch 40 to 50 Rials and 50 to 90 'catti' nutmegs (in Banda). Similarly, (13) 'Sarassa gobaer', purchased for 70 to 80 Rials per corge. (14) 'Tschelleyes' ('chelas') (*shela*) were white checkered cotton textiles with black stripes.

From Nagapatnam the following cloths could be procured for

---

of European Commerce and Traditional Economies, 's-Gravenhage, 1962, Appendix C, pp.221-22, has made use of this memoir to elucidate some varieties of Coromandel cloth.

[3] *Memorie van 1603*, p.xi.

[4] Ibid.

trade in Banda, Amboina, Seeram and other places: (15) 'Salalous' (Sallalos), black and dark blue cloths, purchased for 6-8 Rials per corge. (16) 'Balatscher' (Ballatios), white, black and blue cloths, purchased for 15-17 per corge: these fetched nutmegs according to the quality of the cloth. (17) 'Poleng' (Pelong), 2-3 fathoms long and 5 spans wide, purchased for 12-15 Rials per corge. (18) 'Touloupoucan' (Tulupucan), 1½ fathoms long and 4½ spans wide, purchased for 6-7 Rials per corge, and 10,11, or 12 pieces fetched in Banda 1 *baar* of nutmegs. (19) 'Borneo Laya', 1½ fathoms long and 4½ spans wide, cost 5-6 Rials per corge; 12-13 pieces fetched 1 *baar* of nutmegs.

Masulipatnam provided: (20) 'Mouryn' (Muri), 4 fathoms long, a cheap striped cotton cloth, of two qualities, purchased for 10 Rials per corge; 6-8 pieces fetched 1 *baar* of nutmegs in Banda. 21 'Soutars' (*chautārs*), 7-8 fathoms long, purchased for 20-25 Rials per corge; 1-5 pieces could procure 30-40 'catti' nutmegs. (22) 'Salimpournis' (Salempuris), 8 fathoms long, white cotton cloth, bordered with red stripes, purchased for 25-30 Rials per corge, fetched in Banda 30-40 'catti' nutmegs. (23) 'Cayn Mogo' (Kain Mogo), yellow cotton cloth in the Malaya style, 2 fathoms long and 3½ span wide, purchased for 8 Rials per corge, and 1 corge sold for 1½ *baar* nutmegs. (24) 'Pattamalam', 2 fathoms long and 5 spans wide, purchased for 10-12 Rials per corge; 1 corge could procure 2-4 'baar' nutmegs. (25) 'Cain Mandil' (Kain Mandil), blue cloth with white stripes, 1½ fathoms long and 4 spans wide, purchased for 7-8 Rials per corge; 2 pieces sold for 10-20 'catti' nutmegs in Banda; (26) 'Distaers' (*dastār*), red dyed cotton cloth, 3 fathoms long and 3½ spans wide, purchased for 8 Rials per corge, and a corge sold for 1½ 'baar' nutmegs. (27) 'Cain Coobaer' (Kain Gover), cotton cloth of 'brownish blue with whitish blue stripes', 1½ fathoms long and 5 spans wide, could be purchased for 13-14 Rials per corge; in Banda sold 10 pieces for 1 'baar' nutmegs. (28) 'Cassiopes', half cotton, half silk, striped cloth, 4 fathoms long and 5 spans wide, purchased for 30-35 Rials per corge and sold in Banda apiece for 40-50 'cattis' nutmegs.

From Bengal came: (29) 'Sattou pacooras', white cotton cloths, 6-6½ fathoms long and 5 spans wide, purchased for 16-18 Rials per corge and sold 3-8 pieces for 1 *baar* nutmegs. (30) 'Cassa bassar' (*Khāṣa Bāzār*), red striped cloth, 8 fathoms long and 5 spans wide; 1 piece could fetch 30-40 'cattis' cloves in Moluccas.

(31) 'Gassa Kyttgil' (*Khāṣa* Kitgil), 5 fathmos long and 3 spans wide, purchased for 25-30 Rials per corge; in Banda it procured 20-40 'catti' nutmegs for 1 piece of cloth. (32) 'Rambouty' (Rambuti), white cotton cloth, 8 fathoms long, sold in Makassar for 90-100 Mas (1 Mas = 1 Rial) by the Portuguese to the Malays and Javanese. (33) 'Beiraram' (*bhairon*), white cotton cloth, which cost 160-180 Rials per corge at Malacca or Makassar.

This list is abstracted from the document with the modest aim of contributing to the elucidation of Mughal-period textile terms, towards which only tentative attempts have so far been made.[5]

5 E.g., John Irwin, 'Indian Textile Trade in the Seventeenth Century', in: John Irwin and P.R. Schwartz, *Studies in Indo-European Textile History*, Part I, Ahmedabad, 1966; Irfan Habib, *Atlas of the Mughal Empire*, Delhi, 1982, pp.69-70 ('Glossary of Textile Terms').

Reviews

Muḥammad G̱ẖauṣī Shattārī, *Ghulzār-i Abrār*, ed. Muhammad Zaki, pub. Khuda Bakhsh Oriental Public Library, Patna (distributors: Maktaba Jamia, New Delhi), 1994 (*rect.* 1995), 15+579pp. Paperback. Rs.250.

We have here the first printed edition of one of the greatest, and historically perhaps the most important, of the collections of biographical notices of Muslim religious divines and mystics compiled in the Mughal period. Only an Urdu translation by Faẓl Aḥmad (two editions; 1908, 1975) was available to anyone who did not have access to the very few surviving manuscripts of this work. Six complete manuscripts appear to be known, two in private collections reported by M. Arshad Qureshi (see p.558 of the edition under review) and the remaining four in public libraries (Storey, *Persian Literature - a Bio-bibliographical Survey*, I, 2, No.1310, pp.984-5). The editor has used as his basic text the fairly early (1668) manuscript in the John Ryland Library, Manchester (Lindesiana, p.143, No.185), collating it with the manuscripts at the Royal Asiatic Society, Calcutta, and Salar Jang Museum, Hyderabad. By an oversight the indicators are not explained, but one presumes that *bā* in the footnotes stands for the Calcutta, and *jīm*, for the Hyderabad MS. These two seem to be copies of a single MS, which, at the time of copying had lost its last page, so that both stop at the same point just before the end.

The editor has given only a functional preface, though he does good service by listing the very large number of texts used by the author of *Gulzār-i Abrār*. Arshad Qureshi's foreword to the 1975 reprint of the Urdu translation provides some essential particulars of the author, mainly culled from the *Gulzār-i Abrār*.

The number of persons whose biographies are given by G̱ẖauṣī is quite large: Ivanow counted 575, the Urdu translator, 612. Probably, an index (not unfortunately prepared for the present edition) would give a still larger count. The bulk of the persons noticed belong to the 15th and 16th centuries.

The author was born at Mandu in 1555 (p.525), and educated there. A romantic attachment took him to Agra, where he spent five years, 1575-6 to 1582 (pp.539-44); here probably he enjoyed the personal association with the famous poet Faiẓī, to which he expressly refers (p.415). He went from Agra to Ahmadabad to complete his education (p.544), and when he had just turned thirty (1584), he returned to Mandu, where he now resided, undertaking journeys sometimes to Ujjain, Ahmadabad, and Burhanpur. It was at Mandu that, on his way for *ḥajj*, 'Abdu'l Ḥaqq, the author of *Akẖbāru'l Akhyār*, a much smaller but earlier compilation of biographical notices of Muslim mystics, met the author in 1587 (pp.524-5). 'Abdu'l Ḥaqq's work, to which G̱ẖauṣī refers twice (pp.187,525), probably encouraged him in his resolve of making a much more extensive compilation. He claims in his preface that he entered on this resolution in 1589, and was reinforced in it by seeing in 1599-

1600 the notices of Indian Muslim saints in Abū'l Faẕl's *Akbarnāma* (that is, the latter portion of the *Ā'īn-i Akbarī*) (p.5). This is interesting since Ghauṣī throughout consciously imitates the majestic (or, according to taste, bombastic) style of Abū'l Faẕl. In 1601-2, at Burhanpur, the author had the privilege of being in Akbar's presence, when the Emperor asked why no one had written about the mystics of recent and contemporary times; and Ghauṣī found himself too embarrassed to divulge his project (p.5). But he persevered in his work, collecting his voluminous information. In 1605-6, he began his writing, making the first draft in two years, but completing the final text only in Rajab 1022 (August-September 1614) (pp.532-3). The long period of writing explains why 1020 should be referred to as the current year on p.79. The author dedicates his book to Jahāngīr both in his preface and at the end.

Ghauṣī defines his object as 'reviving the memory of the select circumstances of God-recognising men, from the beginning of 700 [AD.1300] to 1000 [AD 1591-2]' (p.5). Though some of the persons noticed never came to India, it aims in fact at being a comprehensive collection of notices of all Muslim mystics of India of whatever *silsila* affiliation or other hue, and of whatever period, from the 11th century onward to the author's own time. Shi'ite divines are not, however, included.

Ghauṣī belonged to the Shattārī *silsila*, and its adherents are given much prominence. But Ghauṣī is always respectful to other orders, and for earlier periods rather uncritical and easily prone to record reports of miracles. But as we come to the 15th and 16th centeries, he becomes increasingly accurate, and the numerous sources and oral testimony he draws on invite respect. Given the regions he knew best, it is not surprising that Central India and Gujarat appear to be over-represented.

Ghauṣī has obvious affiliations with the Mughal court and seems to have enjoyed some status with the nobility. Yet, there is a succinct criticism of Akbar's religious views on p.377, where Akbar's doubts about Islamic beliefs are attributed, as by Badāūnī, to the open, bitter disputes among theologians. The author tells us that Akbar sought to bring to public gaze the concept of 'Ṣulḥ-i Kul' (Absolute Peace), which was a secret concept of the pantheistic mystics (*ahl-i fanā*). Since this did not succeed, he became embittered with the orthodox and removed them from service. His brief account of the punishment of Shaikh Munawwar, a theologian, condemned to prison by Akbar and dying in 1602-3, is not without pathos. Yet it is hard to improve on his concise biography of Faiẕī, for its accuracy and thoughtful assessment of that important figure in Akbar's circle (pp.414-5).

Besides its importance for the history of ideas and beliefs among Muslims, especially of the sufic world, the work gives much information, often incidentally, of the political history of Gujarāt and Malwa. The author seems to have been well informed of what was happening in the higher counsels of the Mughal Empire, and is notable for his frank references to the atmosphere of suspicion and intrigue which Khusrau's rebellion gave rise to at Jahāngīr's court (pp.51, 486-7).

The present edition lacks historical annotation of any sort; and there are unfortunately some misprints and, in the latter portion, an abundance of unexplained round brackets. But the text, with its difficult vocabulary and unusual constructions, must have caused the editor considerable labour in laying it out. He has now done the necessary spade-work for others to quarry the rich material this work undoubtedly contains. For this he deserves our unstinted thanks.

The price is reasonable; the binding could have been better.

IRFAN HABIB

'Ārif Qandahārī, *Tārīkh-i Akbarī, An Annotated Translation with Introduction*, transl. Tasneem Ahmad, Pragati Prakashan, Delhi, 1993, XVII+315pp. Rs.350.

Almost all the major sources of Akbar's reign have for long been available in full English translations, and Elliot and Dowson have through their selected, translated excerpts introduced the reader to some other sources. But among formal histories, 'Ārif Qandahārī's work is one whose existence was not even known to earlier generations of historians, having been first described by Sri Ram Sharma in 1933. There are two known manuscripts, one preserved at Cambridge (containing corrections in the author's own hand) and the other at Rampur. The work was excellently edited, with collation of both MSS by Nadwi, Dihlawi and Arshi, pub. Rampur, 1962. Now, Tasneem Ahmad has taken the important step of rendering the work into English, and so enabling a larger circle of scholars to appreciate its value for the history of Akbar's reign.

Completed sometime between 1579 and 1581, 'Ārif's work is the first known history of Akbar's reign if one excludes the short account of Akbar in 'Alā'u'ddaula's *Nafā'isu'l Ma'āṣir*, the well known biographical compendium of poets, completed c.1574. 'Ārif Qandahārī's main sources of information, besides the *Nafā'isu'l Ma'āṣir* (which he quotes twice), appear to have been oral (including information derived from his patron Muẓaffar Khān Turbatī, one of Akbar's leading nobles), various documents, and his own observations. It, therefore, gives us many facts that we would not have known about otherwise, for though his work was known to the historian Firishta and to Nahāvandī, the biographer of 'Abdu'r Raḥīm Khān-i Khānān, the major historians of Akbar's reign, such as Abū'l Faẓl, Niẓāmu'ddīn and Badāūnī were unaware of it.

Tasneem Aḥmad offers us not merely a translation that was long needed, but also much useful annotation in which he painstakingly compares the information in 'Ārif with that of other sources, giving complete references. Reasonably enough, he bases his translation on the practically definitive text of the Rampur edition.

Tasneem Ahmad's translation covers the entire text, but lamentably leaves out four pages of later additions by the author, found in the Rampur MS and reproduced at the end of the Editor's introduction to the Rampur ed., pp.22-27. These pages are particularly important because these relate to Akbar's first expedition to Kabul and help in fixing the date of the final closing of the book at 1581. Similarly, the information given in the detailed end-notes by the editors of the Rampur edition seems to have been ignored by the translator while compiling the notes to this translation.

'Ārif Qandahārī's language is undoubtedly difficult, his aim being to compose extremely ornate prose heavily interspersed with verses and Arabic words and phrases. One sympathises, therefore, with Tasneem Ahmad in the task he has had to perform. Inevitably, one comes across points where one's understanding of the meaning of the original text is different. On page 83 of the translation (Akbar's letter to Bairam Khān) there is an obvious error. The word *'mulāzimat'* is here translated as 'service' instead of 'attendance'; and, therefore, the phrase, 'We heard that you were coming to wait on us' has been rendered as 'We have come to know that you intend to continue in the service of the Court'. This misunderstanding of the word '*mulāzimat*' continues throughout, e.g., on page 286, where 'Ārif simply says that he was given an audience, but has been represented as saying, 'I was favoured by being reemployed'.

On the same page a surprising piece of confusion occurs to mar the translation of an entire passage. The text (Rampur ed., p.233) clearly says: 'In the said year the administration of Gujarāt was given to Quṭbu'ddīn Khān Atka and Shihāb Khān, and of Sārangpūr, *sarkār* Mālwa, to Shujā`at Khān ...' The translation, however, reads: 'In the said year *the administration of various places was entrusted to nobles*. The administration of Gujarāt was entrusted to Quṭbuddīn Muḥammad Khān Atga, Shāhab Khān of Sārangpūr', etc. There is no sanction for the italicised sentence in the original text. The further error regarding Sārangpūr is seemingly due to Tasneem Aḥmad's misconception regarding the term *sarkār*. In his introduction Tasneem Aḥmad chides 'Ārif Qandahārī for using *sarkār* as a synonym of *wilāyat*. He has perhaps only the post-1580 meaning of *sarkār* in mind, when after the formation of *ṣūbas* or provinces by Akbar the subdivisions of *ṣūbas* were officially designated *sarkārs*. Before 1580, the *sarkār* was, in fact, the highest division within the Empire and so equivalent to province or *wilāyat*.

Such slips unfortunately mean that in considering the sense of any passage, the researcher would be best advised to check also with the Persian text.

There can be little grouse with the translator for not using diacritical marks; but printing errors might have been checked more carefully. We have, e.g., 'Afif' for 'fief' (p.4); and 'Baruni' for 'Barni' (p.6).

An indulgent view of such manifestations of haste may, however, be taken, since there was possibly some anxiety on the translator's part to bring out the book in time to synchronise with the 450th birth anniversary of Emperor Akbar, an occasion of national celebration in India.

SHIREEN MOOSVI

Shireen Moosvi, *Episodes in the Life of Akbar: Contemporary Records and Reminiscences*, National Book Trust, Delhi, 1994, xv + 131pp., Rs.45.00.

Shireen Moosvi's carefully selected passages from contemporary and near-contemporary texts in this small but competently arranged volume project a revealing biographical profile of perhaps the best known Indian ruler, with the exception of Asoka. What the reader is served with is not only livelier and much more colourful than what one comes across in modern secondary works, but emphasizes features which never came out so clearly in the historical narratives. Interestingly enough, this profile reminds us of the images of Akbar preserved in folklore. Besides being a great military leader and builder of imperial institutions, he also comes out in this book as a man with deep compassion for all living beings, one who respected women, firmly rejected religious formalism and intolerance, disapproved of inhuman practices like slavery, *sati* and polygamy, recognized India as his own and felt deeply involved in its people and culture. These humane facets of Akbar's personality are often overshadowed in the narratives by his military exploits and administrative measures. The folklore about Akbar, originating in his lifetime, has continued to grow, down to the present time (now envoked in films like *Mughal-i Azam* and *Anarkali* for example); it highlights images which bring out his human personality rather than imperial majesty. In exploring the various dimensions of Akbar's personality in the light of contemporary texts, Shireen Moosvi gives substance to such images, which have become especially topical in the context of present-day attempts to rewrite Indian history, one side presenting Akbar as an alien invader, and the other as a Hindu-appeaser. One may thus say that, besides being a delightfully readable book, we have here a significant contribution to the reconstruction of an authentic and meaningful biography of Akbar.

It may, however, be pointed out that while there is little in the present selection of the passages, at whose inclusion one could cavil, it could still be enlarged. One may off-hand mention the *ghazal* composed by Akbar to celebrate his catching of of a black panther in 1562 near Palam in Delhi (reproduced by 'Ārif Qandahārī) or the description of Akbar's conversation with the Mahdavī divine, Miyān Muṣṭafā Bandagī in 1572 (given in a contemporary Mahdavī text, *Majālis* by Shaikh Muṣṭafā Gujarātī).

Regarding the selections made from Akbar's sayings, Moosvi seems to have a tendency to overlook statements reflecting Akbar's early attitudes in matters of religious beliefs, and to be more concerned with that side only which reflected his maturer perceptions.

These minor grouses should not detract from appreciation of Moosvi's care in selection and extreme accuracy in her translations (or revisions of translations) of Persian texts. Lastly, the National Book Trust is to be congratulated for fixing so modest a price, despite seven illustrations in colour and a delightfully designed cover.

IQTIDAR ALAM KHAN

John F. Richards, *The Mughal Empire*, being Vol.I, Part 5, of *The New Cambridge History of India*, Cambridge University Press, 1993; Indian edition, Foundation Books, New Delhi, 1993, xvi + 320 pp., index, 6 maps. Rs.350.

The *New Cambridge History of India* seems designed to provide us with the Sahibs' 'post-colonial' approach to Indian History. It has an exclusively UK-US board of editors; and in its scheme, as set out in the General Editor's Preface (p.xiv), the British conquest becomes 'Transition to Colonialism' (the title of Vol.II), as if the conquest was an internal, indigenous process; and, consequentially, Vol.III is titled 'The Indian Empire', as if the British Empire was really our own (I mean, the natives' own) Empire. It is heartening, however, to find that Professor Richards, one of the associate editors and already known to Indian historians for his significant monograph, *Mughal Administration in Golconda*, Oxford, 1975, should have produced a volume so independent of the brief implicitly set for him by the scheme.

At the very beginning Richards records his disagreement with the view increasingly in fashion (Wink, Perlin) that the Mughal Empire was either illusory as 'Empire' or of little relevance to the main economic and social processes. He speaks in the Preface of his conviction 'that Mughal centralized power was a reality and that its effect on Indian society was considerable', adding reasonably that 'whether this was good or bad is a different question' (p.xv). This basic assumption serves Richards as a major justification for restricting his survey of the Mughal Empire essentially to political history, though he takes the latter in its broadest sense, commenting at length on administrative developments and on the interaction between Mughal polity and the economic, social and cultural environment. One may still cavil at this restriction, for one would look invain in this volume for any adequate survey of culture, especially religious thought, literature and art. Neither Faiẓī, nor Tulsīdās, nor 'Abdu'ṣ Ṣamad nor Bichitr find mention here. But if the *New Cambridge History* editors had set a particular space-limit for him, one may sympathise with his dilemma, for it is hard to see how he could have found space for the other themes without reducing his treatment of political history to a mere chronological statement.

As it is, Richards has succeeded in giving us a readable account of the Mughal Empire, drawing upon the findings of the latest published researches and making his reader feel as if he is participating in an open-minded exploration where all possible strands are being pursued. Some of his few digressions help to sustain the reader's interest, such as those on Mirzā Nathan (pp.107-109) and on Murshid Qulī K͟hān's early career (pp.248-50), while they usually have some message as well to impart. I find Richards to be most at home when he is discussing the details of Mughal administration: he is exceptionally clear both in his comprehension and exposition here. I find his present views on the *jāgīr* crisis (pp.244-46, 292) far more convincing than in his book on Mughal administration in Golconda. Also reassuring is his commonsense acceptance of the contemporaries' view that revenue-farming was a device symptomatic of administrative disintegration (pp.266-68), rather than a process of creative innovation or even statesmanship (as suggested by Bayly, and, following him, by Muzaffar Alam).

Richards draws a very positive economic balance-sheet for the Mughal Empire in the days of its glory in the seventeenth century, and is unable to accept the view that the wars engulfing the whole of the country in the first half of the eighteenth century had no adverse effect on trade (e.g., pp.278-9). He argues, on the basis of 'qualitative evidence', that the Mughal Empire stimulated economic growth (p.285). And he is not willing to concede that this stimulation might have stemmed from a parasitic relationship with agriculture (pp.291-2). On the contrary, he argues that the Mughal Empire broke up owing to contradictions between the very classes that had prospered under its protection or patronage, the Empire lacking the machinery or flexibility to resolve these contradictions (pp. 294-96). Most readers may find the argument interesting; and certainly the present thrust of opinion from authors as diverse as M. Athar Ali, S. Moosvi and H. Mukhia, seems to be against my thesis of 'agrarian crisis' which Richards accurately summarises and firmly rejects (pp.291-2). Though I remain unconvinced, I find the pages Richards devotes to this question as one of the most stimulating parts of the volume.

It is, then, a great disappointment that so promising a volume should be disfigured by so many errors of fact. Panipat is hardly 'a few miles from Delhi', and the 'Ranā of Mewar' did not die at the battle of Khānua (1527) (p.8); the Uzbek commander in Akbar's early years was Khān Zamān, not 'Zaman Khan' (p.16); Āṣaf Khān was not an Uzbek (p.17); Rohtas in the Panjab was not situated on the Indus (p.28); 'Maulana Abdullah' (Sultanpuri) was not the *ṣadr* of the Empire, this office being then held by Shaikh 'Abdu'n Nabī (p.37); the *maḥẓar* of 1579 recognising Akbar's authority in *sharī'at* interpretation was not 'an imperial edict', but a declaration issued by leading theologians (pp.39-40); Shaikh Aḥmad Sirhindī after his arrest (1619) and subsequent release did not travel 'with the Imperial encampment of Jahangir's tour to the Deccan', for Jahāngīr never made such a tour (p.100); after his rebellion in 1622, Khurram was never appointed 'Governor of the Deccan provinces' by Jahāngīr (pp.115, 137); Miyān Mīr, not 'Mulla Mir', was the name of the Qadirī saint (p.151); Sipihr Shukoh, the son of Dārā Shukoh, was not killed along with his father (he married Aurangzeb's daughter fourteen years later) (p.161); Aurangzeb's invasion of Bijapur took place in 1657 (not 1656), and it did not precede, but followed, the death of Muḥammad `Ādil Shāh (p.207); 'Baharji Bohra, the Ismā`īli trader' of Surat is really Virji Vora, a Hindu, not an Ismā'īli (p.209); Sikandar 'Ādil Shāh surrendered Bijapur to the Mughals in September 1686, not 1685 (p.220); there was no 'Murshidabad' in 1696-7 (p.248); and in 1720 Niẓāmu'l Mulk won his victory at Siugaon, not Shakarkhedla (p.273). Map (p.131) 2 is made confusing by a wrong delineation of Mughal boundary after 1647, and on map 5 (facing p.227), one needs to substitute 'Mysore' for 'Bijapur'. This list of slips is not unfortunately exhaustive.

The Bibliography is fairly comprehensive as far as recent work is concerned, but one regrets the absence of references to some of the old classics, such as Moreland, Ibn Hasan and Saran, which have not by any means lost their value. By a curious slip, Noman A. Siddiqi's work on Mughal land-revenue administration, 1707-1750, is put under Akbar, and Ellen Smart's paper on the illiteracy of Akbar, under Imperial Administration (p.305).

While one need not insist on diacritical marks, the spelling system could have been made more consistent: It is odd to have 'Zulfikar Khan' (p.259) instead of 'Zulfiqar Khan', when the consonant concerned is elsewhere represented by 'q' as in 'Murshid Quli Khan' (p.249).

IRFAN HABIB

Sanjay Subrahmanyam (ed.), *Money and the Market in India, 1100-1700*, Oxford University Press, Delhi, 1994, 316 pp. Rs.300.

This is apparently the first volume dealing with medieval India in the 'Oxford in India Readings' series.

Subrahmanyam as Editor contributes an introduction of 56 pages and includes his own paper on bullion influx and prices in the 16th and 17th centuries. He finds most Indian scholars who have written before him on economic history to be rather dull-witted (e.g., remarks on Tapan Raychaudhuri, pp.8-9, though the reviewer, being perhaps similarly slow on the uptake, fails to see any 'contradictions' in Raychaudhuri's exposition) or driven by irrational preconceptions (like Irfan Habib with 'his *desired* Price Revolution', p.208). As for Subrahmanyam himself, the high standards he sets for his sources, enables him to dismiss the rich statistical material in Abū'l Faẓl's *Ā'īn-i Akbarī*, because it is merely 'a normative manual on administration', a surely inept description, but rather typical of the way in which Subrahmanyam deals with Persian material with which in any case he seems quite unfamiliar. One might as well dismiss pre-1947 official statistics because they were 'a part of the larger apologia' of British imperialism, or the data in the Portuguese, Dutch and English records of Mughal times, because these were part of a similar apologia for colonial or mercantilist chicanery. Subrahmanyam's advice to the reader to forget about gold: silver: copper ratios, since these were not 'commodities' (p.208), is a characteristic instance of overlooking evidence that does not suit his own predilections. His own demand in 'Towards a Conclusion' that 'the rate of increase of money supply be largely decomposed in terms of the rate of change of output and that of the inverse-velocity of money' (p.218) merely repeats in long words what Fisher's equation has long set for us; and we know any way that because of lack of the statistics required, these factors would be as much subject to speculation in respect of 16th-century India as of 16th-century Europe.

Among the papers on the 16th century that Subrahmanyam includes in his volume, those by J.F. Richards (on the economy under the Lodīs) and Aziza Hasan (on silver influx in the Mughal Empire) were published long ago, but it is good to see them republished.

I enjoyed the implicit claim in the blurb that the volume is an improvement on the *Cambridge Economic History of India*, Vol.I, which is censured for portraying 'the debate... somewhat monolithically'. Oxford English?

The volume is fairly well-printed.

IRFAN HABIB

Som Prakash Verma, *Mughal Painters and their Work, a Biographical Survey and Comprehensive Catalogue*, Centre of Advanced Study in History, Aligarh/ Oxford University Press, Delhi, 1994, xvi +438 pp., 51 plates (black-and-white). Rs.800.

This is a very important work of reference, indispensable for students of Mughal painting. The result of great industry, it aims at comprehensively cataloguing all paintings of the Mughal school by individual painters belonging to the main Mughal period (c.1550-1700), with biographical data about individual artists culled from all possible sources. All known paintings signed by, or attributed to, a named artist are included. It includes even such paintings as bear no evidence of identity of the artist, but have been ascribed by modern critics to one or other, and, often enough, to different artists, on no better a foundation than perceived peculiarities of style. Verma, however, carefully prefaces such entries with a question mark, indicating his own disavowal of the certainty of the identifications.

Indeed, one major merit of Verma's catalogue is the distinction he makes between actual signature (indicated usually by semi-cursive writing and an expression of self-abasement, *banda*, *k͟hānazād*, *faqīr*, & c.) and contemporary attribution (usually in *nasta'līq* either as direction to particular artists to make particular paintings, as in the book-illustrations of Akbar's reign, or simple record made within the main painting or its margin). Anonymous attribution in Persian inscriptions found on stray paintings must often engender doubt, now that works of famous Mughal artists are known to carry high prices. While Verma is not unduly suspicious, he is right to be vigilant, and to query many attributions accepted by modern art critics. The reader may, for example, see entry no.32 under Bichitr on p.109, which describes a well-known painting, the signature and inscription affixed to which Verma pronounces a forgery.

Verma gives the present whereabouts of each painting recorded, details of where it has been published (adding also whether in colour), and full references to cataloguers' descriptions and other comments on each painting. While no art historian can claim to have seen all or even most Mughal paintings, Verma has himself supplemented the printed literature with personal examinations of major collections in India, UK and US, so that he is often able to add details from his own scrutiny. Nevertheless, throughout the catalogue, his acknowledgement of the work of his fellow art-historians, Das, Skelton, Welch, Beach, Khandalavala, and others, is extensive, even when he holds opinions different from theirs.

In the Catalogue the list of works of each artist is preceded by a summary of what is known about him. This is usually well done with a fairly comprehensive utilisation of Persian sources. I would particularly commend for attention the biography of 'Abdu'ṣ Ṣamad, one of Akbar's famous painters, reconstructed on pp.40-44. Of Manṣūr, the celebrated painter of Jahāngīr's court, whose painting of a tulip is reproduced in colour on the jacket of the book, Verma too gives a notice (pp.261-2), which is quite useful, despite so much having been written already on that artist. Where there are namesakes, and the question of identity is uncertain, e.g. Sūr, Sūrdās, pp.357-61, Verma takes the reader fully into confidence as to the difficulty and generally seems to take a sensible position.

The Catalogue's utility is enhanced by a very competent introduction, giving at the end a useful chronology of illustrated MSS (pp.32-33), and a list of major collections of miniatures. Verma's black-and-white plates may not look attractive on the coffee table, but these include a notable collection of artists' portraits (Plates xxv-li, pp.402-16), which is very appropriate for the Catalogue. The Bibliography is full; the index, given the dictionary-arrangement of the Catalogue itself, is understandably limited to Subjects and Portraits.

The material in this Catalogue will itself need much exploration and analysis. A table on p.24 shows that the Catalogue has notices of 327 painters, of whom as many as 260 belonged to Akbar's reign. Allowing for overlap between different reigns, the entire seventeenth century offers us works of only 131 named artists. Is this because in Akbar's enterprise of book-illustration much greater care was taken to give individuals credit for their work? This would also speak for Akbar's personal interest in the work of ordinary painters in his atelier.

As a book of reference, Verma's Catalogue may be in need of a supplement as time passes, for new catalogues of museums and other collections are bound to appear, fresh discoveries made of Mughal paintings, and new insights and information published. But the basic spade-work has been done; and this is an achievement to be sincerely lauded.

IRFAN HABIB

Iqtidar Ḥusain Siddiqui, *Sher Shah Sur and his Dynasty*, Publication Scheme, Jaipur, 1995, 235 pp. Rs.350.

The first important monograph on Sher Shāh was published by K.R. Qanungo in 1921, of which the second (revised) edition appeared in 1965. Since then much new material has become available. The publication of Iqtidar Ḥusain Siddiqui's *History of Sher Shah Sur* in 1971 took into account a larger store of information and suggested revisions of some of Qanungo's well-known hypotheses. The present work is stated to be a 'thoroughly revised and recast version' of the earlier work, but is, in fact, largely a reprint.

The author has divided his study into eight chapters (against seven chapters in the 1971 edition), by providing a separate chapter on 'Provincial Organization', which in the earlier edition formed a section of Chapter III. An 'Excursus' has been added, showing that the correct tribal name of the dynasty is Sūr, not Sūrī; but it is not clear whether there was any real need for affirming such a well-known fact.

Siddiqui makes it clear that the term *jāgīr* was not in use during the Lodī and Sūr periods, the term *iqṭā'* or *pargana* being then used for territorial assignments, which also differed in nature from the Mughal *jāgīr* (Chapter I, c). Siddiqui's argument over the term *ra'iyat* used by 'Abbās Sarwānī, which was accepted by scholars like Moreland R.P. Tripathi, P. Saran and Qanungo, as standing for 'peasantry' is quite persuasive, and one tends to agree with him that the term was often used not for the peasantry in general, but for *muqaddams*, and other landholders.

Siddiqui's Chapter V on Barmāzīd is quite interesting. It provides ample evidence from the contemporary chronicles on Barmāzīd's Afghan origin as against Rajput argued for by Qanungo.

Chapter VI ('Provincial Organization') contains many insights on the functioning of provincial government, with its territorial units and officials. It brings out the basic differences between *khiṭṭa*, *vilāyat*, and *shiqq* and the position and powers of various functionaries such as *shiqqdār*, *muqta'*, *faujdār*, *amīn*, *munṣif*, etc., are clarified.

Chapter VII on '*Wajh-i ma'āsh*' is well documented and also reveals some of the secular dimensions of the Sūr Administration.

In the present work the frequent mention of the title '*Masnad-i 'ālī*' for nobles like Khawāṣ Khān, Miyān Muḥammad Farmulī, Muḥammad Khān Lodī, Miyān Ḥusain Farmulī, 'Īsā Khān Sarwānī, Ḥusain Khān Lodī, Miyān Bhūa and others makes it quite clear that the holders of this title were very high nobles. One, therefore, regrets the absence of a discussion of this title, which survived, if not in the Mughal empire, then, at least, in the Sikh tradition ('masands' of the Gurus).

The present edilion regrettably suffers from numerous printing errors We may note:'Abas Khan' for 'Abbas Khan' (p.19), '*Tafikh*' for '*Tarikh*' (p.71), 'Sher Shaj' for 'Sher Shāh' (p.74), 'Bihar in 1933-33 A.D.' for 'Bihar in 1532-33' (p.55), 'Durig' for 'During' (p.150), 'machinnery' for 'machinery' (p.151), 'Delhni' for 'Delhi' (p.159), 'sarkars' for 'sawars' (p.169), 'Sevice' for 'Service' (p.198). Even some footnotes appear to have been missed by the printer (p.62, n.3).

The reader needs further to be warned that except for fourteen pages on Hemū in chapter VII (pp.200-13), there is nothing on Sher Shāh's successors to justify the change of title from that of the first edition by the addition of the words 'and his Dynasty'. It would have been better to describe the volume merely as the second edition of the author's work on Sher Shāh rather than make it appear as a new work.

IQBAL HUSAIN

Sukumar Ray, *Bairam Khān*, ed. M.H.A. Beg, Institute of Central and West Asian Studies, University of Karachi, 1992, XXI + 287 pp, 6 plates (3 coloured) and map. Rs.200 ($10 outside Pakistan).

The singular position held by Bairam Khān among the nobles of Humāyūn and Akbar and the role played by him in the re-establishment of the Mughal Empire in India after Humāyūn's death undoubtedly justify a careful biographical study. Professor Sukumar Ray, with his earlier, almost definitive work, *Humāyūn in Persia*, Calcutta, 1948, was certainly the most qualified to attempt the task. He unfortunately died in 1987 without seeing it in print. It has now been published posthumously from Karachi about thirty-four years after it had been written. It is heartening to note that the publication of this work, written by a veteran Indian scholar, should became accessible to readers by the endeavours of colleagues at the Karachi University. This should encourage all of us to look forward to a more active academic collaboration between the historians of our two countries.

Sukumar Ray based his book not only on well-known contemporary histories, from which he culled the major part of his information, but also sifted a large number of lesser known Persian sources. His description of the early career of Bairam Khān is particularly detailed and informative. The first five chapters are devoted to this phase. It was perhaps his acquaintance with the evidence that he had already used while working on his *Humāyūn in Persia* that came handy to him here.

Sukumar Ray adopts throughout a critical approach towards his sources, though one has to note the influence on him of an earlier historiographic tradition in which a biography meant concentrating strictly on the subject without any attempt to explain fully the environment and larger factors, enabling one to see the subject's actions in perspective (a welcome feature, for instance, of Iqtidar Alam Khān's *Political Biography of a Mughal Noble — Mun'im Khān Khān-i Khānān)*.

All readers should be grateful to Professor Riazul Islam who obtained the manuscript from the author and his heirs and to Professor M.H.A. Beg who has so very competently updated the work by his 'Additional Notes', where nearly all the relevant modern works have been suitably utilised. We also learn that the original copy of the main work was at different stages of completion, varying from printed forms to hand-written first draft; the way Ray's text has been salvaged and printed is much to the credit of the editor. Proof-reading too has been carefully done: most of the few misprints the reviewer discovered are already noticed in the corrigenda (pp.263-4). It is, however, rather sad that (by a wrong command to the computer?) Bairam Khān's own name is misspelt 'Bairām Khān' throughout. The map is useful; the illustrations (including colour) well printed. The price too is moderate, placing it within reach of ordinary readers in Pakistan. Hopefully, improvements in trade between the two countries will enable readers in India also to buy it.

SHIREEN MOOSVI

Imperial Mughal Painters, Indian Miniatures from the Sixteenth and Seventeenth Centuries by Amina Okada, translated by Deke Dusinberre, Flammarion, Paris, 1992, 267 illustrations in colour and black-and-white, 240 pp. Price not stated. Also published under the title, *Indian Miniatures of the Mughal Court*, 1992.

The book with numerous full-page illustrations is a gorgeous production. It essentially centres around portraits of the Mughal school. In the first part we are treated to themes like 'A dynasty of Sovereign Patrons', 'Dynastic Portraits' including genealogical-tree portraits (see miniature by Dhanrāj, fig. no.34), and 'Allegorical Portraits'. The book opens with a rather sketchy essay on the origins of the Mughal painting (pp.11-16). The next section 'Court Painters at the Service of Imperial Ideology' (pp.17-26) presents the Mughal emperors' approach to painting. Here the artists' acquaintance with European art (initially with Flemish and German engravings) is examined. It is, however, rather surprising that the background of Persian, Central Asian and indigenous traditions has been ignored as if these did not form sources of art for the Mughal artists nor serve the ends of the patrons' ideology. Apparently these are not considered relevant to our author's concern ('a fresh approach') for perceiving Mughal painting as a tool for glorifying the Mughal emperors and their ancestors.

Mughal manuscript painting, largely inspired by the Persian, had a large area for its subject matter, including legend, fable, history, and even astronomy. However, Okada is mainly concerned with the illustrated historical manuscripts (pp.17-22), since she considers that their illustrations aimed at glorifying Islamic, Mongol and Timurid sovereigns. As a follow-up, the author's selection of illustrations at Akbar's atelier is deliberately one-sided. This may be set forth as a new approach to these illustrations, but it lacks credibility. We know that apotheosizing portraits of the ancestors of Akbar do not find a place in the illustrations of the *Tārīkh-i Alfī*, *Tārīkh-i Khāndān-i Timūrīa*, *Jāmi'ut Tāwarīkh* and *Bāburnāma*. Yet even the *Akbarnama* paintings are viewed by Okada as manifestations of an 'unprecedented glorification of Akbar's policies and political institutions' (p.22).

In fact, it is the seventeenth century which marks a new era in Mughal portraiture with the appearance of the apotheoses and allegorical portraits of the Mughal emperors. The main force behind this process was the concept of a semi-divine sovereignty that generally became accepted at the Mughal court, and was proclaimed by lofty titles for the ruler like 'World-Seizer', 'World-Ruler', etc. The pictorial expression of these concepts became more feasible with the Mughal artists' increasingly close contact with European paintings, especially pictures on Biblical themes and portraits of European rulers. European symbols, such as the cherubs, putties, cupids, orb, terrestrial globe, radiating halo and 'God the Father', could now serve the Mughal artist's purposes while working on an allegorical picture or on an apotheosizing portrait.

Akbar's portraits representing him as a 'superman', or with attributes of divinity, are all posthumous. In the sixteenth- century paintings, Akbar is invariably represented as partaking in the events as an earthly man. Of course, his status as a ruler and as a central figure in textual narratives, naturally tends him to be shown, though not necessarily always, as a hero.

There is no evidence that the symbolic elements of European art inspired Akbar to use painting serve the purpose of the monarch's glorification. His master painters, such as Basāwan, are known for allegorical pictures, but not a single attempt has been traced from Akbar's time to incorporate the European symbolisms in historical miniatures and portraits. Kesavdās, another famous painter of his court, is well known for imitating and adapting European examples, but again without such effort. The illustrated volumes of the Royal Polyglot Bible was presented to Akbar in 1580, paintings of which certainly influenced Mughal painters (see Okada, figs.85 and 86; also see Ebba Koch, 'The Influence of the Jesuit Mission on Symbolic Presentation of the Mughal Emperors' in Christian W. Troll, ed., *Islam in India, Studies and Commentries*, New Delhi, 1982). However, this influence is not reflected in sixteenth-century Mughal portraits. Indeed, Akbar was of too realistic a bent to project himself and his ancestors as men of exaggerated powers or with visible attributes of divinity in painting.

The inclination for documentation was the most likely factor behind the compilation of the MS *Tārīkh-i Alfī* and *Tārīkh-i Khāndān-i Timūrīa*: and this combined with the fondness for painting promoted the tradition of manuscript painting (historical miniatures). Okada's thesis is thus inapplicable to the sixteenth-century portraits and historical illustrations.

It is during the reigns of Jahāngīr and Shāh Jahān, that numerous apotheosizing portraits of Mughal emperors, nobles and saints, begin to appear, especially those executed by Abū'l Ḥasan, Biçhitr, Chitarman, Govardhan and Payāg. In them, the symbols of divinity and sanctity, mostly borrowed from European art, are attached to the figures portrayed. The posthumous portraits of Bābur, Humāyūn and Akbar, executed during the seventeenth century also carried these symbols (figs.41 and 44). Here one could agree with Okada that these paintings represent an attempt at 'glorification' and attribution of a celestial status to the ruler. The famous pictures, 'Jahāngīr shooting at the head of Malik 'Aṁbar' (fig.48), 'Jahāngīr entertaining Shāh 'Abbās' (fig.53) and 'Jahāngīr embracing Shāh 'Abbās' (fig.54) are some of the allegorical pictures designed to sustain the emperor's claims to semi-divine sovereignty.

The second part of the book deals with sixteen imperial Mughal painters, including 'Abdu'ṣ Ṣamad, Mīr Sayyid 'Alī, Basāwan, Kesavdās, Abū'l Ḥasan, Bichitr, Bishandās, Manohar, Miskīn, Payāg, Govardhan and

Manṣūr. After the works already published on the master-painters, especially those by W. Staude, S.C. Welch, M. Abdullah Chughtai, R. Ettinghausen, R. Skelton, M.C. Beach, A.K. Das and the present reviewer, Okada has little new factually to offer. However, her distribution of painters under thematic sub-titles distinctly marking out the individual's *forte* and his contribution to painting is an original exercise. This arrangement also brings into sharper focus the different influences at work at the imperial atelier, though the sequence is sometimes blurred, the work of painters not being presented strictly in a chronological order. For example, under the sub-title 'Painterly Virtuosity' (pp.125-147), Manohar is discussed first, though his active period lasts till late in Shāh Jahān's time; whereas Miskīn, who is taken up next, worked in Akbar's reign. Then, under the sub-title 'The Blossoming of Realist Portraiture in the Seventeenth Century' (pp.148-164), Mīr Hāshim (or Hāshim) is described first, though in portrait painting, Bishandās's work is earlier. Besides, Hāshim remained active during Shāh Jahān's reign while no work of Bishandās in known from that time. Such casualness in arrangement affects the corresponding textual description of the developments taking place in the Mughal school.

In the studies of individual painters, it is rather unfortunate that often pictures attributed by some modern scholars are referred to as 'ascribed' works and not, as they should be, as anonymous works. Also, the pictures containing third-person ascriptions and emperor's autographs are designated 'signed works' (figs.233 and 234). The only argument one can offer on Okada's behalf is that the authenticity of the ascriptions may have little relevance for her since she was looking exclusively for traces of European influences. From this specific point of view, the present volume is fairly successful. But there is one small lapse. While explaining European symbols, Okada (as also E.D. Maclagan, M.C. Beach and Ebba Koch) have overlooked the representation of 'God the Father' in the works of Basāwan (figs.85 and 86) and Bichitr (fig.208). Aḥsan Jan Qaisar, who discussed it first, considers it remarkable since in Bichitr's painting the depiction of God the Father is associated with a Muslim ruler ('The Profane and the Sacred in the Mughal School of Art', *Art and Culture: Felicitation Volume in Honour of Professor S. Nurul Hasan*, Jaipur, 1993).

Beach's identification of the portrait in figure 97, on page 95, of a person with a board under his arm, and offering a coconut, as an early portrait of Kesavdās, is accepted by Okada. However, in this painting the workmanship is quite at variance with that in the other works of that painter. The figure is, in fact, strikingly similar to that of Parsurāma depicted in a miniature of the *Rāmāyaṇa* in Sewai Man Singh II Museum, Jaipur (No.AgG1891, dated 1587). This raises doubt about not only the authenticity of the identification of the figure, but also the genuineness of the picture.

Further, like Beach, Okada does not distinguish between Payāg of Akbar's studio from the Payāg of Shāh Jahān's time. Akbar's Payāg is devoid of any European influence, and this particularly distinguishes him from the later Payāg. Besides, the painter's age (mid-thirties), depicted in his self-portrait in the illustration on folio 195 (*c*.1650-1657) of the MS *Pādshāhnāma* (Royal Library, Windsor No.773) also suggests that the Payāg of Akbar's time was a different artist (his earliest work survives in the MSS of the *Bāburnāma*, *c*.1598-1600).

The study of Manṣūr (pp.216-225), at the end of the volume, under the sub-title 'The Painter of Flora and Fauna' is interesting, but has little to do with the main thrust of the book

Two wrong descriptions of paintings have been noticed. Fig.22 is a portrait of Ṣafdar Khān, not Zain Khān Koka; and Fig.239 cannot be the portrait of the 'Dying 'Ināyat Khān'.

Okada's hypothesis that the historical miniatures, especially the allegorical and dynastic portraits were executed under the Mughal emperors' urge for presenting themselves and their ancestors in the most magnificent form can only be partially true. Still the present volume, so profusely illustrated, well brings out the grandeur and skill of the Mughal school of art. And such an achievement is always to be welcomed.

S.P. VERMA

Margaret H. Case (ed.), *Govindadeva: a Dialogue in Stone*, photographs by Robyn Beeche, Indira Gandhi National Centre for the Arts, New Delhi, 1996, 305 pp. Price: Rs 2000.

This volume comprises a collection of papers presented by a number of distinguished scholars on the theme of the Govind-dev temple and the early history of the Chaitanya sect at Vrindaban. Vrindaban is, perhaps, one of the most remarkable deliberate creations of a holy place. The creation came about in the sixteenth century, by the identification of a site near the village of Dosaich with the legendary Vṛindāvana which till then had been supposed to be the celestial seat of the sports of Lord Krishna. The rise to eminence of the earthly Vrindaban belonged to Akbar's reign which saw the transformation of a petty, recent religious settlement into a reputed temple-town. If the priestly establishments of the temples of Vrindaban, notably Govind-dev and Madan Mohan, owed much to the land grants conferred upon them by Akbar, the great building of the Govind-dev temple (perhaps replacing an earlier one adjacent), completed in 1590, was due to the generous patronage of one of Akbar's premier nobles, the famous Mān Singh of Amber.

The Govind-dev temple, as it was now built, is a notable representative of the architectural tradition fashioned at Fatehpur Sikri; and it is, therefore, only to be expected that the present volume should begin with four essays on the architecture and sculpture of the temple. Nalini Thakur's essay on the building, with its plans and photographs is particularly informative. It is, therefore, rather regrettable that in both the maps accompanying it (figs.2.3 and 2.5 on pp.13-14), there should be such a gross error as the placing of Vrindaban on the wrong side of the Yamuna river (left bank, instead of right bank). George Mitchell investigates the puzzle of the missing sanctuary with its *śikhara*. He seems to have overlooked the following description of the Govind-dev temple given by Maḥmūd Balkhī (*Baḥru'l Āsrar*, ed. Riazul Islam, Karachi, 1980, pp.13-14), who saw it in 1625:

> The said *deora* (temple) is one of the wonderful things of that locality. The first is a building which is conically shaped. Its height is more than a hundred 'yards' (*zira*') and the circle of its interior about 80 'cubits' (*arash*); and from ground to pinnacle, made firm and upright by stone and brick. There are some other buildings on both sides of it. But they are neither so grand nor so large. An idol made of black stone has been fixed in that building, its height around 12 'cubits' and breadth four 'yards'. The building has been constructed near the bank of Jamuna river, and was erected by Rāja Mān Singh, one of the nobles of Emperor Akbar.

This constitutes, perhaps, the most definite evidence about the presence of a high *śikhara* in the original building.

There are two contributions heavily based on the rich Persian and Braj/Rajasthani documentation available on the priests of the Chaitanya sect at Vrindaban and Amber/Jaipur, contributed respectively by Irfan Habib and Monika Hortsmann. Habib's reconstruction of individual biographies from the documents is a most interesting exercise and helps to elucidate a number of matters of the local history of 16th- and 17th-century Vrindaban. The prefatory note on p.132 contains a convenient listing of the three main lines of the Goswāmīs. By some slip it is not stated that the dates after each name are those yielded by records in which the *Goswāmī* is mentioned as alive. Moreover, such dates are omitted in respect of Seo (Shiv) Rām Gosā'in (No.8 in the line of Rūp), the dates being 1648-89 (cf. p.157).

There is a collection of photographs of inscriptions of the Govind-dev temple on pp.280-6; and the decipherments and translations of the two important Sanskrit inscriptions are offered by G.N. Bahura on pp.200-03. On p.287 a *farmān* of Akbar is reproduced, which has already been shown to be a forgery by the late Tarapada Mukherji and Irfan Habib.

Shrivatsa Goswami's two essays, one on iconography (pp.69-114) with numerous illustrations, and the other giving a general interpretation (pp.269-77), are both valuable: in the first he writes as the expert he is, and in the second, he is the perceptive insider who knows that in this world the sacred can never overlook the profane. Kapila Vatsyayan contributes in the beginning a useful introduction summing up the individual thrusts of the twelve essays.

The volume has a descriptive index, which at points consulted by the reviewer, proved to be most serviceable.

The editor explains in her preface why a system of transliteration based on the standard one for Sanskrit was adopted for the book, despite objections from 'many of the contributors'. The editor's reasoning leaves me unconvinced. Ms Case reads not only 'Māna Siṁha' for Mān Singh and 'Visnu Simha' for Bishan Singh, and has *burja* for Pers. *burj*, *parvānā* for Pers. *parwānā*, *sūbā* for Arab. *ṣūba* (then, why not '*farmāna*'?), and so on. Well-known place-names also occur in strange, misleading forms, e.g. 'Gvāliyara', 'Ajmera', 'Jayapura', 'Lāhora' and 'Uḍīsā' for Gwalior, Ajmer, Jaipur, Lahore and Orissa. Such eccentricities divert the reader's attention and must cause him irritation, while opening the gates to illiterate errors and inconsistencies.

Despite this caveat, the editor's work in preparing this volume must in general be deemed commendable; and, though the price is rather stiff, it is hoped that good libraries would acquire it, for the volume not only seriously deals with a worthy theme, it also presents much new material which should lead to further questioning and research.

IQBAL HUSAIN

Contributors

ISHRAT ALAM	Lecturer in History, Aligarh Muslim University.
M. ATHAR ALI	Former Professor of History, Aligarh Muslim University.
FATIMA ZEHRA BILGRAMI	Lecturer in History, Aligarh Muslim University.
FRANÇOISE 'NALINI' DELVOYE	D. Litt. (Sorbonne).
J.S. GREWAL	Former Director, Institute of Advanced Study, Shimla.
IRFAN HABIB	Former Professor of History, Aligarh Muslim University.
NAJAF HAIDER	New College, Oxford.
IQBAL HUSAIN	Former Professor of History, Aligarh Muslim University.
SAIYID ZAHEER JAFRI	Reader in History, Delhi University.
AHSAN RAZA KHAN	Professor of History, Himachal University, Shimla.
IQBAL GHANI KHAN	Reader in History, Aligarh Muslim University.
IQTIDAR ALAM KHAN	Former Professor of History, Aligarh Muslim University.
K.S. MATHEW	Professor of History, Pondicherry University.
SHIREEN MOOSVI	Professor of History, Aligarh Muslim University.
PUSHPA PRASAD	Reader in History, Aligarh Muslim University.
ANIRUDDHA RAY	Professor of Islamic History and Culture, Calcutta University
S. ALI NADEEM REZAVI	Lecturer in History, Aligarh Muslim University.
SOM PRAKASH VERMA	Professor of History, Aligarh Muslim University.
S. INAYAT ALI ZAIDI	Reader in History, Jamia Millia Islamia, New Delhi.
SUNITA ZAIDI	Reader in History, Jamia Millia Islamia.